Recommended by **Teachers**
Trusted by **Toppers**

All in One®

ENTREPRENEURSHIP
Class 12

EVERYTHING YOU NEED TO SCORE

- Simplified Theory
- All Types of Exam Pattern Questions
- CBQs; MCQs, A-R, Case Based
- Board Questions Upto 2025
- Sample Question Papers

CBSE Exams 2026

Author
Shruti Manglik

arihant
SUCCESS AND NOTHING LESS

ARIHANT PRAKASHAN

(School Division Series)

卐 ADMINISTRATIVE & PRODUCTION OFFICES

Regd. Office

'Ramchhaya' 4577/15, Agarwal Road, Darya Ganj, New Delhi -110002
Tele: 011- 47630600, 43518550; Fax: 011- 23280316

卐 *Head Office*

Kalindi, TP Nagar, Meerut (UP) - 250002, Tel: 0121-7156203, 7156204

卐 SALES & SUPPORT OFFICES

Agra, Ahmedabad, Bengaluru, Bareilly, Chennai, Delhi, Guwahati, Hyderabad, Jaipur, Jhansi, Kolkata, Lucknow, Nagpur & Pune.

PO No : TXT-XX-XXXXXXX-X-XX

Published By Arihant Publications (India) Ltd.

For further information about the books published by Arihant, log on to www.arihantbooks.com or e-mail at info@arihantbooks.com

Follow us on

卐 PRICE ₹350.00

PRODUCTION TEAM

Publishing Managers	Cover Designer	Inner Designer
Mahendra Singh Rawat & Keshav Mohan	Salman Shaikh	Ankit Tyagi
Project Head	*Page Layouting*	*Proof Reader*
Saurabh Gupta	Amit Bansal	Apoorvi

Index *cum* Study Planner

One Book- Endless Features
to Help you Succeed

In this Chapter

At the start of each chapter, all the topics of the chapter have been listed, so that students may know what they are going to study.

CHAPTER **02**

Entrepreneurial Planning

In this Chapter...

- Forms of business organisations
- Business plan
- Components of a business plan
- Organisational plan
- Production plan
- Operational plan
- Financial plan
- Marketing plan
- Human resource planning

Sole Proprietorship

As the name suggests, sole means single and proprietor means an owner, thus, it is a form of business which is managed and controlled by a single owner.

One of the oldest, simplest and most commonly used forms of business organisation, which is owned, financed, controlled and managed by only one person is called as sole proprietorship.

It is also referred to as single entrepreneurship or individual proprietorship.

Complete Theory

Each chapter has Complete, Easy to Understand and Simplified theory covering latest syllabus and CBSE Textbook. Theory is developed in such a way that it is suitable for all types of learners.

CHECK POINT 01

1. Which is the oldest simplest and most commonly used form of organisation?
2. State the maximum number of partners in partnership firm.
3. Partnership deed can only be in written form. State true or false.
4. Maximum numbers in a private company is 50. State true or false.
5. State two characteristics of a company.

Check Points

A set of 4-6 Questions given in between the text, helps students to remain connected with the text while studying. They can instantly assess themselves for their understanding.

EXAM PATTERN EXERCISE

Objective Type Questions (1 Mark)

Multiple Choice Questions

1 The scope of operation of sole proprietorship form of business is limited because of
(a) limited finance availabilities
(b) limited managerial abilities
(c) Both (a) and (b)
(d) None of the above

Ans (c) Both (a) and (b)

2 Which of the following forms of business organisations require minimum two persons to start the same? (CBSE Term 1 2021)
(i) Sole proprietorship
(ii) Partnership
(iii) Private company (iv) Public company
(a) (i) and (ii) (b) (iii) and (iv)
(c) (ii), (iii) and (iv) (d) (ii) and (iii)

Ans (d) (ii) and (iii)

Short Answer Type I Questions (2 Marks)

1 The scope of the company's business is determined by certain documents. Name them.

Ans The documents which determine the scope of the company are
(i) Memorandum of association.
(ii) Articles of association.
Also, it should not transgress the provisions of Companies Act, 2013.

2 What is the implication of the feature 'separate legal entity'?

Ans The implications of this feature are
(i) Members are not joint owners of the assets of the company. All assets belong to company itself.
(ii) The company continues to exist, even if all its members die.
(iii) Company can sue and be sued by its members, creditors or third parties.

Exam Pattern Exercise

To make students completely prepared for examination, this Exercise contains Exam Pattern Questions. This exercise covers all types of questions, like; MCQs, Case Based Questions, Assertion-Reason, SA & LA Type Questions. All the questions are fully explained helping students to understand, how to write the answers to get full marks in the exam.

One Book- Endless Features

to Help you Succeed

Case Studies

Case studies are given at the end of the chapter to facilitate the understanding of the practical aspect of the topics discussed, i.e, real life implications.

CASE STUDIES

Case 1

Satya Brata Day : Shree Leathers

Satya Brata Dey

Ever seen a long time outside a shoe store? People waiting in the scorching heat just to buy a pair of shoes? If you haven't, you'll see it outside Satya Brata Dey's Shree Leather Shoe Stores in Calcutta.

From Rags to Riches

One dreary morning in November, 1986, Satya left his home in Jamshedpur and came to Calcutta with little more than the clothes on his back. He wore a pair of corduroy pants, a shirt and a pair of sturdy shoes made by his father. Before he left home, his mother had pressed in his hands a few hundred rupee notes which he brought with him.

Today, Satya Brata Dey is a millionaire, a crorepati. And what gives him the greatest satisfaction is that he provides jobs for people in West Bengal, a state where there are very few industries and over five million unemployed.

When he remembers his father bending over his work table making shoes day after day, tears glisten in his eyes. The tears of love and pride.

He remembers his father's hands that had over the years become hard and tough like the leather he worked with. Today, Satya would give anything to be able to hold those callused, wrinkled hands in his own and invite him to come and see the little boy but Satya's father is no more. Whereas, Satya manages a business worth crores, what he is most proud of is that even today he can make shoes with his own hands.

From his beloved father, Satya learned another important lesson that would come in very handy for him later in life, i.e. dignity of labour. It means the value and worth of working with one's own hands. Because of his background, Satya has great respect for the working man.

In his business, he treats his employees and workmen like family members and they, in turn, give him their undying loyalty. That is one of the secrets of his success.

CHAPTER ASSESSMENT

Objective Type Questions (1 Mark)

1 Which amongst the following is/are the element(s) of operational plan?
(a) Routing (b) Scheduling
(c) Follow-up (d) All of these

2 Kamakshi wanted to raise finance. For this purpose, she decided to prepare a 3 minute summary of business plan's executive summary to awaken the interest of potential investors. This format of presentation of business plan is referred to as
(a) elevator pitch
(b) a pitch deck with oral narrative
(c) a written presentation for external stakeholders
(d) None of these

3 A partnership firm comes to an end on the
(a) retirement of a partner
(b) death of a partner
(c) insolvency of a partner
(d) Any of the above

5 In partnership, ... agreement is much more advisable as disputes can be resolved better with it.

6 The investors focus on four C's of credit character, cash flow, collateral and ....

7 One of the characteristics of company form of organisation is unlimited liability.
State whether this statement is true or false.

8 Proforma income statement summarises all the profit data during the first year of operations of new enterprises.
State true or false.

Short Answer Type I Questions (2 Marks)

9 What is break-even analysis?

10 Why is the scope of operation of sole proprietorship form of business limited?

11 What is a business plan?

12 What is a production plan?

Chapter Assessment

Complete Test of Chapter in Exam format.

Sample Question Papers

To make students practice of examination in real sense, there are 3 Sample Question Papers at the end. All these Sample Questions Papers are exactly prepared on the latest syllabus & pattern of examination.

Sample Paper 1

A Highly Simulated Sample Question Paper for CBSE Class XII Examination

Entrepreneurship

General Instructions

Read the following instructions carefully and follow them

1. This question paper contains 34 questions. All questions are compulsory.
2. This question paper is divided into four sections—Section A, B, C and D.
3. Section A : Questions number 1 to 18 are Multiple Choice Type Questions. Each question carries 1 mark.
4. Section B : Questions number 19 to 24 are Short Answer Type-1 Questions. Each question carries 2 marks. Write answer to each question in 30 to 40 words.
5. Section C : Questions number 25 to 29 are Short Answer Type-II Questions. Each question carries 3 marks. Write answer to each question in 50 to 70 words.
6. Section D : Questions number 30 to 34 are Long Answer Type Questions. Each question carries 5 marks. Write answer to each question in 120 to 150 words.
7. There is no overall choice. However, an internal choice has been provided in Section B, C and D of question paper. A candidate has to attempt only one of the alternatives in such questions.

Time : 3 hours **Max. Marks : 70**

Section-A

1. Which of the following factors is/are involved in sensing opportunities? (1)
I. Ability to perceive and preserve basic ideas.
II. Ability to read the environment.
III. Ability to access the environment.
IV. Ability to harness different sources of information.
Codes
(a) I and II (b) Only I
(c) I and IV (d) I, II and III

2. What is the first stage in the process of innovation? (1)
(a) Idea germination (b) Creativity
(c) Preparation (d) Incubation

eventually help him to establish a place for his brand in the beverage industry.
Identify the field of idea generation used by him. (1)
I. Market driven II. Trading relevant
III. Service sector IV. Creative efforts
Codes
(a) Only IV (b) I and II
(c) Only III (d) All of these

4. The law states that the business and owner are same in the case of sole proprietorship. Which of the following characteristics is highlighted in the above sentence? (1)
(a) Separate entity (b) No separate entity
(c) Limited liability (d) Unlimited liability

Latest Course *Structure*

S.No.	Units	Marks
1.	Entrepreneurial Opportunity	30
2.	Entrepreneurial Planning	
3.	Enterprise Marketing	20
4.	Enterprise Growth Strategies	
5.	Business Arithmetic	20
6.	Resource Mobilisation	
	Project Work	30
	Total	**100**

UNIT I

Entrepreneurial Opportunity

Competencies: *Scanning the environment; Analytical and logical thinking; Innovation and creativity; Decision making; self-confidence.*

Contents

- Sensing Entrepreneurial Opportunities
- Environment Scanning
- Problem Identification
- Idea Fields
- Spotting Trends
- Creativity and Innovation
- Selecting the Right Opportunity

Learning Outcomes

After going through this unit, the student/learner would be able to:

- Comprehend the concept and elements of business opportunity
- Discuss the process of sensing opportunities
- Understand the need to scan the environment
- Enlist the various forces affecting business environment
- Identify the different idea field
- Understand the concept of opportunity and market assessment
- Appreciate the ways in which trends can be spotted
- Understand the process of creativity and innovation
- Transform ideas into business opportunities

UNIT II

Entrepreneurial Planning

Competencies: *Analytical and critical thinking; personal responsibility; determination; Resourceful; collaboration*

Contents

- Forms of business organization- Sole proprietorship, Partnership, Company
- Business Plan: concept, format.
- Components: Organisational plan; Operational plan; Production plan; Financial plan; Marketing plan; Human Resource plan

Learning Outcomes

After going through this unit, the student/learner would be able to:

- Recall the meaning of the various forms of business organization
- Understand the characteristics of the various forms of business organization
- Understand the difference between a Public and Private Company
- Appreciate the reasons for a private company being more desirable
- Appreciate the concept and importance of a business plan
- Describe the various components of Business plan
- Differentiate among the various components of business plan
- Develop a business plan

UNIT III

Enterprise Marketing

Competencies: *Persistence, Negotiation, Collaboration, Ethical behavior, team spirit*

Contents

- Marketing and Sales Strategy
- Branding, Logo, Tagline
- Promotion Strategy

Learning Outcomes

After going through this unit, the student/ learner would be able to:

- Discuss the various marketing strategies used in a business
- Explain Marketing Mix.
- Understand the concept of Branding, Packaging and Labelling
- Describe the various methods of Pricing
- Discuss the various factors affecting the channels of distribution
- Understand the concept and types of sales strategy
- Discuss different tools of promotion
- Appreciate the objectives and different modes of Advertising
- Understand the concept of personal selling, sales promotion, public relations
- Discuss the various techniques of sales promotion

UNIT IV

Enterprise Growth Strategies

Competencies: *Need for achievement, Initiative, Analytical thinking, risk vs reward, collaboration, synergy, leadership*

Contents

- Franchising: Concept, types
- Franchising : Advantages and limitations to franchisor and franchisee.
- Mergers and Acquisition: Concept, reasons and types.
- Reasons for Mergers and Acquisitions.

Learning Outcomes

After going through this unit, the student/learner would be able to:

- Understand the concept of growth & development of an enterprise
- Discuss the concept, types, advantages and limitations of franchising
- Appreciate growth of business through mergers and acquisitions
- Discuss the different types of mergers and acquisitions
- Discuss the reasons for mergers and acquisitions

UNIT V

Business Arithmetic

Competencies: *Arithmetic skills, critical analysis, decision making, self-confidence, problem solving.*

Contents

- Unit of Sale, Unit Cost for multiple products or services
- Break even Analysis for multiple products or services
- Computation of Working Capital
- Inventory Control and EOQ
- Return on Investment (ROI) & Return on Equity (ROE)

Learning Outcomes

After going through this unit, the student/learner would be able to:

- Understand the concept of Unit Cost and Unit Price
- Calculate Break-even point for Multiple products and services.
- Understand the concept of Inventory Control
- Compute the working capital of a business.
- Calculate Return on Investment; Return on Equity and Economic Order Quantity

UNIT VI

Resource Mobilisation

Competencies: *Risk taking, Communication, Persuasion, Networking, Ethical behavior*

Contents

- Capital Market- Concept
- Primary Market - Concept, Methods of issue
- Angel Investor: Features
- Venture Capital: Features, funding.

Learning Outcomes

After going through this unit, the student/learner would be able to:

- Understand the need of finance in Business
- Discuss the various sources of funds required for a firm
- Understand the ways of raising funds in primary market
- Appreciate the Angel Investors and Venture Capitalists as a source of business finance.

PROJECT WORK

1. Business Plan
2. Market Survey

- *10 Marks each for 02 Projects*
- *5 Marks for Numerical Assessment*
- *5 Marks for Viva*

Note:

Students need to complete both the projects. Guidelines for both projects are given in the CBSE Textbook.

Prescribed Books

1. Entrepreneurship - Class XI- C.B.S.E,Delhi
2. Entrepreneurship - Class XII - C.B.S.E.,Delhi
3. Udyamita (in Hindi) by Dr. MMP. Akhouri and S.P Mishra, pub. By National Institute for Entrepreneurship and Small Business Development (NIESBUD), NSIC-PATC Campus,Okhla

Magazines

1. Udyamita Samachar Patra (Monthly, Hindi), Pub. By Centre for Entrepreneurship Development, M.P. (CEDMAP), 60 Jail Road,Jhangerbad, Bhopal-462008.
2. Science Tec. Entrepreneur (A Bi Monthly Publication), Centre for Entrepreneurship Development, M.P (CEDMAP), 60 Jail Road, Jhangerbad, Bhopal -462008
3. Laghu Udhyog Samachar
4. Project Profile by DCSSI

CHAPTER 01

Entrepreneurial Opportunity

In this Chapter...

- Introduction
- Environment scanning
- Problem identification
- Product identification
- Creativity
- Innovation

Introduction

An **entrepreneur** is a person who conceives the idea or discovers an opportunity in the environment and initiates the process of converting the opportunity into business. The process of identifying opportunities in the environment and arranging the resources to exploit the identified opportunity in order to harness long-term gain is called **entrepreneurship**.

An entrepreneur conceives the idea of setting up a business and performs various activities to give shape to business. When business gets a proper shape, it is called an **enterprise**.

Peter F Drucker defined entrepreneur as a person who always searches for opportunity and believes in increasing the value. The basic test of entrepreneur is to identify the business opportunity in the environment and initiate steps to provide and sell goods and services to make the best use of that opportunity.

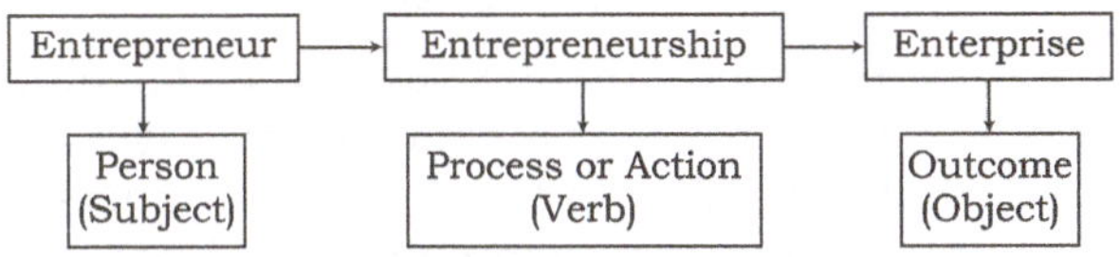

Concept of Entrepreneurship

Business Opportunity

Business opportunity is an economic idea which can be implemented to create a business enterprise and earn profits. Two things should be kept in mind before selecting an opportunity

- Ensure good market for the product, which is to be produced or provided.
- Ensure attractive rate of return on the investment.

All ideas cannot be converted into business. Sometimes entrepreneur conceives an idea and starts the business without analysing the market criteria which results in failure of business.

Elements of Business Opportunity

Before setting up a business, certain elements should be considered which are as follows

- Assured market scope.
- An attractive and acceptable rate of return on investment.
- Practicability of the idea.
- Competency and ability of the entrepreneur to encash it.
- Potential of future growth.

Exploring Opportunities in the Environment

Opportunities exist in the environment, they may exist in the form of needs and problems of the society. An entrepreneur should search for an opportunity suitable to him in terms of profits expected and customers. Thus, an entrepreneur should spot the opportunity, evaluate the idea and through creativity and innovation, build something valuable in the form of enterprise/project.

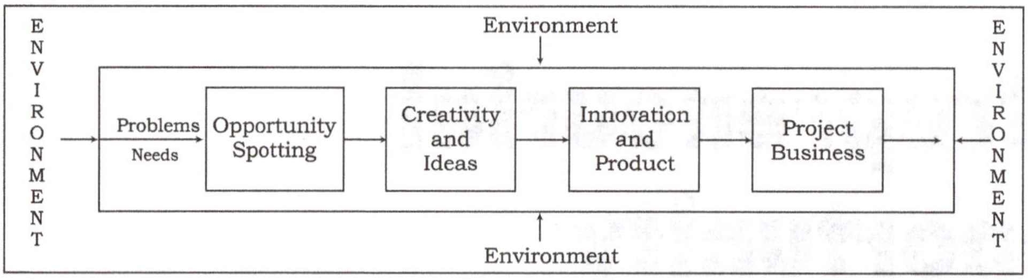

Enterprise Process

Stages of Enterprise Building Process

As depicted in the above diagram, the following stages take place in enterprise building

- Spotting an opportunity by analysing the needs and problems of the society.
- Evaluating the ideas received from different sources to find a creative solution.
- Identifying a product or service through innovation.
- Setting up a project and nurturing it to success.

Thus, sensing entrepreneurial opportunities is a process of converting an idea into an opportunity and then into an enterprise.

Perceiving and Sensing Entrepreneurial Opportunities

The entrepreneurs perceive opportunities, synthesise the available information and analyse emerging pattern that escape the attention of other people. An entrepreneur with a vision is able to persuade others such as customers, partners and employees to see the opportunity, share and support it.

He employs his skill, observation, vision, knowledge and creativity to sense the opportunity.

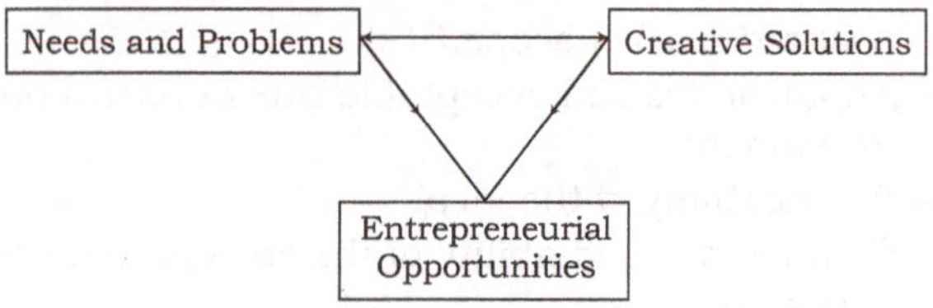

Process of Sensing Entrepreneurial Opportunities

Factors involved in Sensing Opportunities

The most important factors involved in the process of sensing opportunities are as follows

1. **Ability to Perceive and Preserve the Basic Ideas** Perceiving an opportunity or an idea might come from different sources, such as
   (i) **Problem** Many times, a solution to a problem leads to idea generation. e.g. water heaters operated on LPG, is the outcome of low power supply in small towns and villages.
   (ii) **Change** Any change in social, legal or technological aspects, leads to a new business opportunity. e.g. product with zero cholesterol, zero calorie coke, multigrain breads, etc., are results of movement of society towards health consciousness.
   (iii) **Invention** New products or services lead to new business opportunities. e.g. with the development of Android, most of the mobile companies started offering it.
   (iv) **Competition** It is often a source of new and better ideas that results in new business opportunities. e.g. emergence of 3D TVs, curve TVs, etc.
   (v) **Innovation** Creating new things of value as well as new and creative processes that add value to the existing products or services. e.g. computers to tablets.

2. **Ability to Harness Different Sources of Information** There are various sources from which information can be gathered like magazines, books, journals, seminars, friends, etc. Information from these sources should be analysed which helps in the identification of the right opportunity to start a new business.
3. **Vision and Creativity** The entrepreneurs should be able to creatively identify an idea to generate valuable solution to a problem. Creative vision helps the entrepreneurs to convert the solution into business opportunity. Through their vision and creativity, they constantly
   - overcome adversity
   - exercise control over the business
   - make a significant difference

CHECK POINT 01

1. What do you mean by business opportunity?
2. Which two things should be kept in mind while selecting an opportunity?
3. Can a solution to a problem lead to idea generation?
4. Mention the stages of enterprise building process.
5. What do you mean by vision and creativity?

Environment Scanning

Business environment is a set of all those forces and conditions, which are external to the business, but effect the working of a business. These factors may be social, economic, political, legal and other factors. Environment scanning means careful monitoring of an organisation's internal and external environment for detecting early signs of opportunities and threats that may influence its current and future plans.

To scan the business environment, entrepreneurs receive and harness ideas from different sources. Then they convert these ideas into viable projects.

Need for Environment Scanning

'If you don't adapt, you don't endure', is the core idea behind environment scanning.

Organisations have to be constantly aware of the changes taking place in the environment and adapt to those changes to survive and be successful. The right information, combined with the right adaptations, can determine an organisation's future viability. Otherwise, the organisation may fail in future.

Importance of Environment

Sensitivity to environmental factors is crucial for an entrepreneur to succeed in the long-run. The following benefits arise by understanding the environment

Importance of Environment

- → Identification of opportunities to get first mover advantage
- → Formulation of strategies and policies
- → Tapping useful resources
- → Better performance
- → Sensitisation of entrepreneurs to cope up with rapid changes
- → Image building

1. **Identification of Opportunities to Get First Mover Advantage** By keeping in touch with the changes in the external environment, an enterprise can identify opportunities and find strategies to capitalise on the opportunities at the earliest. e.g. LPG rationing led the manufacturers to come out with induction cooker.
2. **Formulation of Strategies and Policies** It helps in identifying threats and opportunities in the market.

   These can serve as the basis of formulation of strategies to counter threats and capitalise on opportunities in the market.

   e.g. the depleting reserves of petrol is a threat for car manufacturers. E-cars or solar powered engines are the outcome of such threats, which forced them to look for alternate sources of energy.
3. **Tapping Useful Resources** If a company has a thorough knowledge of environment, the enterprise can tap resources like financial resources, human resources, physical resources, etc., from the market at economical prices at the right time.

   e.g. Pasco Ltd. should buy wheat for its wide variety of biscuits when the new crop comes in the market, as it is available at cheap prices.

4. **Better Performance** It can be increased with the timely action in dealing with threats and availing opportunities for the purpose of improvement in the performance of the firm.

   e.g. the 'Make in India' scheme declared by the government (a part of political environment) opens new avenues for entrepreneurs to diversify.

5. **Sensitisation of Entrepreneurs to Cope up with Rapid Changes** A keen watch on trends in the environment would help sensitise the entrepreneur to become proactive towards the needs of customers, changing trends, government policy, technology, etc.

   e.g. Reliance Trends keep on changing its clothes with changes in fashion to gain an edge over its competitors.

6. **Image Building** If a company is sensitive to the external environment, it will come out with new products and services or bring out better goods and services to meet customers requirements, which help in image building or reputation of the company. e.g. call-radio taxis with GPS systems, online booking, etc.

Environment Analysis

It is the process of monitoring the economic and non-economic environment, to determine the opportunities and threats to an organisation.

Such an anlysis involves data collection, information processing and forecasting to provide a rational basis for developing goals and strategies for business survival and growth.

It helps entrepreneurs to form their policies and strategies to grab opportunities and overcome threats. Information for environmental scanning can be collected from several sources.

These include

- Verbal information from customers, wholesalers, retailers, distributors, consultants, etc.
- Records of companies.
- Government publications.
- Publications by financial institutions.
- Formal studies conducted by strategic planners.

The data collected is analysed using quantitative and qualitative techniques. The information received is tested for its economic viability against important environmental parameters to arrive at a sound business choice.

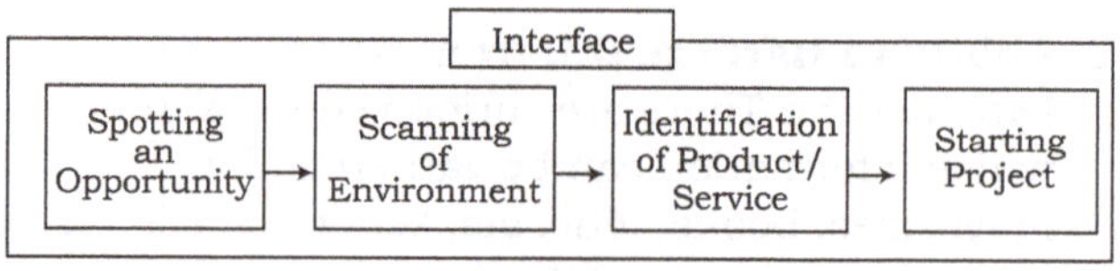

Opportunity-Project Interface

SWOT Analysis Framework

SWOT stands for **Strengths, Weaknesses, Opportunities** and **Threats**. SWOT analysis helps to monitor the environment, both internal and external, therefore, it is also referred to as internal and external analysis.

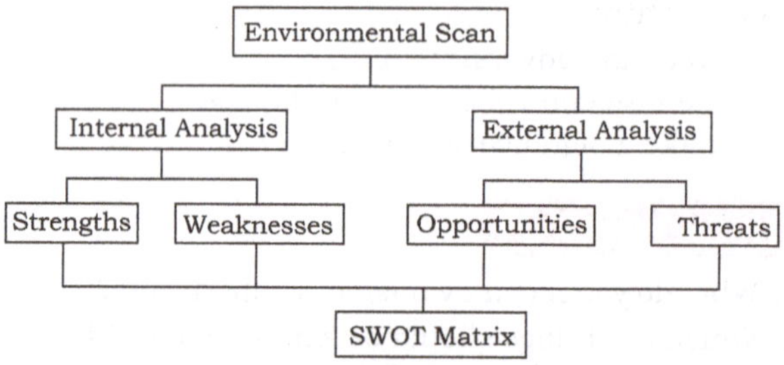

SWOT Analysis Framework

SWOT analysis helps an entrepreneur to decide on a particular opportunity keeping in view his strengths and weaknesses (internal analysis) and the opportunities and threats (external analysis) in the market.

Environmental Factors

Entrepreneurship environment refers to the various forces within which various small, medium and large enterprises operate. These factors exert influence upon each other and do not operate in isolation.

Business environment consists of two levels, i.e., micro environment and macro environment.

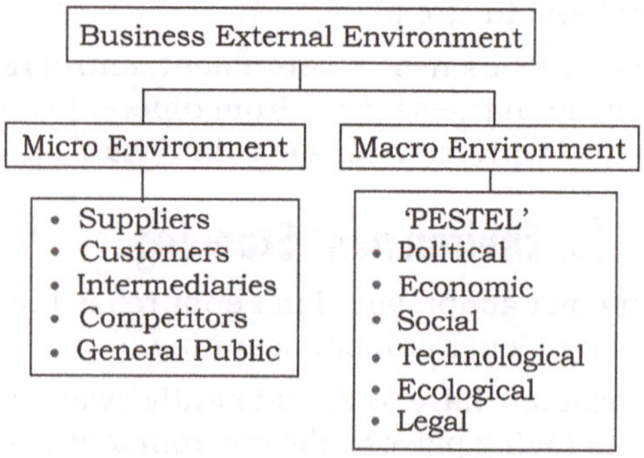

Note *Micro factors are same which have been discussed in class XI.*

Macro Environment These are the factors which affect the industry as a whole. These are Political, Economic, Social, Technological, Ecological and Legal factors, abbreviated as PESTEL. Macro forces refer to all those forces that are part of the larger society and are 'uncontrollable' in nature.

PESTEL Model

Political Factors	Economic Factors	Social/Cultural Factors	Technological Factors	Ecological Factors	Legal Factors
Taxation policy	Interest rates	Population demographics	Government spendings on research	Carbon emissions	Taxation
Government stability	Inflation	Social mobility	New discoveries	Care for environment	Employment
Foreign trade regulations	Business cycles	Income distribution	Focus on technological efforts		Law
	Unemployment	Lifestyle changes	Speed of technological transfer		Monopoly
	Disposable income	Attitude towards work and leisure	Rates of obsolescence		Legislation
	Energy	Levels of education			Environmental protection laws
	Availiability and cost	Consumerism			

e.g. an airline is planning to expand over the next 5 years.

The following would be some of the PESTEL factors, it should consider

1. **Political** It includes political unrest, terrorism, landing rights in foreign countries.
2. **Economic** It includes oil prices, exchange rates, taxation (e.g. VAT on fuel), economic boom or depression (airline revenues are very sensitive to business traffic).
3. **Social/Cultural** It includes change in population size, fashion (e.g. increasing willingness to go on short breaks).
4. **Technological** It includes engine efficiency, new aircraft being planned, better and cheaper video conferencing.
5. **Ecological** It includes concern about the impact of carbon emissions from jet engines, noise, resistance to airport expansion.
6. **Legal** It includes health and safety regulations, consumer legislation (e.g. compensation for cancelled flights), safety and security legislations.

CHECK POINT 02

1. Only internal environment of organisation should be monitored for detecting opportunities. State true or false.
2. What does SWOT stand for?
3. What does micro environment include?
4. State the name of factors for the following items Inflation, taxation, population, new discovery.
5. Name any two sources of information.

Problem Identification

A problem is a road block in a situation which sets up a conflict and forces you to find a solution. When one identifies this road block, it is called as problem identification.

Objectives of Problem Identification

Objectives of problem identification are given below

- It should clearly state the problem.
- To identify target group facing the problem.
- To find the market acceptability of the solution to the problem.

Uses of Problem Identification

Identification of problem helps the entrepreneur in the following ways

- To understand the needs and problems of the market.
- To bring out new products in the market.
- To become creative.
- To increase employment generation.
- To increase national income of the country.

Problems are generally identified by the entrepreneur themselves and sometimes, the problems are present for which the consumers want instant solutions. Here the entrepreneur finds out the solution to their problems by bringing out new products and services.

e.g. most of ready to cook meals are the result of problems faced by youths living by themselves to pursue their careers and studies and also due to the demand generated by nuclear families where females are also working.

Idea Generation

Idea generation is a process of creating, developing and communicating ideas which are abstract, concrete or visual.

It includes the process of developing the idea through creativity and innovation and bringing the concept to reality. Business ideas are an outcome of

- careful analysis of market trends.
- careful analysis of consumer needs.
- serendipity i.e. creation of something or discovery through accident.
- exploring the ways of getting ideas.

Idea Fields

The process of generation of idea can be streamlined by developing an awareness for different 'idea fields'. This will help the entrepreneur in enlarging the scope of thinking.

Thus, idea fields can be defined as convenient frames of reference for streamlining the process of generation of ideas.

Sources of Idea Fields

The various sources of idea are given below

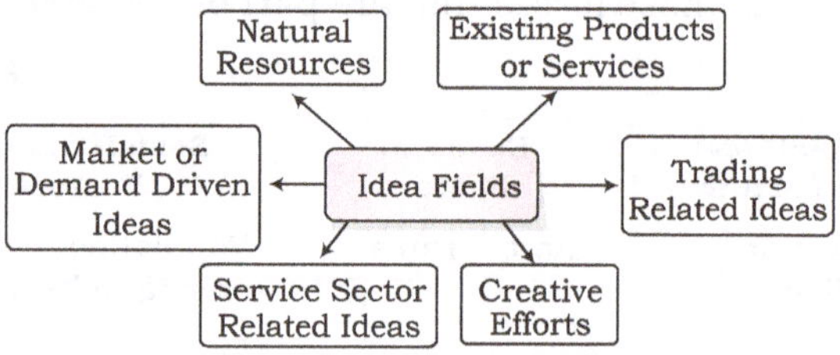

Sources of Idea Fields

1. Natural Resources

Ideas can be generated based on natural resources. A product or service may be desired from forest resources, agriculture, horticulture, mineral, marine or aqua mineral, animal husbandry, wind, the sun and human resources. e.g. if we think of getting ideas in the field of forest resources, we can think of forest produce, wood based products, bio-fertilisers, etc.

Natural Resources and their Uses

Natural Resources	Existing Use	Potential Use
Lumber	Timber	Furniture, craft ideas and other wood based products.
Horticulture	Plant cultivation	Food preservation, canning, freezing and pickling.
Citrus and other fruits	Juices	Selling of preserved fruits for supermarkets and bottled local juices for sale.
Medicinal herbs	Remedies	Medicines and bio-fertilisers.
Clay	Soil	Ceramics, idols, gifts and show-pieces.
Flowers	Selling in market	Selling to floral decorators, florists.
Water resources (sulphur spring, waterfalls)	Domestic and recreational use	Paid tours for visitors and tourists and opening of a water plant.

2. Existing Products or Services

Another field to generate new ideas can be improving the existing products or services.

A great business idea combines skills with imagination and market demand. Entrepreneurs who look at ways to make an existing product or service better can be as successful as those who create and invent products.

They use the latest technology in existing products or make them cheaper by producing them with cost saving method. Quite often we come across a business which is improving on or changing its existing products. There are several reasons for doing so. Changes and improvements help a business to expand and grow.

e.g. in case of Britannia Breads, the company is constantly improving on its existing product and bringing out new variants like Atta bread, multigrains bread, garlic bread, etc, thus, improving and expanding their present product line.

The ideas of changing, improving or adding to existing product, have to be done skillfully or else other problems can arise.

It can benefit the business in the following ways

(i) **Keep up with the Competition** If the products or services are of constantly changing nature, you have to stay aware of the changes and adopt such changes.

e.g. in case of a mobile manufacturing unit, the manufacturer has to constantly upgrade his process with the change in technology.

(ii) **Increase Sales** The main reason for bringing about change and improvement in existing products or services is to increase sales and ultimately their revenue. So, the change should be such that, it helps in increasing the revenues of the business.

e.g. a publishing house engaged in the publication of competitive books ventures into school books. This addition in product line will definitely increase the revenues of the firm.

3. Market or Demand Driven Ideas

One of the important methods of generating an idea is market research. It is an organised effort to gather information about target markets or customers. It includes social and opinion research and is the systematic gathering and interpretation of information about individuals or organisations using statistical and analytical methods and techniques of applied social sciences to gain insight or support decision-making.

Market research is a good source of generating ideas, as it gives information regarding

- Market needs
- Market size
- Level of competition
- General environment
- State of technology

Often, market research and marketing research are used synonymously. However, the distinction is that marketing research is concerned specifically about marketing processes, while market research is concerned with markets.

4. Trading Related Ideas

Trading simply refers to buying goods and services and selling them to the consumers at a profit. Advantages of trading are that it is easier to launch and is less risky.

However, these days trading is not restricted to general stores and small outlets but its scope has enlarged to local trade, import, export, e-commerce, etc. Umbrella markets, departmental stores, chain stores, international companies like Walmart have entered into market, making competition very fierce. To survive in the market, new entrants will have to acquire skills, competencies and knowledge required to launch, manage and expand business opportunities.

5. Service Sector Related Ideas

Service sector is the most growing field these days. The reason being the emerging knowledge societies and advancements in information and technology. Many opportunities can be identified by understanding the linkages to different business activities. Some of the interesting opportunities in service sector are as follows

Food Sector Opportunities Some of the interesting opportunities in food sector are

(i) **Indian Fast Food/Finger Food** While 'pizzas', 'burgers' and 'popcorn' may find a lot of favour from Indians across India and across all age and income groups, the fact remains that almost all regions of India still have their own local fast food options that far outsell the 'imports'.

(ii) **Family Dinner** Special arrangement for family dinner service, like Nirula's offering Indian style 'Plated or Combo' meals, with table service and overall good price value equation, can be used as a service idea in this sector.

(iii) **Sandwich and Salad Parlours** The success of subway in this segment, inspite of inconsistent product quality, poor service and high prices show that this segment has huge potential.

(iv) **Ice-cream and Juice/Beverage Parlours** There is a good opportunity in this sector also. Till now, many start-ups, who had ventured in this segment have not been successful. However, the reason for their failure is a lack of conceptualisation and faulty execution and not lack of market.

(v) **Indian 'Desserts' and 'Snack Food' Chains** In the genre of food and food service chains, one of the biggest opportunities remains in starting national or atleast regional chains offering Indian sweets. Players in 'desserts' and 'snack food' chains are very few. Haldiram, Bikanerwala have done it nationally. There is a huge scope in this genre.

Other Service/Non-food Sector Opportunities
Opportunities present in non-food sectors are as follows

(i) **Speciality Tourism** India is geographically diverse and has a rich heritage. Opportunity in this sector has a huge scope. Creating specialised options for high-end international tourists offers a tremendous opportunity potential.

(ii) **Personal Grooming Salons** Some players like Habib's in hair care, VLCC in slimming and personal grooming, Shahnaz Hussain in beauty care have their chain outlets. Thus, salons also provide a great opportunity.

(iii) **Career Counselling Centres** India is having the maximum number of youths. Presently, 3 million of these likely to go for studies beyond 12th grade. Most of them have little knowledge about job and vocation trends in India and abroad. There is a huge opportunity in this area.

(iv) **Chain of Repair and Maintenance Services for Electric and Electronic Goods** India is seeing a massive increase in the penetration of electrical information products. India's low labour-related service costs can provide a cost-effective solution to the millions which, on the other hand, can generate good returns on investment for the entrepreneur.

6. Creative Efforts

Creativity is an important idea field. It is not only used to spot and harness opportunities but, it can also be applied to develop new products and services.

There are five ways in which creative ideas can be generated

- Develop a new product or service.
- Improve an existing product or service.
- Find a new process or resource for manufacturing a product.
- Find new markets for existing products or services.
- Find a new use of an existing product or service.

Generally, creativity comes as a result of problem solving. Whenever people face problems, to overcome those problems new products and services are created.
e.g., when someone found it difficult and cumbersome to tighten the screw on fixture, the solution came with the invention of self adjusting screwdriver which prevented over tightening.

CHECK POINT 03

1. Problems are not identified by entrepreneurs themselves. State true or false.
2. Can ideas be generated from natural resources?
3. Mention two natural resources alongwith their existing use.
4. Write two service sectors where interesting opportunities can be derived from.
5. Creativity can only be used to develop a new product. State true or false.

Product Identification

After opportunity spotting and scanning of the environment, an entrepreneurial idea should lead to a definite product.

Transforming Idea into Opportunities

Initial spotting of idea, i.e., identifying a basic idea is a random process but, developing idea after scanning environment is a strategic and deliberate process.

All basic ideas undergo a vigorous process of examination, evaluation, analysis and synthesis to identify viable opportunities.

The process of how a basic idea gets converted into an opportunity is depicted in the diagram given below

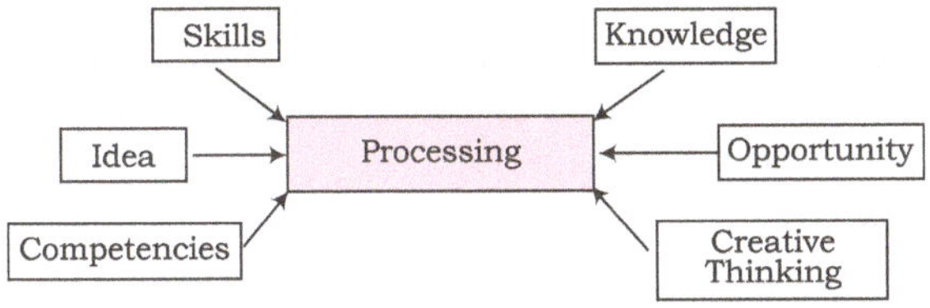

Conversion of Idea into Opportunity

The above figure shows that a strategic positioning is required to convert an idea into an opportunity. It means that knowledge, creative thinking, competencies and skills of an entrepreneur are backed by a thorough processing of the idea through close examination, evaluation, analysis and synthesis leading to an idea evolving as an opportunity.

Idea and Opportunity Assessment

Generating ideas is relatively an easy exercise, especially if it is done in groups. However, to ensure that idea should necessarily become a sound business opportunity, we have to assess it in terms of the potentiality of the opportunity.

The steps involved in this type of investigation are discussed below

Steps in Opportunity Assessment

- Step 1 → Product identification
- Step 2 → Application and use
- Step 3 → Level of operation
- Step 4 → Cost
- Step 5 → Competition
- Step 6 → Technical complexity
- Step 7 → Annual turnover and profit margin

***Step* 1 Product Identification** The ideas should lead to a definite product/service, which an entrepreneur can sell. The proposed product should be such that it can be marketed at a reasonable cost.

Also, it should be analysed in the light of possible product substitutes, preferences of customers, modifications suggested, etc.

If the product is already available in the market, identify the reason for introducing the same product or service.

***Step* 2 Application and Use** Ideas are to be examined for their real life use and application. If it is an existing product, modification should be proposed that should lead to its better use.

***Step* 3 Level of Operation** The level of operation will depend upon the type of product, skill, use of labour and expertise. The entrepreneur should decide whether he/she will produce it in cottage industry, small scale industry or large scale industry.

***Step* 4 Cost** At different levels of operations, cost should be assessed. Also, the price of the competiting products should be known. This will help in determining the sale price.

***Step* 5 Competition** Competitive analysis of a product or service should be done through its demand and supply position.

***Step* 6 Technical Complexity** Whether the product requires certain technology in terms of plant and machinery, training needs and application should be assessed.

It is to be seen whether such requirements could be met locally or will have to be sourced from outside.

***Step* 7 Annual Turnover and Profit Margin** The annual turnover has to be estimated as profits are based on the amount of net sales.

Market Assessment

Once the entrepreneur has assessed the opportunities, he has to assess the market. Selection of product will depend upon market assessment.

The following factors require careful evaluation while assessing the market

1. **Demand** The demand of the product should be assessed on the basis of the market being targeted, viz. local markets, or markets at state, national or international level.

   Also, a study should be conducted on target consumers to assess their tastes and preferences.

2. **Supply and Nature of Competition** The present supply schedule of the competitors should be assessed. Not only this, future supplies by possible new entrants have to be gauzed too.
3. **Cost and Price of Product** The price of the product should be competitively set with regard to existing competitors of the product. Cost reduction in variable costs should be strived to be achieved.

   e.g. if the transportation costs of a competitor are quite high and this lead to wastage during transit, then the entrepreneur should strive to save on his transportation costs to gain an advantage over the competitor.
4. **Project Innovation and Change** Market assessment will require a study of prevailing innovations and changes being carried out by existing entrepreneurs.

   Technological advancements in the field have to be analysed because they may change the quality and influence the cost and price ultimately.

Trend Spotting

It means identification of new trends. It will help the entrepreneur to understand the market and provide service or produce goods according to the market trends.

There are several professional trend spotters, but they charge huge sums of money. So, entrepreneurs can spot these trends themselves by using the following ways

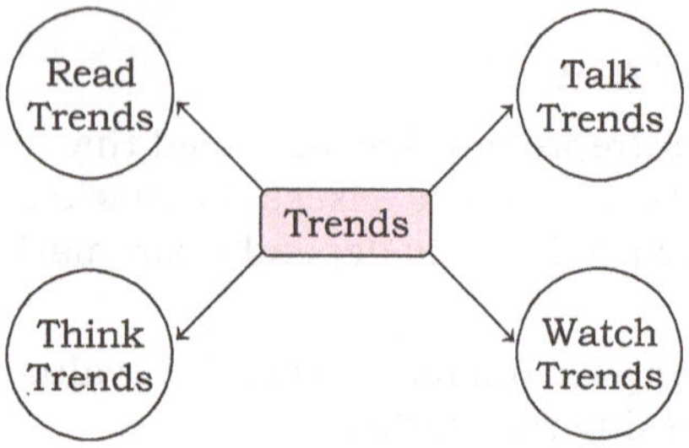

1. Read Trends

Wide variety of information can be collected from various sources as given below

- Read the leading publications.
- Websites related to their business.
- Industry publications.
- Business magazines.
- Major newspapers.
- International trends through websites.
- Influential bloggers.
- Niche bloggers focused on specific aspects of their industry.

The information available from the above sources is vast and every piece of information may not be relevant for the entrepreneurs. They have to make an intelligent choice as to which source is valuable for them and which is not.

For this, they use tech-tools like RSS feeds, e-mails, newsletters or websites and forums to get the information that they want.

2. Talk Trends

Talking to people is an equally important trend-spotting tactic. For this, the entrepreneurs should participate in events organised by specific industry's trade association, whether it is online or offline.

They should also take advantage of social networking tools like social network sites and forums. They can also start or join groups on the networks to know about the latest trends.

It is also important to talk to customers, both online and offline. They should pay attention to what the customers are saying not only on their product, but also on competitor's product.

3. Watch Trends

Observation in the market place is the best way to get on the actual trends. Entrepreneurs can study the habits, preferences and likes and dislikes of the consumers.

If the target consumers of a product are the youth, then, they can visit a mall and observe trends of clothing, eating habits, how youth are engaging themselves in different activities, etc.

They can see which stores are attracting maximum crowd and which are lying vacant. Trade shows are also a great place to get trend ideas.

4. Think Trends

When an entrepreneur begins gathering information regularly, he becomes a trend-spotter. After reading, watching, talking and observing trends, they will use their abilities of thinking, analysing and synthesising to make connections with their business and can come up with a great idea for a new product or a new product line or a new business.

CHECK POINT 04

1. Initial spotting of idea i.e., identifying a basic idea is a strategic proess. State true or false.
2. Name two factors which require evaluation before assessment of market.
3. Professional trend-spotters charge no money. State true or false.
4. When does an entrepreneur become a trend-spotter?

Creativity

It is the first stage in the process of innovation which leads to discovery of opportunity and new venture creation. One of the important tasks demanded from entrepreneurs is to manifest creative ability by conceiving a new product market opportunity and unique value proposition.

It is seen that the new entrants often start their beginning by giving the reason of novelty, usefulness and appropriateness, which are nothing but an extension of creativity. The entrepreneur must try to get first mover advantage by trying new inventions and applying creativity in the organisation to survive and grow.

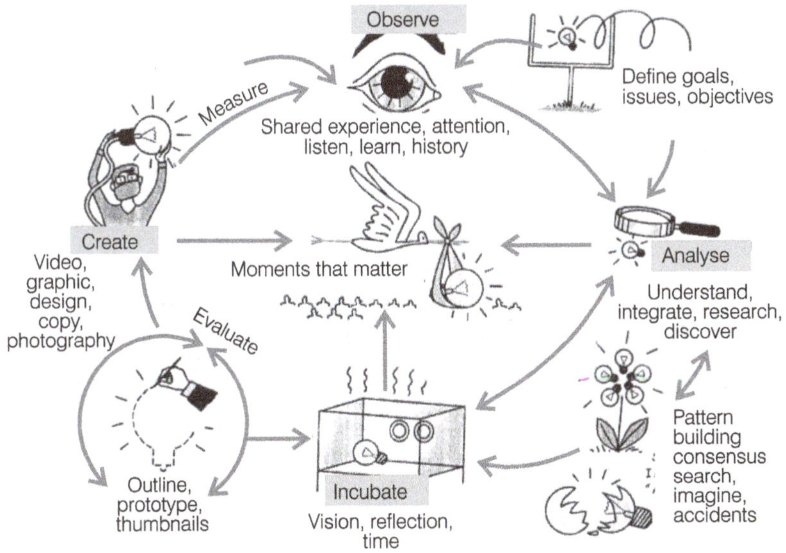

Process of Creativity

The Creative Process

Creativity is important to entrepreneurs. The process of creativity involves the following steps

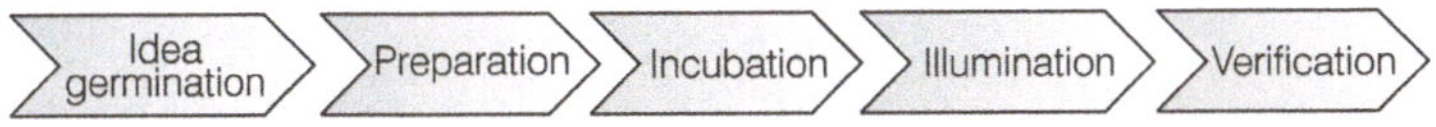

***Step* 1 Idea Germination**

It is the seeding stage, where the new idea grows. The idea germinates from the interest and curiosity of the entrepreneur.

He then explore and exploits it to its best potential. The ideas can also germinate from the need of a specific problem or area of study.

***Step* 2 Preparation**

Now, with the germination of idea, it needs to be implemented. For this, the entrepreneur takes up market research to see whether the product will have any future or not.

***Step* 3 Incubation**

This is the subconscious assimilation of information. This is the transition period.

The entrepreneur think about his idea, its pros and cons, process of its implementation in his mind. Here, the idea starts spreading its roots.

***Step* 4 Illumination**

The fourth stage or the illumination stage occurs when the idea re-surfaces in a realistic way.

The entrepreneur comes with a viable plan to give practical shape to his idea by collecting raw materials, arranging for finance, etc.

***Step* 5 Verification**

This is also called the validation or testing stage. In this, the idea or plan is translated into useful application which has value.

This is the most difficult phase of creativity as obstacles begin to appear. It is a stage when knowledge is developed into application.

Innovation

It is a process of entrepreneurship which involves the translation of a useful idea into an application which has a commercial value.

Innovation is required to work out analytically the details of the enterprise, to develop marketing strategies, to organise, finance and strategies operations.

Elements of Innovation Process

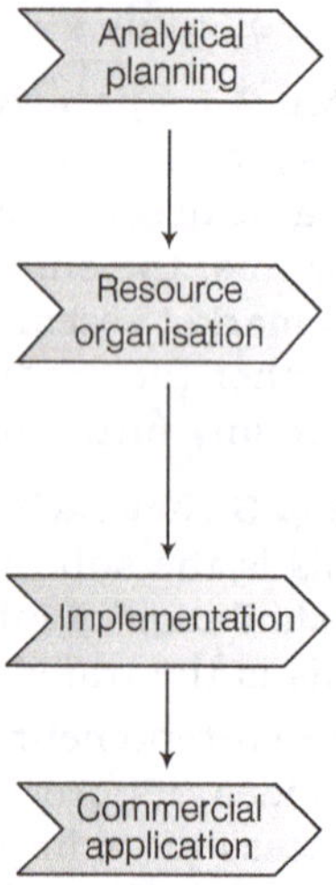

(i) Analytical planning involves
   (a) Identifying the product or service features
   (b) Design
   (c) Resources

(ii) Resource organisation involves
   (a) Human resources
   (b) Material resources
   (c) Technology
   (d) Capital resources

(iii) Implementation involves
   (a) Applying resources
   (b) Delivering results

(iv) Commercial application involves
   (a) Provision of value to customers
   (b) Reward employees
   (c) Satisfy stakeholders

Selecting the Right Opportunity

The entrepreneur should look into various factors before deciding on the opportunity. Even if the opportunity looks promising, an entrepreneur should look into the environmental factors before choosing the best opportunity.

CHECK POINT 05

1. What do you mean by creativity?
2. Mention first two steps involved in the process of creativity.
3. What is meant by innovation?
4. State any one element of innovation process.
5. What is included in commercial application?

EXAM PATTERN EXERCISE

Objective Type Questions (1 Mark)

Multiple Choice Questions

1 Entrepreneur is 'The Person' who always searches for the opportunity and initiates steps to produce and sell goods and services which is 'The Process' and 'The Outcome' is the enterprise. From the following identify 'The Process'. **(CBSE Term I 2021)**

(a) Opportunity (b) Entrepreneurship
(c) Problem identification (d) Both (a) and (c)

Ans (d) Both (a) and (c)

2 An economic idea which can be implemented to create a business enterprise and profit is called **(CBSE Term I 2021)**

(a) Business environment
(b) Business opportunity
(c) Business problem (d) Product identification

Ans (b) Business opportunity

3. Given below are some of the elements of a business opportunity. Identify the correct combination of the elements.

I. Assured market scope
II. Overcome adversity
III. Practicability of the idea
IV. Potential of future growth **(CBSE 2023)**

Codes

(a) I, II and IV (b) I, III and IV
(c) II, III and IV (d) I, II and III

Ans (b) I, III and IV

4 The process of entrepreneurship which involves the translation of a useful idea into an application is called **(CBSE Term I 2021)**

(a) incubation (b) innovation
(c) verification (d) illumination

Ans (b) innovation

5 Which of the following factors does the macro-environment not include? **(CBSE SQP Term I)**

(a) Political and regulatory factors
(b) Customer needs in a given market
(c) Social and demographic factors
(d) Technological changes

Ans (b) Customer needs in a given market

6 A prospective entrepreneur has to find an opportunity which would be suitable for him/her in terms of customers to be served and profits expected.

An opportunity may be derived from spotting and analysing the …… and …… that exist in the environment. **(CBSE Term I 2021)**

(a) needs, market conditions
(b) market conditions, needs
(c) needs, problems
(d) market conditions, problems

Ans (a) needs, market conditions

7 Exploring opportunities in the environment is a process involving various steps.

Arrange the steps in correct order.

(i) Evaluating the ideas received from different sources to find a creative solution.
(ii) Identifying a product or service through innovation.
(iii) Opportunity spotting by analysing the needs and problems that exist in the environment.
(iv) Setting up a project and nurturing it to success.

(a) (i) (ii) (iii) (iv)
(b) (iii) (i) (ii) (iv)
(c) (ii) (iii) (iv) (i)
(d) (i) (iv) (iii) (ii)

Ans (b) (iii) (i) (ii) (iv)

8 An idea should eventually lead to success of the venture of an entrepreneur. Which among the following ideas will an entrepreneur have to select? **(CBSE SQP Term I)**

(a) Basic idea
(b) Any random idea
(c) Idea developed before environmental scanning
(d) Idea developed after environmental scanning

Ans (d) Idea developed after environmental scanning

9 Identify the micro-environmental factors from the following.
(i) General public (ii) Competitors
(iii) Economic (iv) Intermediaries
(v) Legal **(CBSE Term I 2021)**
(a) (i), (ii) and (iii) (b) (ii), (iii) and (iv)
(c) (iii), (iv) and (v) (d) (i), (ii) and (iv)

Ans (d) (i), (ii) and (iv)

10 Nelson started an AC repair shop in his area after doing a diploma course. What idea field is it? **(CBSE SQP Term I)**
(a) Market driven (b) Trading related
(c) Service related (d) Creative efforts

Ans (c) Service related

11 Identify the third element in the innovation process from the given options. **(CBSE SQP Term I)**
(a) Resource organisation
(b) Commercial application
(c) Implementation (d) Analytical planning

Ans (c) Implementation

12 What is the basic test of a successful entrepreneur? **(CBSE SQP Term I)**
(a) Identification of business opportunity
(b) Identification of a problem
(c) Identification of target market
(d) Identification of ways to earn profit

Ans (a) Identification of business opportunity

13 According to the 'PESTEL Model', which factor emphasises the production of goods with minimum environmental damage? **(CBSE Term I 2021)**
(a) Economic (b) Social
(c) Ecological (d) Technological

Ans (c) Ecological

14 Can all ideas be converted into opportunities? **(CBSE SQP Term I)**
(a) Yes, as ideas lead to opportunity
(b) Yes, only if it has assured market scope
(c) Yes, only if there is a good market for the product and rate of return on the investment is attractive.
(d) Yes, if the entrepreneur has enough financial resources.

Ans (c) Yes, only if there is a good market for the product and rate of return on the investment is attractive.

15 Which of the following is not a natural source of ideas? **(CBSE Term I 2021)**
(a) Horticulture (b) Existing products
(c) Agriculture (d) Forests

Ans (b) Existing products

16 Which of the following is not a use of product identification? **(CBSE Term I 2021)**
(a) It helps in increasing national income
(b) It increases employment generation
(c) It should clearly state the problem
(d) It brings out new products in the market

Ans (c) It should clearly state the problem

17 LPG rationing led the manufacturers to come out with induction cooker. Which importance of environment does the above example indicate?
(a) Identification of opportunities to get first mover advantage
(b) Tapping useful resources
(c) Better performance
(d) Image building

Ans (a) Identification of opportunities to get first mover advantage

18 Mr. Dinesh wanted to manufacture an energy efficient AC. He looked into various options and finally narrowed down to one option. He understands that his idea would have to follow a process. Identify the process.
(a) Process of idea germination
(b) Process of creativity
(c) Process of idea generation
(d) Process of idea fields

Ans (b) Process of creativity

19 Arvind planned to start a small fast-food joint in his area after finishing his degree in hospitality management. His plan was to combine and use healthy ingredients like whole wheat flour to make the burger buns.
He knew that he had to start collecting information from different sources which will help him to identify the right opportunity to start his business. From where will Arvind get the necessary information? **(CBSE SQP)**
(a) Magazine
(b) Shows
(c) Family members (d) All of these

Ans (d) All of these

20 WX Ltd. is in the process of innovating a new pen drive especially for teachers which will have a built-in antivirus and which can be worn like a watch so it minimises the problem of losing the pen drive. Which of the given statements aptly describes the situation? **(CBSE SQP Term I)**

(a) This is trend spotting

(b) This is product identification

(c) This is problem solving

(d) This is problem solving by introducing an innovative product

Ans (b) This is product identification

21 Which of the following examples is not a part of the social environmental factor? **(CBSE SQP Term I)**

(a) At the time of Holi, a large number of manufacturing firms get involved in making colours which are used in the celebration of this colourful festival.

(b) A particular channel refrains from showing the advertisement of a particular product as it is banned by the government.

(c) The sale of sarees increases in the months of the year when a large number of marriages take place in India. The saree manufacturing companies make special plans of sale for these months.

(d) (a) and (c) only

Ans (b) A particular channel refrains from showing the advertisement of a particular product as it is banned by the government.

22 Ramesh starts his day by reading all newspapers and has a keen interest towards all business news and articles. He connects the articles with the observations he has made over the years which he knows will eventually lead to business-boosting insights. Identify the way of trend spotting at this level. **(CBSE SQP Term I)**

(a) Read trend (b) Think trend

(c) Watch trend (d) Talk trend

Ans (b) Think trend

23 Which of the following statements correctly explains the concept of creative efforts?

(i) Develop and improve an existing or new product or service.

(ii) Compete with an existing product or service

(iii) Find a new process or resource for manufacturing a product. **(CBSE SQP Term I)**

(a) Both (i) and (iii) (b) All of these

(c) Both (ii) and (iii) (d) Only (i)

Ans (a) Both (i) and (iii)

24 'Safe for Women'- SFW has been a known brand among working women as the company keeps introducing various new innovative products for the safety of women. Their latest product is a pen which can be used as a pocket knife. The product is in huge demand.

Which point of importance of scanning the environment does this news indicate? **(CBSE SQP Term I)**

(a) Formulation of strategies and policies

(b) Tapping useful resources

(c) Image building (d) Better performance

Ans (c) Image building

25 Sohan started a small scale business of manufacturing and marketing pickles and named the same as 'Desi Achar'. He supplied the pickle in the whole city.

Now, he wants to expand his business in other cities. He discussed the same with his father, who suggested to Sohan to properly look into those conditions and forces which are external to a business under which it operates.

On his father's suggestion, Sohan carefully monitors the internal and external environment for detailing early signs of opportunities and threats that may influence its current and future plans. Sohan's father suggested to him about **(CBSE Term I 2021)**

(a) problem solving (b) image building

(c) environment scanning

(d) tapping useful resources

Ans (c) environment scanning

26 VM Ltd is a leading mobile phones manufacturer in India. The company decided to launch a new model which will have inbuilt software for hands-free use and enhance the customer experience through 3D photos.

They are also looking into ideas to use eco-friendly recyclable materials for the body of the phones that may cause negligible damage to the environment. Identify the factor of the PESTEL model discussed here. **(CBSE Term I 2021, SQP)**

(a) Social and Policical
(b) Ecological and Technological
(c) Economic and Social
(d) Legal and Economical

Ans (b) Ecological and Technological

27 Madhu Chandan started the first Organic Mandya store in 2015 on the Bengaluru – Mysuru highway. Today it has grown into a ₹ 25 crore turnover organic retail chain with eight stores. By buying the agricultural products from the farmers and selling them at 'Organic Mandya' stores, Madhu has not only provided a direct market to the farmers, but also has built a ₹ 25 crore turnover organic retail chain.
Which idea field has Madhu Chandan taken up? **(CBSE SQP Term I)**

(a) Natural resources (b) Service sector
(c) Trading related
(d) Existing products or services

Ans (a) Natural resources

28 Saraswati is the managing director of 'Gama Ltd'. The company is manufacturing shoes and wants to enter into the business of trendy ladies shoes market. But before entering into this business she has to assess the market demand and other related variables. Identify from the following the factor which Saraswati will not consider while doing market assessment. **(CBSE Term I 2021)**

(a) Supply and nature of competition
(b) Idea generation
(c) Cost and price of product
(d) Project innovation and change

Ans (b) Idea generation

29 Deepa after graduating from IIM wanted to become an entrepreneur. She identified and analysed the market need, market size and competition and realised that there is an untapped demand for 'Almond milk'. She started supplying 'Almond milk' in different flavours.

She used to get feedback from her customers. Over a period of time 'Almond milk' became popular. Identify from the following the source of idea field chosen by Deepa. **(CBSE Term I 2021)**

(a) Natural resources
(b) Market driven or demand driven idea
(c) Creative efforts
(d) Existing products or services

Ans (b) Market driven or demand driven idea

30 Swami wants to start a new business. Before deciding the type of business, he started identifying the new trends in retail business. He became a member of a trade association. He attended its events both online and offline. He also took advantage of the social networking tools. Which of the following ways of trend spotting did Swami adopt? **(CBSE Term I 2021)**

(a) Watch trend
(b) Think trend
(c) Talk trend
(d) Read trend

Ans (c) Talk trend

31 Monik Ltd. was the market leader in the Mobile Phone industry in 2,000. The company was well known for it's affordable phones. In 2007, a new company launched new mobile models with latest technologies and captured the market. Monik Ltd., did not expect this and lost the entire market share and had to close their operations. Which of the following SWOT analysis framework does this case indicate that Monik Ltd. failed to do? **(CBSE SQP Term I)**

(a) Strengths (b) Weakness
(c) Opportunities (d) Threats

Ans (d) Threats

32 During the pandemic, the worst hit were the families who were infected by the virus and had no source for home cooked nutritious food. 'Chilly Chillz' is a multi-cuisine chain of restaurants operating throughout Delhi by a well-established network of outlets.

The owner of the chain understood the concern and started serving 3 course meal to such families on payment basis. The interested customers had to login the website, select their location and set their menu for the day. This service proved to be a great support for suffering families.
What was the source of generation of basic idea? **(CBSE SQP Term I)**

(a) Innovation (b) Invention
(c) Problem (d) Competition

Ans (c) Problem

33 In a bid to send astronauts to Mars, US space agency Nasa has invited applications for four people to live in a simulated Martian exploration habitat in order to prepare them for the reallife challenges of future missions to the red planet. Nasa started taking applications for participants to live for a year in Mars Dune Alpha, a 1,700-square-foot Martian habitat created by a 3D-printer that is inside a building at Johnson Space Center in Houston.

Identify the macro environment factor which has influenced Nasa to develop Mars Dune Alpha. **(CBSE SQP Term I)**

(a) Political (b) Social
(c) Legal (d) Technological

Ans (d) Technological

34 Hitesh, a fisherman, faced a lot of problems in selling the fish he caught. His entire community was facing this problem and most of the time they had to dump the fish they caught back into the sea. He read a news-paper article on how people have started ordering online for most of the essentials.

He spoke to his fellow fishermen about selling their fish online and started their business with a small delivery truck and an app and slowly and steadily their business started to flourish. What trend has Hitesh spotted? **(CBSE SQP Term I)**

(a) Read trends (b) Watch trends
(c) Talk trends (d) Think trends

Ans (a) Read trends

35 Priya joined a publication company that publishes a monthly magazine "Lifestlye". It covers articles related to fitness, clothing, gadgets, cooking, etc., Priya had joined the clothing division of the magazine. Her divisional head explained her nature of work of the division.

She also informed Priya that in addition to visits to local mall she would have to attend 'Power lunches' on the first monday of every month. Out of the following identify the way of spotting trend, the divisional head is talking about?

(a) Talk trends (b) Read trends
(c) Watch trends (d) Think trends

Ans (c) Watch trends

36 Varun, a student of class XII, observed that a large number of students of the school were using mobile phones.

He also observed that many parents of such students were worried about the content being viewed by their children on mobile phones and were not able to control them.

Being a talented and an intelligent student he decided to develop an app that may help the parents to watch and control children regarding the content being viewed. From the following identify the "idea field" used by Varun to develop the app.

(a) Creative efforts
(b) Trading related ideas
(c) Market driven idea
(d) Natural resources

Ans (a) Creative efforts

37 Rashmi, a teacher of Entrepreneurship, was teaching the steps in the creative process. By the time she was able to explain the first two steps of the process with a number of examples from day-to-day life, the period was over.

She asked the students to read the sequence of the remaining steps to be discussed in the next period.

The remaining steps and their correct sequencing is **(CBSE Term I 2021)**

(a) verification, illumination and incubation
(b) incubation, verification and illumination
(c) illumination, incubation and verification
(d) incubation, illumination and verification

Ans (d) incubation, illumination and verification

38 Which of the following will not take place in enterprise building?

(a) Spotting opportunity by analysing the needs of the society
(b) Identification of product or service through innovation
(c) Setting up a project and nurturing it till its failure
(d) Evaluating ideas received from different sources

Ans (c) Setting up a project and nurturing it till its failure

39 **Assertion** (A) Entrepreneurship is the process of identifying opporunities in the environment and arranging the resources to exploit the identified opportunity.

Reason (R) Entrepreneurship process is exercised to harness long-term gain.

Alternatives

(a) Both Assertion (A) and Reason (R) are correct
(b) Assertion (A) is correct, but Reason (R) is incorrect
(c) Assertion (A) is incorrect, but Reason (R) is correct
(d) Both Assertion (A) and Reason (R) are incorrect

Ans (a) Both Assertion (A) and Reason (R) are correct

40 **Assertion** (A) Needs and problems exists in the environment.

Reason (R) Opportunity is spotted by analysing the environment.

Alternatives **(CBSE SQP Term I)**

(a) Assertion (A) is true, but Reason (R) is false
(b) Both Assertion (A) and Reason (R) are true, but Reason (R) is not the correct explanation of Assertion (A)
(c) Assertion (A) is true and Reason (R) is the correct explanation of Assertion (A)
(d) Both Assertion (A) and Reason (R) are false

Ans (b) Both Assertion (A) and Reason (R) are true, but Reason (R) is not the correct explanation of Assertion (A)

41 **Assertion** (A) A problem is a road block in a situation that forces the entrepreneur to find its solution.

Reason (R) One of the objectives of problem identification is to identify the target group facing the problem. **(CBSE 2023)**

Alternatives

(a) Both Assertion (A) and Reason (R) are true and Reason (R) is the correct explanation of Assertion (A)
(b) Both Assertion (A) and Reason (R) are true, but Reason (R) is not the correct explanation of Assertion (A)
(c) Assertion (A) is true, but Reason (R) is false
(d) Assertion (A) is false, but Reason (R) is true

Ans (a) Both Assertion (A) and Reason (R) are true and Reason (R) is the correct explanation of Assertion (A)

42 **Assertion** (A) E-commerce in India is growing at a rapid pace.

Reason (R) India has a large number of young entrepreneurs with education from premier educational institutes.

Alternatives

(a) Both Assertion (A) and Reason (R) are correct
(b) Assertion (A) is correct, but Reason (R) is incorrect
(c) Assertion (A) is incorrect, but Reason (R) is correct
(d) Both Assertion (A) and Reason (R) are incorrect

Ans (a) Both Assertion (A) and Reason (R) are correct

43

Column I (PESTEL Factors)	Column II (Examples)
A. Legal	(i) Change in fashion
B. Social	(ii) Regulations, rules, taxation rules
C. Political	(iii) Oil prices, exchange rate
D. Economic	(iv) Terrorism, landing right in foreign countries

Codes

	A	B	C	D
(a)	(i)	(ii)	(iii)	(iv)
(b)	(ii)	(i)	(iv)	(iii)
(c)	(iii)	(i)	(iv)	(ii)
(d)	(ii)	(iii)	(iv)	(i)

Ans (b) (ii) (i) (iv) (iii)

44

Column I (Natural Resources)	Column II (Potential Use)
A. Clay	(i) Furniture
B. Lumber	(ii) Medicines
C. Horticulture	(iii) Ceramics
D. Medicinal herbs	(iv) Food preservation

Codes

	A	B	C	D
(a)	(i)	(ii)	(iii)	(iv)
(b)	(ii)	(i)	(iv)	(iii)
(c)	(iii)	(i)	(iv)	(ii)
(d)	(ii)	(iii)	(iv)	(i)

Ans (c) (iii) (i) (iv) (ii)

45

Column I (Trends)		Column II (Sources)
A. Real Trends	(i)	Market places
B. Water Trends	(ii)	Publications, magazines, sites
C. Talk Trends	(iii)	Observation
D. Think Trends	(iv)	Talk to people

Codes

	A	B	C	D		A	B	C	D
(a)	(i)	(ii)	(iii)	(iv)	(b)	(ii)	(i)	(iv)	(iii)
(c)	(iii)	(i)	(iv)	(ii)	(d)	(ii)	(iii)	(iv)	(i)

Ans (d) (ii) (iii) (iv) (i)

46

Column I (Stage)		Column II (Process)
A. Idea germination	(i)	Finding ways for implementation
B. Preparation	(ii)	Sub-conscious period
C. Incubation	(iii)	Testing period
D. Verification	(iv)	Recognisation of opportunity

Codes

	A	B	C	D		A	B	C	D
(a)	(i)	(ii)	(iii)	(iv)	(b)	(ii)	(iii)	(iv)	(i)
(c)	(iv)	(i)	(ii)	(iii)	(d)	(iii)	(ii)	(iv)	(i)

Ans (c) (iv) (i) (ii) (iii)

47

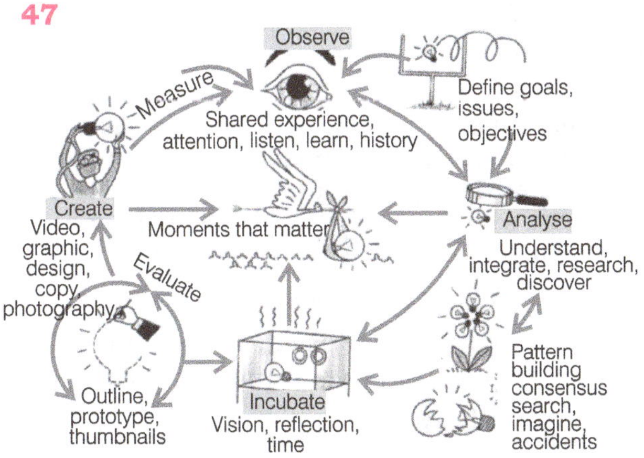

Name the process in given image.

(a) Innovation
(b) Creativity
(c) Opportunity
(d) None of these

Ans (b) Creativity

48 What does the given chart indicate?

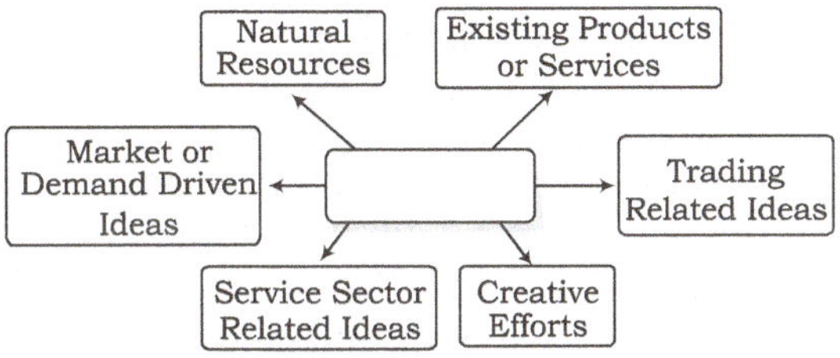

(a) PESTEL model
(b) Sources of idea fields
(c) Idea and opportunity assessment
(d) Creativity process

Ans (b) Sources of idea fields

Fill in the Blanks

49 A prospective entrepreneur has to find an opportunity which would be suitable for him/her in terms of ...... and .... **(CBSE 2020)**

Ans profitability and viability

50 An entrepreneur with a .... is able to pursuade others to see the opportunity.

Ans vision

51 Birla clothing started their business from India to various parts of the world in year 2018.

Company had been successful in its business as people changed in fashion and lifestyle. It is .... factor in PESTEL.

Ans social

52 .... is a process of creating, developing and communicating ideas which are abstract, concrete or visual.

Ans Idea generation

53 .... are convenient frames of reference for streamlining the process of generation of ideas.

Ans Idea fields

54 .... is the first stage in innovation.

Ans Creativity

55 .... stage occurs when the idea re-surfaces in a realistic way.

Ans Illumination

56 Market driven idea is also known as ....

Ans demand driven idea

57 Mohit and Aarti, a talented couple are having three years old son Aarav. Mohit was working with an MNC and was posted in Canada. Aarti is also working as an executive with an IT firm in Noida and is staying with her in-laws in a locality of South Delhi. She wants to admit her son in a good day boarding school, but she could not visit any school.

She discussed her problem with her husband. He advised her to hire a computer operator who could collect data related to admission in nursery class visiting the website of different schools. He also advised Aarti to launch her own website www.nurseryadmission.com and upload the data so collected on it so that this data can also be used by other parents. After following his advice, large number of parents visited the website started by her on an online payment of ₹ 100 per visit. The entrepreneurship concept discussed in the paragraph is ....

Ans product identification

58 Vikrant was always interested in technology driven products. After finishing his engineering degree, he started working on a new walking stick which will help blind people. The stick will be Bluetooth and Wi-Fi enabled which will be connected through an app on the phone which will guide the blind persons about the objects in front of their walking path.

He has started testing the walking stick and found that the stakeholders were satisfied and it had a great value to the customers. Vikrant is in .... stage of innovation process. **(CBSE SQP)**

Ans commercial application

59 Mallika was selling vegetables in her cart along with her mother. They were able to earn a profit of around ₹ 200 every day. Even though the amount was not substantial it was sufficient for a decent living. Mallika often noticed that nuclear families where both husband and wife go to work find it difficult to cook as cleaning and cutting vegetables took a lot of time, so as an entrepreneur she started gathering information regularly and developed a new product line of selling cut vegetables in hygienic packaging. Mallika used .... trend to spot this idea. **(CBSE SQP)**

Ans think trends

State True or False

60 The stage of 'implementation' in the innovation process involves applying resources and delivering results.

Ans True

61 Rate of inflation, business cycles, interest rates, etc. are all part of economic environment.

Ans True

62 Creativity is of utmost importance for an entrepreneur.

Ans True

63 Business environment consists of three levels i.e., SWOT analysis level, micro level and macro level. **(CBSE 2020)**

Ans False. It only consists of two levels i.e. micro and macro level.

64 Britannia company is constantly improving on its existing range of breads and bringing out new variants lie atta bread, multi grain bread, garlic bread, etc. Its source of idea field is market driven.

Ans False. Its source is existing product or services.

65 Environment analysis helps an entrepreneur to decide on a particular opportunity, keeping in view his strengths and weaknesses and opportunities and strengths.

Ans False. The above objective is achieved through SWOT analysis.

66 Innovation is an indication that will help the entrepreneur to understand the market and produce goods or provide services in sync with the market needs, demand and taste.

Ans False. It is market assessment.

67 Ravi created a portable incinerator to be installed in the houses. The dry waste generated at homes can be converted by it into ash that can be used as manure for plants.

He has installed five prototypes of this incinerator in his society to test its working and to prove its value. Ravi is in the verification stage of his product. **(CBSE 2020)**

Ans True

68 Anant and Anandi together took over their family business of furniture. They understood that the present competitors were using online means to sell their products. They decided on a new idea of providing furniture on a rental basis to offices and households and to also start making furniture using the traditional method which caught the attention of the new generation. They opened stores in various cities and started selling through online mode also. They both are using the service related idea field. Mention whether the idea field identified is true or false. **(CBSE SQP)**

Ans False. The idea field is 'Creative efforts'.

69 India has been moving away from plastics for many years and many cities have already issued plastic bag bans. While legislation like this helps to protect our environment and wildlife, a young entrepreneur, Minkesh Sharma noticed that it was a hardship for many Indians. He eventually landed on a combination of natural starch (from potato and tapioca) and vegetable oils to make a bag that looks and feels just like plastic with none of the negative environmental impacts of a plastic vessel.

This was also affordable for all. Characteristics of Minkesh that developed his idea into valuable and successful project are vision and creativity.

Ans True

Case Based Questions

70. Read the following article and answer the questions that follow

Shopping malls are an integral part of the community and a one-stop for all the consumer's needs-from shopping and dining to entertainment and special occasions. Additionally, malls today are synchronising with customer's needs by offering constant engagement, activities and niche campaigns to cater to each target audience that visits the mall. The latest department stores which are opened in malls also want to provide their customers a wholesome experience. They are often hypermarkets having all products under one roof. The concept of 'retailtainment' has been around for quite a while, as upscale malls have slowly transformed into recreational destinations.

A plethora of restaurants serving luscious delicacies has seen massive footfall. Thus, to create memorable experiences, shopping malls strive to provide a high level of engagement by focusing heavily on unique experiential content.

The future malls will integrate virtual and augmented reality, will provide highly immersive retail experience to consumers in the days to come. Deliveries will be carried out using drones and virtual reality will be used as a sales channel. **(CBSE 2023)**

(i) Identify the prominent idea field from the following sentence

'Additionally, malls today are synchronising with customer's needs by offering constant engagement, activities and niche campaigns to cater to each target audience that visits the mall.'

(a) Natural resources (b) Service related
(c) Market driven (d) Creative efforts

Ans (d) Creative efforts

(ii) 'A plethora of restaurants serving luscious delicacies has seen massive footfall in many malls.' The idea field reflected in the given statement is

(a) natural resources (b) service-related
(c) market-driven (d) creative efforts

Ans (b) service-related

(iii) The idea field which is depicted in the sentence 'Deliveries will be carried out using drones and virtual reality will be used as a sales channel' is

(a) natural resources (b) service-related
(c) market-driven (d) creative effort

Ans (d) creative effort

(iv) From the following, which form of business organisation is best suited for owning and managing shopping malls?

(a) Sole proprietorship (b) Partnership firm
(c) Joint stock company (d) Both (a) and (c)

Ans (c) Joint stock company

Note **Joint stock company is covered in Ch-2 ahead.*

(v) From the following, identify the element of macro environment that would play a dominant role in the transformation of shopping malls in future.

(a) Economic (b) Social
(c) Technological (d) Legal

Ans (c) Technological

71 Read the following article and answer the questions that follow

Daan foundation was established in 2019 around the Covid-19 pandemic to help people survive at those times of difficulties. The head of the foundation, Mr. Meet was an enthusiastic entrepreneur and social activist. He was a talented engineer and left his job after working for 10 years to serve the society. Recently, Meet read an article in the newspaper about the death of 5 members of a family due to a rare disease which cannot be diagnosed because the family was middle-class and the tests to diagnose this disease costs a lot.

He was shattered from the news and decided to do something. He gathered all the creative heads of the foundation from different cities and districts and held a meeting asking all the members to give some ideas. Salem, a member suggested that the foundation should start a go- fund-me drive for the needy patients and collect money for them. The whole team loved the idea and started gathering information about the poor patients who are not able to get tested because of high prices. The team analysed the small towns and villages and asked the dwellers about their health issues and within 6 months the team was able to come up with 100 patients that needed the support.

With right aim and goal the foundation was able to gather funds from the drive and helped the needy. They provided certificates and gifts to all the donors and appreciated the team for their efforts.

(i) Which of the following was the main driver for the new drive of the Daan foundation?

(a) Problem (b) Profits
(c) Competition (d) Innovation

Ans (a) Problem

(ii) Which source of idea field is highlighted in the above case?

(a) Natural resources
(b) Human resources
(c) Creative efforts
(d) Market driven

Ans (c) Creative efforts

(iii) "Recently, Meet read an article in the newspaper about the death of 5 members of a family due to a rare disease which cannot be diagnosed because the family was middle-class and the tests to diagnose this disease costs a lot."

Meet used .... trend to generate a new idea.

(a) watch (b) talk
(c) think (d) read

Ans (d) read

(iv) Which macroeconomic factor is tapped by the foundation referring to this sentence, "Daan foundation was established in 2019 around the Covid-19 pandemic to help people survive at those times of difficulties"?

(a) Technological (b) Legal
(c) Social (d) Economical

Ans (c) Social

(v) Identify the vision of Daan foundation from the above case.

(a) Make a significant difference
(b) Exercise control in market
(c) Overcome adversity
(d) All of the above

Ans (a) Make a significant difference

72 Read the following article and answer the questions that follow

Anil and Nash were roommates and worked in an MNC in Delhi. Anil was the finance manager of the company and Nash was in the sales department. Both met in the office and began a strong bond of friendship that later led to renting an apartment near their office.

The apartment was 3 metro stations away from the office building and it took 30 minutes to reach the metro station by taking an auto or e-rickshaw because it took a lot of time to find them. It was the daily struggle to reach the metro station on time and get the ready metro.

But many times, they reached the station late and lose the ready metro and have to wait for some time to board the next one.

Anil and Nash observed that many others were also facing the similar problem because of not getting a ride on the right time.

One evening, Nash suggested Anil that if they provided an easier way to the people to reach the metro stations in their locality as well as other localities then it can be a profitable idea because the scope is wider. So, they asked one of their coder friends to develop a prototype of a mobile application that can register e-rickshaws and autos that dwell nearby so that they can reach to the customers on time. In the meantime, both scanned the neighbourhood and other areas to find the people who can be registered on the application.

After a month, the application was ready and 50 people were registered as drivers with the application. They decided to take the idea to the next level and gave the name "E-Ride" to their venture. They took the initiative of employing more women in this venture. The venture took a downturn at first but with proper planning and marketing, E-Ride became a famous and successful business in not more than 2 years.

(i) Which element of business opportunity was analysed by Anil and Nash?

(a) Higher returns (b) Assured market scope

(c) Potential to succeed

(d) All of the above

Ans (b) Assured market scope

(ii) "Anil and Nash observed that many others were also facing the similar problem because of not getting a ride on the right time."

Which step of idea generation is highlighted in the above sentence?

(a) Spotting the opportunity by identifying problems

(b) Setting up a project

(c) Finding a creative solution to the identified problem

(d) All of the above

Ans (a) Spotting the opportunity by identifying problems

(iii) Identify how Anil and Nash were able to sense the market opportunities?

(a) Identifying the change in business environment

(b) Inventing a new product

(c) Innovation and creativity

(d) None of the above

Ans (c) Innovation and creativity

(iv) .... helped Anil and Nash in grabbing the new opportunity and creating a successful business.

(a) Environment analysis

(b) Trend analysis

(c) Both (a) and (b)

(d) None of the above

Ans (a) Environment analysis

(v) "They took the initiative of employing more women in this venture."

Which factor of macro environment was tapped with this initiative?

(a) Technological (b) Legal

(c) Social (d) Economical

Ans (c) Social

Short Answer Type I Questions (2 Marks)

1 State the two basic qualities of a successful entrepreneur. **(CBSE 2019)**

Ans The two basic qualities of a successful entrepreneur are as follows

(i) He should be innovative.

(ii) He should be willing to take risks.

2 What are the factors involved in sensing opportunities? **(CBSE TBQ)**

Ans Factors involved in sensing opportunities are as follows (Any two)

(i) **Ability to Perceive and Preserve the Basic Ideas** Spotting an idea often leads to identification of opportunities. Sources of emergence of ideas may be from problems, changes in environment, inventions, competitions and innovations.

(ii) **Ability to Harness Different Sources of Information** Information can be gathered from various sources like magazines, journals, books, seminars, trade shows, family and friends, customers, etc.

(iii) **Vision and Creativity** Creativity is bringing out a solution. After solution is identified, vision of the entrepreneur converts the solution into business opportunity.

3 Apart from verbal information from the customers, wholesalers, retailers, distributors and consultants, state any other four sources of collecting information for scanning the environment. **(CBSE 2019)**

Ans The other four sources of collecting information for scanning the environment are as follows
(i) Records of companies
(ii) Government publications
(iii) Publications by financial institutions
(iv) Formal studies conducted by strategic planners.

4 What are the differences between entrepreneur and entrepreneurship?

Ans Differences between entrepreneur and entrepreneurship are

Basis	Entrepreneur	Entrepreneurship
Meaning	An entrepreneur is a person who starts an enterprise.	The process of creation of an enterprise is called entrepreneurship.
Scope	Entrepreneur is a person who perceives opportunity, exploits it and transforms it into something new.	It is the set of activities performed by an entrepreneur to exploit opportunity by combining resources and pursuing the opportunity for long-term gains.

5 Scanning of opportunity is the link between 'sensing opportunities' and 'entrepreneurial success'. Explain this statement with a suitable example.

Ans Scanning of opportunity is a link between sensing opportunities and entrepreneurial success. It is a process of perceiving the needs and problems of people and society and arriving at a creative solution. Entrepreneur has the quality to scan the environment based on his knowledge and experience. He finds an opportunity through this process and converts it into a viable project.

e.g. Nirma brand captured the market by introducing a low priced detergent powder against expensive brands like Surf Excel. Here, the entrepreneur scanned the need for low priced detergent powder requirement of the society, fulfilled it and became successful.

6 Explain 'ability to perceive and preserve basic ideas' as a factor in the process of sensing opportunities.

Ans Entrepreneurs have the ability to perceive and preserve a basic idea and after spotting an opportunity, they are able to synthesise the available information to arrive at creative solutions.

An entrepreneur may spot an idea from the following sources
(i) Problems
(ii) Change
(iii) Invention
(iv) Competition
(v) Innovation

7 What is meant by environment scanning? Why does an enterpreneur need to scan the environment? **(CBSE 2020, TBQ)**

Ans **Environment Scanning** Scanning of environment can be defined as a close examination of the environment to develop an understanding of the socio-cultural, economic, political and other development factors in order to ensure that the perceived entrepreneurial opportunity is compatible with them.

Need to Scan the Environment Environment is constantly changing and if you don't adapt to change, you don't endure. The organisation should gather information on changing conditions and incorporate those wherever and whenever required.

Careful monitoring of external and internal environment is necessary for detecting early signs of opportunities and threats. When right information is combined with right adaptation, the organisation's future viability and growth are ensured.

8 What is PESTEL model? Explain it. **(CBSE TBQ)**

Ans Business environment forces exert pressure on the enterprises. The external environment consists of two levels, i.e. micro environment and macro environment. Micro environmental factors consist of suppliers, customers, intermediaries, competitors, general public.

The macro environmental factors consist of Political, Economic, Social, Technological, Ecological and Legal factors, together known as 'PESTEL'.

9 Read the following newspaper, article and identify and explain the two elements of PESTEL model which have been presented in this article

A popular brand of mobile phones has used repurposed fishing nets in its latest model of smart phones. Fishing nets are made of Nylon which has the basic property of adsorbing moisture and water. Use of this material would make the phones waterproof and dust resistant.

Every year around 6,40,000 tonnes fishing nets end up in oceans, posing a serious threat to the marine ecosystem. According to the Managing Director, Research and Development Department, they are working to replace fossil-based raw materials with bio-based raw materials which are renewable. The company has been researching and developing sustainable materials. **(CBSE 2023)**

Ans The two factors of PESTEL model highlighted are

(a) **Technological** It includes product efficiency, new technology being planned, better and cheaper innovative products.

(b) **Ecological** It includes concern about the impact of carbon emissions from jet engines, care for environment, noise, and resistance to airport expansion.

10 Understanding lifestyle changes and attitude towards work and leisure, Flizon India Ltd. started an online shopping portal offering same day delivery to its customers without any extra charge, on orders above ₹ 500.

The company also installed an online payment security system where there is end-to-end encryption of the banking details of the customer. Identify and state the two environmental factors discussed above. **(CBSE 2020)**

Ans Two environmental factors discussed here are

(i) **Social** It includes changes in lifestyle, fashion etc.

(ii) **Technological** Speed of technology transfer, focus on technology, spending of government and new discoveries, all comprises technological environment.

11 Ram is living in a rural area where there is no school and people are illiterate. He decides to open a retail outlet of computer accessories. As an entrepreneur, do you think his decision is correct? Give reason in support of your answer stating the relevant environmental factor. **(Delhi 2014)**

Ans No, I do not think his decision is correct. The environmental factor to be scanned should be the socio-cultural factor which tells us about the level of education, standard of living, etc.

On scanning the environment, he would be able to assess that the level of education is quite low and because of this, the customer demand will also be low for computer accessories which are demanded by educated population.

12 Enlist any two uses of problem identification. **(CBSE SQP)**

Ans Uses of problem identification are as follows (Any two)

(i) It helps an entrepreneur to bring out new products in the market.

(ii) Understand the problems and needs of the market.

(iiii) Helps the entrepreneur to be creative.

(iv) Increase in employment generation.

(v) Increase in national income of the country.

13 Nayan has just passed his Senior Secondary Examination from a CBSE affiliated school. He wanted to start his own business but was undecided about the nature of the business to be started.

One day, during the morning walk, his grandfather fell down in the park and was injured. He observed that his grandfather often forgot to take his medicines.

He thought that the same problem may be faced by other old people.

He thought to develop a walking stick for old people that could be fitted with some electronic devices connected to the mobile phones of the members of their families which could indicate the location of the old people when they go outside their homes.

He also thought to fit a timer in the stick that could remind them about the time of taking their medicines.

Identify and state the meaning of the concept described in the above para that helped Nayan in structuring his idea of solving the problem. **(CBSE 2017)**

Ans The concept described in the above para is 'problem identification'.

When there is a road block in a situation, which poses a conflict and forces an individual to find a solution, then this road block is a 'problem' and when one identifies this road block, it is called 'problem identification'.

14 Atul's father owned a small piece of agricultural land in Nahan, around 100 kms, away from Chandigarh. During one of his visit to Chandigarh to sell 'Wheat' in Mandi, Atul happened to visit a "flower show" and was surprised to see the response and interest of people for it.

Back home he, decided to convert his agricultural land into a Botanical Garden, to be used, both for growing flowers for sale and organising flower shows

(i) Identify the frame of reference used by Atul for this idea generation.

(ii) State the various sources of the identified concept.

Ans (i) Idea fields

(ii) The various sources of idea fields are

(a) Natural resources

(b) Existing products or services

(c) Creative efforts (d) Service related

(e) Trading related

(f) Market or demand driven

15 Gunjan has just passed her senior secondary examination from a CBSE affilited school. She wanted to start her own business but was unable to decide about the nature of the business. One day during the morning walk her grandfather fell down in the park and was injured.

She observed that her grandfather often forgets to take his medicines. She thought that the same problem may be faced by other old people.

She through to develop an instrument for old people that could be fitted with an electronic device connected to the mobile phones of the members of their family which could indicate the location of the old people when they go outside their homes.

This device was to be kept in their pockets. She also thought to fit a timer in the instrument that could remind the old persons about the time of taking their medicines.

Identify and state the meaning of the concept described in the above para that helped Gunjan in structuring her idea for solving the problem. **(CBSE 2017)**

Ans Product identification an entrepreneurial idea leading to a definite product after opportunity spotting and scanning of the environment is called product identification.

16 Yash was not too keen to take up his family run business of making bamboo baskets. But due to the bad condition of the family business, he had no option except to take up this business. He started thinking about the new ways of using bamboo.

One day while having lunch in a restaurant, he overheard the owner talking about the difficulty in disposing the plastic and thermacol crockery that was being used in the restaurant.

This provided him the stimulus for a new venture creation. Yash started looking into various options of making bamboo plates which could be used in the restaurants.

He discussed the idea with his father who advised Yash that ideas should lead to commercially viable forms in order to survive and grow.

Identify and explain the concept discussed in the above situation. **(CBSE 2019)**

Ans The concept discussed is 'product identification'. The idea should lead to a definite product or service that an entrepreneur could sell.

Also the proposed product should be such that it can be marketed at reasonable cost. Also, it should be analysed in the light of possible product substitutes, preferences of customers, modification suggested etc.

17 While 'assessing the market', explain what is assessed under 'supply and nature of competition'? **(Delhi 2014)**

Ans The following factors are to be assessed under'supply and nature of competition', while assessing the market'

(i) The present supply schedule of the competitors.

(ii) The possible future supply by new entrants.

(iii) Also the market form, whether monopolistic competition or monopoly or oliggopoly should also be assessed.

18 Why is market research conducted?

Ans Doing market research on a regular basis is essential for keeping up with current market trends and maintaining a competitive edge.

Whether an entrepreneur is starting a new business, expanding, or developing new products, conducting market research is essential. It helps to understand target market, increase sales and spearhead business growth.

19 A young man, Vipul, wants to start a business. He is not sure of the type of business he should start. His friends suggested him to seek the help of professionals. He contacted a professional who asked Vipul to pay a big amount for providing the reports and industry updates. Therefore, he decided to search for the reports and industry updates himself.

He started looking for the required information and reports on different websites regularly. He also interacted with people for the type of products they would like to use in future.

In addition to this he visited trade fairs, malls, exhibitions, etc. to assess the on-going trends.

Identify and state the way that Vipul is using for spotting the trend. Also state on more way which will help Vipul in starting his business. **(CBSE 2016)**

Ans Vipul is using the following ways to spot the trends

(i) Read trend (ii) Talk trend and

(iii) Watch trend.

One more way is 'Think trend'.

As an entrepreneur begins gathering all these informations regularly, he will start to developing a "trend-spotter mind". As entrepreneurs absorb and mull over what they have read, heard and observed, they will start making connections and observations that will lead to business-boosting insights.

20 State the elements in innovation process. **(CBSE 2019)**

Ans (i) **Analytical Planning** Carefully identifying the product or service, features, design and resources.

(ii) **Resource Organisation** Obtaining the required resources, materials, technology, human or capital resources.

(iii) **Implementation** Applying the resources in order to accomplish and deliver the results.

(iv) **Commercial Application** Provision of value to customers, reward employees and satisfy the stakeholders.

21 Earlier this week, the World Bank, released its Global Economic Prospects Report. It expects India's Gross Domestic Product (GDP) to contract by 3.2% in 2020-21. There will be a moderate recovery to 3.1% growth in 2021-22.

This means that 2021-22 GDP will be less than what it was in 2019-20. To be sure, India is not the only country which will face this predicament. The East Asian region seems to be the only exception.

Source *Hindustan Times, 14th June, 2020*

Identify and explain the environmental factor stated in the above article.

Ans Economic environment is the environmental factor stated in the above article.

Economic Environment It refers to all the external economic factors that influence buying habits of consumers and businesses and therefore affect the performance of a company. These factors are often beyond a company's control and may be either large scale (macro) or small scale (micro).

While companies often can't control their economic environment, they can evaluate economic conditions before choosing to enter a particular market or industry or pursue other strategies.

22 Drew Stevens, a St. Louis professional speaker and consultant who works with entrepreneurs to quickly understand whether their product or service will make it in the current environment, once said in his conference, "This analysis means the analysis of strengths of your industry, weaknesses of your product and potential threats. It enables you to understand the strengths and flaws from internal such as bureaucracy, product development and cost to external factors such as foreign exchange rates, politics, culture, etc."

Source *Entrepreneurs India*

Identify the analysis which Drew Stevens talked about. Also, explain its meaning.

Ans Drew Stevens talked about SWOT Analysis. It is an analysis undertaken by an organisation to identify its internal strengths and weaknesses as well as its external opportunities and threats.

Short Answer Type II Questions (3 Marks)

1 "An opportunity may be derived from the needs and problems of the society". Comment. **(CBSE TBQ)**

Ans Opportunities often exist in the environment in the form of needs and problems of the society

(i) **Needs** From the case study of La Opala, we can understand how needs of society provide an opportunity. In 19th century, bone China crockery was imported. However, use of cow bone ash restricted its use in India. Jhunjhunwala realised that there is a need for something new. He identified the need of Indian consumers who were becoming affluent and came up with 'La Opala'.

(ii) **Problems** Problems faced by people often lead to creation of opportunities. e.g. electric cars, e-rickshaws, invertors, are all results of the problems faced by the society in the form of rising fuel prices.

2 State the different stages of an 'enterprise process' with diagram. **(CBSE TBQ, 2014, 2012)**

Ans

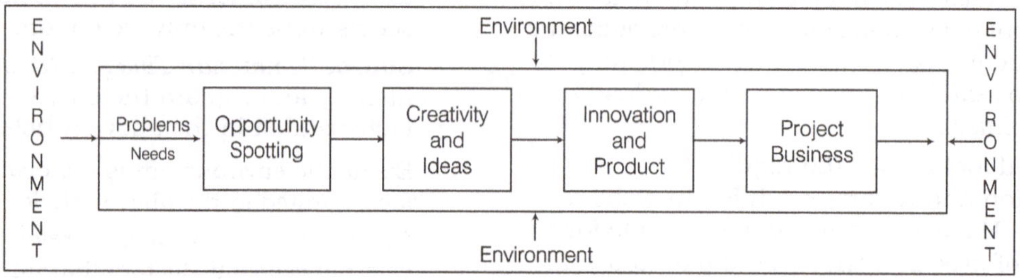

Enterprise Process

The enterprise process diagram shows the different stages of enterprise building, which are as follows

(i) Spotting an opportunity by analysing the needs and problems that exist in the environment.
(ii) Evaluating the ideas received from different sources to find a creative solution.
(iii) Identifying a product/service through innovation.
(iv) Setting up a project and nurturing it to success.

3 Lalita Devi did her post-graduation from Manipur University, Imphal. She had offers to join reputed firms in metropolitan cities like Delhi and Mumbai.

Instead of joining any to these firms, she decided to do some creative work in Imphal. She observed that a special type of chill is grown by the farmers of most of the village around Imphal.

This chilli has a distinct flavour and the pickle made form it has a taste that may be linked by many people in other parts of the country. But the farmers were neither trained in the farming of this kind of chilli on a large-scale nor was there a secured market for their produce.

Lalita Devi met eighteen like-mined women of the area and formed an organisation for doing the business of pickle manufacturing.

Each of them contributed ₹ 2,00,000 towards its capital and were equally responsible for its management.

On one hand, they assured the farmers to purchase the chilli produced by them and on the other hand, the organistion with the help of the local agriculture department arranged for the training of the farmers. They also employed 10 local unemployed graduate girls for doing the various operations of pickel manufacturing.

(i) Name the process that helped Lalita Devi in 'converting an idea into an opportunity'.
(ii) Identify the kind of organisation that Lalita Devi has decided to set-up. **(CBSE 2015)**

Ans (i) 'Sensing entrepreneurial opportunity' is a process of converting an idea into an opportunity and then into an enterprise. Enterprenuers are people with vision and after spotting the opportunity are able to synthesise the available information and analyse emerging patterns that escape the attention of other people. They are also able to persude others such as partners and employees to see the opportunity, share and support it.

(ii) The kind of organisation that Lalita Devi has decided to set-up is 'cooperative organisation'. Cooperative organisation is a corporate form of business organisation. It operates not only for profit, but also to provide some benefits of services to its members and even to society at large.

The Indian Cooperative Society Act, 1912, defines cooparative in Section 4 as, "Society which has its objectives as the promotion of economic interests of its members in accordance with cooperative principles.

4 Ankit is into the business of manufacturing low-cost diesel cars in Germany. He is earning good profits and ambitiously considering overseas expansion. He scans the environment for finding out the opportunities and threats that may influence his current and future plans.

He zeroes down on India as a potential place for his business expansion as Indian Government has announced favourable trade regulations. On selling the first lot of cars in India, the Indian Government noticed that the emissions from these cars were above the permissible limit.

The government asked him to make necessary modification in his cars if he wanted to continue business in India. He readily agreed to meet the emission norms set by the Indian Government.

Quoting the lines from the above paragraph identify any two environmental factors.

(CBSE 2016)

Ans Two environmental factors affecting Ankit's business are

(i) **Political Environment** The political environment consists of the forces concerning management of public affairs and their impact on business. It includes political conditions in the country and attitude of the government towards businesses and business policy. Lines from the paragraph which are indicative of this environment are

"He zeroes down on India as a potential place for his business expansion ... trade regulation".

(ii) **Legal Environment** The business has to function within the framework of laws and regulations of the country which make up its legal environment.

Lines from the paragraph which are indicative of this environment are "The government asked him ... Indian Government".

5 What is meant by 'problem identification'? State its any two objectives and also give an example of 'problem identification'.

(CBSE 2015)

Ans When there is a road block in a situation which poses a conflict, then this road block is a problem and when this road block is identified, then it is called 'problem identification'.

Two objectives of 'problem identification' are as follows

(i) To identify the target group facing the problem.

(ii) To find the market acceptability of the solution to the problem.

e.g. most of the ready to cook meals are the results of the problems faced by the youths living by themselves to pursue their careers and studies and also due to the demand generated by nuclear families where females are also working.

6 There are various sources of idea fields like nature resources, existing products or services, creative efforts, etc. The enterpreneurs who look at ways to make an existing product or service better, have a number of reasons for this. Giving example, explain any two such reasons. **(CBSE 2020)**

Ans Refer to topic 'Existing products or services' on page 7.

7 Explain how 'demand' and 'project innovation and changes' help an entrepreneur in assessing the market?

(CBSE 2013)

Ans **Demand** The demand for a product or service has to be assessed taking into account the various factors. The demand assessment will be based on the size of market being targeted, i.e. local market, market at state level or national/international market.

It will also involve a study of the target groups of consumers, their preferences, tastes and other related variables.

Project Innovation and Changes Market assessment will require a study of prevailing innovations and changes being carried out by existing entrepreneurs.

Technological advancements in the field have to be analysed because they may change the quality and influence cost and price ultimately.

8 Describe briefly the ways in which an entrepreneur spots trend. **(CBSE 2017)**

Ans Various ways in which an entrepreneur spot trends are (Any three)

(i) **Read Trends** They regularly read the leading publications and websites affecting their business. This could include industry publications, trade association sites, major newspapers, key business magazine, thought leaders and influential bloggers.

(ii) **Talk Trends** They get involved in specific industry's trade association and in attending events and in talking to customers both online and offline. They also take advantage of social networking tolls like Linkedin and Facebook.

(iii) **Watch Trends** They make it a point to regularly go where their target customers hang out. The entrepreneur spends some time simply watching and observing what people eat, doing, wearing, using etc.

(iv) **Think Trends** As they absorb and mull about what they've read, head and observed they'll start making connections and observations that will lead to business boosting insights.

9 Give the meaning of 'Innovation'. State the elements in the innovation process. **(CBSE 2016)**

Ans Innovation is a process of entrepreneurship which involves the translation of a useful idea into an application which has a commercial value. Innovation is required to work out analytically the details of the entreprise, to develop marketing strategies, to organise, finance and strategise operations.

Elements of innovation process are given below

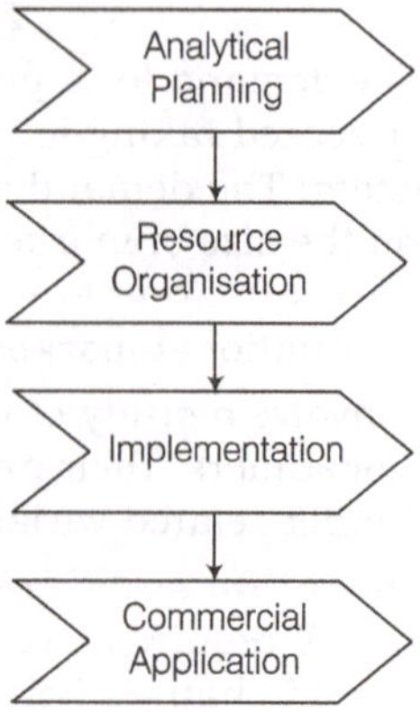

10 Explain the first three steps in the process of idea and opportunity assessment. **(CBSE 2019)**

Ans Refer to topic 'Idea and opportunity assessment' on page 9.

Long Answer Type Questions (5 Marks)

1 Enlist the various sources which lead to the emergence of basic ideas and briefly explain them. **(CBSE TBQ)**

Or "Ability to preceive and preserve basic ideas" is an important factor involved in the process of sensing opportunities. Identify and state any three sources that lead to emergence of these basic ideas. **(CBSE 2023)**

Ans Various sources which lead to the emergence of basic ideas are as follows

(i) **Problem** Often a problem leads to the emergence of an idea,
e.g. solar lamps due to problem of irregular electricity supplies in suburbs and villages.

(ii) **Change** Changes in the environment in social, legal, technological aspects, lead to new opportunities.

(iii) **Invention** Development of new products or services, etc., are sources of ideas.

(iv) **Competition** It leads to emergence of ideas as the firms are always thinking in terms of beating the competition.

(v) **Innovation** Value addition to existing products and services through creative processes leads to an innovated product/ service.

2 State any four benefits of understanding the business environment relevant to an enterprise. **(CBSE 2016)**

Ans Understanding the business environment is relevant to an enterprise because of the below stated benefits

(i) **Identification of Opportunities to Get First Mover Advantage** By being always vigilant (careful) and aware, an enterprise can identify the opportunities at the earliest. e.g. LPG rationing led the manufacturers to come out with induction cooker.

(ii) **Formulation of Strategies and Policies** The threats are always present from the competitors, for which counter strategies have to be formulated to combat (tackle) competition.

Also, opportunities can only be capitalised by suitable strategies and policies.

e.g. the depleting reserves of petrol is a threat for car manufacturers. E-cars or solar powered engines are the outcome of such threats, which forced them to look for alternate sources of energy.

(iii) **Tapping Useful Resources** If a company has a thorough knowledge of environment, the enterprise can tap resources like financial resources, human resources, physical resources etc, from the market at economical prices at the right time. e.g. Parle should buy wheat for its wide variety of biscuits when the new crop comes in the market, as it is available at cheap prices.

(iv) **Better Performance** It can be increased with the timely action in dealing with threats and availing opportunities for the purpose of improvement in the performance of the firm.

e.g. the 'Make in India' scheme declared by the government (a part of political environment) opens new avenues for entrepreneurs to diversify.

3 What is meant by 'Analysis of environment'? State any four sources of collection of information for environmental scanning. **(CBSE 2019)**

Ans Refer to topic 'environment analysis' on page 4.

4 Explain the process of transformation of an idea into a viable opportunity with the help of a diagram. **(CBSE 2019)**

Ans Refer to topic 'Transfoming idea into opportunities' on page 8 and 9.

5 Before identifying a feasible product or process, an idea should be tested along certain parameters which involves a number of steps. Explain the first four steps. **(CBSE 2013)**

Ans First four steps are

(i) **Identification** Identification of a product or service is the first step. The idea provides the concept of the product or service.

Already existing products guide the entrepreneur in understanding the scope of innovations that can be undertaken.

If a totally new product is to be launched, then the policy related with advertising, sales promotion, popularising are to be effectively prepared.

A critical analysis of the product in light of the competition to be faced, choices of the customers, extent of the customers, etc., is to be made.

(ii) **Evaluation of Use and Application** The present use of the product/service is to be found out. This helps in innovating the existing product and in increasing the dependability on the product.

(iii) **Level of Operation** Depending on the nature of the enterprise, the production is undertaken, the enterprise can be small scale, medium scale or large scale industry. Quantity of production is considered. Requirement of labour, technical experts, skilled labour, etc., all are to be considered.

(iv) **Cost** The per unit cost of production is different for different levels of operations. Is the cost competitive? This is to be answered as the price of the product depends on it.

6 Explain the various factor involved in assessing the market while selecting a product or service. **(CBSE SQP)**

Or While assessing the market, an entrepreneur has to prepare details on four factors, one of them being 'project innovation and change'. Explain briefly the other three. **(CBSE 2018)**

Or State any two factors while assessing the market. **(CBSE SQP)**

Or State any four factors that an entrepreneur has to take into consideration while assessing the market. **(CBSE 2016)**

Ans (i) **Demand** The demand assessment will be based on the size of market being targeted, i.e., local markets, market at state level or national international market.

It will also involve a study of the target groups of consumers, their preferences, tastes and other related variable.

(ii) **Supply and Nature of Competition** While assessing market, supply position is also studied by entrepreneurs. A complete picture of quantities of the product made available in the market by all the existing players should be made available. It should take into account future supplies from possible entrants in the field.

(iii) **Cost and Price of Product** It is important to determine the cost of the product and its comparison with available products in the market.

Cost variable of competitors in terms of transportation delays, wastage, storage, etc, have to be studied to spot cost advantage. This will influence the delivery mechanism of the identified product or service.

(iv) **Project Innovation and Change** Market assessment will require a study of prevailing innovations and changes being carried out by existing entrepreneurs.

Technological advancements in the field have to be analysed because they may change the quality and influence the cost and price ultimately.

7 Explain by giving any four points why 'market assessment' is needed for an entrepreneurship.

Ans Market assessment is important as it helps the entrepreneur in (any four)

(i) **Demand Analysis** This refers to the assessment of the willingness and ability of the customers to buy products or services.

It analyses the economic status and expenditure pattern of the customers, their needs and number of potential customers.

(ii) **Understanding Supply and Competition in the Market** It tells about the number of enterprises with their name and share in the market. It also tells about strengths and weaknesses of the product, the credit terms and trade practices followed by enterprises.

(iii) **Determining Cost and Price of Product** The entrepreneur should consider the cost of material, labour, overheads and other expenses to determine the price.

Pricing is a process of fixing a monetary value to the product or service against its utility. It mainly depends on cost of products, already in market.

(iv) **Understanding the Existing Trade Practices** The enterprise may involve intermediaries to understand the existing trade practices in the market. This study would indicate the distribution pattern.

(v) **Project Innovation and Changes** Technological advancements in the field have to be analysed because they may change the quality and influence the cost and price.

8 Bunty, a fitness freak NRI, had done his masters in nutritional sciences from UK, during his vacations, he was disappointed to see that no gymnasium in Delhi had a workout module to suit his requirement. Anyhow, Fitness Fine Gymnasium of his friend offered him freedom to exercise the way he wanted.

In short time, Bunty became popular amongst the other members because of his knowledge, experience, competency, tactics and tips on exercising. He now explored deeply his curiosity of starting a Gymnasium in Greater Kailash 2, having a fusion of both diet and exercise under one roof.

He conducted a market research and subconsciously assimilated a whole data bank of information pertaining to lifestyle, interests, etc. of people in and around the area.

He approached his father for financial help of ₹ 25 lakhs as he had ₹ 20 lakhs only.

The ground floor of his flat was to be converted into a gymnasium. He started networking and negotiating with the manufacturers who could provide him with customised machines of his choice.

"One of the first task demanded of an entrepreneur is to manifest ability through the conceiving of new product market propositions". Identify and explain the steps involved in this process being initiated by Bunty. **(CBSE SQP)**

Ans The process initiated by Bunty is enterprise building. For explanation, refer to text on page 2.

9 Dr. Bhim is a senior cardiologist and is concerned about the depleting health index. He researched and found that proper eating habits can improve the quality of life. He initiated 'MediBytes', a unique canteen, where the food is provided as per one's health needs.

The food served at 'MediBytes' has no fast food and no aerated drinks. It provides zero oil food with all the basic nutrients required for the body.

Initially health conscious, 'MediBytes' is planning to open their branches in other locations also.

(i) Identify and explain the idea field that was explored by Dr. Bhim.

(ii) State any two idea fields with examples other than the one identified in (i) above. **(CBSE 2018)**

Ans (i) **Service Sector Ideas** Entrepreneurial opportunities are not only restricted to the manufacturer. Service sector is the most growing field these days, the world over, thanks to emerging, knowledge societies and advancements in information and tecnology. So, new opportunities can be idenfitied by understanding the linkages to diffierent business activities.

(ii) Two other ideas fields are

(a) **Market Driven or Demand Driven Ideas** Market research yields valuable data about trends of supply, demand and consumer preferences. Market research is a key factor to maintain competitiveness over competitiors.

(b) **Creative Efforts** Apart from applying creativity to spot and harness opportunities, it can also be applied to develop new products and services.

There are basically five ways in which creative ideas can be generated

- Develop a new product or service.
- Improve an existing product or service.
- Find a new process or resource for manufacturing a product.
- Find new markets for existing products or services.
- Find a new use of an existing product or service.

A very useful concept to bear in mind is that, most often creative products and services are born as results of problem solving.

10 Rajeev has just completed his B.Tech and wants, start his own business. He knew that the demand of electricity in India was increasing day-by-day, whereas its generation was not sufficient. Rajeev shared his views with some of his friends and they all decided to start the business of electricity generation. They experimented various methods and ultimately succeeded in electricity generation through garbage. They all were very happy as India is also facing the problem of garbage disposal.

(i) Identify and explain the source of "idea field" from where the idea had been generated by Rajeev and his friends.

(ii) Also explain two other sources of idea fields with the help of example. **(CBSE 2016)**

Ans (i) Rajeev and his friends generated the idea from demand driven or market driven. One of the important methods for generating ideas is to carry out a market research.

Such a study yield valuable data about trends of supply, demand and consumer preference. Market research is any organised effort to gather information about target markets or customers

(ii) Two other sources of idea are

Refer to topic of 'Sources of idea fields' on page 6.

11 'One of the keys to business success is to anticipate what the market will want or need.' Since, it is not possible for an entrepreneur to see into the future, there is one best way. This 'best way' will help the entrepreneur to understand the market and produce goods or provide services accordingly.

(i) Identify the concept discussed in the above lines.

(ii) Explain any three ways in which an entrepreneur can perform the activities related to the concept identified.

(CBSE 2015)

Ans (i) The concept discussed in the question is 'market assessment'. Market assessment helps an entrepreneur to know about the market potential by studying factors like demand, supply sources, nature of competition, etc.

(ii) For market assessment, the tool used is 'trend spotting'. Trend spotting helps the entrepreneurs to come out with the products, which are according to the trends of the market.

Three ways in which entrepreneurs can spot trends are

(a) **Read Trends** Wide variety of information can be collected from various sources as given below

- Read the leading publications.
- Websites related to their business.
- Industry publications.

- Business magazines.
- Major newspapers.
- International trends through websites.
- Influential bloggers.
- Niche bloggers focused on specific aspects of their industry.

(b) **Talk Trends** Talking to people is an equally important trend-potting tactic. For this, the entrepreneurs should participate in events organised by specific industry's trade association, whether it is online or offline.

They should also take advantage of social networking tools like social network sites and forums. They can also start or join groups on the networks to get the latest trends.

It is also important to talk to customers, both online and offline. They should pay attention to what the customers are saying not only on their product, but also on competitor's product.

(c) **Watch Trends** Observation in the market place is the best way to get on the actual trends. Entrepreneurs can study the habits, preferences and likes and dislikes of the consumers.

If the target consumers of a product are the youth, then they can visit a mall and observe trends of clothing, eating habits, how youth are engaging themselves in different activities.

They can see which stores are attracting maximum crowd and which are lying vacant. Trade shows also are a great place to get trend ideas.

12 Why is trend spotting important for the success of business? Explain the four ways in which an entrepreneur spots trends. **(CBSE 2023)**

Ans **Trend Spotting** It means identification of new trends. It will help the entrepreneur to understand the market and provide service or produce goods according to the market trends. There are several professional trend spotters, but they charge huge sums of money.

For various ways in which an entrepreneur spot trends, refer to Q.No. 8 of short answer type II (3 Marks).

13 Idea germination is the seeding stage of a new idea in the creative process. Explain the next four stages in the process. **(CBSE 2018)**

Or

The first step in the creative process is 'Idea Germination'. State the other steps of this process. **(CBSE 2015)**

Ans (i) **Preparation** On the basis of the idea, interest and curiosity the need is adjudged by the entrepreneur and he starts looking for the answer to implement that idea.

If the idea is to launch a new product or service then market research is conducted.

(ii) **Incubation** This is the subconscious assimilation of information. This is the transition period.

(iii) **Illumination** In this period of illumination the idea re-surfaces is realistic way and entrepreneur comes out with viable plan to give practical shape by collection raw material, arranging funds, policy making for the implementation of idea.

(iv) **Verification** Also called the validation or testing stage. This is where the idea is verified to prove that it has value. This is the most difficult phase of creativity as obstacles begin to appear.

This is the developing stage in which knowledge is developed into application.

14 Why is creativity important and explain the creative process? **(CBSE SQP)**

Ans Creativity is important to entrepreneurs because it is the first stage in the process of innovation, providing the stimulus for opportunity discovery and new venture creation.

Creative Process Refer to text on page 11.

15 Kavita has observed that there can be a good market for hand-knitted cotton and woollen trendy garments for small kids up to the age of three years.

She thought of starting a small enterprise for the same.

She also ensured that the enterprise will require 10-15 trained workers and an investment of rupees two lakhs.

This will give 40% annual return on investment.

(i) Quoting lines from the above para, identify and give the meaning of the entrepreneurship concept being stated in the above para.

(ii) Also, state the elements of the concept identified in (i) above. **(CBSE 2017)**

Or What is meant by innovation? Explain the elements in the innovation procss. **(CBSE 2023)**

Ans (i) The entrepreneurship concept discussed in the above para is 'innovation'. It is a process of entrepreneurship which involves translation of a useful idea into an application which has commercial value.

The lines from the above para which help to identify the stated concept are, "Kavita has observed .... for the same."

(ii) **Elements of Innovation Process** Refer to text on page 12.

16 Ms. Zambrano and Mr. Son are both successful entrepreneurs. However, they differ greatly in their opportunity searching behaviour. First, Mr. Son actively searched for opportunities and he examined many ideas, while Ms. Zambrano did not look for ideas at all.
Second, Mr. Son selected the best idea out of many ideas that he considered, while Ms. Zambrano took the only idea available and put it into action. Third, Mr. Son systematically and carefully assessed all his ideas before exploiting the best one, while Ms. Zambrano used her intuition.

We label entrepreneurs like Mr. Son purposeful entrepreneurs and those like Ms. Zambrano accidental entrepreneurs; they differ in whether they actively search for opportunities and in whether they satisfice when selecting an opportunity.

Source *Front.Psychol.,28th January, 2021 https://doi.org/10.3389/fpsyg.2020.592994*

How can an entrepreneur explore opportunities in the environment?

Ans Refer to text on page 2.

CASE STUDIES

Case 1

Bull in a China Shop

La Opala is India's only opal glassware maker and ready to take on global competition.

La Opala

In the 19th century, it was common to import good China crockery in return for opium exports from Calcutta. However, bone China crockery never really caught on, because it used cow bone ash. Even today, food is served on glass plates at traditional weddings for this reason. The porcelain and glass tableware market in India has always been strong. However, after independence and under foreign exchange restrictions, crockery imports tapered off and the market was filled with small manufacturers with products of suspect quality.

A small glass kiln, Radha Glass, at Madhupur in Bihar, has been making tea shop glasses, jars that are found in the neighbourhood grocery shop and hurricane-lamp shades for decades. The eldest son of the family, Sushil Jhunjhunwala, inherited his father's business in the mid-1980s.

Jhunjhunwala realised that nothing big could had happen, if he stuck to traditional glass products and was persuaded to look around. He got an idea when, in late 1980s, during a trip to South Korea, he came across an opaque white glass called 'opal'. Impressed by its look, he decided to manufacture it with the use of imported machinery and La Opala was born in 1988. Jhunjhunwala's timing was almost perfect because of liberalisation and the Indian middle-class affluence began to bloom after 1991 and every middle-class home was gifted one or two La Opala sets at a wedding. "The idea was to bring out an elegant product, Indianise it and make it readily available at an affordable price. Also, the attractive oven-proof designs were a welcome change from the heavy porcelain and China tableware that dominated the Indian market at that time", recalls Jhunjhunwala.

In 1996, Jhunjhunwala started a handmade lead-crystal glassware unit in collaboration with Doosan of South Korea. It was a well-placed investment because labour rates in the main crystal manufacturing countries were high and also because the Indian middle-classes were developing a penchant for good glasses. Solitaire, handmade, lead-crystal glassware making has now matured with 1,100 tpa production and annual sales at ₹ 18 crore. There are about 150 skilled workers who hand-carve crystal at the Madhupur plant.

In 2007, Jhunjhunwala started a second plant in Sitarganj near Haldwani in Uttarakhand, attracted by the hill-state tax regime and its proximity to Delhi's fancy market.

Now, the plant capacity has just been doubled to 8,000 tpa at an investment of ₹ 22 crore. La Opala, a silent performer, has reported sales of ₹ 157.66 crore and a PAT of ₹ 22.8 crore for the year ended March 2013, an increase of 34% in revenue from ₹ 117.5 crore sales, with PAT of ₹ 12.6 crore, in the previous year.

La Opala is the only opal glassware manufacturer in India and holds 40% of the ₹ 400 crore estimated opal glassware market, in competition with global brands like Corelle of Corning, US and Luminarc of France.

Courtesy Business India magazine, 27th May to 9th June, 2013 issue

1 How did Jhunjhunwala adapted his business to changing environment?

Ans When Sushil Jhunjhunwala inherited his father's business in mid-1980s, it was a small set-up making tea shop glasses and jars with no growth prospects. During a visit to South Korea, he came across an opaque white glass called 'opal' and he decided to use it to manufacture elegant crockery to target the newly emerging affluent middle-class. Thus, he adapted his business to the changing environment and was able to achieve tremendous success.

2. By quoting the lines, identify the elements of business opportunity, as sensed by Jhunjhunwala while starting a handmade lead-crystal glassware unit in collaboration with Doosan of South Korea.

Ans The elements of business opportunity are as follows

(i) **Assured Market Scope** "Jhunjhunwala's timing was almost perfect because of liberalisation and the Indian middle-class affluence began to bloom after 1991, and every middle-class home was gifted one or two La Opala sets at a wedding. The idea was to bring out an elegant product, Indianise it and make it readily available at an affordable price".

(ii) **An Attractive and Acceptable Rate of Return on Investment** "It was a well-placed investment because labour rates in the main crystal manufacturing countries were high and also because the Indian middle-classes were developing a penchant for good glasses."

(iii) **Potential for Future Growth** "Solitaire, handmade, lead-crystal glassware making has now matured with 1,100 tpa production and annual sales at ₹ 18 crore. There are about 150 skilled workers who hand-carve crystal at the Madhupur plant. In 2007, Jhunjhunwala started a second plant in Sitarganj near Haldwani in Uttarakhand."

3 Give any two entrepreneurial functions which Sushil Jhunjhunwala performed.

Ans Two entrepreneurial functions are

(i) Innovation and creativity

(ii) Risk taking

Case 2

Meals-on-Wheels

How many of you have travelled long distance in Indian trains? Wouldn't it be great to order food of your choice online while booking your train ticket, so that it can be delivered at your seat in the train? That's exactly the service TravelKhana offers to train travellers.

The Idea

Travel is a passion for the founders of TravelKhana and there is considerable work done in the Indian internet space in this sector. However, they felt, once a passenger buys a ticket, there is very little that technology has to offer in terms of the passenger's needs being fulfilled for food, local transport and local lodging. This is an even bigger problem for the train passengers and there is a huge gap between demand and supply. Being someone who has suffered several times while travelling, Pushpinder came up with this idea of capitalising on this opportunity.

TravelKhana is a market place that connects passengers with several restaurants on the Indian rail network. It offers a variety of choices to a railway passenger, so that the passengers can order food as per their liking and at their price point while they are travelling. Travelkhana.com is a service for transforming the experience of the railway passenger. TravelKhana aims to solve a 'food-on-the-move' issue by making available fresh, tasteful food to 'Indian Railways' commuters. Travelling in India is plagued by inefficiencies and their mission is to remove those inefficiencies through operational excellence.

The Founder

Pushpinder Singh, CEO and Chief Architect of TravelKhana has a Masters degree in Computer Science from BITS-Pilani and a B.Tech from IT-BHU. He has over 15 years of software and technology industry experience, particularly focused around the product industry, besides having played the role of CTO in 2 of his earlier successful ventures.

Pushpinder was most recently the VP Technology and acting CTO for INCA Informatics. He has, in the past, provided sustenance, continuity and providing thrust to an existing world leading product (Quark Xpress). Creation and contribution has been a hallmark of his career and he has been instrumental in creating and taking to market multiple products of repute at Quark, ARI Labs and Aplion Networks.

Start-up and Growth

We all know that Indian Railway is one of the biggest networks in the world. It's been a backbone of Indian transport for more than 50 years and will always be. There are new trains launched after every budget, along with new or extended train routes. 8 billion people travel in India by train annually and out of them 10% are premium users.

The TravelKhana automated platform, tracks trains in real time across India and ensures that fresh food is delivered to the passengers as per their choice in real time. It also helps vendors and restaurants in terms of effective and efficient fulfillment. Additionally, it completes an entire fulfillment cycle right from the point of ordering to delivery, customer feedback and reconciliation.

TravelKhana currently operates by offering a call centre interface as well as a web interface to passengers. The web version is currently in beta and still undergoing changes.

These interfaces will be followed with a Mobile App and an SMS version. TravelKhana will take your order with a minimum of 1 hour of lead time before the train arrival at a particular station.

The company tied up with travel agents who sell railway tickets. Travelkhana.com provides them free paper to print their tickets in return for advertisement space on the back of the ticket. What better way to reach out to your target audience! Travelkhana.com also offers each agent a login ID to the Travelkhana.com website in case passengers want to book their meals while booking their tickets.

TravelKhana currently operates in 30 cities and is rapidly expanding across the railway network. Now, they are looking at adding several cities across the Indian map and increasing the market size. They also plan to focus on acquiring the internet customer using a focused marketing campaign and to work along with vendors such that a delightful customer experience can be provided to the customers each time with reliable deliveries and excellent quality of products each time an order is placed.

This will require efficient logistics as well as managing that the quality of food is consistent with each delivery. TravelKhana has tie-ups with about 200 vendors across 50 railway stations in the North and West and has plans to expand to other regions by pulling in venture capital.

Once the rail business stabilises, Singh also intends to extend the convenience to bus passengers.

Funding

The founders have invested ₹ 20 lakhs (approximately), so far in addition to the accrued revenues from services. The promoters have further committed ₹ 30 lakhs to the venture. They are also looking for raising an angel round now and are at various stages of discussions with potential investors.

1 Pushpinder Singh, CEO and Chief of TravelKhana, followed various stages in developing his project.
Explain them by quoting the lines from the case study.

Ans The various stages in developing a project are as follows

(i) **Spotting an Opportunity by Analysing the Needs and Problems of the Society** "This is an even bigger problem for the train passengers and there is a huge gap between demand and supply. Being someone who has suffered several times while travelling, Pushpinder came up with this idea of capitalising on this opportunity".

(ii) **Identifying a Product or Service Through Innovation** "TravelKhana aims to solve a 'food-on-the-move' issue by making available fresh, tasteful food to 'Indian Railways' commuters".

(iii) **Setting up a Project and Nurturing it to Success** "TravelKhana currently operates in 30 cities and is rapidly expanding across the railway network".

2 'Opportunities exist in the environment'. Do you agree?

Ans Yes, opportunities are present in the environment, generally in the form of needs and problems of the society. In this case also, Pushpinder Singh capitalised on the problem faced by him by turning it into an opportunity.

CHAPTER ASSESSMENT

Objective Type Questions (1 Mark)

1 Entrepreneur is a person who
(a) conceives the idea to start a business
(b) earns income for himself
(c) Both (a) and (b)
(d) None of the above

2 The important method for generating ideas about market trend of supply, demand, consumer preference, competition degree, etc. is considered as
(a) market research (b) innovation
(c) creativity (d) None of these

3 While selecting an opportunity, an entrepreneur has to ensure
(a) good market for the product
(b) suitable rate of return
(c) Both (a) and (b)
(d) None of the above

4 'Suppliers' constitute a part of
(a) internal environment
(b) micro environment
(c) macro environment (d) None of these

5 Which of the following step is also entailed the testing stage of the creative process?
(a) Incubations (b) Innovation
(c) Preparation (d) Verification

6 ……… means identification of new trends.

7 There are ………… stages in the creative process.

8 Entrepreneur initiates the process of converting the opportunity into business. State true or false.

9 Sensitivity of environmental factors is crucial for an entrepreneur to succeed in the short-run. State true or false.

Short Answer Type I Questions (2 Marks)

10 What is the purpose to scan the environment?

11 Draw the enterprise process diagram.

12 What is PESTEL model? Explain it.

13 Mention any two ways in which an entrepreneur spot trends.

Short Answer Type II Questions (3 Marks)

14 What do you mean by business opportunity? Discuss its elements.

15 Discuss briefly importance of environment.

16 Write a short note on SWOT analysis framework.

Long Answer Type Questions (5 Marks)

17 Enlist the various sources which lead to the emergence of basic ideas.

18 Elaborate the factors involved in sensing opportunities.

19 Discuss the steps involved in investigation of ideas.

20 Comment on the following diagram.

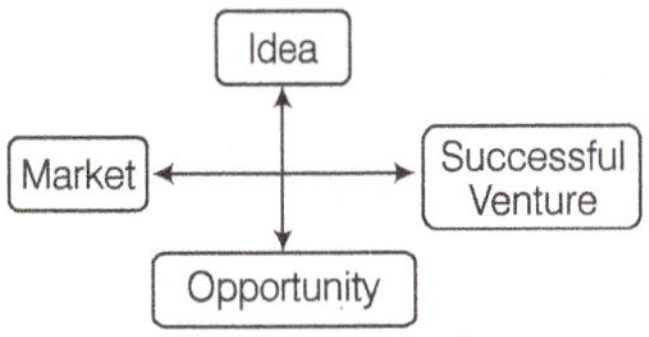

Entrepreneur

For explanations scan the given QR Code

CHAPTER 02

Entrepreneurial Planning

In this Chapter...

- Forms of business organisations
- Business plan
- Components of a business plan
- Organisational plan
- Production plan
- Operational plan
- Financial plan
- Marketing plan
- Human resource planning

Forms of Business Organisation
(Private Sector Enterprises)

The commonly opted forms of private sector enterprises are

– Sole Proprietorship
– Partnership
– Company
– Joint Hindu Family Business
– Co-operative Organisation

Since, entrepreneurs are highly motivated by independence and monetary gains, these five forms fufil the basic requirement of entrepreneurs well, which makes them the most desirable structure to commence a venture.

Sole Proprietorship

As the name suggests, sole means single and proprietor means an owner, thus, it is a form of business which is managed and controlled by a single owner.

One of the oldest, simplest and most commonly used forms of business organisation, which is owned, financed, controlled and managed by only one person is called as sole proprietorship.

It is also referred to as single entrepreneurship or individual proprietorship.

According to **ET Elbourne**, "Sole proprietorship is a business initiated and operated by one individual who carries all financial and administrative responsibilities, employing such assistants as may be necessary".

According to **Edward Elbourne**, "Sole proprietorship is a business unit whose ownership and management are vested in one person. The individual assumes all risks of loss or failure of the enterprise and receives all profits from its successful operations".

Characteristics of Sole Proprietorship

Main characteristics of sole proprietorship are as follows

Characteristics of Sole Preprietorship

- Individual ownership
- Individual management and control
- Individual Financing
- Unlimited liability
- Sole beneficiary
- Easy formation and closure
- No separate legal entity
- Limited area of operation/scope

1. **Individual Ownership** The business is exclusively owned by a single person.
2. **Individual Management and Control** All affairs of the business like what is to be done, how it is to be done and when it is to be done, etc., are managed and controlled by the sole proprietor.

However, competent people can also be employed for efficient management.

3. **Individual Financing** Proprietor arranges all finance through personal sources, which can also be from friends and other family members. He can also take loans and debts from financial institutions.
4. **Unlimited Liability** The proprietor and the business are considered to be the same and in case the assets of the business are not sufficient to pay liabilities, his/her personal property can also be used to pay off the business debts.
5. **Sole Beneficiary** The sole proprietor is entitled to all the profits and losses of the business.
6. **Easy Formation and Closure** Starting and closing this form of business is very easy as there are minimum legal formalities subjected to this form.
7. **No Separate Legal Entity** Owner and business are considered as one and the same. With the death of the owner, business also comes to an end.
8. **Limited Area of Operation/Scope** The scope of operations is limited due to
   - limited finance availabilities.
   - limited managerial abilities.

Suitability of Sole Proprietorship Form of Business

The success or failure of an enterprise depends upon the intelligence, competence and sensible decision-making capacity of the entrepreneur. Basically, this type of form is suitable when

- Capital requirement is limited.
- Confidentiality/Secrecy is important.
- Market for the product is local.
- Goods are of artistic nature or demands customised approach.
- Quick decision-making is necessary.
- Size of the venture is small.

Partnership

A partnership is an association of two or more persons as co-owners, to carry on, a business and to share its profits and losses. Thus, two or more persons may form a partnership by making a written or oral agreement to carry a business jointly and share its proceeds.

This is most accepted business form for small-scale and medium-scale businesses.

According to **John A Shubin**, "Two or more individuals may form partnership by making written or oral agreement that they will jointly assume full responsibility for the conduct of business".

According to **Indian Partnership Act, 1932**, "Partnership is a relationship between persons who have agreed to share the profits of a business carried on by all, or any of them acting for all".

Characteristics of Partnership

The essential characteristics of partnership are as follows

Characteristics of Partnership

- Two or more persons
- Agreement
- Profit sharing
- Unlimited liability
- Implied authority
- Mutual agency
- Utmost good faith
- Restriction on transfer of shares
- Continuity

1. **Two or More Persons** Partnership is formed by entering into a contract. So,
   - there must be at least two persons to enter into a contract to form partnership.
   - minors cannot be admitted to a partnership, because they are incompetent to enter into contract, but they can be admitted to the benefits of a running firm.
   - minimum number is 2 and maximum number of partners is 50.
2. **Agreement** When the partners enter into a contract, that means they make an agreement which can be oral or written. Written agreement is advisable as it helps in resolving disputes, if any. A written agreement between partners is referred to as **partnership deed**.
3. **Profit Sharing** The profits of the partnership business are shared amongst the partners in an agreed ratio. It should be kept in mind that sharing of profits is the main feature of this form of organisation. Partnership is not formed for charity.
4. **Unlimited Liability** The liability of partners is individually and collectively unlimited. This means that their personal properties can also be disposed off to pay the firm's debts. The creditors can claim their dues from anyone of them or all of them.

5. **Implied Authority** Any partner can act on behalf of the firm and his acts bind the firm.
6. **Mutual Agency** The business of the firm can be carried on by all the partners or any one of them acting for all. Thus, every partner is a principal as well as an agent.

   This means
   - each partner is liable for the acts performed by other partners.
   - each partner can bind other partners and the firm by his acts done in an ordinary course of business.
7. **Utmost Good Faith** Mutual trust and confidence is the main strength of partnership. Every partner should act honestly and give proper accounts to other partners.
8. **Restriction on Transfer of Shares** No partner can sell or transfer his shares to anybody else without the consent of the other partners. If a partner wants to discontinue, he can do so with the consent of other partners.
9. **Continuity** A partnership continues until all partners desire to continue it.

   Legally, a firm dissolves on the retirement, death, bankruptcy, lunacy or disability of a partner, if not otherwise provided in the partnership deed.

Suitability of Partnership Form of Business

Partnership form is suitable when more investments and better managerial efficiency is required. Partnership form of business should be a choice when

- Capital and managerial requirements are higher as compared to that of sole proprietorship.
- Enterprise falls in the category of being a small or medium scale enterprise.
- Direct contact with the customers is essential.

Consequences for Non-registration of a Partnership Firm

Partnership firms in India are governed by Indian Partnership Act, 1932. While it is not compulsory to register your partnership firm as there are no penalties for non-registration, it is advisable since the following rights are denied to an unregistered firm

- A partner cannot file suit in any court against the firm or other partners for the enforcement of any right arising from a contract or any right conferred by the Partnership Act.
- A case cannot be filed against a third party for claiming any right conferred by a contract.
- The firm or any of its partners cannot claim a set off (i.e. mutual adjustment of debts owned by the disputant parties to one another) or other proceedings in a dispute with a third party.

Joint Stock Company

Joint stock companies are evolved because the resources and life span of both sole proprietorship and partnership form of organisations are limited, while their liability is unlimited.

So, keeping step with the changing time, organisations faced growing needs for

- Capital
- Managerial talent and skills
- Limited liability

Thus, joint stock company as a modern form of business organisation emerged to meet the requirements of large sized business. Joint stock company means a voluntary association of persons, formed for some common objectives, with capital divisible into units of equal value called shares and with limited liability. Company is basically a creation of law, i.e. it is brought to life by law and can be put to death by law only.

In terms of **Companies Act, 2013**, "A company means a company incorporated under the Companies Act, 2013 or under any of the previous company law, [Section 2 (20)]."

In common law, a company is a 'legal person' or legal entity', separate from and capable of surviving beyond the lives of its members.

According to **Professor LH Haney,** "A joint stock company is a voluntary association of individuals for profit, having a capital divided into transferable shares, the ownership of which is the condition of membership".

Characteristics of a Company

A company is distinct from other forms of organisations because of the following characteristics

Characteristics of a Company

- Voluntary association
- Artificial person
- Separate legal entity
- Common seal
- Limited liability
- Transferability of shares
- Diffusion of ownership and management
- Number of members
- Limitation of action
- Winding up

1. **Voluntary Association** A company is a voluntary association of two or more than two persons, joining hands out of their free will, to form a company. A single person cannot constitute a company except in the case of one person company.
2. **Artificial Person** A company is created by law. Though, it has nobody and no conscience, it still exists as a person, having a distinct personality of its own and like a natural person, it can buy, sell and own property, sue others and be sued by others.
3. **Separate Legal Entity** A company has an entity or personality, which is absolutely independent and separate from the entity of its members. This implies that a company cannot be held liable for the actions of its members and *vice-versa.*
4. **Common Seal** Every company has a common seal with the name of the company engraved on it. Since, the company being an artificial person cannot sign, the common seal of the company is affixed on all the documents where the signature of the company is needed. Common seal is equivalent to the signature of the company.
5. **Limited Liability** It implies that the maximum liability of a member is limited to the unpaid value of shares held by a member or guarantee given by him. e.g. if a member holds 20 shares of ₹ 100 each, on which he has paid ₹ 60 per share, then his maximum liability will be limited to only ₹ 800, i.e. @ ₹ 40 per share on 20 shares held by him.
6. **Transferability of Shares** Shares of a company are freely transferable, i.e. if a member no longer desires to hold shares of a company, he can transfer them to somebody else. In a private company, there are certain restrictions to transfer shares, but the right to transfer shares is not denied by the company.
7. **Diffusion of Ownership and Management** In this form of organisation, there exists separation of ownership from management. As the shareholders (i.e. the owners) are scattered across the country, they give the right to manage the affairs of the company to the Board of Directors. Hence, through the Board of Directors, the company is managed in a democratic manner.
8. **Number of Members**

   Private Company

   Minimum required members = 2

   Maximum members = 200 (excluding employees)

   Public Company

   Minimum required members = 7

   Maximum members = No limit
9. **Limitation of Action** The scope of company is determined by
   - The Indian Companies Act, 2013
   - Memorandum of Association
   - Articles of Association

   If the company transgresses the limits as specified in the above documents, then it can lead to winding up of the company.
10. **Winding Up** Since, a company is born out of law, therefore, it can be terminated or winded up as per the provisions of law as stated in the Companies Act, only.

Forms of Company

An entrepreneur under the company form of organisation has option to incorporate an enterprise as a

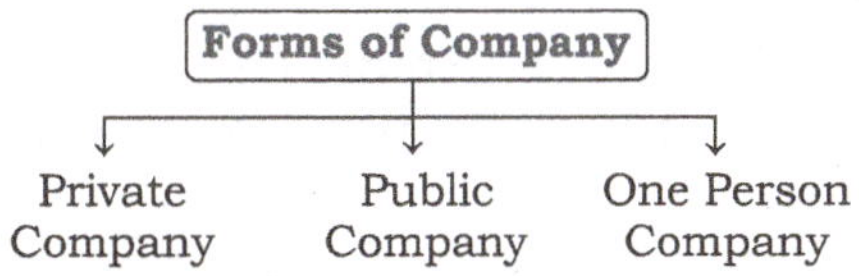

1. **Private Company** Private company means a company having a minimum paid-up share capital as may be prescribed and which by its articles
   - Restricts the right to transfer its shares.
   - Except in case of one person company, limits the number of its members to two hundred–(excluding present and past employees).
   - Prohibits any invitation to the public to subscribe for any securities of the company.
2. **Public Company** Under Section 3 (i), (ii) of the Companies Act, "Public company means a company which is not a private company and has a minimum paid-up share capital as may be prescribed".

The characteristics exhibited by a public company are as follows
- A public company has a minimum requirement of seven people to commence business, with no upper limit to membership.
- It does not restrict any transfer of shares.
- It invites public to subscribe for its shares, debentures and public deposits.
- It uses the word 'Limited', at the end of its name.

3. **One Person Company** As per provision of Section 2(62) of the Companies Act, 2013, one person company means a company which has only one person as member. It is a company incorporated as a private company which has only one member.

   Any natural person (should not be minor) who is an Indian citizen whether a resident in India or not i.e., NRI, shall be eligible to incorporate a one person company and appoint nominee of an OPC.

Why Private Company is More Desirable

A substantial number of entrepreneurs prefer to form a private company because of the following privileges enjoyed by it

(i) Only 2 members are required to form a private company as against the minimum requirement of 7 members for a public company.

(ii) Only 2 directors are required to constitute the quorum to validate the proceedings of the meetings.

(iii) Private companies are not required to file a prospectus and neither the statement in lieu of prospectus.

(iv) Private company can commence its business immediately after receiving certificate of incorporation. It does not need to obtain a certificate to commence business.

However, it has to submit the following documents with the Registrar

(a) Declaration of the company directors that every subscriber to the memorandum has paid for the value of share taken by him.

(b) The company should file with the Registrar a verification of its registered office.

(v) Holding of a statutory meeting or filing of a statutory report is not required by a private company.

(vi) A non-member cannot inspect the copies of the final accounts filed with the Registrar of a company.

(vii) Maintaining an index of members is not required by a private company.

(viii) A private company may have 2 directors.

Suitability of Company Form of Organisation

Company form of organisation should be chosen by an entrepreneur if
- The venture that he is opting for is of heavy and basic industry type.
- Large-scale operations are involved.
- The business has requirement for huge capital.
- The business involves heavy risks.
- The business opted for is technologically complex and sophisticated and requires the services of experts and professionals.

Joint Hindu Family Business

Hindu Undivided Family business is a unique form of business as this is only present in Indian society. HUF is governed by Hindu Law.

As defined under Hindu Law, "a family which consists of male lineally descended from a common ancestor and includes their wives and unmarried daughters". It arises from status and not from legal contracts.

For HUF to come into existence, there should be
– minimum two members in a family.
– existence of ancestral property.

Characteristics of HUF

Following are the main characteristics of HUF

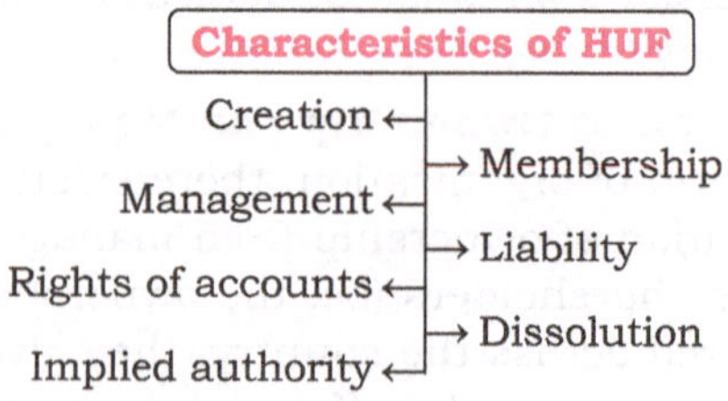

1. **Creation** It arises by status or operation of Hindu Law.
2. **Membership** A male member becomes a member by merely taking birth in a family. Even an adopted child can be admitted to HUF.
3. **Management** The eldest male member manages the affairs and is known as the 'Karta' of HUF. Other members are known as 'coparceners'.
4. **Liability** Karta has an unlimited liability whereas, the coparceners have limited liability.
5. **Rights of Accounts** Only the Karta can check the accounts.
6. **Dissolution** Hindu Undivided Family continues until two members in a family exist. However, if all members mutually agree, HUF can be dissolved.
7. **Implied Authority** Only Karta has the implied authority to bind the HUF and this is the reason he has an unlimited liability.

Cooperative Organisation

This form is different from any other form whether corporate or non-corporate because it operates not for profit but to provide some benefits or services to its members and even to general public by fighting against some social evil.

e.g. in a consumer cooperative, the aim is to provide quality goods at cheaper prices to its members by eliminating the middlemen.

The **Indian Cooperative Societies Act, 1912** defines cooperative society in Section 4 as, "Society which has its objectives as the promotion of economic interests of its members in accordance with cooperative principle".

According to **HC Calvert**, "Cooperation is a form of organisation wherein, persons voluntarily associate together as human beings on the basis of equality for the promotion of the economic interest of themselves."

Characteristics of Cooperative Organisation

Fundamental features of a cooperative organisation are as follows

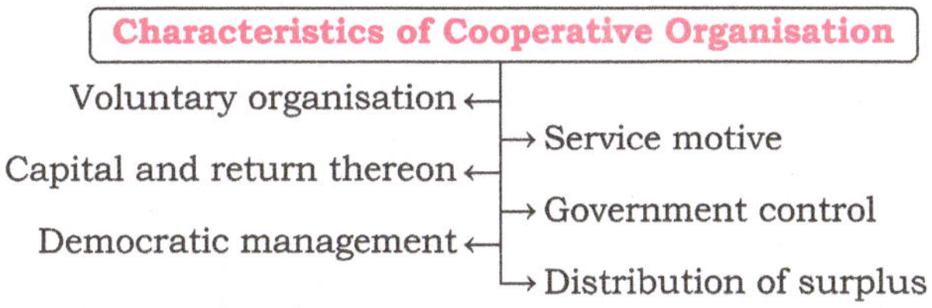

1. **Voluntary Organisation** A cooperative organisation is a voluntary association of persons. Everyone having a common interest is free to join a cooperative society irrespective of caste, creed, religion or political affiliation.

   Also, a member after giving proper notice can leave the society and will get back his capital according to the rules of the society. But no member can transfer his shares to another person.
2. **Service Motive** The main aim of a cooperative society is to provide some services or benefits to its members and even to general public by fighting against some social evil.
3. **Capital and Return Thereon** The capital of a cooperative society is raised from its members through issue of shares. A member can subscribe to maximum 10% of the total share capital or ₹ 1,000 whichever is higher.

   The members can be paid dividend on the capital contributed by them, subject to a maximum rate of 9% as per Cooperative Societies Act, 1912.
4. **Government Control** In India, the activities of cooperative societies are regulated according to the provisions of Cooperative Societies Act, 1912 and various State Cooperative Acts and also Multi-State Cooperative Act.

   These societies are required to submit their annual reports and accounts to the concerned Registrar of Cooperatives.

5. **Democratic Management** Co-operative organisation's management is vested in the hands of the managing committee elected by the members on the basis of 'One member-one vote'. Thus, democracy is the keynote of co-operative society's management.
6. **Distribution of Surplus** After giving dividends to the members, the surplus of profits, if any, is distributed among the members on the basis of goods purchased by each member from the society.

CHECK POINT 01

1. Which is the oldest simplest and most commonly used form of organisation?
2. State the maximum number of partners in partnership firm.
3. Partnership deed can only be in written form. State true or false.
4. Maximum numbers in a private company is 50. State true or false.
5. State two characteristics of a company.

Business Plan

Planning can be defined as "thinking in advance, what is to be done, when it is to be done, how it is to be done and by whom it should be done".

Before starting business venture, an entrepreneur needs to gather information about internal and external environment that may affect his business and form strategies and objectives in harmony of the environment. It is an intellectual thinking process, with the organised foresight, which is quite essential for an intelligent action.

Entrepreneur needs to workout in detail all the relevant external and internal elements involved in starting a new venture and then running it successfully which can be achieved through the preparation of a business plan.

Meaning of the Business Plan

A business plan is basically a written representation of an entrepreneur's vision for his business. It is a comprehensively written document prepared by an entrepreneur describing formally all the external and internal factors involved in starting a new venture.

It is a comprehensive project report which not only includes the entire range of activities which are being planned in the business, but also

- helps to understand the feasibility and viability of the proposed venture.
- facilitates in assessing and making provisions for the bottlenecks in the progress and implementation of the idea.
- discusses the potential for success of the project alongwith the risk factors involved.

So, it can be concluded that business plan is a formal statement of a set of business goals, the reason why they are thought to be attainable and a plan for reaching those goals, with complete understanding of internal and external factors affecting those goals.

Business Plan : A Decision-making Tool

Business plans are considered as decision-making tools due to the following

- Describe all necessary inputs for the enterprise.
- Explain the mode of utilisation of the resources.
- Detail the strategies for the execution of the project.
- Outline the desired goals.
- Assess market sensitivity and the profitability of the venture.

Scope of Business Plan

An effective business plan should represent all aspects of a business and sub-plans should be prepared to cover all aspects relating to

- marketing
- finance
- operations
- human resources
- legal compliance
- intellectual property rights

Who Should Write the Plan?

Preparing a business plan requires knowledge of diverse business disciplines. Ideally, a business plan should be prepared by the entrepreneur himself, with the advice and input derived from

- lawyers
- accountants
- marketing consultants
- engineers
- internet sites
- officially appointed or established banks, specialised financial institutions or agencies to promote entrepreneurship
- friends, relatives, mentors, etc.

The entrepreneur should assess his/her own skills and seek assistance where he is lacking his expertise. He can also hire a consultant to draw up the plan.

Importance of Business Plan

The business plan is valuable to all stakeholders such as the entrepreneur himself, potential investors, venture capitalists, banks, financial institutions, suppliers, customers, advisors, etc., as it provides a road-map for starting a new venture.

Road map is required to start a venture because of the following reasons

- A business plan helps in determining the viability of the venture in the designated market.
- It guides the entrepreneur in planning his activities such as
  - (a) identifying the resources required.
  - (b) obtaining licenses, if required.
  - (c) meeting with the legal requirements as desired by the government.
- A business plan helps in satisfying the concerns, issues and queries of each group of people interested in the venture.
- It provides room for self-assessment and self-evaluation by requiring the entrepreneur to think through various scenarios and plan ways to avoid obstacles.
- At times, a business plan also helps to identify the obstacles which cannot be overcome, suggesting to terminate the venture while still on paper, thereby saving time and money.
- Business plan is an important tool for procuring funds. Any investor, before investing in a venture is interested in knowing about 4 Cs to access the credit worthiness of the entrepreneur and the business.

  These 4 Cs are – Character, Cash flow, Collateral and Contribution towards equity.

  And it is the business plan which reflects the entrepreneur's credit history, his ability to make payments against debt and interest and the amount of equity invested by him. So, it helps a business to raise funds by providing the relevant information.
- A business plan gives a clear indication to the entrepreneur, investors and the government regarding
  - (a) What an entrepreneur is doing?
  - (b) Why he/she is doing it?
  - (c) How he/she will do it?

So, keeping the above points in view, it could be concluded that although writing a good business plan can't guarantee success but it can go a long way towards reducing the odds of failure.

Formats of a Business Plan

The depth and detail in the business plan depends on the size and scope of the proposed new venture. There is no fixed content for a business plan as it varies according to the entrepreneur's goals and audience. Thus, it is common to have three or four formats as follows for the same business plan

1. **Elevator Pitch** It is basically a 3 minute summary of the business plan's executive summary.

   This format is often used as a teaser to awaken the interest of the potential investors, customers or strategic partners.
2. **A Pitch Deck With Oral Narrative** This format presents the business plan in the form of an entertaining slide show complemented with an oral narrative.

   It is meant to trigger discussion and awaken the interest of the potential investors and induce them to read the written presentation.

   It includes executive summary, important graphs showing financial trends and key decision-making benchmarks.
3. **A Written Presentation for External Stakeholders** It includes a detailed, well written and pleasingly formatted plan targeted at external stakeholders.
4. **An Internal Operational Plan** It is a detailed plan describing planning details that are needed by management, but may not be of interest to external stakeholders.

Format/Outline of a Business Plan

1. Introductory page
   - (i) Name and address of business
   - (ii) Name(s) and address(s) of principal(s)
   - (iii) Nature of business
   - (iv) Statement of financing needed
   - (v) Statement of confidentiality of report
2. Executive summary—Three to four pages summarising the complete business plan.
3. Industry analysis
   - (i) Future outlook and trends
   - (ii) Analysis of competitors
   - (iii) Market segmentation
   - (iv) Industry and market forecasts
4. Description of venture
   - (i) Product(s)
   - (ii) Service(s)
   - (iii) Size of business
   - (iv) Office equipment and personnel
   - (v) Background of entrepreneurs
5. Production plan
   - (i) Manufacturing process (amount subcontracted)
   - (ii) Physical plant
   - (iii) Machinery and equipment
   - (iv) Names of suppliers of raw materials
6. Operational plan
   - (i) Description of company's operation
   - (ii) Flow of orders for goods and/or services
   - (iii) Technology utilisation
7. Marketing plan
   - (i) Pricing
   - (ii) Distribution
   - (iii) Promotion
   - (iv) Product forecasts
   - (v) Controls
8. Organisational plan
   - (i) Form of ownership
   - (ii) Identification of partners or principal shareholders
   - (iii) Authority of principals
   - (iv) Management team background
   - (v) Roles and responsibilities of members or organisation
9. Assessment of risk
   - (i) Evaluate weakness of business
   - (ii) New technologies
   - (iii) Contingency plans
10. Financial plan
    - (i) Proforma income statement
    - (ii) Cash flow projections
    - (iii) Proforma balance sheet
    - (iv) Break-even analysis
    - (v) Sources and applications of funds
11. Appendix (contains backup material)
    - (i) Letters
    - (ii) Market research data
    - (iii) Leases or contracts
    - (iv) Price lists from suppliers

CHECK POINT 02

1. "Business plan is an oral document prepared by an entrepreneur." Do you agree?
2. "An effective business plan should represent all aspects of a business." State true or false.
3. Should engineers write a business plan?
4. What are the 4 C's required to know before investing in a venture?
5. Which format is often used to awaken the interest of investors?

Components of a Business Plan

Depending upon the entrepreneur's experience, knowledge and purpose, generally a business plan outlines sequentially following components or parts

- Organisational plan
- Production plan
- Operational plan
- Financial plan
- Marketing plan
- Human resource planning

I. Organisational Plan

The organisational plan is that part of the business plan that describes the proposed ventures form of ownership, i.e. whether it is

- sole proprietorship
- partnership
- joint hindu family
- company
- corporation

Their are four basic categories under which any business falls. These are as follows

1. **Manufacturing** Business that makes a tangible product.
2. **Wholesale** Business that buys products in bulk from the manufacturers to be sold in smaller lot to retailers.
3. **Retail** Business that sells directly to the final consumers for final satisfaction.
4. **Service** Business that sells intangible products such as time or expertise.

Each type of business differs significantly in terms of

- commencement procedures
- legal constraints
- financial requirement
- accounting methods
- marketing and promotional strategies
- risk and liability

So, before selecting the form of ownership, firstly, it is necessary to categorise the business.

Also, each form of ownership has important, implications on taxes, liability, continuity, financing and ownership.

As we already know, 'no form is the best form'. So, an entrepreneur should select that form which best suits his business category and its needs and that would ensure long-term effectiveness of the enterprise and profitability.

Elements of Organisational Plan

The organisational plan is that part of the business plan which describes the proposed venture's opted form of ownership.

An organisational plan throws light on

- the terms and conditions associated with the selected form.
- lines of authority and responsibility of members of the new venture.
- the names, designation, addresses and resumes of the members.
- stake of members in the organisation.
- roles and responsibilities of each member.
- procedure for solving conflicts/disputes amongst members.
- forms of payment for the members of the organisation.
- voting rights, managerial and controlling rights of the members.

The above information provides the potential investor with a clear understanding of the organisational structure.

Importance of Organisational Plan

Organisational plan is very important for both, the entrepreneur as well as the investors, as it

- specifies the types of skills needed and the roles that will be performed by the members, i.e. by defining its formal organisation.
- represents the attitudes, behaviours, dress code, communication styles, etc., thus, defining the informal organisational culture.

II. Production Plan

Production is the most important activity of an enterprise because it is through this process that raw materials are transformed into finished products.

According to **Kimball and Kimball Jr**, "The planning of industrial operations, involves four considerations, namely, what work shall be done, how the work shall be done and lastly, when and by whom the work shall be done".

Being highly complex and tedious, the manufacturing operation needs to be well planned.

This venture mostly face the following situations

1. **No Manufacturing Involved** If the new venture does not include any manufacturing function, i.e. it is a trading business, then this section is eliminated from the plan.
2. **Partial Manufacturing** If the entrepreneur plans to partially manufacture some of the parts and outsource or subcontract for other processes, then the production plan should describe
   - name and location of subcontractors.
   - reasons for their selection.
   - cost and time involved.
   - any contracts that have been completed by them.
   - any other relevant information.
   - a clear mention of what entrepreneur intends to do himself and what he plans to get done from outside.
3. **Complete Manufacturing** If the entrepreneur plans to carry out the whole manufacturing process by himself, then he/she needs to describe
   - the physical plant layout.
   - the machinery and equipment required to perform the manufacturing operations.
   - raw materials and suppliers names, addresses, terms and conditions.
   - cost of manufacturing.
   - any future capital equipment required, etc.

Objective of a Production Plan

The objective of a production plan in the words of **Alford** and **Beathy** is "Picturising ahead every step in a long series of separate operations, each step to be taken in the right place of the right degree and at the right time and each operation to be done at maximum efficiency".

So, a production plan helps to plan the work in such a manner that one can clearly form an idea about

- production schedule and/or budget.
- machinery, equipment required.
- manufacturing method and process involved.
- plant layout.
- time, motion and work study.
- manpower requirement.
- inventory requirement.

III. Operational Plan

Where the production plan aims at 'plan your work', the operational plan ensures 'work your plan'. It is basically related to how a business proposes to put its plan in action.

According to **Wright**, "Operational plan is a system whereby there is achieved a smooth and coordinated flow of work within the factory so that, by planning and control of all the productive operations in all the stages of manufacture, the final product is completed in accordance with the plans".

So, operational plan is a blue print prepared in advance of actual operations, to

- ensure orderly flow of materials in the manufacturing process, right from the acquisition of raw materials to the completion of the product.
- facilitate continuous production, lesser work-in-progress and minimisation of wastage.
- coordinate the work of engineering, purchasing, production, selling and inventory management.
- describe the flow of goods or services from production point to the consumers.
- introduce a proper system of quality control.
- undertake the best and most economic production policies and methods.

Objectives of Operational Plan

An operational plan aims at getting desired manufacturing results in terms of

- quantity
- quality
- time
- place
- cost

Thus, the objectives of an operational plan are as follows

- Planning for production in advance of operations.
- Establishing the exact route for each individual items in the part of the assembly line.
- Setting starting or finishing dates for each important assignment or work.
- Regulating the orderly movement of goods throughout the entire manufacturing cycle.

Elements of Operational Plan

In order to achieve the above mentioned objectives, the following elements of the operational plan need to be specifically addressed

Elements of Operational Plan

- Routing
- Scheduling
- Dispatching
- Follow-up
- Inspection
- Shipping

1. **Routing** It is a process concerned with determining exact route or path a product/ service has to follow right from raw material till its transformation into finished products.
2. **Scheduling** This means deciding the time frame within which each operation would be completed. It simply means fixation of time, day, date when each operation is to be commenced and when it is to be completed.
3. **Dispatching** It means issuing necessary orders, instructions and guidelines relating to the work to be performed. It initiates the production process.
4. **Follow-up** This element relates to evaluation and appraisal of work performed. It is helpful in early detection of errors and helps all entrepreneur to
   - Develop ways to review the present situation with regard to materials, work-in-progress and finished goods.
   - Evolve ways to expedite the performance of those departments which lag behind.
   - Remove obstacles in the way of production by suggesting remedial measures.
5. **Inspection** This means comparing materials, product or performance with established standards. Products can be tested in specified laboratories or new methods or strategies can be evolved to ensure pre-determined standard quality of the product.
6. **Shipping** This section goes beyond the manufacturing process and describes the flow of goods or services from production to the consumers.

All the above discussed elements help us to make a successful operational plan.

Factors affecting Operational Plan

Operational plan is greatly affected by
- nature of venture
- type of product/service
- scale of operation
- technology involved

CHECK POINT 03

1. Write two elements of organisational plan.
2. Organisational plan does not specify the types of skills needed. State true or false.
3. State any one objective of production plan.
4. Mention any one objective of operational plan.
5. What do you mean by inspection?

IV. Financial Plan

Finance is the life blood of any organisation and is the most important pre-requisite to establish any business. Availability of finance enables the entrepreneur to bring together the 5Ms of business, i.e. Men, Material, Machines and Methods, the fifth 'Money' is finance itself.

An entrepreneur before drawing out the financial plan,must keep in mind the following factors
- Financial requirements.
- Sources of raising funds.
- Exact assessment of the revenue, cost, profits, cash flows, dynamics, stock of inventory, loans, etc.

So, a financial plan is basically a projection of key financial data about
- the potential investment commitment needed for the new venture.
- economic feasibility of the enterprise.

Objective of Financial Plan

The financial plan must be able to explain to any potential investor how the entrepreneur plans to meet all financial obligations and also to maintain his liquidity in order to pay for debt and to provide good return on investment.

Financial Plan

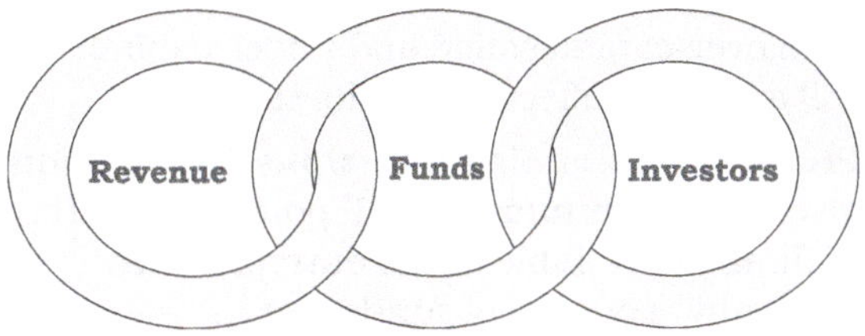

Elements of Financial Plan

An entrepreneur makes use of several financial projection techniques and tools to draw up a financial plan. Generally, a financial plan needs 3 years of projected financial data to satisfy any outside investors. To simplify, the financial plan is so designed that the entrepreneur and the investors could have a clear picture of
- How much funds are required?
- Where will the funds come from?
- How are they disbursed?
- The amount of cash available.
- General financial well-being of the new venture, i.e. probable revenue forecast for the first year atleast.

Components of Financial Plan

Major financial items that should be included in the financial plan are as follows

Components of Financial Plan

- Proforma investment decisions
- Proforma financing decisions
- Proforma income statement
- Proforma cash flow
- Proforma balance sheet
- Break-even point
- Economic and social variables

1. **Proforma Investment Decisions** This part of financial plan highlights how the business proposes to invest its assets, so as to be able to generate highest possible returns.

   This part clearly specifies the amount of investment required to be made in fixed as well as working capital. In this plan, an entrepreneur should mention investment required for
   - land and building.
   - machinery and plant installation cost.
   - preliminary expenses.
   - margin for working capital.
   - expenses on research and development.
   - investment in short-term assets viz. raw material, level of cash, etc.

   This part helps an entrepreneur to plan for optimum capital structure for his business as both over-capitalisation and under-capitalisation will adversely affect the business.

2. **Proforma Financing Decisions** This section gives a brief summary of all potential sources of finance available to the entrepreneur. Typically, sources of funds are
   - Owners, i.e. owner's funds.
   - Outsiders i.e. borrowed funds.

   An entrepreneur should select the best overall mix of financing, so that
   - The cost of capital and the financial risk stands minimsed.
   - Return on investment and profitability stands maximised.

3. **Proforma Income Statement** This section of the financial plan gives the projected net profit of the business based on projected revenues and projected expenses. While estimating the projected revenues for the year, 'sales by month' must be estimated first by using forecasting techniques.

   Any of the following techniques can be made use of while making sales projections for the month
   - Marketing research.
   - Industry sales.
   - Survey of buyers' intentions.
   - Expert opinions.
   - Financial data on similar start-ups.
   - Some trial experiences of self or others.

4. **Proforma Cash Flow** This part reflects the projected cash available with the enterprise as a result of subtracting projected cash payments from projected cash receipts.

   Cash flow results only when actual cash is received or paid. Credit sales or outstanding expenses are not considered in this section as they do not result in flow of cash.

   The entrepreneur may find it difficult to project cash flows as determining the exact monthly receipts and payments is not easy.

   So, they prefer a simple determination of 'Cash in Less Cash Out' which helps to give them a fast indication of cash position.

   Also, while working out the projected cash flows, entrepreneurs follows a conservative approach.

5. **Proforma Balance Sheet** This document helps the enterprise to reflect the position of the business at the end of its first year. A summary of the projected assets, liabilities and net worth of the entrepreneur is depicted through proforma balance sheet.

6. **Break-even Point** The break-even point is that level of volume of production at which firm neither makes a profit nor a loss. Here, the total revenue is equal to the total cost of a firm at a given level of capacity.

   This section of the plan projects the number of units to be sold or sales volume to be achieved to break-even.

   Calculation of Break-even Point (BEP) is quite useful for the entrepreneur as it helps in assessing
   - the minimum level of output to be produced.
   - the effect of change in quantity of output upon the profits.
   - the selling price of the product.
   - the profitable options in the line of production.

7. **Economic and Social Variables** In view of the social responsibility of business, the abatement costs, i.e. the cost of controlling the environmental damage should also be stated in the plan.

   It is always advisable to mention the following socio-economic benefits expected from the proposed investments in the financial plan
   - employment generation
   - import substitution
   - ancillarisation
   - export promotion
   - local resource utilisation
   - development of the area

   If it is not possible to quantify the expected benefits, then each point should be carefully analysed and its importance should be stated in this section.

V. Marketing Plan

This plan describes the market conditions and strategies related to how
- products/services will be distributed,
- priced,
- promoted and
- where to be distributed

The marketing plan is a significant element in the business plan of a new venture, as it highlights how a business plan makes a place for itself in a competitive market by providing answers to three basic questions, they are

1. **Where have We Been?** This segment focuses on
   - some history of the market place.
   - marketing strengths and weaknesses of the new venture.
   - market opportunities and threats.
2. **Where do We want to Go?** This primarily addresses the marketing objectives and goals of the enterprise in the next 12 months.
3. **How do We get There?** This question discusses
   - the specific marketing strategy that will be implemented.
   - when it will occur.
   - who will be responsible for the monitoring of activities.

Normally, the entrepreneur should prepare an annual marketing plan each year so as to gel well with the changing business environment and its forces.

Facts needed for Market Planning

The facts that are needed for market planning are as follows

- Who are the users, where are they located, how much do they buy, from whom do they buy, and why?
- How have promotion and advertising been employed and which approach has been most effective?
- What are the pricing changes in the market, who has initiated these changes, and why?
- What are the market's attitudes concerning competitive products?
- What channels of distribution supply consumers and how do they function?
- Who are the competitors, where are they located and what advantages/disadvantages do they have?
- What marketing techniques are used by the most successful competitors and by the least successful?
- What are the overall objectives of the company for the next year and 5 years hence?
- What are the company's strengths and weaknesses?
- What are one's production capabilities regarding product?

Steps in Preparing a Marketing Plan

Investors give a great weightage to this section of business plan to assess the chances of success of a business.

So, an entrepreneur should prepare a comprehensive and detailed marketing plan.

The steps involved in marking a marketing plan are as follows

1. **Business Situation Analysis** This section starts with addressing the question, 'where we have been?'

   In case of an existing enterprise, a review of past performance and achievements of the enterprise are stated in this part but in case the venture is new, then the following issues are addressed
   - personal profile of the entrepreneur.
   - emphasis on products development.
   - what 'needs' it satisfies.
   - any other enterprise/experience of the entrepreneur.
   - any marketing segmentation, if planned.

2. **Identify the Target Market** This section identifies the target consumers for a business, so that marketing strategies could be aimed towards them. Identification of target consumers involve
   - deciding what the general market or industry wishes to buy on the basis of market research or industry analysis.
   - dividing the market into smaller groups (segmentation), based on

   (a) Consumer's characteristics viz.
   - Geographic (state, country, etc)
   - Demographic (sex, age, etc)
   - Psychographics (personality, life style, etc)

   (b) Buying situation viz.
   - Buying conditions (time available, etc)
   - Usage
   - Desired benefits (features of product)
   - Select segment or segments to target.
   - Develop a marketing plan integrating according to product, price, distribution, promotion.
3. **Conduct SWOT Analysis** A successful marketing plan needs to consider the strengths and weaknesses of the new venture to ensure its success.

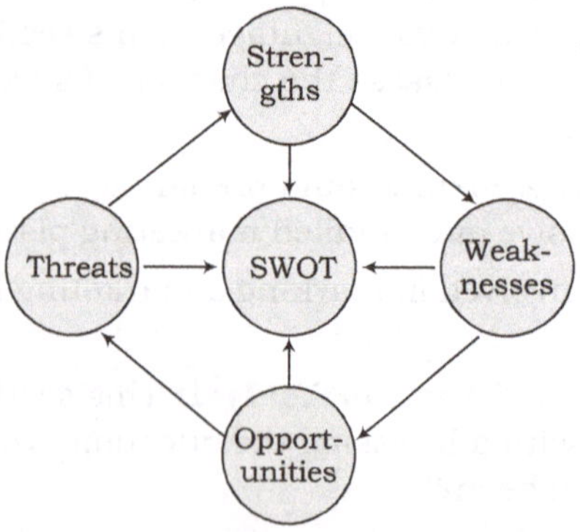

SWOT Analysis

So, it is important for the entrepreneur to consider in the target market his/her enterprise's

- Strengths
- Weaknesses
- Opportunities
- Threats

All these together make the acronym 'SWOT'.

4. **Establish Goals** 'Where do we want to go?' is answered well by establishing
   - Realistic, attainable and well defined goals and objectives for the enterprise.
   - Quantifying the goals, so that they could be measured for control purposes.
   - Setting standards to measure those goals which are qualitative in nature.
   - Limiting, the goals to a specific number so that there are no chaos, confusions or overlapping.
5. **Define Marketing Strategy** 'How do we get there?' demands specific activities to be outlined to meet the enterprise's established goals and objectives.

   The marketing strategy and action plan comprises of decisions pertaining to the following 4P's
   - Product
   - Price
   - Promotion
   - Place
6. **Implementation and Monitoring of the Plan** Evolving a marketing plan is not a mere formality. It is meant to be a commitment by the entrepreneur to a specific strategy.

   It is important for the entrepreneur to be flexible and be prepared to make adjustments if necessary in the plan.

VI. Human Resource Plan/ Manpower Planning

An organisation's performance and resulting productivity are directly proportional to the quantity and quality of its manpower.

So, human resources (men) are of paramount importance for the success of an organisation.

According to **Hicks and Gullet**, "The people working in a firm make it what it is".

So, in order to build up loyal, efficient and dedicated personnel, entrepreneur needs to pay adequate and proper attention to human resource planning.

Manpower planning thus helps to assess

1. **What Kind of People are Required?**

   To carry on its operations effectively, each organisation needs manpower with the necessary qualifications, skills, knowledge, experience and aptitude for work.

   So, in this section, an entrepreneur must clearly state

   - What kind/type of person is required to be hired for getting his work done?
   - As each person would have different position, duties and responsibilities, it becomes imperative for the entrepreneur to clearly workout a wide range of personnel ranging from managers, supervisors, administrators, engineers, technical, skilled and unskilled class.

     Nature of business activity helps entrepreneur to a large extent in deciding the type of manpower required.

2. **How Many People are Required?**

   This question deals with the number of personnel the enterprise needs. The important factors to be considered before deciding the number of personnel needed are

   - The total work to be done.
   - How much work can an average person do in a specified period of time?
   - Level of absenteeism expected.
   - Rate of labour turnover.
   - The present number of employees.
   - The future plans for expansion and diversification.

3. **How Will they be Selected?/ How to Procure Personnel?**

   Procurement of 'right person, at right job, at the right time' is the objective of human resource plan.

   So, in this section, an entrepreneur clearly mentions the strategies, methods, policies, rules and regulations pertaining to manpower

   - Recruitment
   - Selection
   - Training

CHECK POINT 04

1. What are 5 M's of business?
2. Financial plan explains how the entrepreneur plans to meet all financial obligations. State true or false.
3. State important components of manpower.
4. Company's strengths and weaknesses analysis is necessary for human resource plan. Is it true or false?
5. With the name of 4 P's of marketing strategy.

EXAM PATTERN EXERCISE

Objective Type Questions (1 Mark)

Multiple Choice Questions

1 The scope of operation of sole proprietorship form of business is limited because of

(a) limited finance availabilities
(b) limited managerial abilities
(c) Both (a) and (b)
(d) None of the above

Ans (c) Both (a) and (b)

2 Which of the following forms of business organisations require minimum two persons to start the same? **(CBSE Term I 2021)**

(i) Sole proprietorship
(ii) Partnership
(iii) Private company (iv) Public company

(a) (i) and (ii) (b) (iii) and (iv)
(c) (ii), (iii) and (iv) (d) (ii) and (iii)

Ans (d) (ii) and (iii)

3 This form of business organisation has a limited area of operation due to availability of limited finance and limited managerial abilities **(CBSE 2023; Term I 2021)**

(a) joint stock company
(b) partnership
(c) sole proprietorship (d) Both (a) and (c)

Ans (c) sole proprietorship

4 Which of the following is not a public sector enterprise? **(CBSE Term I 2021)**

(a) Departmental undertaking
(b) Public corporation
(c) Sole tradership (d) Government company

Ans (c) Sole tradership

5 Which of the following is not a disadvantage of sole proprietorship form of business organisation? **(CBSE Term I 2021)**

(a) Limited capital
(b) Quick decision-making
(c) Limited managerial ability
(d) Limited continuity

Ans (b) Quick decision-making

6 A company is called an artificial person because .... **(CBSE SQP Term I)**

(a) it does not have the shape of a natural person
(b) it cannot be sued in the court of law
(c) it is invisible and intangible
(d) it exists in the eyes of law

Ans (d) it exists in the eyes of law

7 What is the minimum number of members required to start a public company? **(CBSE SQP Term I)**

(a) 2 (b) 5
(c) 7 (d) 50

Ans (c) 7

8 The business of partnership firm can be carried out by all the partners or any one of them acting for all. This highlights the following characteristic of partnership. **(CBSE Term I 2021)**

(a) Agreement (b) Utmost good faith
(c) Mutual agency (d) Implied authority

Ans (c) Mutual agency

9 (i) Each partner is liable for acts performed by other partners.
(ii) Each partner can bind other partners and the firm by his acts done in the ordinary course of business.

Which feature of partnership is highlighted by these two statements? **(CBSE SQP Term I)**

(a) Implied authority (b) Utmost good faith
(c) Mutual Agency (d) Agreement

Ans (c) Mutual Agency

10 'It is an artificial person created by law' is a characteristic of which of the following forms of business organisation? **(CBSE Term I 2021)**

(a) Company (b) Partnership firm
(c) Sole proprietorship (d) Both (a) and (b)

Ans (a) Company

11 In which of the following forms of business organisation there exists separation of ownership from management? **(CBSE Term I 2021)**

(a) Sole proprietorship (b) Partnership
(c) Company (d) Both (b) and (c)

Ans (c) Company

12 Being an artificial person, a company cannot sign the documents. Hence it uses a .... on which its name is engraved for the same. **(CBSE Term I 2021)**

(a) trademark (b) logo
(c) patent (d) common seal

Ans (d) common seal

13 Which form of business organisation can commence business immediately after incorporation? **(CBSE SQP Term I)**

(a) Public company (b) Private company
(c) Partnership (d) Sole proprietorship

Ans (b) Private company

14 Which of the following feature applies only to a public company? **(CBSE SQP Term I)**

(a) Can start business after incorporation
(b) Has a restriction up to 200 members
(c) Can invite public to subscribe for its shares
(d) Directors are not required to obtain qualification shares

Ans (c) Can invite public to subscribe for its shares

15 A comprehensively written document prepared by the entrepreneur describing all the relevant internal and external elements in starting a new venture is called **(CBSE Term I 2021)**

(a) marketing plan (b) business plan
(c) financial plan (d) operational plan

Ans (b) business plan

16 The business plan

(a) helps in determining the viability of the venture in a designated market
(b) helps in providing guidance to the entrepreneur in organising his/her planning activities
(c) provides room for self-assessment and self-evaluation
(d) All of the above

Ans (d) All of the above

17 Partnership form of organisation was developed due to the inherent limitations of sole proprietorship. One of them is limited capital, identify the other two? **(CBSE SQP Term I)**

(a) Limited managerial ability, limited continuity
(b) Limited continuity, unlimited liability
(c) Limited managerial ability, unlimited liability
(d) Lack of secrecy, limited continuity

Ans (a) Limited managerial ability, limited continuity

18 .... section of the business plan generally begins with the "mission statement" by the entrepreneur describing the size, scope and nature of the enterprise. **(CBSE SQP Term I)**

(a) Description of business venture
(b) Introductory profile (c) Industry profile
(d) Entrepreneur's biodata

Ans (a) Description of business venture

19 Amar and Akbar started a partnership firm to help the poor and needy. They collected money from various agencies and used it to benefit all those who are in dire need. Which characteristic are they violating? **(CBSE SQP Term I)**

(a) Agreement
(b) Unlimited liability
(c) Profit sharing
(d) Utmost good faith

Ans (c) Profit sharing

20 .... plan is that part of the business plan which describes the proposed venture's opted form of ownership.

(a) Operational (b) Production
(c) Organisational (d) Business venture

Ans (c) Organisational

21 Which of the following plans help to plan the work in such a manner that one can clearly form an idea about plan layout?

(a) Operational plan
(b) Production plan
(c) Marketing plan (d) Financial plan

Ans (b) Production plan

22 .... component of a financial plan helps to ascertain the highest possible returns on investment. **(CBSE SQP Term I)**

(a) Proforma investment decision
(b) Proforma income statement
(c) Proforma cash flow
(d) Proforma balance sheet

Ans (a) Proforma investment decision

23 Routing is an element of which of the following components of business plan? **(CBSE Term I 2021)**

(a) Production plan (b) Operational plan
(c) Organisational plan (d) Financial plan

Ans (b) Operational plan

24 Which of the following is not a component of financial plan? **(CBSE Term I 2021)**

(a) Economic and social variables

(b) Follow-up (c) Break-even analysis

(d) Proforma investment decisions

Ans (b) Follow-up

25 'How products/services will be distributed, priced and marketed' is described by which of the following components of a business plan? **(CBSE Term I 2021)**

(a) Marketing plan (b) Production plan

(c) Operational plan (d) Financial plan

Ans (a) Marketing plan

26 The component of the business plan that goes beyond the production process by describing the market conditions and strategies related to products/services to be distrubuted is called **(CBSE Term I 2021)**

(a) production plan (b) marketing plan

(c) operational plan

(d) organisational plan

Ans (b) marketing plan

27 Karan has learnt the art of zardozi work from his grandfather and father. He opened a designer boutique exclusively for bridal wear all by himself. He introduced new designs in his work which is highly appreciated by everyone. What form of business organisation is operated by him? **(CBSE SQP Term I)**

(a) Sole proprietorship

(b) Partnership

(c) Private company

(d) Public company

Ans (a) Sole proprietorship

28 Divij and Ayaan were partners in a transport business. With a view to expand, they thought of changing the form of business where their liability will be limited.

To keep a control over the business, they decided to sell shares to friends, families and some employees. Which form of business they adopted?

(a) Public limited company

(b) Private limited company

(c) Cooperative organisation

(d) None of the above

Ans (b) Private limited company

29 Sen wanted to start a spare parts manufacturing unit. These spare parts will be used for the production of electric vehicles. For preparing the business plan he took the help of lawyers, accountants and marketing consultants. A detailed plan that will be needed by the management was prepared. The plan was not target at external stakeholders.

Which format of business plan was used by Sen? **(CBSE Term I 2021)**

(a) Elevator pitch

(b) A pitch deck with oral narrative

(c) A written presentation for external stakeholders

(d) An internal operational plan

Ans (d) An internal operational plan

30 Vani, Shiva, Bhanu and Kumar are good friends. They are the students of Class IX and are studying in the same school. They were admitted at the age of 5 years and did not fail in any class. They want to start a retail business. Can they form a partnership? **(CBSE Term I 2021)**

(a) They can form a partnership after taking permission for the parents.

(b) They can form a partnership after taking permission from their school principal.

(c) They can form a partnership because they are more than two persons.

(d) No, they cannot form a partnership because all of them are minors.

Ans (a) They can form a partnership after taking permission for the parents.

31 In the drive to make the world 'plastic free', Aru designed a machine to convert single-use plastic into very small granules that could be used for making low cost roads. Her machine worked with the help of solar energy.

She put her idea before the venture capitalists by making an entertaining slide show and oral narration. She also presented the executive summary of her proposed venture and a few key graphs. The format of business plan used by Aru is **(CBSE 2020)**

(a) elevator pitch

(b) a pitch deck with oral narrative

(c) a written presentation for external stakeholders

(d) an internal operational plan

Ans (b) a pitch deck with oral narrative

32 'Moderma Cameras Ltd'. are the manufactures of security cameras. Their research team came up with a new idea of manufacturing drones with security cameras that will give a 360° view of entire building. They needed huge finance for the same. The company came to know about a consortium of venture capitalists who were ready to invest in new ideas.

The managing director got an appointment with them and started the preparation of a business plan to be presented to them. The plan was to make an informative PowerPoint presentation showing the key graphics of financial trends.

It was meant to trigger discussion and interest among the members of the consortium through reading the written presentation. Which of the following formats of the business plan is being used by the company? **(CBSE Term I 2021)**

(a) An internal operational plan
(b) A pitch deck with oral narration
(c) Elevator pitch
(d) A written presentation for external stakeholders

Ans (d) A written presentation for external stakeholders

33 Bhawna, Maya and Advik's interior design business was taking off in a big way. Their talent was in high demand. Now, the trio needed to hire more employees.

Since the needs of their company were changing, they reviewed their personal circumstances, finances, and goals. They decided to legally organise their organisation into one with a limited liability. Identify the type of organisation the trio will form. **(CBSE SQP Term I)**

(a) Partnership (b) Public company
(c) Private company (d) Company

Ans (c) Private company

34 Sankalp Singh Parihar cultivates the world's most expensive Miyazaki variety of mangoes at his farm in Dhedagoua village in Madhya Pradesh. The Miyazaki variety of mangoes he grows at his farm sell at ₹ 2.5 lakh per kg in Japan. In India he got a price of ₹ 21,000 per kg, but he is yet to launch sales and is focusing on propagating the variety now. He intends to plant more saplings and make the mangoes affordable for Indians and sell it for as little as ₹ 2,000 per kg. He plans in such a manner that economic feasibility can be achieved in a few years.

Which part of the business plan highlights economic feasibility? **(CBSE SQP Term I)**

(a) Organisational plan (b) Financial plan
(c) Operational plan (d) Marketing plan

Ans (b) Financial plan

35 Rajan, son of a humble soldier of the Indian army, did not have the resources to prepare for a medical entrance exam, but decided to launch a venture that would help others achieve their dreams. His startup, launched in July 2020 with zero investment, has clocked a turnover of ₹ 35 lakh in just 10 months and he has achieved it all as a one-man army.

The start up prepares Group C employees of the Department of Post for the Limited Departmental Competitive Exams (LDCE) that qualifies them for their next promotion in the department. He realised that there was no training centre or coaching class for the aspirants so he marketed his classes for this specific group.

Which step is involved in this marketing plan? **(CBSE SQP Term I)**

(a) Identify the target market
(b) Conduct SWOT analysis
(c) Establish goals
(d) Define marketing strategy

Ans (a) Identify the target market

36 Ravi Mohan is in the process of developing the business plan of a shoes manufacturing unit which he wants to start in an industrial area of Kanpur. He is in the process of developing a component of his business plan wherein he has to detail the kinds of people required their number and the process of their selection.

Which of the following components of his business plan he has to develop after this? **(CBSE Term I 2021)**

(a) Marketing plan (b) Financial plan
(c) Operational plan (d) Organisational plan

Ans (d) Organisational plan

37 Hemant approached his father seeking ₹ 5,00,000 for his new venture. He had planned to start a computer assembling unit. Though his father was in a position to give him the money he still insisted that he should take a loan from the bank which will make him more responsible.

When Hemant approached the bankers, they asked for a business plan. Hemant was not sure as to who can help him in preparation of the business plan. Who among the following can prepare the business plan? **(CBSE SQP)**

(a) Lawyers (b) Accountants

(c) Marketing consultants

(d) All of these

Ans (d) All of these

38 Varun along with his friends had a brilliant idea to manufacture an air conditioner which will also act as an air purifier. The idea was new and the market did not have such a successful product. For starting the unit, they were in need of huge funds, so they decided to approach Shankar, a successful businessman and who is also a venture capitalist. However, Shankar said that he was very busy and if they could pitch their idea within a span of 3 minutes, he was ready to hear it.

Which format of business plan will Varun and his friends would have to use? **(CBSE SQP)**

(a) Elevator Pitch

(b) A pitch deck with oral narrative

(c) A written presentation for external stakeholders

(d) An internal operational plan

Ans (a) Elevator Pitch

39 Amaze Ltd., is a company engaged in the manufacturing of air-conditioners. The company has four main departments Purchase, Marketing and Sales, Finance and Warehousing. As the demand for the product grew, the company decided to recruit more employees in the Finance department and Marketing and Sales departments.

Identify the component of the business plan which will help the Human Resource Manager to decide and recruit the required number of persons for each department. **(CBSE SQP Term I)**

(a) Marketing plan (b) Financial plan

(c) Manpower plan (d) Organisational plan

Ans (c) Manpower plan

40 Vinita, Bhavana, Rani and Nandini are all good friends in the age group of 15-17 years of age. All of them decided together to start a business venture of making soaps at home using natural ingredients. They decided to name their venture as 'O & HM' meaning Organic and Home Made.

They spoke about their venture to their parents and asked them if their business could be registered so that it will be easy to divide the profits. Vinita suggested that they should register it as a partnership firm. Can they form a partnership firm? **(CBSE SQP)**

(a) No, they cannot form a partnership firm since all of them are minors

(b) Yes, they can form a partnership firm

(c) No, since minimum number of people required to form a partnership is 10

(d) None of the above

Ans (a) No, they cannot form a partnership firm since all of them are minors

41 Sindhuja was extremely good at making traditional sweets which she had learnt from her grandmother. She decided to start selling the sweets through advertising in social media. Her business picked up and she got a lot of orders from clients all across India.

Seeing her huge success, her friend Raman advised that she should open a shop in the market area to expand her business. He expressed interest in the business and was ready to invest money so that they could do the business together.

What form of business organisation does Raman and Sindhuja start? **(CBSE SQP Tem I)**

(a) Sole proprietorship (b) Partnership

(c) Private company (d) Public company

Ans (b) Partnership

42 Which of the following is not a consequence for non-registration of a partnership firm? **(CBSE Term I 2021)**

(a) The creditors cannot claim their dues.

(b) A partner cannot file a suit aganist the firm in a court of law for enforcement of any right arising out of the contract.

(c) A right arising from a contract cannot be enforced in any court by or on behalf of the firm against any third party.

(d) The firm or any of the partners cannot claim a set-off against a third party.

Ans (a) The creditors cannot claim their dues.

43 Assertion (A) A male member becomes a member of HUF by merely taking birth in a family.

Reason (R) HUF does not arise by status or operation of Hindu Law.

Alternatives

(a) Assertion (A) is correct, but Reason (R) is incorrect

(b) Assertion (A) is incorrect, but Reason (R) is correct

(c) Both Assertion (A) and Reason (R) are incorrect

(d) Both Assertion (A) and Reason (R) are correct

Ans (a) HUF arises by status or operation of Hindu Law.

44 Assertion (A) A sole proprietorship does not need to be registered.

Reason (R) Therefore, it is an expensive manner of commencing business. **(CBSE Term I 2021)**

Alternatives

(a) Assertion (A) is correct, but Reason (R) is incorrect

(b) Assertion (A) is incorrect, but Reason (R) is correct

(c) Both Assertion (A) and Reason (R) are incorrect

(d) Both Assertion (A) and Reason (R) are correct

Ans (a) Sole proprietorship is an inexpensive manner of commencing business.

45 Assertion (A) A company which is suffering huge losses can be shut down only by following the procedures laid down in Companies Act.

Reason (R) A company can be born as well as liquidated only by law. **(CBSE SQP Term I)**

Alternatives

(a) Assertion (A) is true, but Reason (R) is false

(b) Both Assertion (A) and Reason (R) are true, but Reason (R) is not the correct explanation of Assertion (A)

(c) Assertion (A) is true and Reason (R) is the correct explanation of Assertion (A)

(d) Both Assertion (A) and Reason (R) are false

Ans (c) Assertion (A) is true and Reason (R) is the correct explanation of Assertion (A)

46

Column I (Characteristics)	Column II (Type of Organisation)
A. One person makes all the decision	(i) Company
B. Unlimited liability	(ii) Hindu undivided family
C. Common seal	(iii) Partnership
D. Member by birth	(iv) Sole proprietor

Codes

	A	B	C	D		A	B	C	D
(a)	(ii)	(i)	(iii)	(iv)	(b)	(iv)	(iii)	(i)	(ii)
(c)	(iv)	(i)	(ii)	(iii)	(d)	(iii)	(ii)	(iv)	(i)

Ans (b) (iv) (iii) (i) (ii)

47 Match the following characteristics of a joint stock company as given in Column I with their meanings as given in Column II. **(CBSE Term I 2021)**

Column I	Column II
A. Artificial person	(i) It has an independent status separate from its members.
B. Separate legal entity	(ii) The liability of the shareholders is limited to the extent of the amount of shares held.
C. Limited liability	(iii) It can be terminated as per the Companies Act.
D. Winding up	(iv) It is created by law and has a distinct personality of its own.

Codes

	A	B	C	D		A	B	C	D
(a)	(iv)	(i)	(ii)	(iii)	(b)	(i)	(ii)	(iii)	(iv)
(c)	(iv)	(iii)	(ii)	(i)	(d)	(iii)	(iv)	(ii)	(i)

Ans (a) (iv) (i) (ii) (iii)

48

Column I (Process)	Column II (Elements)
A. Determine exact path	(i) Follow-up
B. Fixation of time, day etc	(ii) Dispatching
C. Initiation production	(iii) Routing
D. Appraisal of work	(iv) Scheduling

Codes

	A	B	C	D		A	B	C	D
(a)	(ii)	(i)	(iv)	(iii)	(b)	(iv)	(iii)	(i)	(ii)
(c)	(iv)	(ii)	(i)	(iii)	(d)	(iii)	(iv)	(ii)	(i)

Ans (d) (iii) (iv) (ii) (i)

49

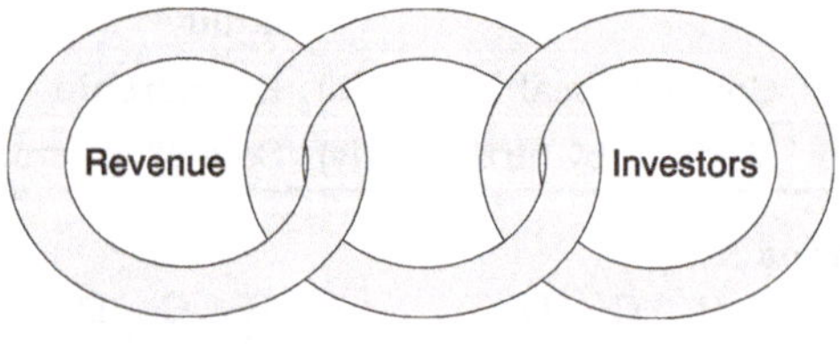

From the given figure, state the third element of financial plan.

(a) Funds (b) Government
(c) Entrepreneur (d) None of these

Ans (a) Funds

50

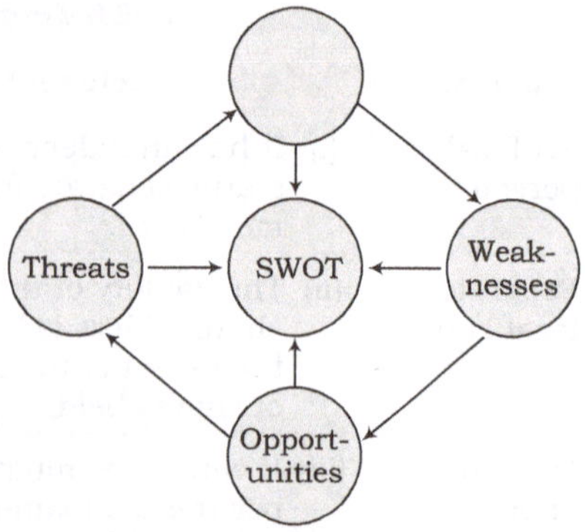

From the given figure, name the fourth element of consideration in SWOT analysis by an entrepreneur.

(a) Saungs (b) Strength
(c) Social environment
(d) None of the above

Ans (b) Strength

Fill in the Blanks

51 .... form of business in suitable when size of the venture is small.

Ans Sole proprietorship

52 .... helps to understand the feasibility and viability of the proposed venture.

Ans Business plan

53 The process of initiating production in accordance with pre-conceived production plan is said to be ..... .

Ans dispatching

54 Production plan aims at 'plan your work', whereas .... plan aims at 'work your plan'.

Ans operational

55 Prabhav is a budding entrepreneur who is about to pitch in his idea to a group of investors. For presenting his business plan he has made a teaser of about three minutes to awaken the interest of the potential investors. Prabhav is using .... from of presenting business plan. **(CBSE SQP)**

Ans elevator's pitch

56 Divyansh is the CEO of a company and he always pay special attention to the recruitment of personnel. He himself supervises all the interviews and decides upon the personnel to be selected.

He keeps a close eye on manpower required by different departments and how they are to be recruited. He firmly believes that the people working in a firm make it what it is. Here, Divyansh pays attention to ....

Ans manpower planning/human resource planning

57 Ansh and Vansh entered into a partnership, by opening their catering firm. However, they did not get their firm registered. One of their clients refused to pay them for a catering contract. They .... file a case against him for claiming their rightful dues.

Ans cannot

58 Piyush and Ramesh are engaged in wholesale business of pulses. They buy pulses directly from farmers in bulk and sell in small lots to the retailers. Both of them known their roles and responsibilities.

They have also laid down the procedure for solving conflicts between them, if any. All the above information is described in a important component of a business plan. The component is .... **(CBSE 2020)**

Ans organisational plan

State True or False

59 A company cannot be held liable for the actions of its members and members cannot be held liable for the actions of the other members.

Ans True

60 The minimum number of members required to form a public company is 7 and minimum number of directors required are 3.

Ans True

61 The scope of business plan is quite extensive and it covers all aspects relating to marketing, finance, operations, human resources, legal compliance etc.

Ans True

62 'Description of venture' is the cover page of the business plan.

Ans False. Introductory profile/general introduction is the cover page of the business plan.

63 Entrepreneurs need to work out in detail all the relevant external and internal elements involved in starting a new venture and then running it successfully and this can be achieved through the preparation of a strategy.

Ans False. The above can be achieved through the preparation of a business plan.

64 To supplement her family income, Alia decided to start a boutique in her home. She employed a tailor, bought a machine and other raw material required and started her venture. Alia has started a sole proprietorship firm.

Ans True

65 Aditya and Siddhartha are partners in a firm which manufactures leather belts. Due to health issues, Aditya is forced to retire. Aditya's minor son Varun, is admitted in the firm. At the end of the year, the firm suffered a loss of ₹ 1,00,000. Varun can be asked to bear his share of loss.

Ans False. Minors can be admitted only to share the benefits of a partnership firm.

66 There are public rumours that the affairs of XYZ company are not in order and huge sums of money had been mis-appropriated. Sumit, who is not a member of the company wants to inspect the books of the company. However, a non-member cannot inspect the books of the company.

Ans True

67 Shekhar was working with Vishal as a production manager. For smooth flow of work, he had to pay attention towards various elements and to ensure predetermined quality of products, he had to compare the performance with established standards. The component of business plan discussed above is 'Operational plan'.

Ans True

Case Based Questions

68 Read the following article and answer the questions that follow

Medha was a bright student in school and got an opportunity to study in the US after finishing school. She met John there, and developed a strong bond. In 2019, Medha and John started a new venture after finishing their Masters in Business Administration. Medha and John were always fond of sweets and delicacies, therefore, they started "American Bakers" manufacturing and selling various kinds of American sweet savories like waffles, biscuits, cookies, pudding, etc. John suggested that a new business like this would be very suitable in a developing country like India.

In 2020, when Covid-19 hard hit the world, American Bakers saw a decline in business and was at the verge of dissolution. The warehouse had a wide stock of raw material that would go as sunken stock and would be a huge expense for them.

Suddenly, Medha had an idea to bake and package the products in small packaging and sell them through online platforms. As, packaging was an essential activity in the lockdown they were able to hire daily wage workers to continue working.

Medha and John connected to the investors of the company and gave them a short summary of their plan. The investors gave a green light to the plan and it was the time for correct execution.

American Bakers started selling their products through different channels that were available at that time and generated sufficient funds that will help in running the business.

(i) Which type of organisation is "American Bakers"?

(a) Joint venture (b) Partnership
(c) Sole proprietorship (d) Corporation

Ans (b) Partnership

(ii) "John suggested that a new business like this would be very suitable in a developing country like India."

Which of the following step is involved in the marketing plan of Medha and John?

(a) Conducting SWOT Analysis
(b) Establishing goals
(c) Identify target market
(d) All of the above

Ans (c) Identify target market

(iii) "Medha and John connected to the investors of the company and gave them a short summary of their plan. The investors gave a green light to the plan and it was the time for correct execution."

Which of the following formats is used by Medha and John to persuade the investors?

(a) Elevator pitch
(b) Internal operational plan
(c) A pitch deck (d) A written presentation

Ans (a) Elevator pitch

(iv) Which type of business plan will represent the economic feasibility of "American Bakers" after generating sufficient funds from the idea?

(a) Organisational plan
(b) Financial plan
(c) Marketing plan (d) Production plan

Ans (b) Financial plan

(v) "As, packaging was an essential activity in the lockdown they were able to hire daily wage workers to continue working."

Which of the following is highlighted in the above sentence?

(a) Entrepreneurial creativity
(b) Production planning
(c) Promotional planning
(d) Manpower planning

Ans (d) Manpower planning

69 Read the following article and answer the questions that follow

Techie Corp. is a known and famous business around the globe that manufactures and sells variety of products and services. The ownership of the company is divided through its shares to its shareholders and the management is looked upon by a team of directors. Recently, the board of directors has guided the senior manager of research and development team to initiate a new product development process. For this, the manager has asked the employees to gather ideas.

Michael, one of the assistant managers managing the marketing department suggested that one of his friends is an inventor and has created self-tapping shoes for tap dance practice. The senior manager asked Michael to bring the product and get it checked by the engineering department. After product checking, a deal was signed between the company and the inventor to sell the product rights to the company. After finalising the deal, the management made some changes in the product and was all ready to launch it.

The marketing department was asked to identify the target audience and run a scan for any threats and risks. The target audience was the dance classes and tap-dance performers in cities and big towns. The pricing was set at a low level for the initial stages and the management planned to contact universities and colleges after six months of checking the performance of the product.

The finance department developed a written statement with the projected expenses and revenues of the new product launch and it was estimated that the new product will result in net profit in the following year and will be an economical choice.

The product was successfully launched and generated good sales in the first year for the company. Altogether, it created a good value for the company.

(i) Which type of market analysis and scanning would help Techie Corp. in knowing the potential for its new product?

(a) Financial analysis
(b) Market analysis

(c) Environment scanning
(d) SWOT analysis

Ans (d) SWOT analysis

(ii) Techie Corp. is .... type of organisation.
(a) joint stock company
(b) partnership
(c) joint venture (d) sole proprietorship

Ans (a) joint stock company

(iii) "The pricing was set at a low level for the initial stages and the management planned to contact universities and colleges after six months of checking the performance of the product."
Which business plan is highlighted in the above text?
(a) Marketing plan
(b) Organisational plan
(c) Manufacturing plan
(d) Operational plan

Ans (d) Operational plan

(iv) Which of the following documents represents the expected revenues and expenses?
(a) Proforma balance sheet
(b) Proforma income statement
(c) Proforma cash flow
(d) Proforma financial plan

Ans (b) Proforma income statement

(v) Which of the following plan is most suitable for analysing the new product and development strategies?
(a) Manufacturing plan
(b) Economic plan
(c) Organisational plan
(d) Marketing plan

Ans (d) Marketing plan

Short Answer Type I Questions (2 Marks)

1 The scope of the company's business is determined by certain documents. Name them.

Ans The documents which determine the scope of the company are
(i) Memorandum of association.
(ii) Articles of association.

Also, it should not transgress the provisions of Companies Act, 2013.

2 What is the implication of the feature 'separate legal entity'?

Ans The implications of this feature are
(i) Members are not joint owners of the assets of the company. All assets belong to company itself.
(ii) The company continues to exist, even if all its members die.
(iii) Company can sue and be sued by its members, creditors or third parties.

3 Give the meaning of 'implied authority' and 'mutual agency' as characteristics of a partnership form of business organisation. **(CBSE 2023)**

Ans The characteristics are as follows
(i) **Implied Authority** Any partner can act on behalf of the firm and his acts bind the firm.
(ii) **Mutual Agency** The business of the firm can be carried on by all the partners or any one of them acting for all. Thus, every partner is a principal as well as an agent. This means each partner is liable for the acts performed by other partners and each partner can bind other partners and the firm by his acts done in an ordinary course of business.

4 State any two characteristics of partnership which overcome the inherent limitations of sole proprietorship form of business organisation. **(CBSE 2023)**

Ans Characteristics of partnership that overcome the inherent limitations of sole proprietorship are
(i) **Continuity** A partnership continues until all partners desire to continue it. Legally, a firm dissolves on the retirement, death, bankruptcy, lunacy or disability of a partner, if not otherwise provided in the partnership deed.
(ii) **Utmost Good Faith** Mutual trust and confidence is the main strength of partnership. Every partner should act honestly and give proper accounts to other partners.

5 Why is a company called an 'artificial person'? **(CBSE 2019)**

Ans A company is created by law. Though it has no body and no conscience, it still exists as a person, having a distinct personality of its own and like a natural person, it can buy, sell and own property, sue others and be sued by others. Therefore, it is called an artificial person.

6 What do you mean by one person company?

Ans One person company means a company which has only one person as member. It is a company incorporated as a private company which has only one member. Any natural person who is an Indian citizen whether a resident in India or not, i.e. NRI, shall be eligible to incorporate a one person company and appoint nominee of an OPC.

7 Rajiv and Ramesh entered into a verbal agreement to form a firm. They agreed to share its profits. Their business was running smoothly. One day a dispute arose between Rajiv and Ramesh regarding the profit sharing ratio.

Rajiv and Ramesh regarding the profit sharing ratio. Ravjiv decided to move the court and enforce his rights against the firm and Ramesh.

Will Rajiv succeed? Give reasons in support of your answer. **(CBSE 2018)**

Ans No, Rajiv will not succeed. Rajiv and Ramesh have entered into partnership by merely agreeing on terms orally. Their firm is not registered.

According to the provisions of Indian Partnership Act, 1932, if a firm is not registered then a partner cannot file suit in any court against the firm or other partners for enforcement of any right arising from an agreement or any right conferred by the Partnership Act.

8 Radhika after graduating from college went back to her home town in Meghalaya. It was a small town with very few job opportunities. The Karbi tribal women in that area were uneducated but still practiced the method of obtaining traditional colours from natural wild herbs.

Their most popular dye was indigo obtained from the leave called 'sibu'. Using these colours, they added variety to their textiles. The women were mainly confined to their homes and they did not know how to make a living out of their talent. Shiela went from door to door analysed the problem that existed.

She thought of setting up a voluntary association of rural women who would be able to join and leave the organisation at their own will without any coercion or intimidation.

(i) Name the process which helped Shiela in converting an idea into an opportunity.

(ii) Identify the kind of organisation that Shiela has decided to set-up.

Ans (i) Sensing entrepreneurial opportunity.

(ii) Cooperative organisation.

9 What is a business plan? **(CBSE TBQ)**

Ans A business plan is basically a written representation of an entrepreneur's vision for his business. It is a formal statement of a set of business goals, the reason why they are thought to be attainable and a plan for reaching those goals with complete understanding of internal and external factors affecting those goals.

10 'Safe Wheelers' is an upcoming cab service. The promoters knew that they are entering a highly competitive market.

They gathered information on existing cab services and changing customer preferences and incorporated those observations into their operations.

In order to reach the customers promptly, they developed an 'App' to book, track and trace the cabs 24 × 7.

To create an environment of trust all drivers were grouped into two shifts 6 am – 6 pm for female drivers and 6 pm – 6 am for male drivers. GPS system were installed in all cabs to monitor their movements.

The fare payment could be either by an e-wallet or through the 'Safe Wheellers Smart Card'. As soon as the services were launched, they were a grand success.

Identify and explain the concept that helped the company to succeed. **(CBSE 2018)**

Ans The concept discussed is business plan. Before starting a business, an entrepreneur needs to gather information about internal and external environment that may affect his business and form strategies and objectives in harmony with the environment.

This is achieved through the preparation of business plan. It is a comprehensive project report including the entire range of activities which are being planned in the business.

11 "Preparing a good business plan can't guarantee success, but it can go a long way towards reducing the odds of failure." Justify this statement by giving any two points. **(CBSE 2023)**

Ans (i) The business plan is valuable to all stakeholders such as the entrepreneur himself, potential investors, venture capitalists, banks, financial institutions, suppliers, customers, advisors, etc., as it provides a road-map for starting a new venture.

(ii) At times, a business plan also helps to identify the obstacles which cannot be overcome, suggesting terminating the venture while still on paper, thereby saving time and money.

Also, it is the business plan which reflects the entrepreneur's credit history, his ability to make payments against debt and interest and the amount of equity invested by him. So, it helps a business to raise funds by providing the relevant information.

Thus, keeping the above points in view, it could be concluded that although writing a good business plan can't guarantee success but it can go a long way towards reducing the odds of failure.

12 What is elevator pitch? **(CBSE TBQ)**

Ans Elevator pitch is a format of presenting a business plan. It is basically a three minute summary of the business plan which is used as a teaser to awaken the interest of the potential investors, customers or strategic partners.

13 Rahul wants to start a small shoe manufacturing factory. As a part of his business plan, he prepared an 'entertaining slide show and oral narrative' that was meant to trigger discussion and create interest in potential investors for reading the written presentation.

Identify and explain the format of the business plan referred in the above paragraph. **(CBSE 2015)**

Ans The business plan referred to in the above paragraph is 'A pitch-deck with oral narrative'. This format presents the business plan in the form of an entertaining slide show complemented with an oral narrative.

It is meant to trigger discussion and awaken the interest of the potential investors and induce them to read the written presentation.

It includes executive summary, important graphs showing financial trends and key decision-making benchmarks.

14 State any four items of physical infrastructure that should be mentioned in the description of a business plan. **(CBSE 2016)**

Ans Four items of physical infrastructure that should be mentioned in the description of a business plan are

(i) **Raw Material** Whether indigenous or imported, sources of supply etc.

(ii) **Labour** Type of labour required, provision for their training, number of manpower required etc.

(iii) **Utilities** These include power, fuel, water, gas, electricity etc.

(iv) **Pollution Control** The sewage system and the sewage treatment plant, water harvesting system, arrangement for dumping and disposing of the other types of wastes or emission, all need to be discussed in the plan.

15 Sanjiv was developing a business plan for his organisation. While working on the financial plan, he realised that his financial requirements will be for fixed assets and their installations, preliminary expenses, working capital, expenses on research and development and investment in short-term assets *viz.* raw material, level of cash, etc.
To decide on the sources of funds for the venture, he tried to ensure the selection of the best overall mix of financing for the enterprise.

(i) Identify the elements of financial plan discussed here.

(ii) Why is it important for an entrepreneur to ensure the selection of the best overall mix of financing for the enterprise?

Ans (i) (a) Proforma investment decisions.

(b) Proforma financing decisions.

(ii) The entrepreneur's job is to ensure the selection of the best overall mix of financing for the enterprise so that

(a) the cost of capital and the financial risk stands minimised.

(b) Return on investment and profitability stands maximised.

16 What is a proforma income statement? **(CBSE TBQ)**

Ans This section of the financial plan gives the projected net profit of the business based on projected revenues and projected expenses. While estimating the projected revenues for the year, 'sales by month' must be estimated first by using forecasting techniques.

17 Shruti, Neelabh and Shewtabh decided to start their own business of manufacturing steel utensils. They also finalised to set-up the manufacturing unit in Orissa as labour is available there at a very low rate.

They also decided about the sources for the procurement of required funds and all the relevant external and internal factors affecting this venture.

Identify the document which is required to be prepared by the entrepreneurs for the above decisions. State any one point of importance of this document. **(CBSE 2016C)**

Ans Financial plan. One point of importance of financial plan is that it ensure timely availability of funds in right volume.

18 How is target market identified while preparing the marketing plan? State. **(CBSE 2016)**

Ans (i) Deciding what the general market or industry entrepreneur wishes to pursue.

(ii) Divide the market into small groups.

(iii) Buying situations.

(iv) Select segment and develop a marketing plan.

19 Give the meaning of 'Business situation analysis' and 'Identification of the target market' as steps in preparing the marketing plan. **(CBSE 2015)**

Ans Refer to text on page 53 and 54.

20 Explain 'SWOT analysis' as a step in preparing a marketing plan. **(CBSE 2023)**

Ans SWOT stands for Strengths, Weaknesses, Opportunities and Threats. SWOT analysis helps to monitor the environment, both internal and external. Therefore, it is also referred to as internal and external analysis. SWOT analysis helps an entrepreneur to decide on a particular opportunity keeping in view his strengths and weaknesses (internal analysis) and the opportunities and threats (external analysis) in the market.

21 Description of business venture is an important component of a business plan. Physical infrastructure is one of the key elements covered under this. State about

(i) utilities, and

(ii) production process as part of the physical infrastructure. **(CBSE 2020)**

Ans (i) **Utilities** These include power, fuel, water, gas, electricity, etc. Business plan needs to clearly state

(a) Type of utilities required

(b) Loan sanctioned

(c) Sources and quality of water used; quantum of coal, coke, oil, etc., required and the suppliers of the same.

(ii) **Production Process** A mention of the process involved in production, the installed licensed capacity of the plant, technology to be used, whether available locally or imported, shifts involved, needs to be present in the business plan.

This phase enables the entrepreneur to evaluate whether his venture is feasible or not.

22 Sukrit is a green entrepreneur who has launched a new water conserving apparatus for urban houses by the name of 'JALASHAY'. This apparatus is a compact system to be installed on the roof of the houses to harvest rainwater.

The uniqueness of the system is that it has an inbuilt water treatment mechanism that makes the water ready for use as soon as it is collected.

Sukrit has set up laboratories to test the water quality with the established standards. By doing so, he is paying specific attention to one of the important elements of the operational plan.

Identify the element and explain one more element of this plan. **(CBSE 2020)**

Ans Sukrit is paying attention to 'Inspection'. This means comparing materials, product or performance with established standards.

Products can be tested in specified laboratories or new methods or strategies can be evolved to ensure pre-determined standard quality of the product. One more element of this plan is **Routing** It is a process concerned with determining exact route or path a product/ service has to follow right from raw material till its transformation into finished products.

23 It's a basic tenet of business–before you can make money you have to figure out how to spend it. Drafting a budget is a key way to help you turn your dreams for business success into reality.

Using this vital tool, you can track cash on hand, business expenses and now much revenue you need to keep your business growing–or at least afloat. By committing these numers to paper, your chances of succeeding with your business are helped by anticipating future needs, spending, profits and cash flow.

It also may let you spot problems before they mushroom, so that you can switch gears.

"It's like a road-map for your company," says Victor Butcher, of Butcher Financial Services in Memphis, Tenn., a former president of the Tennessee Society of Certified Public Accountants' Memphis Chapter who advises small businesses. You need the road-map to understand where you're going with your business.

Source *INC Magazine*

Identify the type of plan stated in the above article. Also mention any four components of it.

Ans Financial plan is the type of plan stated in the above article.

Components of financial plan include

(i) Proforma investment decisions.
(ii) Proforma financing decisions.
(iii) Proforma income statement.
(v) Proforma cash flow.

24 A recent survey conducted jointly by FICCI and Indian Angel Network revealed that 70 percent of startups across the country have been impacted by Covid 19 while as many as 12 per cent have had to halt operations altogether.

These are difficult times that no one was prepared to deal with. The prolonged lockdown had a massive impact on the startup ecosystem. Given that they rely largely on a constant flow of capital and investments, which due to the pandemic came to a complete standstill.

With the ongoing crisis, to keep startups afloat has become quite a challenge. However, this challenge can be eliminated if entrepreneurs adapt to the current times, adopt new strategies, and are open to experiments and pivot their business plans. That's because the pandemic has not only affected our present but also our future.

Source *Entrepreneur Magazine–August, 2020*

Keeping in mind this article, state any two things which should be written by start up companies in their manpower planning component of business plan? **(CBSE SQP)**

Ans Start up companies should write following things under the component manpower planning (Any two)

(i) **What Kind of People are Required** Every organisation needs the right person with the right qualifications, skills, experience and aptitude to work.

So, the organisation should be clear to know as to what kind of personnel is required as per the nature of business activity.

(ii) **How Many People are Required** They should also estimate the number of personnel require keeping in mind the total work and survival in the present situation and planning for future growth.

(iii) **How to Procure Personnel** The next step is to recruit, select and train the right personnel.

Short Answer Type II Questions (3 Marks)

1 Explain any three characteristics of partnership. **(CBSE SQP)**

Ans Refer to text on page 41.

2 The business assets of an organisation amount to ₹ 2,50,000 and its unpaid liabilities ₹ 3,00,000.

What are the alternatives available to the creditors if

(i) the organisation is a sole proprietorship firm.

(ii) the organisation is a partnership firm with Raghu and Rahul as partners.

(iii) the organisation is an Hindu Undivided Family.

Ans (i) In case of sole proprietorship, the creditors can claim the personal property of the sole proprietor to recover the deficiency of ₹ 50,000.

(ii) In case of partnership, the personal assets of both the partners or either one of the partners could be used to recover the deficiency.

(iii) In case of Hindu Undivided Family, the personal assets of Karta could be used to recover the deficiency.

3 Two years ago Gopal started manufacturing low fat, sugar-free ice-cream on a small scale basis in his home town, Visakhapatnam. After some time his ice-cream became popular among health conscious young customers and old persons specially those having diabetes or some heart ailment.

Because of the popularity of the ice-cream the demand has increased manyfold. Gopal is unable to meet the same, because of his limited managerial ability and limited capital. Gopal also felt that whenever he fell sick his business was temporarily closed.

To overcome this problem he decided to admit in the business his friend Mohan who has recently completed his MBA and is ready to invest money for the expansion of the business. Mohan advised Gopal to get their firm registered.

(i) State three limitations indicated in the above para from which Gopal's business suffered.

(ii) Why did Mohan advise Gopal to get the firm registered? **(CBSE 2017)**

Ans (i) The three limitations from which Gopal's business suffered on account of it being a sole proprietorship business are as follows

(a) Limited managerial ability

(b) Limited capital

(c) Limited life of a business concern.

(ii) Mohan advised Gopal to get the partnership firm registered because a non-registered firm suffers from the following limitations

(a) A partner cannot file suit in any court against the firm or other partners for the enforcement of any right arising, from a contract or any right conferred by the Partnership Act.

(b) A case cannot be filed against a third party for claiming any right conferred by a contract.

(c) The firm or any of its partners cannot claim a set off (i.e., mutual adjustment of debts owned by the disputant parties to one another) or other proceedings in a dispute with a third party.

4 Kareem after completing his XII class from his village school joined the course of electrician in an ITI in a town near his village. On completion of this course, he tried for a government job but could not get the same. He therefore, decided to work as a helper to a renowned electrician of the area. After working with him for 2 years, he decided to start his own electrician shop in the village.

For this, he purchased equipments of ₹ 10,000 and hired a shop at a monthly rent of ₹ 2,000. He himself managed the shop.

(i) Identify the kind of business organisation set-up by Kareem.

(ii) State any four characteristics of the identified form of business organisation. **(CBSE 2015)**

Or Explain any three charateristics of sole proprietorship. **(CBSE SQP)**

Ans (i) The business organisation set-up by Kareem is 'Sole proprietorship'.

(ii) Four characteristics of this form of business organisation are as follows

(a) **Individual Ownership** The business is exclusively owned by a single person.

(b) **Individual Management and Control** All affairs of the business are managed and controlled by the sole proprietor.

(c) **Sole Beneficiary** The sole proprietor is entitled to all the gains and suffer all the losses of the business.

(d) **Easy Formation and Closure** Starting and closing this form of business is very easy as there are minimum legal formalities subjected to this form.

5 Prerna is a sole proprietor. Over the past decade, her business has grown from operating a neighbourhood corner shop, selling accessories such as artificial jewellery, bags, hair clips and nail art to a retail chain with three branches in the city.

Although, she looks after the varied functions in all the branches, for better management of the business she is thinking to convert her sole proprietorship into some other form of business.

She also has plans to open branches countrywide. However, she is afraid of the fact that in case the business incurs losses, her personal property may be called upon to pay the business debts.

She is also feeling that she may not be able to effectively manage a large business because of her deteriorating health.

(i) Identify and explain the features of sole proprietor business highlighted in the above case.

(ii) Also suggest to her the form of business organisation which will help her in continuing her business, stating reason in support of your answer. **(CBSE 2019)**

Ans (i) The following are the features of sole proprietor business highlighted in the above case

(a) **Individual Ownership** The business is exclusively owned by a single person.

(b) **Individual Management and Control** All affairs of the business are managed and controlled by the sole proprietor.

(c) **Unlimited Liability** The sole proprietor's personal property can be used to pay the business debts.

(ii) The form of business organisation which will help her in continuing her business is a joint stock company as it fulfills the growing needs for capital, managerial talent and skills and limited liability.

6 What are the drawbacks associated with non-registration of a partnership firm?

Ans Refer to text on page 42.

7 "Before operationalisation of a Hindu Undivided Family Business, its Karta has to fulfil certain legal formalities." Explain any three such legal formalities. **(CBSE 2016)**

Ans The legal formalities required to be fulfilled by Karta are given below

(i) **Apply for PAN** The Karta is required to obtain a Permanent Account Number (PAN) for the HUF. PAN is a mandatory requirement for the formation of HUF as all the financial transactions shall carry PAN.

(ii) **Open a Bank Account** After PAN has been allotted, the Karta is required to open a bank account in the name of the HUF. Only transactions related to HUF should be routed through this account.

(iii) **Other** Official stationery such as letter heads, envelopes etc, should be printed with HUF's name for official communication. Also, the Karta will have to invest in tax saving instruments and file tax returns on behalf of the HUF.

8 (i) What is meant by a 'Business plan'?

(ii) State any one importance of writing a business plan for each of the given interest groups

(a) Investors

(b) Entrepreneurs **(CBSE 2018)**

Ans (i) Refer to Q. No. 9 of short answer type I questions (2 Marks).

(ii) (a) A business plan helps in determining the viability of the venture. Therefore, it is important for investors.

(b) It is important for entrepreneur because it helps him to plan his activities.

9 Mahesh is a young man of 20 years. He has completed a tailoring course from an industrial training institute. He wants to start a big-size tailoring shop in a modern locality where young men and women working in various multinational companies live.

He went to one of his friends who had completed a diploma course in textile designing to discuss about the opening of the tailoring shop. His friend advised him to prepare a written document describing formally all the relevant external and internal elements involved in starting a new venture.

It will not only help in understanding the feasibility and viability of the proposed venture but also facilitate in assessing and making provisions for the bottlenecks in the progress and implementation of the idea.

State any six points of importance of the concept discussed by Mahesh with his friend. **(CBSE 2017)**

Or This document is valuable to the entrepreneur, potential investors, venture capitalists, banks, financial institutions, new personnel's suppliers, customers, advisors and others who are trying to familiarise themselves with the business venture, its goals, and objectives. State any four reasons for the importance of this document. **(CBSE SQP)**

Ans The concept or document discussed in the given case is 'Business plan'.

Six points of importance of business plan are as follows

(i) A business plan helps in determining the viability of the venture in the designated market.

(ii) A business plan helps in satisfying the concerns, issues and queries of each group of people interested in the venture.

(iii) It provides room for self-assessment and self-evaluation.

(iv) A business plan also helps to identify the obstacles which cannot be overcome, suggesting to terminate the venture while still on paper.

(v) Business plan is an important tool for procuring funds.

(vi) A business plan gives a clear indication to the entrepreneur, investors and the government regarding.

(a) What an entrepreneur is doing.

(b) Why he/she is doing it.

(c) How he/she will do it.

10 Rashi has done her Acharya degree in Ayurveda from Trichy. She is planning to start a small scale enterprise of making herbal face care and body care products by the name 'Skinatural'. She makes use of her extensive knowledge about herbs to create products that can suit all skin types.

She is also taking care of the allergen factor as the products have to be applied on skin. She is planning to offer only dry mix of the herbs to be blended by the user at the time of use. Create an introduction for her product relating to the 'product details' in the business plan which will help her to attract the customers. **(CBSE 2020)**

Ans **Product Details**

'Skinatural' is planning to launch a whole new series of herbal face care and skin care products. These products are made from herbs and are the brainchild of our entrepreneur Rashi, who has done her Acharya degree in Ayurveda from Trichy.

These products are formulated to suit all skin types. The allergen factor has also been taken care of. These products will be offered as dry-mix and are quite economical. They will give your face and skin a healthy glow and save you from the harmful effects of chemical based beauty products.

11 Kartik works as a production analyst at 'Shree Tyres.' During the board meeting for the financial year 2022-23, the target production of tyres of the year was decided at 6 lakh units.

The Managing Director of the company asked Kartik to prepare a blueprint in advance and 'work your plan.'

He also added that this blueprint will ensure orderly flow of materials in the manufacturing process from the beginning to the end.

Identify and explain the component of 'business plan' being discussed by the Managing Director. **(CBSE 2023)**

Ans The component of business plan highlighted is production plan.

Production is the most important activity of an enterprise because it is through this process that raw materials are transformed into finished products.

According to Kimball and Kimball Jr, "the planning of industrial operations, involves four considerations, namely, what work shall be done, how the work shall be done and lastly, when and by whom the work shall be done".

Being highly complex and tedious, the manufacturing operation needs to be well planned.

A production plan helps to plan the work in such a manner that one can clearly form an idea about

(i) Production schedule and/or budget.

(ii) Machinery, equipment required.

(iii) Manufacturing method and process involved.

(iv) Plant layout.

(v) Time, motion and work study.

(vi) Manpower requirement.

(vii) Inventory requirement.

12 Picturising ahead every step in a long series of separate operations, each step to be taken in the right place, of the right degree and at the right time.

Each operation is to be done at maximum efficiency.

This is the objective of one of the components of a business plan.

(i) Identify the component.

(ii) There are three situations before the venture under this component. Explain briefly those three situations. **(CBSE 2018)**

Ans (i) The component is operational plan.

(ii) The following are the elements of operational plan

(a) **Description of Company's Operation** This plan contains the detailed description of company's operation related to routing, scheduling, dispatching, follow-up etc.

(b) **Flow of Orders for Goods and Services** It contains full description related to how orders will flow from the customers and how they will be fulfilled.

(c) **Technology Utilisation** It also contains description related to utilisation of technology. This helps in improving the quality of the products and services.

13 What are the key areas for a sound financial plan to work? **(CBSE TBQ)**

Ans Finance is the life-blood of any organisation and is the most important pre-requisite to establish any business. An entrepreneur before drawing out the financial plan, must keep in mind the following factors

(i) Financial requirements.

(ii) Sources of raising funds.

(iii) Exact assessment of the revenue, cost, profits, cash flow dynamics, stock of inventory, loans, etc.

So, in a financial plan an entrepreneur basically projects financial data about the following key areas

(i) The potential investment commitment needed for the new venture.

(ii) Economic feasibility as the enterprise. So, a financial plan explains to any potential investor how the entrepreneur plans to meet all financial obligations and also to maintain the liquidity of the business and to provide good returns to investors.

14 Explain any four factors which affect the formulation of a financial plan. **(Delhi 2014)**

Ans Finance is one of the most important pre-requisite to establish an enterprise. Availability of finance facilitates the entrepreneur to bring together men, material, machines and methods to produce goods and services.

The following four factors affect the formulation of a sound financial plan

(i) **Financial Requirements** The financial requirements of a new project or even for an existing venture should be assessed before drawing up the financial plan.

(ii) **Sources of Raising Funds** The various sources from which funds could be raised should be identified.

(iii) **Exact Assessment of Related Concepts** The revenue, cost, profits, cash flow dynamics, stock of inventory, etc., should be exactly assessed to draw up an effective plan.

(iv) **Economic Feasibility of the Proposed Investment** The plan should also be indicative of the general financial well-being of the new venture or proposed investment.

15 You are Ravi and you have planned to start manufacturing a new brand of chocolates aiming at teenagers. Your company 'Delight' has already been manufacturing and selling biscuits since 2010. The success of biscuits has encouraged you to move ahead into the chocolate industry.

Keeping in mind the steps involved in preparation of the marketing plan, draft a marketing plan, explaining the first three steps. **(CBSE SQP)**

Ans For first three steps involved in marketing plan, refer to text on page 53 and 54.

16 Karan finished his graduation from Polytechnic college in the year 2018. He had specialised in repairing of electronic goods. After few months of his graduation, he met his uncle who has a small factory manufacturing electronic circuits used in Television.

His uncle informed Karan that he could no longer run the unit so Karan decided to take over the factory. His uncle had two workers.

Karan was able to get a huge order of supplying 10,000 units of electronic circuits every month from a popular TV manufacturing company in India.

He knew that to meet the orders timely he has to employ more people. In order to do so he decided to formulae manpower planning.

Describe the factors that Karan has to keep in mind while formulating manpower plan.

Ans Karan has to formulate manpower planning keeping in mind the following

(i) **What Kind of People are Required** To carry on its work, each organisation needs personnel with the necessary qualifications, skills, knowledge, experience and aptitude for work.

(ii) **How Many People are Required** This question deals with the quantity of personnel the enterprise needs. Presently, the factory has just two employees, so Karan will need atleast ten workers to achieve the production target every month.

(iii) **How to Procure Personnel** As the next step in manpower planning, entrepreneur clearly mentions the strategies, methods, policies, rules and regulations pertaining to employees. He can approach his own polytechnic college and recruit fresh graduates.

Long Answer Type Questions (5 Marks)

1 What is a partnership deed? List out the various contents of partnership deed.

Ans Partnership deed is a written agreement between persons to carry on a business as partners and share gains arising out of business. A partnership deed is necessary for avoiding any misunderstanding and can serve as a proof during litigation.

Some contents of a partnership deed are as follows

(i) Name of the firm.
(ii) Nature of the business.
(iii) Name of partners.
(iv) Place of business.
(v) Amount of capital to be contributed by each partner.
(vi) Profit sharing ratio between partners.
(vii) Loans and advances from the partners and the rate of interest thereon.
(viii) Drawings allowed to partners and the rate of interest charged thereon.
(ix) Maintenance of accounts.
(x) Duties, powers and obligations of partners.

2 "In spite of certain restrictions imposed on a private company, it enjoys certain privileges under the Companies Act and a substantial number of entrepreneurs prefer to form a private company". Comment. **(CBSE 2019)**

Or

Enlist two points as to why a private company is more desirable than a public company. **(CBSE SQP)**

Ans **Privileges of Private Company over Public Company** Refer to text on page 44.

3 Differentiate between public company and private company.

Ans Difference between public and private company

Basis	Public Company	Private Company
Minimum Number of Members	Its minimum number of members are 7.	Its minimum number of members are 2.
Maximum Number of Members	No limit.	200 (excluding its past and present employees).
Minimum Number of Directors	There are minimum 3 directors.	Its minimum number of directors are 2.
Public Invitation of Capital	It is free to invite the public to subscribe for its shares and debentures.	It cannot invite the public to buy its shares and debentures.
Commencement of Business	After obtaining the certificate of incorporation, it has to further obtain certificate of commencement of business before it is allowed to commence business.	It can commence business immediately after obtaining certificate of incorporation.
Transfer of Shares	No restriction on transfer.	Restriction on transfer.

4 How many choices are there to start a business by a businessman? Explain them. **(CBSE TBQ)**

Ans A businessman has following choices to start a business

(i) **Sole Proprietorship** As the name suggests, sole means single and proprietor means an owner, thus, it is a form of business which is managed and controlled by a single owner. One of the oldest, simplest and most commonly used forms of business organisation, which is owned, financed, controlled and managed by only one person is called as sole proprietorship.

(ii) **Partnership** A partnership is an association of two or more persons as co-owners, to carry on, a business and to share its profits and losses.

Thus, two or more persons may form a partnership by making a written or oral agreement to carry a business jointly and share its proceeds.

(iii) **Joint Stock Company** Joint stock companies have evolved because the resources and life span of both sole proprietorship and partnership form of organisations are limited, while their liability is unlimited.

(iv) **Joint Hindu Family/HUFs** Hindu Undivided Family business is a unique form of business as this is only present in Indian society. HUF is governed by Hindu Law.

(v) **Co-operative Organisations** This form is different from any other form whether corporate or non-corporate because it operates not for profit but to provide some benefits or services to its members and even to general public by fighting against some social evil. e.g. in a consumer cooperative, the aim is to provide quality goods at cheaper prices to its members by eliminating the middlemen.

5 In addition to 'number of persons', 'profit sharing' and 'agreement', there are various other features of partnership. Explain any six such features. **(CBSE 2020)**

Ans Refer to topic 'Characteristics of partnership' on page 41 and 42.

6 Explain any six characteristics of company. **(CBSE SQP)**

Ans Refer to text on page 43 and 44.

7 Why is a business plan valuable for an entrepreneur? Explain with the help of any four points. **(CBSE 2020)**

Ans Refer the topic 'Importance of business plan' on page 47.

8 An entrepreneur is doing an industry analysis. While he/she is analysing his/her competitors in his/her line of business that the competitors are far better in their business plans and their execution.

Should the entrepreneur add unique selling point in the existing plan to get a creative niche above others or should he/she go for a completely different line of business, where the competition is less and he/she is easily able to place his/her feet in the market? Give reasons. **(CBSE TBQ)**

Ans I think that instead of venturing out towards a different line of business where the competition is less, the entrepreneur should add Unique Selling Point (USP) in the existing plan to get a creative niche above others. The reasons for this decision could be

(i) The competitors are better only in terms of their business plans and its execution and not in terms of product quality. So, by adding a USP in their existing plan, they might be able to fight competition.

(ii) He is familiar with the current industry and thus, better equipped to succeed.

(iii) Running is no solution. What will he do when competition in the other business also increase?

9 Identify and explain formal statement of business goals with the plan for reaching those goals along with background, information about the organisation and team attempting to reach those goals.

How is the statement valuable to the entrepreneurs, customers, advisors and others who are trying to familiarise themselves with the venture, its goals and objective? Explain with the help of any six ways. **(CBSE 2019)**

Ans The business plan is valuable to the entrepreneur, potential investors, venture capitalists, banks, financial institutions, new personnel's suppliers, customers, advisors and others who are trying to familiarise themselves with the venture, its goals and objectives. The business plan

(i) Helps in determining the viability of the venture in a designated market.

(ii) Help in providing guidance to the entrepreneur in organising his/her planning activities as such

(a) Identifying the resources required.

(b) Enabling obtaining of licenses, if required.

(c) Working out with legal requirements as desired by the government.

(iii) Helps in satisfying the concerns, quarries and issues of each group of people interested in this venture.

(iv) Provides room for self-assessment and self-evaluation, requiring entrepreneur to think through various scenarios and play ways to avoid obstacles.

(v) Though not desirable, at times, business plan helps to realise the obstacles which cannot be avoided or overcome, suggesting to terminate the venture while still on paper without investing further time and money.

(vi) As the investors/lenders focus on the four Cs of credit, i.e. character, cash flow, collateral and equity contribution, it is the business plan which reflects the entrepreneur's credit history, the ability to meet debt and interest payments and the amount of personal equity invested thus serving as an important tool in funds procurement.

10 Abhimanyu Industries Ltd. had a team of professionals and experts to draft a comprehensive yearly document with all the relevant details of internal and external elements in meaning the venture. This document acts as a decision-making tool for the management.

The Chief Executive Officer of the company always pays special focus on one element of this document that ensures the orderly flow of materials from raw state to finished product with a proper system of quality control, as according to him work your plan' is more important than 'plan your work.

(i) Identify the 'comprehensive yearly document' being prepared by Abhimanyu Industries.

(ii) How is this plan a 'decision-making tool for the management?

(iii) Identify the element that is the priority of the CEO of the company.

(iv) Why is the element as identified in (iii) important? **(CBSE 2019)**

Ans (i) Business plan

(ii) Business plans are decision-making tools (Any four)

(a) Describing all necessary inputs for the enterprise.

(b) Explaining the mode of utilisation of the resources.

(c) Detailing the strategies for the execution of the project.

(d) Outlining the desired goals.

(e) Assessing market sensitivity and the profitability of the venture.

(iii) Operational plan

(iv) Importance of operational plan is as follows (Any four)

(a) Ensuing orderly flow of materials in the manufacturing process from the beginning (raw state) to the end (the finished products).

(b) Facilitating continuous production, lesser work-in-progress, minimisation of wastage.

(c) Co-ordinating the work of engineering, purchasing, production, selling and inventory management.

(d) Describing the flow of goods/services from production point to the consumers.

(e) Introducing a proper system of quality control.

(f) Undertaking the best and most economic production policies and methods.

11 The Covid-19 pandemic has ushered an era of new business opportunities for many businesses.

Rajat, an entrepreneur, designed a unique N-95 face mask which would not only filter the air inhaled but also change its colour when the mask is no longer good for use.

Not only this, it would also send an alert in case the user of the mask comes in contact with any virus in the air. The idea sounds good and marketable, but Rajat needs to impress the investors to fund his idea. Rajat prepared a three-minute summary of the business plan executive summary to awaken the interest of the potential funders, customers or strategic partners. **(CBSE 2023)**

(i) Give the meaning of 'business plan' and identify the format of business plan used by Rajat.

(ii) Explain three formats of business plan other than the one identified in (i) above.

Ans (i) A business plan is basically a written representation of an entrepreneur's vision for his business. It is a comprehensively written document prepared by an entrepreneur describing formally all the external and internal factors involved in starting a new venture.

The depth and detail in the business plan depends on the size and scope of the proposed new venture. There is no fixed content for a business plan as it varies according to the entrepreneur's goals and audience.

Thus, it is common to have three or four formats as follows for the same business plan.

Rajat has used an elevator pitch

Elevator Pitch It is basically a 3 minute summary of the business plan's executive summary. This format is often used as a teaser to awaken the interest of the potential investors, customers or strategic partners.

(ii) Other formats of business plan are as follows

(a) **A Written Presentation for External Stakeholders** It includes a detailed, well written and pleasingly formatted plan targeted at external stakeholders.

(b) **An Internal Operational Plan** It is a detailed plan describing planning details that are needed by management, but may not be of interest to external stakeholders.

(c) **A Pitch Deck With Oral Narrative** This format presents the business plan in the form of an entertaining slide show complemented with an oral narrative.

12 Define organisational plan. A business can be classified in how many categories? **(CBSE TBQ)**

Ans An organisational plan is that part of the business plan that describes the proposed venture's form of ownership, i.e. whether it is

(i) sole proprietorship
(ii) partnership
(iii) joint hindu family
(iv) cooperative society
(v) joint stock company

A business, having whichever form of ownership, can be categorised as follows

(a) **Manufacturing Business** A business that makes a tangible product.

(b) **Wholesale Business** A business that buys products in bulk from the manufacturer to be sold in smaller lots to the retailers.

(c) **Retail Business** A business that sells directly to the final consumer for final satisfaction.

(d) **Service Provider** A business that sells intangible goods such as time and expertise, e.g. insurance companies, banks, etc.

13 AB Ltd., manufacturing light bulbs decided to start manufacturing of ceiling fans. They formed a sister concern by the name 'Cool Air Ltd.' The new company was in need of some investment and for the same they had approached a bank. They had submitted a business plan to the bank stating all the necessary details.

They had mentioned very clearly in the plan that they will be manufacturing the blades and have decided to outsource the required motor parts. The plan spoke about the reason for outsourcing along with the contracts with subcontractors.

(i) Explain the component of the business plan along with its related sub part.

(ii) The business plan further gave details about the money which will be invested by the owners and how much they are expecting to borrow. Explain the component of the business plan along with its related sub part. **(CBSE SQP)**

Ans (i) Component of business plan is production. Production is the most important activity of an enterprise, because it is here that transformation of raw material into finished product takes place with the help of energy, capital, manpower and machinery.

The sub-part related to it is partial manufacturing. If some or all the manufacturing process is to be subcontracted or outsourced, then it is referred to as partial manufacturing. It should describe

(a) name and location of subcontractor(s)

(b) reasons for their selection

(c) cost and time involved

(d) any contracts that have been completed etc.

In such cases, a clear mention of what the entrepreneur intends to do himself and what he plans to get it done from outside is required.

(ii) Component of business plan is financial plan. Financial plan is a projection of key financial data about the potential investment commitment needed for the new venture and economic feasibility of the enterprise.

The related sub-part is proforma financing decision. This section summarises all the projected sources of funds available to the venture to raise finance from. Typically, sources of funds are owner's funds and borrowed funds. The entrepreneur's job is to ensure the selection of the best overall mix of financing for the enterprise so that the cost of capital and the financial risk stands minimised, and return on investment and profitability stands maximised.

14 Briefly explain the objectives of an operational plan. **(CBSE TBQ)**

Ans Refer to text on page 50.

15 What is a marketing plan? Why is it required in business enterprise? **(CBSE TBQ)**

Ans The marketing plan is a significant element in the business plan of a new venture, as it highlights how a business plan is to make place for itself in a competitive market by providing answers to three basic questions

(i) Where have we been?
(ii) Where do we want to go?
(iii) How do we get there?

A good marketing plan helps a business to reach its target audience, boost its customer base and helps its customers to understand why its product/service is better than its competitors.

A marketing plan is required by a business as

(i) it helps the business to identify its target market and understand how its product or service meets the consumer's needs.
(ii) it helps the business to identify its competitor and assess what its target customers think about competitor's strengths and weaknesses.
(iii) it helps the business to position its brand, products or services so that its target customers visualise its business as better than or different from its competitors.
(iv) it sets specific, measurable goals and timeframes for its marketing activities.
(v) it helps the business to map out a strategy to reach its target audience, including the messages, channels and tools it will use.

16 Explain any six components of a financial plan. **(CBSE 2020)**

Ans Refer to topic 'Components of financial plan' on page 52.

17 "Having a solid strategy is crucial at any phase of your business, whether you're just starting up or growing an existing venture. Like weather conditions, the needs and challenges of your business change.

A business plan will help you understand your challenges better and outline specific goals and courses of action that are needed to improve. In a way, a business plan is like your car's GPS. It gives you direction and focus and speeds up your journey through all the necessary steps.

After writing business plans with my clients, it becomes easy for us to track their progress, review what goals have already been accomplished and what's still lying on the back burner, identify what changes should be made and discuss what direction the business should be headings.
Source *Forbes Magazine, 16th June, 2017*

Keeping in mind the above article, explain the need of business plan for a business.

Ans Refer to topic 'Importance of business plan' on page 47.

CASE STUDIES

Case 1

Satya Brata Day : Shree Leathers

Satya Brata Dey

Ever seen a long time outside a shoe store? People waiting in the scorching heat just to buy a pair of shoes? If you haven't, you'll see it outside Satya Brata Dey's Shree Leather Shoe Stores in Calcutta.

From Rags to Riches

One dreary morning in November, 1986, Satya left his home in Jamshedpur and came to Calcutta with little more than the clothes on his back. He wore a pair of corduroy pants, a shirt and a pair of sturdy shoes made by his father. Before he left home, his mother had pressed in his hands a few hundred rupee notes which he brought with him.

Today, Satya Brata Dey is a millionaire, a crorepati. And what gives him the greatest satisfaction is that he provides jobs for people in West Bengal, a state where there are very few industries and over five million unemployed.

Parents had a Strong Influence on His Life

Satya's mother was always a strong woman and still is, even at the age of 80. She believed in herself and encouraged Satya to do the same. 'Son, she would say stroking his unruly hair into place, No matter what you do, always win, remember that, always win'. Satya learned his lesson well. He won. And he won against great odds.

Satya's father owned a small shop in Jamshedpur where he made shoes. His shoes were so sturdy that they could last 20 years. As a teenager, Satya often went to his father's shop and helped him in making shoes. That's where he learned the fine art of making sturdy, good looking shoes at a reasonable cost.

It was this apprenticeship under a master shoemaker like his father that taught Satya very early in life, a priceless craft. Little did he knew, that what he was learning in his father's humble shop in Jamshedpur, would someday make him a millionaire, a 'crorepati' in Calcutta. He would have laughed if someone had told him back then, that someday, he would create jobs for hundreds of people with this priceless craft that he learned from his father.

When he remembers his father bending over his work table making shoes day after day, tears glisten in his eyes. The tears of love and pride.

He remembers his father's hands that had over the years become hard and tough like the leather he worked with. Today, Satya would give anything to be able to hold those callused, wrinkled hands in his own and invite him to come and see the little boy but Satya's father is no more. Whereas, Satya manages a business worth crores, what he is most proud of is that even today he can make shoes with his own hands.

From his beloved father, Satya learned another important lesson that would come in very handy for him later in life, i.e. dignity of labour. It means the value and worth of working with one's own hands. Because of his background, Satya has great respect for the working man.

In his business, he treats his employees and workmen like family members and they, in turn, give him their undying loyalty. That is one of the secrets of his success.

What? Start Your Own Business? That's Despicable

In Satya's Bengali community running one's own business was not much respected. Starting a business was looked down upon. Businessmen were seen as people who amassed wealth at the cost of others.

They took too much risk. What if the business failed? What would you do then? On the other hand, a secure government job was quite a another thing.

Becoming a babu in a government department was coveted. Once you got your foot in the door, nobody could fire you and whether you worked or not, the government paid you and even when you retired, the government care of you. It gave you a pension.

It was like your father-in-law's house. You were always a well-looked after guest.

The second best thing to be a government employee was being in 'service', getting a job in someone else's business or in somebody's private business enterprise, you did not get good marriage proposals as the government employee would but there was still a hope for you. You had a job.

Making Shoes was Low in the Prestige Ladder

It was bad enough to do a risky thing like running one's own business, but making shoes? That was truly low down in the prestige ladder of the community. Satya had faced this kind of prejudice before. He remembers well, the days he used to go to his father's shop after school to help out. One day his father's friend said to him, 'Why do you let your son come here and waste his time? Doesn't he have anything better to do? He should learn skills that would get him a job instead of doing this'.

Satya remembered this comment made by his father's friend as he wandered down the streets of Calcutta looking for a place where he could start a business of making shoes. Thank goodness, he had learned the trade and art of making good shoes.

There were no jobs available and last thing he wanted to do was join the ranks of the unemployed. But Satya had never considered looking for a job.

Satya Dreamed Big but Reality Hit Hard

Ever since Satya was four or five, he knew he wanted to have his own business. In Jamshedpur, he would look at the TISCO (Tata Iron and Steel Company) Plant and says to himself, 'Someday I will have a factory like this'.

Hot, tired and hungry, Satya wandered down the streets of Calcutta looking for a place that could be his showroom or shop. At the corner of a deserted street, he spotted a rundown showroom that was for rent. He used the money his mother gave him to pay the rent and moved in. It was his home and 'showroom' rolled in one.

The 'showroom' was rat and cockroach infested. The paint on the walls was peeling. It was dingy, dirty and dimly lit. The windows were filthy and you could hardly see through them. The floor had several layers of dust caked with moisture. But for Satya, it was his dream showroom. It was his place.

Every night Satya washed his pants and shirt and hung them to dry. Often his corduroy pants were still wet in the morning. He wore the wet pants anyway and hoped that his body heat would dry them during the course of the day. 'I was sweeper, painter, salesman, owner everything rolled into one', says Satya.

Never be afraid to dream big, he advises. 'You can make your dreams come true'.

Even as he dreamed his big dreams, he continued to live in the filthy, run-down showroom.

He set about cleaning and fixing it. He swept and mopped until the floor shone. Then, he cleaned the windows with soap and water until they sparkled and finally he painted the walls until the showroom looked bright and attractive and ready for business.

Satya Started his Business

Satya started his business venture with buying six pairs of ladies chappals. He was determined not to borrow money from anybody. He sold the chappals at ₹ 69 each and made a little profit, which he invested to buy more chappals. After a few months Satya made a profit of ₹ 300 which thrilled him to no end. Now he was really in business.

Satya's Business Philosophy Develops Satya's showroom was in new market. In those days 'New Market used to close by 6 pm. After 6 or 7 pm, the whole area used to be dark and deserted. But Satya opened his shop before anyone else and kept it open for long after others had closed theirs.

He did this even if there were no customers. What if there was one customer who needed shoes late in the day when the other shops were closed?

Gradually over a period of time, Satya started to manufacture the shoes that he sold in his store. He positioned his shoes as poor man's of shoes of good quality and inexpensive. He kept his margins low, so that he could attract a large number of customers.

Even though his shoes were meant to attract the low-income customers, many ministers and business people also bought his shoes. Soon satisfied customers brought their friends and family and his business started to grow by leaps and bounds.

He had a winning combination for success, the quality was good and the price was right. A shrewd businessman that Satya is, he kept other manufacturers products as well, so the customers could compare and see that Shree Leathers shoes were cheaper and better.

Customer Service is of Prime Importance

Customer service is always very important at Shree Leathers Stores. Satya offers his customers tea, coffee or coke at his store, so that they would sit, spend some time and buy more than they had originally come to buy. Satya told the story of a woman, who was standing outside his store one day waiting for a sari shop across the street to open.

His salesman invited her in and asked her to sit and wait in the store. She came in and sat down in the comfortably air-conditioned store. The salesman offered her coffee. She had some. She started to look at the different shoes displayed in the store. Without anyone trying to sell her anything, she ended up buying 12 pairs of shoes.

'We don't just sell shoes. We make our customers feel good. That's what brings them back', says Satya Brata Dey.

One day a man was in a hurry to catch a train to Raipur. He came to the store bought his shoes and rushed to the train station. But soon he came back and bought four more pairs. He continues to come back to the store everytime when he is in Calcutta and is one of Satya's best customers. About 15% of his customers are from out of town.

Cut Out the Middleman

Since, Satya manufactures his own shoes, there are no middlemen to pay. He can afford to sell his shoes at a lower price than Bata and other large companies who have huge overheads. If he has to import something from abroad such as material for soles, which he gets from the UK, he imports it directly from the manufacturer there. Thus, once again he avoids paying the middlemen.

He Keeps his Employees Happy and Motivated

Satya firmly believes that motivating the staff and keeping them happy is critical for the success of any business. A disgruntled or unhappy employee will not provide good customer service and customer service is what keeps people coming back and that is what makes the business successful.

'How do you motivate your staff?', I asked.

'I have staff who have been with me right from the very beginning. I treat them like family. I keep them in good humour. I spend time talking with them and help in solving their problems. My staff members don't feel like employees. They feel like they are the owners'.

Satya has a small team of dedicated managers who work long hours, sometimes as much as from 6 am until mid-night.

The third important key to a successful business is paying the vendors and suppliers on time, says Satya. He loses his temper, if his vendors and suppliers are not paid on time.

Sources of Stress

Some of Satya's biggest sources of stress are government authorities. The small bureaucrats and government employees harass for no reason whatsoever, he says. To illustrate his point, he told the following story.

Satya was getting a new showroom constructed. He had taken permission from the Calcutta Municipal Corporation and everything was legal and above board. The construction started and then one day out of the blue, some policemen arrived and ordered the work to be stopped. They demanded a huge bribe. Satya's manager negotiated and settled for a lower sum. But when Satya came to know of it, he was furious and refused to pay a single paisa.

He said he wasn't going to bribe. He contacted some higher authorities in the police department and the government and the policemen left. The work continued. Then one day, a couple of the Calcutta Municipal Corporation employees arrived.

They started finding faults with the construction. Now, they wanted a bribe. Once again, he had to approach the higher authorities to solve the problem. These kinds of harassment and hassles cause unnecessary delays and make doing business stressful.

Growing, Franchising

Shree Leathers has about 15 outlets in Eastern India. He has only one showroom of his own; the rest are all franchises. There is such a great demand for his franchises that people come with recommendations from the Prime Minister and the Finance Minister. Some people come with briefcases full of money requesting a franchise. But Satya Brata is very choossy about giving franchises because the quality and his hard won reputation are very important to him.

Satya's shoes are sold in many countries abroad such as Greece, Austria, Netherlands, Germany, UK, USA, Singapore and Saudi Arabia. But in these countries they are sold as non-brand name shoes.

Satya has reached a point in life when expansion has taken on a new meaning and purpose, expansion for its own sake doesn't mean much to him. He makes enough money and expansion would only mean more stress for him. But creating jobs is important to him. West Bengal doesn't have many industries and jobs are scarce. He feels that it would be selfish of him not to expand. He wants to create as many jobs as he can.

He believes that creating jobs is the best service he can do for the society. He employs about 150 people in his factory and outlets and in addition, if each of his fifteen franchises employs about 10 people, then Satya has created employment for atleast 300 people. It's a win-win situation.

Shree Leathers is worth crores today. The young man who came to Calcutta with only the clothes on his back and a fistful of money has come a long way. His secret? Hard work, dignity of labour and big dreams.

1 In an Indian mindset, specially in Bengali community which livelihood options were favoured? (Give in a sequence).

Ans The livelihood options which were favoured in Bengali community are as follows

(i) Secure government job is the first choice as it gives job security and also a comfortable retired life.

(ii) Second best option is getting employed with somebody's else's business.

(iii) Running own business was not much respected.

2 What are the main reasons for success of Satya Brata Dey's Shree Leathers business? Give in points.

Ans There are many factors which attributed to the success of Shree Leathers. They are as follows

(i) **Dignity of Labour** Satya had great respect for the working man as he himself worked hard for it.

(ii) **Pursuing his Dreams** He had decided that he would do his own business of shoes.

(iii) **Hard Work** When he started, as he says, 'I was sweeper, painter, salesman, owner everything rolled into one', he did hardwork which paid him back.

(iv) **Customer Service and Customer Satisfaction** It was the prime focus of Satya Brata Dey.

(v) **Employee Satisfaction** He believes that motivating the staff and keeping them happy is critical for the success of any business.

He always treats them like family. He keeps them in a good humour and spend time talking with them and solving their problems.

3 What route has 'Shree Leathers' taken for growing its business?

Ans (i) **Franchising** Shree Leathers has about 15 outlets in Eastern India and only one showroom of his own. All the 15 outlets are franchises.

(ii) **Exporting** He sells his shoes in many countries like Greece, Austria, Netherlands, Germany, UK, USA, Singapore and Saudi Arabia. There, he sells his shoes as non-branded shoes.

4 What is the greatest satisfaction for him?

Ans Greatest satisfaction for Satya Brata Dey is to give employment to many. In all, he directly employs around 150 people and another 150 are employed through his franchises. This satisfaction is due to the fact, that once he was also unemployed and he knows the sufferings of that phase, so he gains great satisfaction in giving employment to the unemployed.

5 What is a franchise?

Ans Franchise is an arrangement where authorisation is granted by a company to sell or distribute its goods or services in a certain area, in return for their payment of royalties and conformance to standardise operating procedures.

Case 2

Quest of Independence Effects Form's Selection

William C Durant, the founder of general motors, started a variety of entrepreneurial ventures, primarily in the fields of insurance, real estate and construction. None of them really took off.

Once he hitched a ride to work with a friend, nothing that his friend's new 'buggy' rode smoother than any he had been in. New design in the buggy's springs was the reason for this.

Durant, on learning that the Coldwater Road Cart Company made the buggies with the improved springs, immediately offered to buy the company for $ 1,500. For this, he had to borrow $ 2,000 from Citizen National Bank of Flint and made two sample buggy carts.

Within a week, the buggy was sold, leaving orders for 600 buggy carts and there was no turning back and the turning point came in 1904, when Buick Manufacturing Company offered Durant partnership, as they were both in need of fresh source of capital and the famed selling abilities of Durant. But, Durant agreed to come in only if he could have absolute managerial control and finally took over the Buick Company.

1 'Buick Company' is a private company or a public company?

Ans As the name does not end with the word 'private limited', therefore, it can be inferred that Buick Company is a public company.

2 Why did the Buick Manufacturing Company offered Durant a partnership proposal?

Ans Buick Manufacturing Company made an offer of partnership to Durant because

(i) they needed fresh source of capital.

(ii) they needed Durant's marketing skills.

3 Who is the founder of general motors?

Ans William C Durant is the founder of general motors.

Case 3

Exactly 3.875 Inches Across Weighs 1.6 Ounces Have 178 Sesame seeds and 19% fat in every McDonald Burger world across

Ray Kroc, the President of McDonald's, did not invent or even improve the hamburger. He invented a new way of marketing hamburgers.

The Original McDonald's restaurant was a small hamburger stand in San Bernardino, California. Two brothers, Maurice and Richard McDonald, ran the stand.

Kroc was a 52 years old salesman of multimixers, the mixers the McDonald brothers used to make their shakes.

When Kroc received an order for eight multimixers — enough to make forty milkshakes at once from these brothers, he flew out to see the business for himself.

With sales of over $3,50,000 a year, McDonald's was one of the most successful little restaurants in America, which had the potential to expand among the country.

When Kroc flew in and formed a partnership with them and took care of franchising their business, they signed on the dotted line. Kroc's marketing strategy aided around

(i) rigidly following McDonald brothers' original recipes even after buying them out.

(ii) rigidly ensuring that every customer from Anchorage to Miami get an identical product.

Many great fortunes have been based on a single marketing insight.

1 What was the reason behind the success of Ray Kroc?

Ans The reason for success of Ray Kroc was his new way of marketing hamburgers.

2 Kroc's marketing strategy aided around which principles?

Ans His marketing strategy focused on

(i) Rigidly following McDonald's brothers' original recipes even after buying them out.

(ii) Rigidly ensuring that each customer across the globe got the same product.

3 McDonald's lays its focus on which 'P' of the marketing mix?

Ans McDonald's lays its focus on its 'product' by highlighting the distinct features of its hamburgers.

CHAPTER ASSESSMENT

Objective Type Questions (1 Mark)

1 Which amongst the following is/are the element(s) of operational plan?

(a) Routing (b) Scheduling
(c) Follow-up (d) All of these

2 Kamakshi wanted to raise finance. For this purpose, she decided to prepare a 3 minute summary of business plan's executive summary to awaken the interest of potential investors. This format of presentation of business plan is referred to as

(a) elevator pitch
(b) a pitch deck with oral narrative
(c) a written presentation for external stakeholders
(d) None of these

3 A partnership firm comes to an end on the

(a) retirement of a partner
(b) death of a partner
(c) insolvency of a partner
(d) Any of the above

4 Ab Ltd. was into manufacturing security cameras for household and commercial buildings. Their research and development team came up with a new idea of manufacturing drones as security cameras which will give a 360-degree view of the entire building.

They needed huge finance for the same. The company MD Sharath heard of this group of venture capitalists who are ready to invest in new ideas. He seeked an appointment with them and started preparation of a business plan to be presented before them.

His plan was to make an informative power point presentation showing key graphs of financial trends. It was meant to trigger discussion among the members. Which format of business plan is Sharath using?

(a) Elevator pitch
(b) A pitch deck with oral narrative
(c) A written presentation for external stakeholders
(d) An internal operational plan

5 In partnership, ... agreement is much more advisable as disputes can be resolved better with it.

6 The investors focus on four C's of credit character, cash flow, collateral and ....

7 One of the characteristics of company form of organisation is unlimited liability.

State whether this statement is true or false.

8 Proforma income statement summarises all the profit data during the first year of operations of new enterprises.

State true or false.

Short Answer Type I Questions (2 Marks)

9 What is break-even analysis?

10 Why is the scope of operation of sole proprietorship form of business limited?

11 What is a business plan?

12 What is a production plan?

13 What is elevator pitch?

14 How many sources of funds are available for arranging funds for business?

Short Answer Type II Questions (3 Marks)

15 Describe the content of an organisational plan.

16 Write the steps in preparing a marketing plan.

17 What is the difference between partnership and company?

Long Answer Type Questions (5 Marks)

18 What are the key areas, for a sound financial plan to work?

19 Mention the features of a company.

20 What is a financial plan? What are its objectives?

21 Explain the investment decision under the financial plan. In which areas should the investment be made on the basis of priority?

For explanations scan the given QR Code

CHAPTER 03

Enterprise Marketing

In this Chapter...

- Meaning of marketing strategy
- Product mix
- Price mix
- Place and place mix
- Promotion
- Sales strategy

Meaning of Marketing Strategy

A strategy is basically a comprehensive plan for achieving an organisations' objectives. Marketing is the process of exchange of goods and services for money or something valuable. So, on the basis of these two concepts, marketing strategy means a comprehensive plan to facilitate and promote exchange of goods and services.

Marketing strategy is defined by **David Aaker** as "A process that can allow an organisation to concentrate its resources on the optimal opportunities with the goals of increasing sales and achieving a sustainable competitive advantage". Marketing strategy includes all basic and long-term activities in the field of marketing that deal with the analysis of the strategic initial situation of a company. It also includes the formulation, evaluation and selection of market-oriented strategies and contributes to the goal of the company and its marketing objectives. It is composed of several stategies for growth as well as interrelated components of the marketing mix.

Meaning of Marketing Mix

Marketing mix refers to the ingredients or the tools on the variables which the marketing mixes in order to interact with a particular market.

Marketing mix consists of a list of the important elements or ingredients that make the marketing system and a list of forces that shape the marketing operation of a firm.

According to **Philip Kotler**, "A marketing mix is the mixture of controllable marketing variables that the firm use to pursue the sought level of sales in the target market."

According to **WJ Stanton**, "Marketing mix is the term used to describe the combination of the four inputs which constitute the core of a company's marketing system, i.e. the product, the price structure, the promotional activities and the distribution system."

Components/Elements of Marketing Mix

The 4Ps that make up a typical marketing mix are Price, Product, Promotion and Place.

Marketing Mix- 4P's

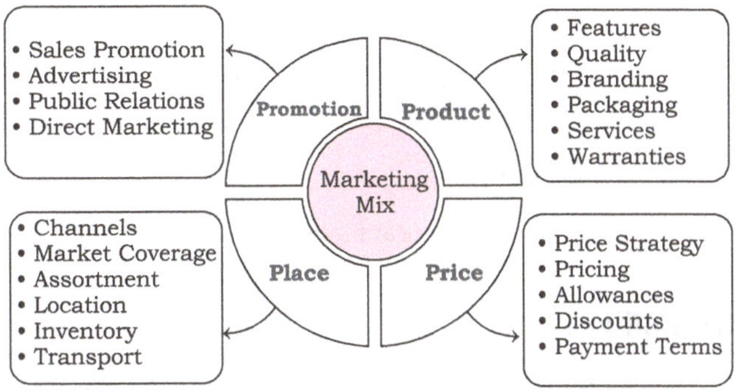

However, now-a-days, the marketing mix increasingly includes several other Ps like *Packaging, Positioning, People* and even *Politics* as vital mix elements.

Product Mix

Product refers to the item actually been sold, i.e. goods or services or 'anything of value', which is offered in the market for exchange. The product must deliver a minimum level of performance, otherwise even the best work on the other elements of the marketing mix will not benefit the organisation.

The product will typically look into the following factors

- What does the customer want from the product/ service? What needs does it satisfy?
- What features does it have to meet these needs?
  - (a) Are there any features you've missed out?
  - (b) Are you including costly features that the customer won't actually use?
- How and where will the customer use it?
- What does it look like? How will customers experience it?
- What size(s), color(s), and so on, should it be?
- What is it to be called?
- How is it branded?
- How is it differentiated from the competitors?

Product mix involves planning and developing the right type of product that will satisfy fully the needs of customers. A product has several dimensions like size and weight of the product, volume of output, product quality, brand name, package, warranties, etc.

These dimensions are collectively called product mix. The components of product mix are branding, labelling and packaging.

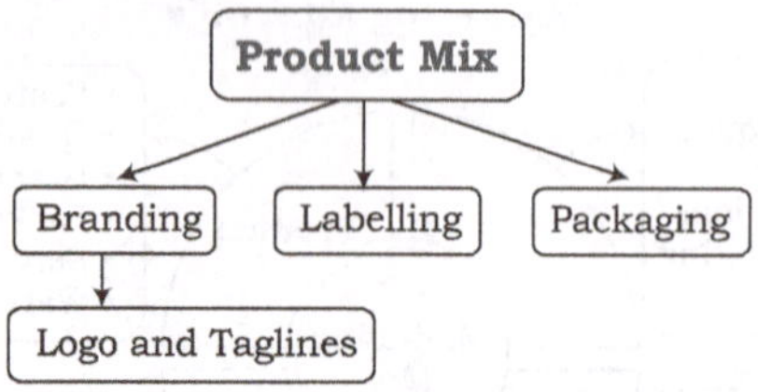

Components of Product Mix

Branding

It is the most important element of product mix. A producer has to decide whether the firm's products will be marketed under a brand name or a generic name. Generic name refers to the name of the class of the product, e.g. car, television, shoes, etc.

If products were sold by their generic names, then it would be very difficult for the marketers to distinguish their products from that of the competitors. Therefore, most marketers give a 'name' (brand) to their products, which helps in identifying their products from that of their competitors.

Thus, 'Branding' can be defined as a process, a tool, a strategy, an orientation whereby a name, a sign, or a symbol, etc., is given to a product by the entrepreneur so as to differentiate its product from the rival products.

According to **Philip Kotler**, "Branding is endowing products and services with the power of **a brand**."

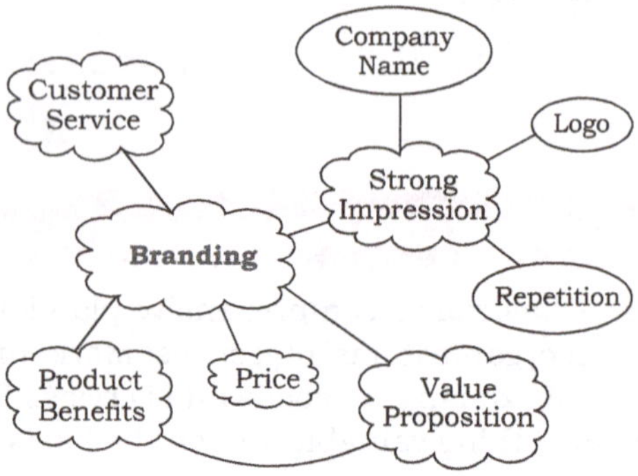

Importance of Branding

Brand

'Brand' is a comprehensive term used to denote a name, term, sign, symbol, design or combination of them, with a view to

– identify the products of one's firm.
– differentiate them from those of their competitors.

The three components of brand are as follows

1. **Brand Name** A part of a brand which can be spoken is referred to as brand name. It is like naming a new born child. e.g. Mercedes, Coke, Lays, etc.
2. **Brand Mark** It is that part of a brand which cannot be spoken but can be recognised. It is non-utterable. It appears in the form of a symbol, design or distinct colour scheme. e.g. 'Girl' of Amul, 'Maharaja' of Air India, etc.
3. **Trademark** A brand or a part of a brand that is given legal protection against its use by other firms is called a trademark. It is essentially a legal term. It confers upon its owner, the exclusive right to use the brand name and brand mark. e.g. [swoosh] is the trademark of Nike.

Qualities/Characteristics of a Good Brand

A good brand name should be distinct and be able to stand out among competitors. In selecting a brand name, entrepreneur should ask himself what he wants to achieve. While selecting a brand name, an entrepreneur should choose a name which is

- short, simple and easy to pronounce, e.g. Nano, LG, etc.
- noticeable, easy to recognise and remember, e.g. 'girl' of Amul.
- pleasing, impressive when uttered, e.g. Zodiac, Kodak, etc.
- neither obscene, negative, offensive or vulgar, i.e. focus should be on positive attributes, e.g. Ujala, Swift, etc.
- adaptable to packaging, labelling requirements, to different advertising media and languages.
- linked to product, symbolically eye catching, e.g. Hajmola, Hair and Care, etc.
- contemporary, capable of being registered and protected legally, e.g., brand mark of Nike and Pepsi etc.

Entrepreneur's Perspective on Brand Name

Entrepreneur can follow different policies in choosing brand name keeping in mind the range of products offered by him/her.

Various types of brands available are

Types of Brand Name
- → Individual brand name
- → Family brand name
- → Corporate names
- → Alpha-numeric names

1. **Individual Brand Name** Under this strategy, an entrepreneur chooses a distinct name for each of his offering, i.e. each product is promoted on the basis of a separate brand name.

   e.g. Hindustan Unilever Limited (HUL) has been concentrating on its core business area i.e. soaps and detergents and has emerged as the clear leader in the toilet soap industry.

   The company has launched many line extensions and variants to leverage the high brand equity of its powerful brand names, *viz.*

   Lifebuoy Brand standing for 'Good health' Lifebuoy liquid, Lifebuoy Personal, Lifebuoy Plus and Lifebuoy Gold to cover various price sub-segments in the health segment.

   Liril Brand name with the 'freshness' concept.

   Lux Brand name for 'beauty soap for film stars'.

   Thus, HUL has ensured for itself a presence in all segments using new brand launches.

2. **Family Brand Name** Under this strategy, an entrepreneur chooses a common or a successful family name for their several products. He can use his own name or the company's name may be used for all the products. It is also referred to as 'Umbrella Branding'. e.g. **Ponds** is a mother brand name used for shampoos, talcum powder, cold creams, face-wash, etc.

   Maggi is a brand name for noodles, sauces, masalas, etc.

   Amul is used to market a large variety of dairy products *viz.* milk, ghee, butter, chocolate, etc.

3. **Corporate Names** Entrepreneurs can choose to utilise their corporate name or logo together with some brand names of individuals products, e.g. Godrej, Tata, Bajaj, etc.

4. **Alpha-numeric Names** Entrepreneurs have an option to brand their product alpha-numerically.

   An alpha-numeric name often signifies its physical characteristics, thus creating a distinctive identity of the product.

   e.g. SX4, i20, Liv52, etc.

Logo

Logo is the short-term for logotype and is an identifying symbol for a product/service or a business. 'Logo' is an important feature or part of branding. It is a graphic mark of emblem used to aid and promote instant public recognition.

Logos are either purely graphic (symbols/icons) or are composed of the name of the organisation (a logotype or word mark).

Some logos are given below

Purpose of a Logo

Logo serves the following purposes

- Logos are an important aspect of business marketing. As the company's graphical representation, a logo acts as an anchor for the company's brand.
- Corporate logos are intended to be the 'identity' of an enterprise by graphically displaying its uniqueness.
- Through a set colour combination, fonts, images, impression and/or patterns, logos provide essential information about a company and helps customers to relate it to an enterprise's core brand.
- Enterprises normally resort to logos as a shortcut to advertising.
- Logos act as the key visual component of an enterprise's overall brand identity.

Tagline

Taglines are basically simple but powerful messages that help to communicate an enterprise's goals, mission, distinct qualities, etc. Thus, a tagline is a short text which conveys a thought effectively.

'Tagline' and 'tag' are American terms. In **UK**, they are called 'end lines' or 'straplines', **Germans** call them as 'claims', **French** refer to them as 'signatures', while **Belgians** call them as 'baseline'. They can come in the form of

- questions
- statements
- exclamations

The basic purpose behind a tagline is to create a memorable dramatic phrase that will sum up a product.

e.g. **Popular Taglines**

Amul's Message 'A gift for someone you love'.

Rasna 'I love you, Rasna'.

McDonald 'I'm lovin it'.

Weekender 'Wear your attitude'.

Raymond's Suiting 'The complete man'.

Yamaha Bike 'The rugged personality'.

Savdhan India 'India fights back'.

Packaging

This is the second element of product mix after branding. It refers to the act of designing and producing the container or wrapper of the product.

In other words, packaging means packing or wrapping goods to look attractive as well as secure safety i.e.,

- holding together the contents
- protecting product while passing through distribution channels.

According to **Stanton**, packaging refers to "All the activities involved in designing and producing the container or wrapper for a product."

According to an **Entrepreneur**, "Packaging is the wrapping material around a consumer item that serves to contain, identify, describe, protect, display, promote and otherwise make the product marketable and keep it clean."

There are three levels of packaging, as discussed below

1. **Primary Package** which encloses the actual commodity.
2. **Secondary Package** which is the layer of cover added to the primary package for its protection.
3. **Transportation Package** refers to further packaging components necessary for storage and transportation.

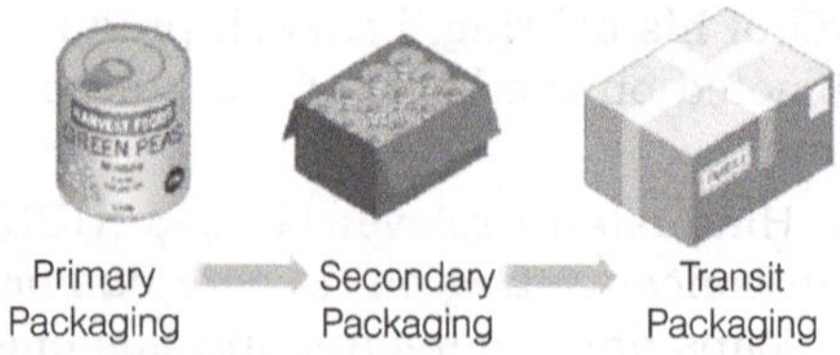

Functions/Importance of Packaging

Packaging is important because it helps in

- Product identification
- Product protection
- Product promotion

– Product differentiation
– Easy handling
– Maintaining rising standards of health and sanitation
– Innovational opportunity for promoting the product

Labelling

Labelling is that part of branding which enables product identification. It is the display of information about a product on its container, packaging, or the product itself. Label may be in the form of simple tag attached to the product or complex graphics that are part of the package.

According to **Philip Kotler** and **Ronald E Turner**, "Labelling is part of packing and consists of printed information that describes the product, appearing on or with the package."

Functions/Importance of Labelling

Labelling is important because of the below mentioned reasons

– It describes the product and specifies its contents.
– It helps in the identification of the product or brands.
– It helps to grade the products.
– It helps in the promotion of the products.
– It helps in providing information as required by law.

Intellectual Property Rights

Intellectual Property (IP) rights are the legally recognised exclusive rights to the creations of the mind.

Under Intellectual Property Act, owners of such property are granted certain exclusive rights to a variety of intangible assets such as copyrights, trademarks, patents, industrial design rights and trade secrets.

These are as follows

1. **Patents** It grants an inventor the right to exclude others from making, using, selling, offering to sell and importing an invention for a limited period of time, in exchange for the public disclosure of the invention.

   The following inventions are patentable
   - Art, process, method, or manner of manufacture
   - Machine, apparatus or other articles
   - Substances produced by manufacturing
   - Computer softwares which have technical applications or can be used with hardware
   - Product patent for food/chemical/medicines or drugs
2. **Copyright** It gives the creator of original artistic or literary work, exclusive rights to use it, usually for a limited time. It applies to a wide range of creative, intellectual or artistic forms of work like musical composition, poems, plays, etc.
3. **Industrial Design** It protects the visual design of objects that are not purely utilitarian. It can be a 2D or 3D pattern to produce a product, industrial commodity or handicraft.
4. **Trademark** It is a recognisable sign, design or expression which distinguishes a product or a service from its competitors.
5. **Trade Secret** Any confidential business information which provides an enterprise a competitive edge is considered as trade secret.
   e.g. Coca-Cola formula.

CHECK POINT 01

1. What do you mean by marketing strategy?
2. Define marketing mix.
3. Mention the components of marketing mix.
4. What are the components of product mix?
5. Name the three levels of packaging.

Price Mix

Price refers to the value that is put on a product. It represents the sum of values that consumers are willing to exchange for the benefit of having or using the product. Price of a product depends upon
– cost of production. – segment targeted.
– ability of the consumer to pay.
– market forces of demand and supply.

Price is the only revenue generating element among the 4Ps, the rest being cost centres.

Pricing Strategies/Methods

Pricing strategy refers to the method that the entrepreneur uses to price his/her products or services. All entrepreneurs, large or small, determine the price of their products and services keeping in view production cost, labour charges, advertising expenses, etc. and then add on a certain percentage so as to earn some profit, based on their pricing strategies, each tied with an overall business plan.

Some pricing strategies are discussed below

Pricing Strategies
- → Cost-plus pricing
- → Penetration pricing
- → Creaming or skimming
- → Variable pricing

1. Cost-plus Pricing

It is the most common technique of pricing where the manufacturer charges a price to cover the cost of producing a product plus a reasonable profit.

This method of pricing is typically based on manufacturing estimates. Estimates of the production costs are made to

- justify planned capital expenditure
- determine likely production costs for new or modified products
- focus attention on areas of high cost

So, estimates are made of the resources required, the cost of these resources and the time for which they will be used. On the basis of these estimates, the price is determined.

Advantages of Cost-plus Pricing

The advantages of this method of pricing strategy are as follows

- The entrepreneur knows exactly the amount of expenditure that has been incurred in producing a product and therefore, profit margin can be added accordingly, which helps in achieving the desired revenue for a firm.
- It is the simplest method to decide the price of the product.
- It helps in evaluating the reasons for escalations in expenses. Because of availability of company's own ready data, corrective action can be taken immediately.

Disadvantages of Cost-plus Pricing

Some disadvantages of this method are as follows

- This method does not take into account the future demand for a product which should be the base for deciding the price of the product.
- It also does not take into account the competitor's actions and their effect on the pricing of the product.
- It can result in the company overestimating the price of a product because this method includes sunk cost and ignores opportunity cost of self-owned assets. Also, profit margin added to the cost can be biased.

2. Penetration Pricing

Under this pricing strategy, the price of the product is initially set at a price lower than the prevailing market price to attract new customers and increase its market share.

Penetration pricing is most commonly associated with a marketing objective to increase market share or sales volume, rather than to make a profit in the short-run. The price is raised later when the market share is gained.

e.g. toothpaste sold at low price in remote rural areas.

Advantages of Penetration Pricing

The advantages of this method of pricing strategy are as follows

- It can result in fast diffusion and adoption, resulting in an increased market share quickly. This strategy can take the competitors by surprise, not giving them time to react.
- It can create goodwill among the early users and create more trade by word of mouth.
- It leads to cost control and cost reduction pressures from the very beginning, thereby leading to greater efficiency.
- It discourages the entry of competitors/new firms in the market because low price acts as a barrier to entry.
- It can create high stock turnover.
- High stock turnover generates enthusiasm and support in the distribution channels.

Disadvantages of Penetration Pricing

The various disadvantages that this method suffers from are as follows

- The main disadvantage of this method is that it establishes long-term price expectations for the product and image preconceptions for the brand and the company. This makes it difficult to raise price later on.

  Also, it is perceived that this pricing strategy only attracts bargain hunters or switchers and they will stop consuming the product when its price rises.
- Another disadvantage is that low profit margins may be inadequate for a business to sustain and survive in long-run.

3. Creaming or Skimming

In this type of pricing strategy, entrepreneurs set their prices higher, so that fewer sales are needed to break-even. Selling a product at a high price, sacrificing high sales to gain a high profit is therefore 'skimming' the market.

This strategy is usually employed to reimburse the cost of investment on the original research and is commonly used in the electronics market where a new range, such as smartphones are initially dispatched into the market at a high price.

This strategy targets the early adopters of a product or a service.

Early adopters have a relatively lower price sensitivity because of the following factors

– Their need for the product outweighs the economic considerations.
– They have greater understanding of the product's unique features.
– They have higher disposable income.

But this strategy is employed only for a limited duration to recover most of the investment made to develop the product. To enhance its market share, the entrepreneur is required to follow other pricing strategies in the long-run.

Advantages of Skimming Price

This price strategy gives an entrepreneur the following advantages

- It helps the entrepreneur to recover the research and development costs associated with the new product quickly.
- This strategy best suits an entrepreneur who caters to consumers who are quality conscious rather than price conscious.

Disadvantages of Skimming Price

This price strategy gives an entrepreneur the following disadvantages

- This strategy can backfire if competitors introduce same product at lower price. Also, business will lose its customers of other segments if the customers perceive that it is the general policy of the business to sell its products at an inflated price.
- This strategy cannot be implemented if there are strict legal and government regulations regarding consumer rights.
- If the consumers become aware that it is the policy of the business to follow this strategy, then they will not buy the product when it is introduced. They will wait till the prices are lowered.

4. Variable Pricing

It is a marketing approach that permits different rates to be extended to different customers for the same goods and services.

This approach is generally followed for businesses where dickering or bargaining over the price of goods is considered the norm.

e.g street vendors who sell various types of small goods. Also, this method is witnessed in the process of bidding or discounted price being offered in case of bulk purchases.

Examples of this strategy are as follows

- Difference in order size by the customers.

  e.g. the soft drink bottle of 200 ml of a company is sold for ₹ 8, while a 2000 ml bottle is sold for ₹ 55 (it should have been priced at ₹ 80, if a uniform price had been followed).
- Difference in anticipated business from different customers.

  e.g. the school fee for the second child is charged at a lower rate by schools.
- Difference in the bargaining power of the customer.

  e.g. the price of unbranded/assembled items of computers are charged differently depending upon a consumer's awareness and his bargaining power.
- Difference in the ability of the consumer to pay.

  e.g. different price is charged by public distribution shops run by the government for wheat, rice, etc., depending on the income groups.

Advantages of Variable Pricing

The advantages that this method of pricing gives are as follows

- Sellers can use this method of pricing to sell those goods and services that they have not been able to sell at original price.
- By selling their products at variable price, the sellers are able to earn a modest profit and recoup their investment in the product.

Disadvantages of Variable Pricing

The disadvantages of this method are as follows

- It can lead to losing other customers who paid full price for their purchase if they find out that another customer was able to purchase the same product at a lower price.
- Goodwill of the business is adversely affected.

CHECK POINT 02

1. State any one factor affecting pricing decisions.
2. Which pricing strategy help the entrepreneur to recover the research and development cost quickly?
3. Give one advantage of penetration pricing.
4. What do you mean by variable pricing?
5. In which pricing strategy, goodwill of the business is adversely affected?

Place and Place Mix

In marketing, place refers to the point of sale. To catch the eye of the consumer and make it easy for him to buy, is the main aim of a good distribution or 'place' strategy. In fact, the mantra for a successful retail business is 'location, location and location'.

Place Mix (Distribution)

Place mix is also referred to as 'distribution mix'. The prime concern of distribution mix is to make sure the timely delivery of products to the customers at the right time and at the right place through various channels of distributions.

A channel of distribution or trade channel is defined as the path or route along which goods move from producers or manufacturers to ultimate consumers.

This channel consists of producers, consumers or users and various middlemen like wholesalers, selling agents and retailers.

According to **McCarthy**, "Any sequence of institutions from the producer to the consumer including one or any number of middlemen is called the channel of distribution."

Therefore, this channel bridges the gap between the point of production and the point of consumption, thereby creating time, place and possession utilities.

A channel of distribution usually consists of three types of flows, which are

- Downward flow of goods from producers to consumers.
- Upward flow of cash payments for goods from consumers to producers.
- Flow of marketing information in both downward and upward direction, i.e.
    (a) Information moves downward in the form of information on new products, new uses of existing products, etc., from producers to consumers.
    (b) Information moves upward in the form of feedback on wants of consumers, suggestions, complaints, etc., from consumers to producers.

Different Types of Channels of Distribution

An entrepreneur has a number of alternative channels available to him for distributing his products. These channels are broadly divided into four types, which are as follows

1. **Producer-Customer** (Direct channel-zero level)
   This is the simplest, shortest and the most economical channel of distribution, in which producers sell their products directly to the consumers.
   There is no middleman involved in this channel of distribution. A producer may sell directly to the consumers through
   – door-to-door sales persons. – direct mail.
   – his own retail stores.
   This method is generally used by
   - big firms to sell industrial products of high value.
   - small producers or producers of perishable commodities also sell directly to local consumer.

   Producer → Customer

2. **Producer-Retailer-Customer** (Indirect–one level) This channel of distribution involves only one middleman called 'retailer'.

   Under it, the producers sell their products to big retailers, who in turn sell to the ultimate consumers.

   This channel relieves the manufacturer from the burden of selling goods and also gives him control over the process of distribution.

   This method is suitable for the marketing of
   - consumer durables.
   - products of high value.

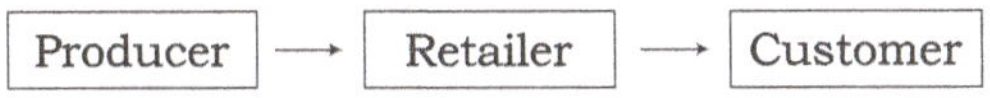

3. **Producer-Wholesaler-Retailer-Customer** (Two levels) This is the most common and traditional channel of distribution, involving two middlemen, *viz.*, wholesalers and retailers.

   Here, the producer sells his product to the wholesalers, who then sell it to retailers, and retailers finally sell to consumers. This channel is suitable for producers
   - having limited finance.
   - having narrow product line.
   - who need the expert services and promotional support of wholesalers.

   This channel is suitable for products having a widely scattered market.

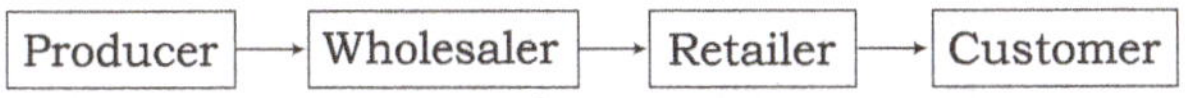

4. **Producer-Agent-Wholesaler-Retailer-Customer** (Three levels) This is the longest channel of distribution in which three middlemen, *viz.*, agent (or distributor), wholesaler and retailer are involved.

   The producer handover his entire output to agents/distributors and the agents distribute the product among wholesalers, who then distribute it among a number of retailers, who finally sell it to the ultimate consumers. This channel is suitable for marketing of various industrial products.

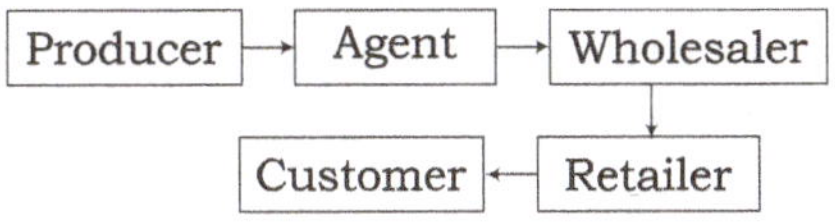

Different Channels of Distribution at a Glance

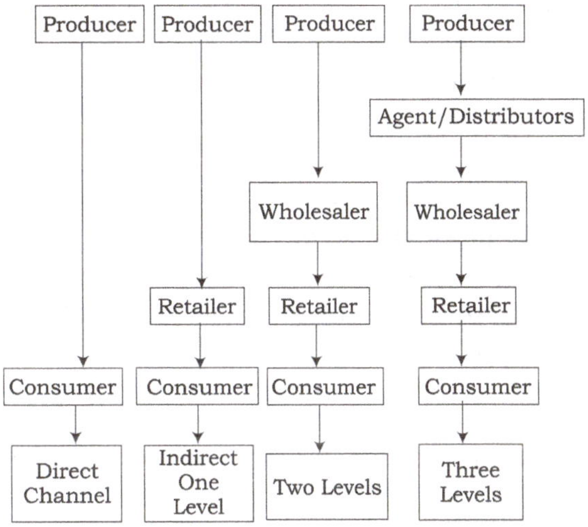

Factors Considered for Selection of Channel

Before selecting a channel of distribution, an entrepreneur should keep in mind the following factors

1. Considerations Related to Product

While selecting a channel of distribution, entrepreneurs should take care of following factors related to the quality and nature of product, which are as follows

(i) **Unit Value of the Product** If the product is very costly, like gold ornaments or industrial machinery, then it is best to use a small distribution channel. On the other hand, for less costly products, long channels can be used.

(ii) **Standardised Products** These are those products in which there is no scope of alteration and their cost is pre-determined, e.g. thermos flask of Milton. For such products, long distribution channels can be used.

(iii) **Customised Products** These products are those which are made according to the discretion of the customers and there is scope for alteration,

e.g. furniture. For such products, direct channel should be used.

(iv) **Perishability** Smaller channels of distribution should be used for goods of perishable nature, such as fruits, vegetables, milk, etc. For durable goods, longer channels can be used.

(v) **Technical Nature** If a product is of technical nature, then it is better to supply it directly to the consumers, so as to explain its technicalities in detail, e.g. machines.

2. Considerations Related to Market

The following considerations related to market need to be analysed by the entrepreneur before taking the final decision

(i) **Number of Buyers** If the number of buyers is large, then long chain of distribution should be opted, but if the number of buyers is small, then smaller channels should be considered.

(ii) **Types of Buyers** Buyers are commonly classified as

- General buyers
- Industrial buyers

For general buyers, long chain of distribution should be used and short-chain for industrial buyers.

(iii) **Buying Habits** A manufacturer should opt for a long channel of distribution if his financial position does not permit him to sell goods on credit and the buyers are in the habit of making credit purchases.

(iv) **Buying Quantity** If goods are bought in small quantities, then long channel of distribution should be used.

(v) **Size of Market** If the market area of the product is scattered, then long channels should be opted.

3. Considerations Related to Manufacturer/Company

The following considerations related to a manufacturer/company need to be closely analysed

(i) **Goodwill** If a manufacturer enjoys good reputation, then he need not depend on middlemen. He can open his own branches easily.

(ii) **Desire to Control the Channel of Distribution** If the manufacturer wants to control the channel of distribution, as in the case of electronic goods sector, then he should opt for shorter channels.

(iii) **Financial Strength** A company having a strong financial base can go in for shorter channels. But financially weak companies have to rely on longer channels.

4. Considerations Related to Government

This is also an important factor while deciding the channel of distribution, e.g. only a license holder can sell medicines in the market according to the law of the government.

So, the manufacturer of medicines should take care that the distribution of his product only takes place through such middlemen who have the requisite license.

5. Other Factors

Certain other factors required to be given due consideration are

(i) **Cost** A manufacturer should select such a channel which is cost-effective.

(ii) **Availability** If a desired channel is not available, then the available channel should be chosen.

(iii) **Possibilities of Sales** Such a channel which has a possibility of large sale should be given preference.

CHECK POINT 03

1. What is the mantra for successful retail business?
2. Define place mix.
3. Mention different types of channels of distribution.
4. If the market area of the product is scattered, then which type of distribution channel should be adopted?

Promotion

Promotion, in marketing, refers to raising customer awareness about a product or brand, generating sales and creating brand loyalty.

It includes all the activities undertaken to make the product or services known to the user and trade.

In the words of **Prof. William J Stanton**, "Promotion is that element in an organisation's marketing mix that serves to inform, persuade and remind the market of a product and/or the organisation selling it, in hope of influencing the recipients' feelings, beliefs or behaviour."

Promotion Strategy

Promotion strategy is a comprehensive plan that aims at finding an appropriate market for a product or service and utilising all aspects of promotion such as advertising and discounts used to promote the product or a service in a particular market.

A business may choose from among the following approaches or strategies to promote its products/services

1. Above The Line (ATL) Approach

This type of promotion focuses on advertising to a large audience. It uses mass media methods of promotion such as

- Advertisements in press.
- Online banner advertisements.
- Place advertisements on billboards.
- Website development.
- Television and cinema advertising.

2. Below The Line (BTL) Approach

Below the line methods of promotion are specific, memorable activities focused on targeted groups of consumers. These promotional techniques are under the control of an organisation and include

- Sponsorship
- Sales promotion
- Public relations
- Personal selling
- Direct marketing

3. Through The Line (TTL) Approach

Through the line approach refers to a promotional strategy involving both above and below the line approaches used by a business to reach their customer base and generate conversions. In this approach, one form of advertising points the target to another form of advertising, thereby crossing the 'line'.

Promotion Mix

Promotion mix refers to the combination of promotional tools used by an organisation to reach the targeted market.

According to **Philip Kotler** and **Gray Armstrong**, "The promotion mix is the specific blend of advertising, public relations, personal selling, and direct-marketing tools that the company uses to persuasively communicate customer value and build customer relationships."

The various promotional tools are as follows

- Advertising
- Personal selling
- Sales promotion
- Public relations

Advertising

Advertising is a paid form of non-personal communication designed to persuade potential customers to choose a product or a service over that of a competitor.

American Marketing Association defines advertising as, "Advertising is any paid form of non-personal presentation and promotion of ideas, goods or services by an identified sponsor".

Objectives of Advertising

The objective of advertising is to increase profit by increasing sales. Advertising achieves this objective by

- making business and product name familiar to the public.
- creating goodwill and building a favourable image.
- offering specific products or services.
- educating and informing the public.
- attracting customers, so that they search for more information about the products or services offered by the business.

Rules of Advertising

Following four rules should be considered while planning any advertising

1. **Aim** Before drafting out an advertisement, the primary or basic purpose of advertisement should be kept in mind.
2. **Target** Target should be considered, i.e. from which sector of the public are we trying to achieve a response? e.g. male, female, adult, teenager, child, mother, father, etc.
3. **Media** Keeping in mind, the aim and the target, the next decision relates to which of the available media will be the most suitable? e.g. TV, radio, press or internet, etc.
4. **Competitors** The actions of the competitors should also be analysed. What are the competitors doing?, Which media channel do they use? Are they successful? Can you improve on their approach and beat them in competition?

These rules should be strictly adhered to, before finalising an advertisement plan.

Developing Effective Advertising (AIDA)

Good advertising generally elicits the following four responses from its target audience, commonly denoted by the acronym AIDA

1. **Attention** (A) An effective advertisement should catch the attention of the audience and stand out amidst the cluster of competing advertisements.
2. **Interest** (I) It arouses interest regarding the company's product or service and delivers a sufficient impact on its audience through its message or offering.
3. **Desire** (D) An effective advertisement should create a desire to gather more information on the offering or to crave for ownership.
4. **Action** (A) It spurs an action which prompts the potential customers to purchase the product or the service.

Commonly Used Media for Advertising

The commonly used media are as follows

Commonly Used Media for Advertising

- Stationery
- Window display or office front
- Press advertising
- Radio
- Television
- Direct mail
- Outdoor
- Ambient
- Cinema
- Point of sale
- Online
- Directory listings

1. **Stationery** Stationery, which includes letterheads, envelopes and business cards, is a means by which the business image or 'name identification' is projected.

   Good quality stationery, used with care and attention and with a high standard of presentation, portrays a positive image of the business.
2. **Window Display or Office Front** The external presentation of the business office or shop is one of the principal ways of establishing and promoting the business image. An attractive, well-maintained exterior with clear, bold sign, windows bright and attractively presented, scrupulously clean and well lit at night and neatly arranged displays, all project an attractive company image and give reasons to customers to buy its products or services.
3. **Press Advertising** This is a commonly used form of general advertising and includes advertising in print media such as newspapers, magazines and journals. This form of advertising is suitable for image building, information dissemination and sales campaigns.
4. **Radio** It is considered to be an ideal medium due to its ability to reach specific target groups such as teenagers, housewives, etc.

   Radio advertising covers spot advertisements which usually last for 15 to 30 seconds, promotions or talkback/RJ discussions. Most radio stations offer packages which include production and extension of the radio campaign through their websites.
5. **Television** It is a powerful advertising medium because it creates impact through sight, sound and movement. But, high cost of advertising on this medium often makes it prohibitive for small businesses.
6. **Direct Mail** This is a very broad category, covering direct communication with the consumer through e-mail, post or fax. It includes newsletters, catalogues and letters.
7. **Outdoor** This form of advertising is done outdoors and includes static advertising such as billboards, backs of street benches and bus shelters or mobile advertising displayed on buses, trains, taxis or towed signage.
8. **Ambient** It refers to any form of advertising that occurs in a non-standard medium outside the home and usually where the consumer is most likely to be.

   It includes advertising on the back of shopping receipts or toilet doors at the cinema, or placing branded coasters at the local clubs, or projecting onto buildings, advertising inside lifts or distributing branded cups.
9. **Cinema** Advertisers can opt to advertise their products through cinema advertising. The advertisements are run in the beginning of the movie or during intermissions.
10. **Point of Sale** This type of advertising is at the point, where the consumer makes purchase decision through floor stickers, in-store digital advertising, shopping trolley signage, shelf or counter posters or playing interviews about the product in store. This method of advertising prompts purchases.

11. **Online** Advertisers can post their advertisements on their own site or on other sites, or they can create link to their websites through other sites or advertise by publishing blogs, offering online product games and through social networks and forums.
12. **Directory Listings** Many consumers use business directories to find a supplier or seller of a specific product or service.

    So, entrepreneurs should get their business registered in various directories which include the yellow or white pages, union directories, trade directories or local business directories.

    e.g. Just Dial is a part of this advertising media, which is a online as well as a telephonic directory.

CHECK POINT 04

1. Define promotion.
2. State various approaches of promotion.
3. Mention any one rule of advertising.
4. What is the full form of AIDA?
5. Mention any two commonly used media for advertising.

Personal Selling

Personal selling means selling products personally. It involves oral presentation of message in the form of conversation with one or more prospective customers for the purpose of making sales.

Kotler and Armstrong define personal selling as, "Personal presentation by the firm's sales force for the purpose of making sales and building customer relationship".

Under personal selling, companies appoint sales persons, who contact with prospective buyers to create product awareness and preferences with the aim of making sales.

In the act of making a final sale, a salesperson plays three different roles

– Role of a persuader. – Role of a service provider.
– Role of an informant.

From the above discussion, it can be inferred that personal selling possesses the following features

- It is a personal form of selling.
- It leads to development of relations.
- It involves oral conversation.
- It has a narrow coverage.
- It has the feature of flexibility.

Qualities of a Good Salesman

A good salesman should possess the following qualities

- A salesman should be good looking, healthy and smart in appearance.
- He should be fully conversant with technical knowledge of the product.
- He should be pleasing, polite and courteous. Apart from having good oratory skills, he/she should also be a good listener.
- He should not give false and misleading information about the product.
- He should be patient and confident.
- He should be of pleasing personality. Being polite will always win customers.
- Salesperson should try to understand the needs of the customers and try to match them with the products available.

Sales Promotion

Sales promotion relates to short-term incentives that encourage or promote the purchase or sale of a product or a service. Sales promotion initiatives are often referred to as 'below the line activities'.

According to **Philip Kotler**, "Sales promotion consists of a diverse collection of incentive tools, mostly short-term, designed to stimulate quicker and/or greater purchase of particular products/services by consumers or the trade".

Sales Promotion Activities

The major sales promotion activities are as follows

Sales Promotion Activities
- → Consumer promotions
- → Business promotions
- → Trade promotions
- → Sales force promotions

1. **Consumer Promotions** The promotion activities directed towards the final consumers are referred to as consumer promotions activities.

Important sales promotion activities of this segment are as follows

- Point of purchase display material which includes
  - (i) **Dangler** A sign that sways when a customer walks by.
  - (ii) **Dump Bin** A bin full of products dumped inside.
  - (iii) **Lipstick Board** A board on which messages are written in crayon.
  - (iv) **Necker** A coupon placed on the neck of the bottle, etc.
- In-store demonstrations, samplings and celebrity appearances.
- Competitions, coupons, lucky draw, sweepstakes and games.
- On-pack offers, discount, rebate, multipacks, product combination and bonuses.
- Loyalty reward programmes.

2. **Business Promotions** The promotion activities targeted towards the business customers are referred to as business promotions activities.

   Important activities of this segment are as follows
   - Seminars and workshops.
   - Conference presentations.
   - Trade show displays.
   - Telemarketing and direct mail campaigns.
   - Newsletters.
   - Event sponsorship.
   - Capability documents which include the information necessary to support production, testing and deployment of an affordable strategy.

3. **Trade Promotions** These promotional activities are targeted towards retailers and wholesalers. Some typical activities of this segment are
   - Reward incentives linked to purchase or sale.
   - Reseller staff incentives.
   - Competitions.
   - Corporate entertainment.
   - Bonus stock.

4. **Sales Force Promotions** The sales promotion activities used to encourage members of the sales force are referred to as sales force promotions. Some important activities belonging to this segment are
   - Commissions.
   - Sales competitions with prizes or awards.

Public Relations

It is a deliberate, planned and sustained effort to establish and maintain mutual understanding between an organisation and its stakeholders by obtaining favourable publicity, building a good corporate image and handling or heading off unfavourable rumours, stories and events.

A Stakeholder

Stakeholders are various groups which can influence or pressurise a business decision-making activity and have an impact on its marketing performance.

These groups comprise of
- clients/customers staff
- strategic partners
- government
- financial institutions
- shareholders
- media
- local community

Tools of Public Relations

Typical tools of public relations include
- News creation and distribution in the form of media releases.
- Special events such as news conferences, grand openings and product launches.
- Speeches and presentations.
- Educational programmes.
- Annual reports, brochures, newsletters, magazines and audio-visual presentations.
- Community activities and sponsorships.

CHECK POINT 05

1. Define personal selling.
2. Write any two qualities of good salesman.
3. What do you mean by sales promotion?
4. What do you understand by stakeholders?
5. Mention any two tools of public relations.

Sales Strategy

A sales strategy is a plan that positions a **company's** brand in such a way, that it gains a competitive advantage in its segment. Successful strategies help the sales force focus on target market customers and communicate with them in relevant and meaningful ways.

A strategic sales plan not only involves a quick understanding of market opportunities, threats and target markets, but also the strengths and weaknesses of the competitors.

Successful sales strategies communicate to the sales force how their products and services can solve the customers' problems, so that they can target the right customers at the right time.

Significance of Sales Strategy

An effective sales strategy is important for a business because of the below mentioned reasons

- Planning an effective sales strategy requires looking at long-term sales goals and analysing the business sales cycle.
- It helps business owners and managers to gain a more precise knowledge of sales intervals, seasonal changes and motivating factors about the sales team.
- After creating long-term sales strategy based on long-term goals, sales managers create monthly and weekly sales strategies. This allows for short-term performance evaluation of sales team and allows to take remedial action if targets are not achieved.

Types of Sales Strategy

There are basically two types of sales strategy to meet an enterprise's sales objectives, *viz* direct and indirect sales strategy. These are as follows

1. **Direct Sales Strategy** Under this strategy, salesmen attack the competitors directly. While talking to the customers, they talk about each feature of the competitor's product and compare it to theirs. This strategy is also termed as negative selling approach.
2. **Indirect Sales Strategy** Under this strategy, salesmen apply more subtle techniques by demonstrating features and benefits of their products or services without ever mentioning the name or features of competitor's products.

   This is more sophisticated positive sales strategy which requires research and analysis of the competition.

Components of Sales Strategy

Components of sales strategy are classified into four types

1. **Product Placement** It is basically an advertising technique used by companies to place the product in market through various social media network. Businesses can use the social network pages to communicate with it's customers.
2. **Promotion** It refers to all such activities which intend to inform customers about the products of the company and persuade them to buy these products.
3. **Testimonials** Customers testimonials and feedback should regularly be posted on the company's site and should be readily available for prospects to read or watch. This lends authenticity to the claim made by a business with regards to its products or services.
4. **Core Selling Strategies** There are a number of strategies available for the sales personnel to carry out their responsibilities and duties effectively. But, the success of these strategies depends on the identification and analysis of those factors that are treated as drivers of selling strategy formulation.

Functions of Sales Strategy

The two main functions of sales strategy are as follows

1. **New Customer Acquisition** A sales strategy lays out steps and methods necessary for targeting customers in different stages.

   Potential customers need communication that introduces the brand and product/service to them and shows, how it can solve their problems.

   Sales strategy facilitates this communication and helps in expanding the customers base.
2. **Customer Retention** Retaining existing customers, so that they don't deviate towards competitors is the second important function to be performed by sales strategy. Current customers require more personal communication about new features or benefits to keep them engaged. Promotions and referral discounts work to motivate current customers to spend their money and spread the benefit of the product to others.

Considerations while Formulating Sales Strategy

The following considerations should be carefully analysed and reviewed by a business before formulating a sales strategy
- Market knowledge.
- Awareness of competitor's activities.
- Awareness of current trends.
- Detailed business analysis.

These considerations are crucial for a successful sales strategy. Small business owners or those formulating a sales strategy for a first time should hire a professional consultant for formulating an effective sales strategy.

CHECK POINT 06

1. Define sales strategy.
2. State any one point of importance of sales strategy.
3. How many types of sales strategies are there? Mention them.
4. Mention any two core selling strategies.
5. Specify one function of sales strategy.

EXAM PATTERN EXERCISE

Objective Type Questions (1 Mark)

Multiple Choice Questions

1 The 'Marketing strategy' and 'Action plan' comprise of decisions pertaining to which of the following? **(CBSE 2020)**

(a) Potential hazards present in the competitive environment
(b) Product, place, price, promotion
(c) Customer's characteristics
(d) Quantifying goals of the organisation

Ans (b) Product, place, price, promotion

2 Which of the following is not a component of product mix? **(CBSE 2020)**

(a) Branding (b) Labelling
(c) Packaging (d) Promotion

Ans (d) Promotion

3 Farhan Akhtar driving Royal Enfield bike in 'Bhaag Milkha Bhaag' is an example of

(a) product placement (b) promotion
(c) testimonials (d) core selling strategies

Ans (a) product placement

4 'Brand' word has originated from the word 'Brandr' which means 'to burn' in

(a) French (b) German
(c) Norwegian (d) None of these

Ans (c) Norwegian

5 'Maharaja' of Air India is **(CBSE SQP)**

(a) brand name (b) brand mark
(c) brand (d) trademark

Ans (b) brand mark

6 .... act as the key visual component of an enterprise's overall brand identity.

(a) Brand name (b) Logo
(c) Tagline (d) Packaging

Ans (b) Logo

7 .... pricing strategy is employed only for a short duration as it is not viable in the long-run.

(a) Penetration (b) Cost-plus
(c) Skimming (d) Variable

Ans (c) Skimming

8 The associated cost of promotion is the highest in case of

(a) advertising (b) personal selling
(c) sales promotion (d) publicity

Ans (b) personal selling

9 .... promotional activities are targeted towards retailers and wholesalers.

(a) Consumer promotions
(b) Business promotions
(c) Trade promotions (d) None of these

Ans (c) Trade promotions

10 In the act of making a final sale, a sales person plays a role of

(a) a persuader (b) a service provider
(c) an informant (d) All of these

Ans (d) All of these

11 Which of the following is not a component of brand? **(CBSE SQP)**

(a) Brand name (b) Brand mark
(c) Logo (d) Trademark

Ans (c) Logo

12 Which of the following are the four rules when planning any advertising activity? **(CBSE SQP)**

(a) Aim (b) Competitors
(c) Media (d) All of these

Ans (d) All of these

13 Advertising is **(CBSE SQP)**

(a) a paid form of communication
(b) selling products personally
(c) a deliberate effort done to establish and maintain mutual understanding between organisation and public
(d) it relates to short-term incentives

Ans (a) a paid form of communication

14 Sales strategy is important because

(a) it creates awareness about business environment
(b) it helps in measuring short-term performance of sales team
(c) Both (a) and (b) (d) None of these

Ans (c) Both (a) and (b)

15 XY Limited manufactures plastic buckets. The CEO wants to select a distribution channel for his buckets. The factor(s) related to the product to be kept in mind is/are

(a) unit value of product
(b) perishability
(c) technical nature
(d) All of the above

Ans (d) All of the above

16 Priyam composed a music piece for a song and the lyrics were written by him. He wishes to legally protect his creation. He can get a **(CBSE SQP)**

(a) patent for lyrics and music piece
(b) copyright for lyrics and music piece
(c) copyright of the lyrics and patent for the music piece
(d) trademark for the complete song

Ans (b) copyright for lyrics and music piece

17 'Balls red' is a SSI producing cricket and tennis balls. To promote its products, it wants to advertise on TV but its Chartered Accountant advises the CEO of the firm against it.

The reason behind this could be

(a) limited scope of TV
(b) high cost associated with it
(c) limited exposure
(d) All of the above

Ans (b) High cost of advertising on the television medium makes it prohibitive for small businessess.

18 The 'Umbrella branding' is **(CBSE SQP)**

(a) Entrepreneur opts to use a common or successful family name for their several products.
(b) Entrepreneurs choose to utilise their corporate name or logo together with some brand names of individual products.
(c) Entrepreneur uses alpha-numeric names to signify physical characteristics of the product.
(d) Entrepreneur chooses distinct names for each of his offerings.

Ans (a) Entrepreneur opts to use a common or successful family name for their several products.

19 Various approaches may be used by a company to promote its products. One of them is the use of mass media methods by designing a promotion strategy that aims at establishing brand identity. Identify promotion strategy.

(a) Below the line
(b) Through the line
(c) Above the line
(d) None of the above

Ans (c) Above the line

20 Krishiv manufactures lamp shades in his cottage industry where labour intensive techniques are used.

He is selling these lamp shades under the brand name 'U-lite'. They are in great demand as now-a-days interior designers are using lamp shades to give an aesthetic look to the houses they design. For Krishiv, the per unit cost of each lamp shade is ₹450 and he sells it for ₹ 900.

Similar lamp shades are available in the market and on online website in the range of ₹ 1,000-₹ 1,100 per unit. The pricing strategy used by Krishiv is the one where the price of the product is initially set at a price lower than the eventual market price to attract new customers.

His objective is to increase the sales volume, rather than to make profit in the short-run. The pricing strategy adopted by Krishiv is **(CBSE 2023)**

(a) cost plus pricing
(b) penetration pricing
(c) skimming pricing
(d) variable pricing

Ans (b) penetration pricing

21 Which of the following statements is related to 'Below- the-Line' promotion approach that a company can use to promote its products? **(CBSE 2023)**

(a) It targets mass audience
(b) It targets identified small groups
(c) It helps in establishing brand identity
(d) It includes conventional media like print, online, television and cinema advertising

Ans (b) It targets identified small groups

22 Prabhas is the creative head of an advertising agency. His latest project is to design a campaign for super food for children in the age group of 6 months to 2 years. He develops a jingle in Hindi as well as in English language to reach out to the maximum audience of the market segment. By doing this, he is not only informing and selling the product but also improving the image of the business. When any advertising activity is planned, there are four rules to be considered.

From the following, identify the rule/rules that are taken into consideration by Prabhas in the above case **(CBSE 2023)**

I. Aim II. Target
III. Media IV. Competitors

Codes

(a) Only I (b) I and II
(c) I, II and III (d) I, II and IV

Ans (c) I, II and III

23 .... channel of distribution completely relieves the manufacturer from the problem of distribution and is suitable for marketing of industrial products.

(a) Producer-customer
(b) Producer-retailer-customer
(c) Producer-wholesaler-retailer-customer
(d) Producer-agent-wholesaler-retailer-customer

Ans (d) Producer-agent-wholesaler-retailer-customer

24 Vinit innovated a new pen which can read any text when placed on top of a page or newspaper which definitely helps blind and old people who are unable to read, he wishes to legally protect his product. He can get a **(CBSE SQP)**

(a) Patent (b) Copyright
(c) Trademark
(d) Geographical Indication

Ans (a) Patent

25 Vector Ltd., is in the Fast Moving Consumer Goods Industry. They introduced a new variety of biscuits in the market. It has high fibre content with different new flavours incorporating various multigrains. State which promotion strategy should be used by Vector Ltd.? **(CBSE SQP)**

(a) Below the line (b) Through the line
(c) Above the line (d) None of these

Ans (c) As per this promotion strategy, focus is paid on advertisement for the large audience through television etc.

26 Harjot is planning to set-up a unit for manufacturing biodegradable bags of different sizes by processing the sugarcane bagasse. She also plans to be fully relieved of the problem of distribution and thus decides to hand over her entire output to the selling agents. The channel of distribution used by Harjot is **(CBSE 2020)**

(a) zero level (b) one level
(c) two level (d) three level

Ans (b) one level

27 Which of the following is not a purpose served by logo?

(a) Logo acts as an anchor for the company's brand.
(b) Enterprises resort to logos as a long and cost increasing factor of advertising.
(c) Corporate logos are intended to be the identity of an enterprise.
(d) Logo act as the key visual component of an enterprise's overall brand identity

Ans (b) Enterprises resort to logos as a long and cost increasing factor of advertising.

28 **Assertion** (A) Labelling acts as a silent salesman.

Reason (R) It helps in the promotion of products by attracting the attention of customers and providing required information.

Alternatives

(a) Both Assertion (A) and Reason (R) are correct
(b) Assertion (A) is correct, but Reason (R) is incorrect
(c) Assertion (A) is incorrect, but Reason (R) is correct
(d) Both Assertion (A) and Reason (R) are incorrect

Ans (a) Both Assertion (A) and Reason (R) are correct

29 **Assertion** (A) Advertising costs are passed on to consumers in the form of higher prices.
Reason (R) Advertising helps in increasing sales and thereby reducing costs.

Alternatives

(a) Both Assertion (A) and Reason (R) are correct
(b) Assertion (A) is correct, but Reason (R) is incorrect
(c) Assertion (A) is incorrect, but Reason (R) is correct

(d) Both Assertion (A) and Reason (R) are incorrect

Ans (b) To meet the increased cost of products due to expenditure on advertising, price of the product is raised.

30 Given below are the types of brands available in the market. Match them correctly with their meaning.

Column I (Brands)	**Column II** (Meaning)
A. Individual brand name	(i) Signifies physical characteristics and is generally used or mobile handsets.
B. Family brand name	(ii) Entrepreneurs can choose to utilise their corporate name or logo together with some brand names of individual products.
C. Corporate name	(iii) Entrepreneurs choose a common or a successful family name for their several products.
D. Alpha-numeric names	(iv) Entrepreneur chooses a distinct name for each of his offering.

Codes

	A	B	C	D		A	B	C	D
(a)	(iii)	(ii)	(iv)	(i)	(b)	(i)	(ii)	(iii)	(iv)
(c)	(iv)	(iii)	(ii)	(i)	(d)	(ii)	(iii)	(iv)	(i)

Ans (c) (iv) (iii) (ii) (i)

31 Given below are the levels of packaging. Match them correctly with their meaning.

Column I (Levels of Packaging)	**Column II** (Meaning)
A. Primary packaging	(i) Refers to further packaging components necessary for storage and transportation.
B. Secondary packaging	(ii) It endoses the actual commodity.
C. Transportation packaging	(iii) It is the layer of cover added to the primary package for its protection.

Codes

	A	B	C		A	B	C
(a)	(iii)	(ii)	(i)	(b)	(ii)	(iii)	(i)
(c)	(i)	(iii)	(ii)	(d)	(iii)	(i)	(ii)

Ans (b) (ii) (iii) (i)

32 Give below are some tools of promotion mix. Match them correctly with their objectives.

Column I (Tools of Promotion Mix)	**Column II** (Objectives)
A. Advertising	(i) To reach a mass audience with a specified message.
B. Personal selling	(ii) Dealing with individual customers.
C. Sales promotion	(iii) To appeal to a mass audience to create awareness.
D. Publicity	(iv) To stimulate short-term sales or spur impulse purchases.

Codes

	A	B	C	D		A	B	C	D
(a)	(iii)	(ii)	(iv)	(i)	(b)	(ii)	(iii)	(i)	(iv)
(c)	(i)	(ii)	(iv)	(iii)	(d)	(iv)	(ii)	(ii)	(iii)

Ans (a) (iii) (ii) (iv) (i)

33

Identify the type of advertising depicted in the given image. **(CBSE SQP)**

(a) Point of sale (b) Ambient

(c) Outdoors (d) Direct mail

Ans (b) Ambient

34

Identify the promotion strategy shown in the image above. **(CBSE SQP)**

(a) Below the line (b) Above the line

(c) Through the line

(d) Both Below the line and Above the line

Ans (a) Below the line

Fill in the Blanks

35 .... is defined as, "a process that can allow an organisation to concentrate its resources on the optimal opportunities with the goals of increasing sales and achieving a sustainable competitive advantage".

Ans Marketing strategy

36 .... is the mixture of controllable marketing variables that the firm uses to pursue the sought level of sales in the target market.

Ans Marketing mix

37 A .... is either a tangible or an intangible offering that is required to satisfy the needs and aspirations of a consumer.

Ans product

38 'Maggi' is an example of ....

Ans umbrella branding/family brand name

39 .... is a simple but powerful message that helps to communicate an enterprise's goals, mission, distinct qualities and so much more. **(CBSE 2020)**

Ans Tagline

40 Komal has started an herbal toothpaste manufacturing unit. She has decided about the logo, packaging format and labelling of the product. Her friend Neha asked her whether she has taken care of the legally recognised exclusive rights of other manufacturers in the industry before taking the above stated decisions. Here, Neha asked Komal about ....

Ans intellectual property rights

41 PapTap is a soft drink company. It sells 200 ml bottle for ₹ 8 and 2,000 ml bottle for ₹ 55. The company follows .... strategy.

Ans variable pricing

42 .... relates to short-term incentives that encourage or promote the purchase or sale of a product or a service.

Ans Sales promotion

43 .... approach of promotion focuses on advertising to a large audience.

Ans Above The Line (ATL)

44 .... is a plan that positions a company's brand in such a way that it gains a competitive advantage in its segment.

Ans Sales strategy

45 'Uber' company providing cab services through mobile app is an example of .... sales strategy.

Ans direct

46 .... sales strategy allows a business to cover a wide geographical market and to sell to a large customer base.

Ans Indirect

State True or False

47 The components of product mix are branding and labelling only.

Ans False. The components of product mix are branding, labelling and packaging.

48 I Phone XI is an example of corporate brand name.

Ans False. It is an example of alpha-numeric brand name.

49 Brand is a name, term, sign, symbol or design or a combination of them which is intended to identify the goods or services of one seller or a group of sellers.

Ans True

50 Stakeholders are various groups which can influence or pressurise a business decision-making activity and have an impact on its marketing performance.

Ans True

51 In UK, they are called 'end lines', 'end lines' or 'strap lines'. Germans call them as 'claims'. French refer them as 'signatures', while Belgians call them 'base lines'. Concept discussed here is tagline. State true or false.

Ans True

52 With it's help the consumers are able to identify the products of a firm and are also able to differentiate them from those of the competitors. Here, concept discussed is marketing mix. State true or false.

Ans False. 'Brand' is discussed here.

53 Primary package encloses the actual commodity.

Ans True

54 Kundan Jewellers manufactures gold ornaments, specialising in Kundan jewellery. They should use a small distribution channel for marketing their products.

Ans True

55 Adhiraj has just started his business of selling designer kurtas. He should follow Below The Line (BTL) approach to promote his merchandise.

Ans True

56 Floor stickers, in-store digital advertising, shopping trolley signage, shelf or counter posters etc. are all examples of point of sale media.

Ans True

57 Direct sales strategy is referred to as 'positive selling'.

Ans False. Direct sales strategy is referred to as negative selling as sales persons highlight the negative aspects of competitor's product.

Case Based Questions

58 Read the following article and answer the questions that follow

Torts Limited started its business in New Delhi in 2014 as a start-up providing freshly created flower bouquets to its customers. It then expended to become a fully-grown décor company in 2019. The management of Torts Limited procures fresh flowers directly from the farmers and has guided them to not use any fertilizers because the motto of the company is to provide organic and freshly picked flowers for their precious occasions. The CEO of the company once stated in one of his speeches that the reason for such growth and development of the company is the use of different online platforms for their promotion. The products and services of their company are listed on various platforms like Facebook, Youtube, etc. The company also has its pages on all social media platforms that encourage two-way communication with the customers. The CEO also stated that initially they charged low prices from their customers to gain trust and attract more customers. Altogether, the business and marketing strategies of the company have helped the company in reaching its goals and the company has grown more than double in terms of its revenue and customer base.

(i) "The company also has its pages on all social media platforms that encourage two-way communication with the customers."

Which of the following promotion strategies was adopted by Torts Limited?

(a) Below the line (b) Above the line
(c) Through the line
(d) None of these

Ans (a) Below the line

(ii) Which concept of enterprise marketing and growth is highlighted in the case of Torts Limited?

(a) Sponsorship (b) Planning
(c) Sales promotion (d) All of these

Ans (c) Sales promotion

(iii) "The management of Torts Limited procures fresh flowers directly from the farmers and has guided them to not use any fertilizers because the motto of the company is to provide organic and freshly picked flowers for their precious occasions." The above statement represents that .... value is promoted by the company.

(a) equality and justice
(b) enhanced services
(c) environmental concerns
(d) All of the above

Ans (c) environmental concerns

(iv) "The products and services of their company are listed on various platforms like Facebook, Youtube, etc."

Which element or means of advertising has been used by the company to attract customers?

(a) Office front
(b) Digital marketing
(c) Radio (d) Display media

Ans (b) Digital marketing

(v) The technique of charging low prices in the initial life of a business is called ....

(a) price skimming (b) variable pricing
(c) penetration pricing (d) cost-plus pricing

Ans (c) penetration pricing

59 Read the following article and answer the questions that follow

Hitesh's father owned a pharmacy in his local town. The pharmacy "Truepill Medicines" was very famous in the town and nearby because Hitesh's father always tried different and new techniques to attract customers. The staff was very polite and customers were handled with utmost care.

After graduating from a reputed business college, Hitesh went on to propose an investment deal to his father. He asked his father to grant him the permission of opening three new Truepill Medicine branches in the nearby cities. His father agreed and Hitesh started planning for the venture. The first pharmacy was opened in six months and Hitesh used a unique technique to attract customers. He used different coupons for the first month of inception of the pharmacy which were placed on the neck of medicine bottles and customers get discounts after bringing them back to the pharmacy.

His salesmen also contacted the customers at the time of giving them the medicines needed and told the customers that their medicines are from legible sources and those they do not stock or sell any expired items. In this way, a positive worth of mouth transferred from the salesmen to the customers. Hitesh also created a website for the pharmacy where customers can pre-book their orders and delivery will be made within 24 hours.

In about 2 years, he was able to open the three shops and all these shops were using unique modern day techniques to gain and retain customers. Hitesh's presence of mind and new ideas made the local town pharmacy, a famous brand.

(i) Which of the following distribution channels can be used by Truepill?

(a) Two level (b) Indirect one level
(c) Direct zero level (d) None of these

Ans (a) Manufacturer-wholesaler-retailer-customer

(ii) "He used different coupons for the first month of inception of the pharmacy which were placed on the neck of medicine bottles and customers get discounts after bringing them back to the pharmacy."

Which of the following techniques is used by Hitesh?

(a) Dangler (b) Dump bin
(c) Lipstick Board (d) Necker

Ans (d) Necker

(iii) Which component of a sales strategy is highlighted in the above case of Truepill Medicines?

(a) Promotion
(b) Testimonials
(c) Placement of product
(d) All of the above

Ans (a) Promotion

(iv) "His salesmen also contacted the customers at the time of giving them the medicines needed and told the customers that their medicines are from legible sources and those they do not stock or sell any expired items."

The .... type of sales strategy was used by the salesmen.

(a) direct sales strategy
(b) indirect sales strategy
(c) product placement
(d) None of the above

Ans (b) indirect sales strategy

(v) "Hitesh also created a website for the pharmacy where customers can pre-book their orders and delivery will be made within 24 hours."

Which of the following promotion strategies was adopted by Torts Limited?

(a) Below the line (b) Above the line
(c) Through the line (d) None of these

Ans (b) Above the line

Short Answer Type I Questions (2 Marks)

1 What does the marketing strategy of a company include?

Ans A marketing strategy is composed of several strategies for growth as well as interrelated components called the marketing mix. So, a company's marketing strategy may include

(i) Choice of channels of distribution.
(ii) Pricing strategy.
(iii) Choice of advertising media.
(iv) Choice of sales promotion techniques.

2 Given the same product and the same market, why is it necessary to adopt different types of market mix? Give reasons. **(CBSE 2010)**

Ans In case of the same product and the same market, it becomes necessary for the entrepreneur to compete with the competitors.

It is important to bring some changes in its product mix, price mix, promotional mix and distribution mix, so as to influence the consumer of the product. So, when the product and market are same, there is a need of different market mix.

3 What is branding? How is it useful?

Ans Branding is the process of giving a name, sign or a symbol to a product in order to distinguish it from products of similar nature.

Branding is useful as it helps in
(i) identification of product.
(ii) differentiation of product.

4 What are the factors that affect branding?

Ans The factors that affect branding are as follows
(i) Image of product among customers.
(ii) Quality maintained by the concerned brand.
(iii) Status and recognition of product.
(iv) Monitoring and identifying customers preferences.

5 Identify the term that is used to identify the products of one firm and differentiate them from those of the competitors. Also, explain the term. **(CBSE 2023)**

Ans Brand is a comprehensive term used to denote a name, term, sign, symbol, design or combination of them, with a view to identify the products of one firm and differentiate them from those of their competitors.

6 Differentiate between trademark and brand mark. **(CBSE TBQ)**

Ans Differences between trademark and brand mark are (Any two)

Basis	Trademark	Brand Mark
Meaning	A brand or a part of a brand that is given legal protection against its use by other firms is called a trademark. It confers upon its owner the exclusive right to use the brand name and brand mark.	A brand mark is that part of a brand which cannot be spoken but can be recognised. It appears in the form of a symbol, design or distinct colour scheme.
Concept	It is a narrow concept, as it is a brand mark that is given legal protection.	It is a broader concept, as it includes trademark.
Example	is the trademark of Nike.	'Maharaja' of Air India is the brand mark.

7 What do you understand by 'Corporate brand' name? Give an example.

Ans When an entrepreneur uses a common name or successful corporate name for their several products, it is known as corporate branding or umbrella branding,

e.g. LG uses LG as brand name for its various range of electronic products like TV, Refrigerator, Air conditioner, etc.

8 What is the purpose of logo? **(CBSE TBQ)**

Ans Logo serves the following purposes (Any four)
(i) It acts as an anchor for the company's brand.
(ii) It graphically displays the company's uniqueness.
(iii) It provides essential information about a company and helps customers to relate to its core brand.
(iv) It is a shortcut to advertising.
(v) It acts as the key visual component of an enterpris's overall brand identity.

9 How does 'tagline' help a company or a product?

Ans 'Tagline' is a small amount of text which servers to clarify a thought and creates a memorable dramatic phrase. These are powerful messages that help to communicate an enterprise's goals, mission and distinct qualities,

e.g. Raymond's tagline is 'The complete man'.

10 Barle Agro Ltd. is a famous name for bottled beverages like cold coffee, flavoured milk, iced tea, etc. Now the company is planning to introduce a range of fresh fruit smoothies giving competition to big multinational and Indian brands.

The company has a very effective marketing department. Create a tagline and an individual brand name for the upcoming product range of Barle Agro Ltd. **(CBSE 2020)**

Ans **Tagline** 'Smoothies are Healthy and Tasty'.

Brand Name Frumoothies.

11 Komal has started a herbal toothpaste manufacturing unit. She has decided about the logo, packaging format and labelling of the product. Her friend Neha asked her whether she has taken care of the legally recognised exclusive rights of other manufacturers in the industry before taking the above stated decisions.

Identify and give the meaning of the concept about which Neha asked Komal. **(CBSE 2017)**

Ans The concept about which Neha asked Komal is 'Intellectual Property Rights'. These rights are the legally recognised exclusive rights to the creations of the mind. Under Intellectual Property Act, owners of such property are granted certain exclusive rights to a variety of intangible assets such as copyrights, trademarks, patents, industrial design right and trade secrets.

12 Shilpi Ltd., started the manufacturing of herbal toothpase. They researched that large number of established enterprises were also manufacturing the similar type of products.

The company fixed the price of their toothpaste on 'cost-plus method' of pricing 'after some time the company realised that they were not getting good response regarding their toothpaste from the customers and the market share of their toothpase was less than 0.5%.

Since their product was new, they decided to change the pricing method so that initially they could get more customers.

(i) Identify the new pricing method that was adopted by Shilpi Ltd.

(ii) State any two advantages of the new pricing method identified in (i) above. **(CBSE 2017)**

Ans (i) Shilpi Ltd. adopted the policy of penetration pricing.

(ii) The advantages of this method of pricing strategy are as follows

(a) It can result in fast diffusion and adoption, resulting in an increased market share quickly. This strategy can take the competitors by surprise, not giving them time to react.

(b) It can create goodwill among the early users and create more trade by word of mouth.

13 Identify the intermediaries involved in the indirect selling mode. **(CBSE 2011)**

Ans The intermediaries involved in indirect selling are

(i) **One Level Channel** Manufacturer → Retailer → Customer

(ii) **Two Level Channel** Manufacturer → Wholesaler → Retailer → Customer

(iii) **Three Level Channel** Manufacturer → Distributor/ Agent → Wholesaler → Retailer → Customer

14 Identify the channel of distribution. **(CBSE 2013)**

(i) When the quantity of the product sold is very small.

(ii) When the product has a seasonal value.

Ans (i) When the quantity of the product sold is very small, then direct channel of distribution should be used.

(ii) When the product has a seasonal value, then long channels should be used.

15 Imagine that you have started selling FMCG goods, then what kind of promotional strategies will you be using? **(CBSE TBQ)**

Ans If I have started dealing in Fast Moving Consumer Goods (FMCG), then I will use Above The Line (ATL) promotional strategies because FMCG goods have a very wide consumer base with customers from all walks of life.

ATL promotion uses mass media methods such as print, television and cinema and focuses on advertising to a large audience, which would be suitable for my business.

16 Above the line approach of advertising suffers from certain disadvantages. Give any two.

Ans Above the line approach suffers from certain disadvantages. Two of them are as follows

(i) Making a message memorable to a large audience is not easy.

(ii) This method is also very expensive.

17 Why should we advertise? **(CBSE TBQ)**

Ans We should advertise (Any four)

(i) to make business and product name familiar to the public.

(ii) to create goodwill and build a favourable image.

(iii) to educate and inform the public about the products and services.

(iv) to offer specific products or services.

(v) to motivate customers to find out more about our products and services.

18 What is AIDA? **(CBSE TBQ)**

Ans Good advertisement generally elicits the following four responses from its audience, which are generally denoted by the acronym, AIDA

(i) **Attention** (A) It should catch the eye of the customer.

(ii) **Interest** (I) It should arouse an interest among the prospective customers towards the product/service.

(iii) **Desire** (D) It should create a desire to learn more or crave ownership.

(iv) **Action** (A) It should prompt the potential customers to make the final purchase.

19 Sales strategy is of immense use for sales representatives. How?

Ans A strategic sales plan not only involves a quick understanding of market opportunities, threats and target markets, but also the strengths and weaknesses of the competitors. Successful sales strategies communicate to the sales force how their products and services can solve the customers' problems, so that they can target the right customers at the right time.

20 What is a sales strategy? Differentiate between its types. **(CBSE SQP)**

Or Explain the different types of sales strategies. **(CBSE TBQ)**

Or Differentiate between the direct selling mode and the indirect selling mode. **(All India 2014)**

Ans A sales strategy consists of a plan that positions a company's brand or product to gain a competitive advantage. There are two types of sales strategy, *viz.* direct sales strategy and indirect sales strategy.

In direct sales strategy, sales people talk about each feature of the competitor's product and compare it to theirs. The term 'negative selling' refers to the direct sales approach.

In indirect sales strategy, sales person apply more subtle techniques by demonstrating features and benefits not available with the competitor's products or services without ever mentioning them by name. This more sophisticated, 'positive sales strategy' requires research and analysis of the competition.

21 Evaluate the two approaches used in sales strategy by a company while retaining it's present customers and when attracting new customers. **(CBSE SQP Term II)**

Ans Potential customers need communication that introduces the brand and product or service in ways which shows how it can solve their problems.

Current customers require more personal communication about new features or benefits to keep them engaged. Promotions and referral discounts work to motivate current customers to spend their money and to spread the word to others.

22 As the world market becomes increasingly competitive, a variety of sales promotion techniques need to be implemented by marketers in order to stand out among their competitors.

Overtime, as consumers become increasingly sensitive towards the sales promotion strategies, marketers need to identify the most suitable sales promotion strategy to be implemented in their products (i.e., monetary or non-monetary sales promotion strategies).

In order to increase the number of consumers; purchasing behaviours and avoid any potential negative perception.

This article has revealed that besides serving as a short-term profit marketing strategy, sales promotion has the potential in helping the marketers to achieve long-term profits through influencing the consumer's self-perception and self-satisfaction and in the development of loyal customers. In other words, sales promotion has benefited both the marketers and the consumers at the same time.

Source *Global Journal of Management and Business Research (E) Volume XV Issue V Version 1, 2015.*

Mention any four types of sale promotion techniques and explain any one technique briefly.

Ans Types of sale promotion techniques are

(i) Rebate

(ii) Discount

(iii) Lucky draw

(iv) Samples

Samples Under this method, the producer distributes free samples of his product among the consumers.

Short Answer Type II Questions (3 Marks)

1 "All business planned for sales volumes and revenues, resource quantities, costs and expenses etc."

Identify the concept involved in the above planning and state any two benefits of this concept. **(CBSE 2016)**

Ans The concept involved in the above planning is 'marketing strategy'. Marketing strategy means a comprehensive plan to facilitate and promote exchange of goods and services.

Marketing strategy is defined by **David Aaker**, as "A process that can allow an organisation to concentrate its resources on the optimal opportunities with the goals of increasing sales and achieving a sustainable competitive advantage".

Two benefits of this concept are

(i) It helps an organisation to increase its sales.

(ii) It helps an organisation to optimally use its resources.

2 What are the qualities of a good brand name? **(CBSE TBQ)**

Ans Qualities of a good brand name are as follows (Any six)

(i) It should be short, simple and easy to pronounce.

(ii) It should be noticeable, easy to recognise and rememberable .

(iii) It should be pleasing and impressive when uttered.

(iv) It should not be obscene, negative, offensive or vulgar.

(v) It should be adaptable to packaging and labelling requirements.

(vi) It should be linked to the product and also symbolically eye catching.

(vii) It should be contemporary and capable of being registered and protected legally.

3 Flipkart, an e-trading business giant, started operations with online selling of goods. People who wanted to buy at ease at anytime. Through its quality service and timely delivery and return policy it has crafted a position for itself. It has developed its logo very attractive. The brand value has increased a lot.

(i) What do you understand by 'brand'?

(ii) What is a logo? Give any two functions that logo serves.

Ans (i) **Brand** Brand is a name, term, symbol, design or contribution of them, which helps to identify a product and differentiate it from the products of competitors.

(ii) **Logo** It is a graphic mark of emblem used to aid and promote instant public recognition.

Functions performed by logo are

(a) Logos act as key visual component of an enterprise's, overall brand identity.

(b) Enterprises normally resort, to logos as a shortcut to advertising.

4 Will you, as an entrepreneur, use the base pricing method for consumable items? Justify your answer.

Ans Yes, as an entrepreneur, I would like to use the base pricing method for consumable products. As we know, that in case of base price method, a base price or list price is fixed for the commodity and varying discounts are offered to various categories of customers after considering the requirements and mode of transactions.

5 Explain 'cost-plus pricing method' of pricing with a suitable example. **(CBSE 2014)**

Ans This is the most common technique of pricing where the manufacturer charges a price to cover the cost of producing a product plus a reasonable profit. This method of pricing is based on manufacturing estimates.

Estimates are made of the resources required, the cost of these resources and the time for which they will be used. On the basis of these estimates, the price is determined. e.g. a shirt manufacturer may arrive at the selling price on the basis of the following information

Estimated cost of cloth ₹ 70

Estimated cost of labour ₹ 12

Estimated cost of overheads ₹ 8

Profit @ 20% [20% of (70+12+8)] ₹ 18

∴ Selling price of shirt is ₹ 108, i.e. 90 + 18

6 Explain the disadvantages of skimming price method. **(CBSE TBQ)**

Ans The disadvantages of skimming price method are as follows (Any three)

(i) This method will lose its relevance if competitors also lower their price.

(ii) If the customers perceive that it is the policy of the business to premiumly price its products, then the business will lose customers of other segments also.

(iii) This pricing strategy cannot be implemented if there are strict and legal government regulations regarding consumer rights.

(iv) This strategy can backfire if customers decide to wait till prices are lowered.

7 Distinguish between cost-plus pricing method and variable pricing method.

Ans Differences between cost-plus pricing method and variable pricing method are (Any three)

Basis	Cost-plus Pricing Method	Variable Pricing Method
Price of Product	Price remains fixed as it includes cost-plus fixed profit.	Price varies as it depends on person to person.
Barga-ining	It is almost nil as cost and profit margin are all set in advance.	Heavy bargaining as price depends on paying capacity of customers.
Quantity	Quantity purchased has no effect on price of the product.	The price reduces with increase in quantity purchased of the product.
Profit	Profit margin is known in advance as it is fixed.	Profit is not known as it depends on the bargaining and negotiations.

8 State the advantages of 'cost plus' method of pricing. **(CBSE 2015)**

Ans The advantages of 'cost-plus' method of pricing are as follows

(i) The entrepreneur knows exactly the amount of expenditure that has been incurred in producing a product and profit margin can be added accordingly, which helps in achieving the desired revenue for a firm.

(ii) It is the simplest method to decide the price of the product.

(iii) It helps in evaluating the reasons for escalations in expenses. Because of availability of ready data, corrective actions can be taken immediately.

9 'Smart Look Ltd'. launched a 'Smart television' in the market after lot of research and development. This television had many new features which distinguished it from the existing televisions in the market.

To recover the investment a high price was determined for the television even then the demand was very high. The quality conscious customers were ready to pay the high price as they understood the product's value and its features.

(i) Identify and explain the 'pricing strategy' used by 'Smart Look Ltd'.

(ii) State two advantages and two disadvantages of this pricing strategy. **(CBSE 2016 C)**

Ans (i) In case of skimming price, goods are sold at higher prices so that fewer sales are needed to break-even.

(ii) **Advantages of Skimming Price** This price strategy gives an entrepreneur the following advantages

(a) It helps the entrepreneur to recover the research and development costs associated with the new product quickly.

(b) This strategy best suits an entrepreneur who caters to consumers who are quality conscious rather than price conscious.

Disadvantages of Skimming Price This price strategy gives an entrepreneur the following disadvantages

(a) This strategy can backfire if competitors introduce same product at lower price. Also, business will lose its customers of other segments if the customers perceive that it is the general policy of the business to sell its products at an inflated price.

(b) This strategy cannot be implemented if there are strict legal and government regulations regarding consumer rights.

10 Identify and explain the type of pricing method used by the following companies

(i) Toothcare, a new brand in the field of toothpastes decided to launch their small packs at a cost of ₹ 5 only which will be sold in the rural market to capture more market share.

(ii) Drinko Ltd., decided to sell their new energy drink initially only in the urban market. The marketing and finance team decided together that 200 ml tetra pack will be sold at ₹ 10 and 1,000 ml will be sold at ₹ 40.

(iii) Bukno, a start-up firm in the field of Artificial Intelligence decided to sell their voice enabled vacuum cleaner in the market for ₹ 1,00,000 for a limited time period to cover the initial research and development costs. **(CBSE SQP Term II)**

Ans (i) **Penetration Pricing** It is a pricing strategy where the price of a product is initially set at a price lower than the eventual market price, to attract new customers. The strategy works on the expectations that customers will switch to the new brand because of the lower price.

(ii) **Variable Price Method** Variable pricing is a marketing approach that permits different rates to be extended to different customers for the same goods or services. The approach is often employed in cultures where dickering over the price of goods is considered the norm, or potential buyers are allowed to participate in a bidding situation, such as in an auction.

(iii) **Creaming or Skimming** In this pricing method, goods are sold at higher prices so that fewer sales are needed to break even.

Selling a product at a high price, sacrificing high sales to gain a high profit is therefore 'skimming' the market. Skimming is usually employed to reimburse the cost of investment of the original research for the product.

11 Mother Dairy dealing in dairy products and fruits and vegetables sells it various products like milk, curd, cheese, fresh vegetables, etc., through its own outlets.

It also deals in frozen vegetables, processed food like fruit juices, jams, pickle, etc. Its slogan is 'Happy People, Happy Food.' It success its milk requirement from dairy cooperatives.

(i) What is the tagline of Mother Dairy?

(ii) What type of distribution channel is adopted by Mother Dairy? Explain.

Ans (i) Tagline –'Happy People, Happy Food'.

(ii) **Direct Distribution Channel** For explanation refer to text on page 92.

12 State by giving any three points how direct channel of distribution is helpful to producers. **(CBSE 2023)**

Ans **Producer-Customer** (Direct channel-zero level) This is the simplest, shortest and the most economical channel of distribution, in which producers sell their products directly to the consumers. This channel is helpful in following ways

(i) There is no middleman involved in this channel of distribution.

(ii) A producer may sell directly to the consumers through — door-to-door sales persons or direct mail or through his own retail stores.

(iii) This method helps the firms to sell industrial products of high value as well as small producers or producers of perishable commodities to sell directly to local consumer.

13 Varshini started her high-end boutique in a posh locality, but she was not aware of how to make her boutique popular in the area. Suggest some measures for it. **(CBSE TBQ)**

Ans Varshini has started a high-end boutique in a posh locality. So, her target customers are rich and affluent people. So Below The Line (BTL) promotional activities will be suitable for her, which include

(i) Sponsorships

(ii) Sales promotion techniques

(iii) Building public relations

(iv) Personal selling

(v) Direct marketing

Since, Varshini deals in providing designer clothes, so sales promotion techniques would be best suited for her. These activities will help to promote her brand.

14 How does the 'nature of products' and 'nature of market' affect the selection of channels of distribution? **(Delhi 2014)**

Ans Nature of product greatly affects the choice of channel of distribution, as is depicted in the chart given below

Nature of Products	Channel of Distribution
Costly products	Zero or one channel of distribution
Less costly products	Two or three channels of distribution
Standardised products	Two or three channels of distribution
Customised products	Zero channel of distribution
Perishable products	Zero channel of distribution
Durable products	Two or three channels of distribution
Technical products	Zero channel of distribution

15 Give the important activities of business promotions.

Ans The promotion activities targeted towards business customers are referred to as business promotions activities. Important activities of this segment are as follows

(i) Holding seminars and workshops.
(ii) Conference presentations.
(iii) Trade show displays.
(iv) Telemarketing and direct mail campaigns.
(v) Newsletters.
(vi) Event sponsorship.
(vii) Capability documents which include the information necessary to support production, testing and deployment of an affordable strategy.

16 "Personal selling is a better method of sales promotion than advertisement". How? Explain with the help of any three points. **(CBSE 2014)**

Ans Personal selling in most simple terms, means selling products personally. It involves oral presentation of message in the form of conversation with one or more prospective customers for the purpose of making sales.

Personal selling is a better method of sales promotion than advertisement because of the below mentioned reasons

(i) It encourages impulsive purchases.
(ii) It helps in increasing the present level of sales.
(iii) Its cost is moderate.

17 Mention any two techniques of sales promotion with example. **(CBSE 2013)**

Ans The two techniques of sales promotion are

(i) **Quantity Plus** In this, seller offers quantity at no extra cost. e.g. 30% extra with Kissan Jam.
(ii) **Contests** Consumers are invited to participate in contests and gain awards. e.g. two free train tickets to Manali.

18 What is sales promotion? State its objectives.

Ans Sales promotion refers to those sales activities that supplement both personal selling and advertising, co-ordinates them and also helps to make them effective.

Its objectives are as follows

(i) To introduce new product in the market.
(ii) To increase sales in slack season.
(iii) To create goodwill among present as well as prospective customers.

19 As a young entrepreneur, you are investing in a book stall. What kind of sales promotion techniques would you adopt? Explain in brief.

Ans As an entrepreneur, while starting a book stall, I would like to follow the following sales promotion techniques

(i) **Discount** I will provide 1% or 2% more discount as compared to the competitors. It will promote my sales.
(ii) **Free Gifts** On purchase of course books, I will provide the customers printed book covers free of cost. It will help in bringing them again and again. Moreover, these printed book covers will advertise my book shop.

I hope, if I will follow the above mentioned sales promotion techniques, it will definitely fetch high sales.

20 What are the main public relations tools? **(CBSE TBQ)**

Or Enlist any four main public relation tools. **(CBSE SQP Term II)**

Ans The main public relations tools are

(i) News creation and distribution.
(ii) Hosting special events such as news conferences, grand openings and product launches.
(iii) Speeches and presentations.
(iv) Conducting educational programmes.
(v) Distributing annual reports, brochures, newsletters, magazines and audio-visual presentations.
(vi) Conducting community activities and sponsorships.

21 What is meant by a 'sales strategy' ? State how a successful sales strategy helps the sales force? **(CBSE 2023)**

Ans A sales strategy is a plan that positions a company's brand in such a way, that it gains a competitive advantage in its segment. Successful strategies help the sales force focus on target market customers and communicate with them in relevant and meaningful ways.

Successful sales strategies communicate to the sales force how their products and services can solve the customers' problems, so that they can target the right customers at the right time.

An effective sales strategy is important for a business because of the below mentioned reasons

(i) Planning an effective sales strategy requires looking at long-term sales goals and analysing the business sales cycle.

(ii) It helps business owners and managers to gain a more precise knowledge of sales intervals, seasonal changes and motivating factors about the sales team.

(iii) After creating long-term sales strategy based on long-term goals, sales managers create monthly and weekly sales strategies. This allows for short-term performance evaluation of sales team and allows taking remedial action if targets are not achieved.

Long Answer Type Questions (5 Marks)

1 What does 'product' mean in marketing mix? Explain the various elements of product mix.

Ans Product is anything that can be offered to a market for attention, acquisition or consumption. It includes physical objects, services, personalities, places, organisations and ideas.

Elements of Product Mix The various elements/ components of product mix are

(i) **Branding** Brand is a name, term, sign, symbol or design or a combination of them which is intended to identify the goods or services of one seller or group of sellers and to differentiate them from those of the competitors.

Branding, therefore, is an effective differentiation strategy used to distinguish their offerings from that of competitors, e.g. we can identify and differentiate between two soaps, like Dove and Pears.

(ii) **Labelling** It is an act of displaying information about a product on its container, packaging or product itself.

(iii) **Packaging** It is an act of designing a wrapper, covering of the product. It is an important element for consumer good companies to achieve a comparative advantage.

2 In order to distinguish their products from that of their competitors, the marketers give some names to their products. After identifying the concept, name and give two examples each of its different types.
(CBSE 2017)

Ans In order to distinguish their products from that of their competitors, the marketers give some names to their products. This concept is referred to as 'brand name'. It is that part of brand which can be spoken. e.g., Mercedes, Coke etc. Brand names can be classified as

(i) **Individual Brand Name** Under this strategy, an entrepreneur chooses a distinct name for each of his offering, i.e., each product is promoted on the basis of a separate brand name.

For e.g., Hindustan Unilever Limited has a separate brand name for different soaps marketed by it, such as Lux, Liril, Lifebuoy etc. Similary ITC has a separate brand name for biscuits (Sunfeast) and a separate brand name for Cigarettes (Wills).

(ii) **Family Brand Name** Under this strategy, an entrepreneur chooses a common or a successful family name for their several products. He can use his own name or the company's name may be used for all the products. It is also referred to as 'Umbrella Branding'. e.g., **Ponds** is a mother brand name used for talcum powder, cold creams, face-wash, etc. **Maggi** is a brand name for noodles, sauces, masalas, etc.

(iii) **Corporate Names** Entrepreneurs can choose to utilise their corporate name or logo together with some brand names of individuals products, e.g, Godrej, Tata, etc.

(iv) **Alpha-numeric Names** Entrepreneurs have an option to brand their product alpha-numerically. An alpha-numeric name often signifies its physical characteristics and is generally used for mobile handsets, e.g., i phone 6S, etc.

3 Give the meaning of 'skimming method of pricing'. State any two advantages and two disadvantages of this method of pricing.
(CBSE 2023)

Ans In this type of pricing strategy, entrepreneurs set their prices higher, so that fewer sales are needed to break even. Selling a product at a high price, sacrificing high sales to gain a high profit is therefore 'skimming' the market.

This strategy is usually employed to reimburse the cost of investment on the original research and is commonly used in the electronics market where a new range, such as smart phones are initially dispatched into the market at a high price.

This price strategy gives an entrepreneur the following advantages

(i) It helps the entrepreneur to recover the research and development costs associated with the new product quickly.

(ii) This strategy best suits an entrepreneur who caters to consumers who are quality conscious rather than price conscious.

This price strategy gives an entrepreneur the following disadvantages

(i) This strategy can backfire if competitors introduce same product at lower price. Also, business will lose its customers of other segments if the customers perceive that it is the general policy of the business to sell its products at an inflated price.

(ii) This strategy cannot be implemented if there are strict legal and government regulations regarding consumer rights.

4 Lalit a small entrepreneur is manufacturing portable fans with the brand name 'P-FAN'. These fans are in great demand. He finds that the cost of production of per unit of the fan is ₹ 800 and he can sell the same at ₹ 1,000 per fan. The competitors in the market are selling this type of fan at the rate of ₹ 1,200. Lalit's objective is not to earn profit in the short-run but to capture the largest market share. His expectation is that the customers will be attracted towards the new brand because of lower price.

Identify the method of pricing adopted by Lalit to capture the substantial portion of the market. Also state any two advantages of this method of pricing. **(CBSE 2016)**

Ans The method of pricing adopted by Lalit is 'Penetration pricing'. Under this pricing strategy, the price of the product is initially set at a price lower than the prevailing market price to attract new customers and increase its market share. Penetration pricing is most commonly associated with a marketing objective to increase market share rather than make a profit in the short-run. The price is raised later when the market share is gained.

Two advantages of this pricing strategy are

(i) It can result in fast diffusion and adoption, resulting in an increased market share quickly. This strategy can take competitors by surprise, not giving them time to react.

(ii) It can create goodwill among the early users and create more trade by word of mouth.

5 M/S Ramlal & Sons started manufacturing oximeters which has a great demand in this time of Covid 19' for domestic use and otherwise also it is an equipment in demand by the medical professionals.

While fixing the selling price for the same Ramlal wants to adopt a method where he can just cover the cost and earn a nominal amount of profit. His sons advised him to fix the price initially at a higher rate and then reduce the price when the demand has reduced.

According to them this method would help them earn a good profit. He hired an agent, Satish, who advised him to initially keep the prices low to attract the market and then he can slowly and gradually increase the price. In the given context answer the following questions **(CBSE SQP)**

(i) Identify and explain the method that Ramlal is planning to adopt.

(ii) Explain the method of pricing suggested by Ramlal's sons and his agent respectively.

Ans (i) The method that Ramlal is planning to adopt is cost plus pricing. In this technique, the manufacturer charges a price to cover the cost of producing a product plus a reasonable profit.

Cost plus pricing is typically based on a manufacturing estimate. Estimates of the costs associated with manufacturing tasks are made for many reasons.

In principle, estimates are made of the resources required (For example, materials, labour and equipment), the cost of those resources and the time for which they will be used.

From these factors, an estimate of the costs of carrying out a manufacturing process is made.

(ii) The method of pricing suggested by Ramlal's sons is 'prices skimming'. The method of pricing suggested by Ramlal's agent is 'penetration pricing'.

Price skimming is usually employed to reimburse the cost of investment of the original research into the product commonly used in electronic markets when a new range, such as smartphones, are firstly dispatched into the market at a high price.

This can be attributed to their need for the product outweighing their need for economics, a greater understanding of the product's value, or simply having a higher disposable income. This strategy is employed only for a limited duration to recover most of the investment made to build the product.

Penetration pricing is a pricing strategy where the price of a product is initially set at a price lower than the eventual market price to attract new customers. The strategy works on the expectations that customers will switch to the new brand because of the lower price. Penetration pricing is most commonly associated with a marketing objective of increasing market share or sales volume, rather than to make profit in the short-term. The price will be raised later once this market share is gained.

6 Differentiate between 'Penetrating pricing' and 'Skimming pricing'. State the situations when 'Penetrating pricing' and 'Skimming pricing' are useful. Also state any two disadvantages each for penetrating pricing and skimming pricing. **(CBSE 2020)**

Ans Difference between penetrating pricing and skimming pricing

Basis	Penetrating Pricing	Skimming Pricing
Pricing Strategy	Price of the product is set at a price lower than the prevailing market price.	Prices are set high.
Objective	To increase market share.	To reimburse the cost of investment on original research.

Situation when Penetrating Pricing is Used It is used when the marketing objective is to increase market share rather than to make a profit in the short-run.

Situation when Skimming Pricing is Used It is used when the cost of investment on the original research is high.

Disadvantages of Penetration Pricing

(i) The main disadvantage of this method is that it establishes long-term price expectations for the product and image preconceptions for the brand and company.

(ii) Another disadvantage is that low profit margins may be inadequate for a business to sustain and survive.

Disadvantages of Skimming Pricing

(i) This strategy can backfire, if competitors lower their price.

(ii) This strategy cannot be implemented, if there are strict legal and government regulations regarding consumer rights.

7 'Mittil Ltd' is a leading company for manufacturing of soft toys for children. The company is in the process of developing a prototype for a talking pillow, 'Talk O Hug', which would enable parents to convey messages to their children when they are away at work.

The mechanism is such that the message is recorded in the device in the pillow and the moment the child touches the pillow, the speaker sensors would repeat the message recorded by the parents for their children. Though an innovation for India, imported versions of this product are already available in the market.

The management wanted to devise a pricing strategy to target the 'switchers' present in the market.

(i) Identify the pricing strategy that the management is planning to adopt. State the marketing objective of the company behind this pricing decision.

(ii) State any two advantages and one disadvantage of adopting this pricing policy to 'Mittil Ltd.'

(iii) Keeping in mind the nature of the product, suggest the distribution channel that would suit the company for distributing 'Talk O Hug'. **(CBSE 2018)**

Ans (i) The pricing strategy being followed is 'Penetration pricing'. The marketing objective of their pricing strategy is to increase market share.

(ii) The two advantages of this strategy are as follows

(a) It can create goodwill among the early users and create more trade by word of mouth.

(b) It can create high stock turnover.

One disadvantage is that low profit margins may make it difficult for the business to sustain and survive.

(iii) The channel of distribution that would suit the company is

Producer → Retailer → Customer

8 Explain any four factors to be taken into consideration for selecting channels of distribution related to a market. **(CBSE 2016)**

Or Explain the factors affecting channels of distribution with relation to market considerations. **(CBSE SQP Term II)**

Ans Factors to be taken into consideration for selecting channels of distribution related to a market are (Any four)

(i) **Number of Buyers** If the number of buyers is large, then long chain of distribution should be opted, but if the number of buyers is small, then smaller channels should be considered.

(ii) **Types of Buyers** Buyers are commonly classified as

(a) General buyers (b) Industrial buyers

For general buyers, long chain of distribution should be used and short-chain for industrial buyers.

(iii) **Buying Habits** A manufacturer should opt for a long channel of distribution if his financial position does not permit him to sell goods on credit and the buyers are in the habit of making credit purchases.

(iv) **Buying Quantity** If goods are bought in small quantities, then long channel of distribution should be used.

(v) **Size of Market** If the market area of the product is scattered, then long channels should be opted.

9 Explain in short, the various elements of the promotion mix.

Ans The various elements of promotion mix are as follows

(i) **Advertising** Advertising is a paid form of non-personal communication designed to persuade potential customers to choose a product or a service over that of a competitor. It is a planned and consistent activity that aims at keeping the name of the business uppermost in the mind of the consumer.

(ii) **Personal Selling** Personal selling involves oral presentation of message in the form of conversation with one or more prospective customers for the purpose of making sales.

Under personal selling, companies appoint salespersons, who contact with prospective buyers to create product awareness and preferences with the aim of making sales.

(iii) **Sales Promotion** It relates to short-term incentives that encourage or promote the purchase or sale of a product or a service.

(iv) **Public Relations** It is a deliberate, planned and sustained effort to establish and maintain mutual understanding between an organisation and its stakeholders by obtaining favourable publicity and building a good corporate image.

10 What are the rules for advertising? **(CBSE TBQ)**

Or A company dealing in pharmaceuticals plans to promote its products through advertising and does not deter from making false claims. Give the rules of advertising of the company.

Ans The rules for effective advertising are

(i) **Aim** Before formulating an advertising, the basic purpose of advertising should be identified.

(ii) **Target** The second rule is identification of target potential customers, so that advertisements could be directed towards them.

(iii) **Media** Keeping in mind the aim and target, the next important decision relates to selecting an appropriate media for advertising.

(iv) **Competitors** The last consideration relates to the acts of the competitors. Before deciding upon the final draft, the important questions to be considered are

(a) What are the competitors doing?

(b) Which media channel do they use?

(c) Are they successful?

(d) Can we improve on their approach and beat them in competition?

The above rules help in formulating an effective advertisement.

11 Suggest any six techniques to Sonu, which will help him in boosting the sales. **(CBSE 2010)**

Or

Assuming you plan to manufacture detergent powder, how would you assess the size of the market of your locality? What strategies would you adopt to sell the product? **(CBSE 2010 C)**

Ans To get any information related to market or product, the entrepreneurs use market research.

The strategies adopted to sell the product are as follows

(i) **Price off or Rebate** It is generally offered to the customers to increase sales. In this method, offer price is less than normal price.

(ii) **Samples** In this method, the manufacturer distributes free samples to the customers to get popularity for his product.

(iii) **Contests** In this method, the customers are invited to participate in the contests like writing a slogan on the product, suggesting good name for a new product and gain awards for the best one.

(iv) **Coupons** In this method, the seller offers a discount coupon on the purchase of specified products.

(v) **Quantity Plus** Sometimes, the manufacturer offers extra quantity of product at same price for a short period.

(vi) **Free Gifts** In this method, the customer is given free gifts on purchase of product. e.g. cup with coffee, toothbrush with toothpaste, etc.

12 Aryan started a Super Specialty Store, 'Sampada'. It's products are sourced from hand picked suppliers. These products are sold under Sampada's own brand. Its promotion strategy is very specific and focuses on targeted groups of customers. The purpose of this promotions strategy is to develop the brand 'Sampada' by creating awareness among the customers.

To do this, Sampada's Facebook and Twitter pages encourage two-way communication with customers. These social media channels provide a platform through which Sampada can interact with customers. It can then assess their opinions about the brand.

(i) Identify the promotion strategy adopted by Sampada.

(ii) List the activities that are included in the strategy identified in (i) above for creating brand awareness.

(iii) Also, explain the promotion strategies other than the one identified in (i) above.

(CBSE 2019)

Ans (i) The promotion strategy adopted by Sampada is Below The Line (BTL) approach.

(ii) Refer to topic 'Below The Line (BTL) approach' on page 95.

(iii) Other promotion strategies are as follows

(a) Refer to topic 'Above The Line (ATL) approach' on page 95.

(b) Refer to topic 'Through The Line (TTL) approach' on page 95.

13 The fundamentals that guide e-commerce marketing, the four Ps of product, person, place, and price are all essential in their own ways.

The digital transformation that has guided the e-commerce boom in the last two years has helped brands and retailers hone optimising those core tenets, contributing to the drive towards expanded stores of first-party consumer data.

With the eventual phase out of third-party cookies, there has been a divestment in those legacy identifiers, which has given smart brands and retailers more actionable, intelligent data.

In short, better data has largely solved the first three of the four Ps; brands and retailers can now deliver the right product to the right person through the right channel with increased efficacy.

The only variable that is in desperate need of optimisation is pricing. As retailers begin mapping their holiday sales strategies, focusing on pricing can help on multiple fronts, including managing supply and demand as well as offering personalisation in an increasingly price sensitive consumer climate.

Source *Jonathan Treiber Contributo (Forbes–22nd October, 2011, 12:25 pm EDT)*

(i) 4Ps are related to which concept of entrepreneurship?

(ii) Explain its meaning and any one element/ component of 4Ps.

Ans (i) 4Ps are related to marketing mix.

(ii) Marketing mix refers to the ingredients or the tools on the variables which the marketing mixes in order to interact with a particular market.

Marketing mix consists of a list of the important elements or ingredients that make the marketing system and a list of forces that shape the marketing operation of a firm.

For component of marketing mix/4Ps, refer to text on page 85.

14 'Memes' have emerged as a lucrative profession for its creators.

Last week, when Zomato acquired Uber Eats, competitors took no time to engage with users through this new-age content marketing tool, which had become an instant hit when it began life on social media a few years ago.

However, generating memes on Instagram, TikTok and Facebook is now starting to become an integral part of marketing budgets for brands that want to stay relevant and topical online. These brands are using popular meme pages such as Laughing Colours, Confused Atma and Sarcastic Indian across social media.

A consumer brand spends ₹ 1,000- ₹ 50,000 on a meme. A page with a million likes charges ₹ 1,000- ₹ 1,500 for visibility on Facebook and around ₹ 3,000 for Instagram, creators said. And, depending on the category of influencers, TikTok charges between ₹ 5,000 and ₹ 3 lakh.

Earlier, meme pages used to make money mainly through Google advertisements, videos or cross promotions. Today, they rack up anywhere between ₹ 10 lakh and ₹ 4-6 crore in yearly turnover.

Some brands that have been active with meme marketing include OnePlus, Truecaller, Dream11, LG and Big Bazaar, apart from big players in the e-commerce and soft drinks space.

Brands use memes for promotions, taking a dig at competition, and for product launches.

The demand for memes as a marketing tool increases ahead of festive seasons and occasions like the Cricket World Cup or Indian Premier League matches.

Usually, a brand engages with meme creators for two-three memes a week.

Source *Economic Times, 31st January, 2020*

In context of the above article, answer the following questions.

(i) Identify and explain the component of marketing mix enumerated in the above article.

(ii) Explain in detail the elements of the component of marketing mix identified in (i) above. **(CBSE SQP)**

Ans (i) The component of marketing mix is 'promotion'. It refers to all the activities undertaken to make the product or service known to the user and trade.

This can include advertising, word of mouth, press reports, incentives, commissions and awards to the trade.

(ii) **Elements of Promotion Mix** Refer to Q. No. 9 of long answer type questions (5 Marks).

CASE STUDIES

Case 1

Creating Value through Marketing Mix

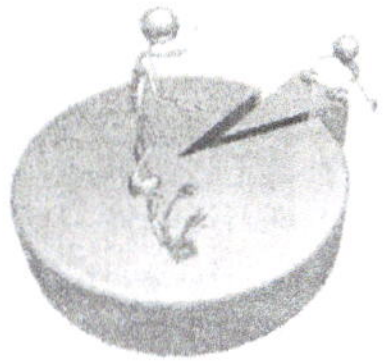

In increasingly competitive markets, consumers have a greater choice of where they buy their goods and services. For an organisation to meet its business objectives, it has to find out what the consumers require and then identify the best way in which it can satisfy these needs and wants. Creating a competitive advantage can be difficult.

A unique marketing strategy with clear objectives is vital to ensure effective promotional activity. Since, opening its first store in 1913, Aldi has established itself as one of the most reputable retailers in the global business market by providing great value and quantity. Aldi's goal is simple. 'To provide our customers with products they buy regularly and ensure that those products are of the highest possible quality of guaranteed low prices.

Aldi's products are sourced from hand-picked suppliers whose products are sold under Aldi's own brand labels. Aldi's main marketing objective is to grow its market share within the UK grocery market. With the economic crisis came an increased demand for value for money. Market research identified that 80% of Aldi's customer base also shopped at other supermarkets.

These customers spent around £20 billion per year in the other stores. Aldi's marketing strategies, therefore focused on generating customer loyalty. Aldi focused its marketing efforts on encouraging customers that are already familiar with the brand to shop at Aldi more often.

Another key focus of Aldi's marketing strategy is on demonstrating that Aldi brands are of equal quality to well known brands such as Heinz and Fairy Liquid. To do this, Aldi's ran blind taste tests amongst a cross section of shoppers.

These confirmed that the majority of consumers that liked the famous brands also liked Aldi's brands.

These findings formed the basis to Aldis 'Like Brands' marketing campaign.

This provided Aldi with a platform to communicate its quality and value messages effectively. Aldi's immediate challenge for the 'Like Brands' campaign was to increase market share from 2.3% to 2.5%. Although, this sounds very little, the retail grocery market is very large. A single 0.1% is worth an extra £65 million revenue.

This case study focuses on the marketing strategies used by Aldi to increase its market share and encourage loyal customers.

The Marketing Mix

The Chartered Institute of marketing describes the term marketing as 'The process responsible for identifying, anticipating and satisfying consumer requirements profitably'. This places consumers at the heart of every organisation. The marketing mix is often referred to as the 4 Ps.

It involves creating a unique blend of the right product, sold at the right price, at the right place, using the most suitable methods of promotion. A marketing mix is a complex set of variables.

The marketing mix of every business will be different. Aldi's mix focuses on providing high quality products that are cheaper alternatives to famous brands.

Aldi's marketing mix therefore focuses on

(i) Product–'high quality' 'Like Brands'.

(ii) Price–Aldi offers lower prices than its competitors, without compromising on quality.

(iii) Place–Aldi outlets are expanding globally.

(iv) Promotion–Aldi uses a combination of above the line and below the line promotions with a focus on its 'Like Brands' and 'Swap and Save' campaigns.

Balancing the Mix

Organisation need a balanced marketing mix to meet the needs of their customers. Aldi's focus is on offering the best possible quality products at the lowest possible prices. Every buyer for Aldi, from fresh fruits and vegetables to meats and electronics, is an expert in his field. They look for products from around the word. This enables them to get the finest quality products that Aldi then sells under its own brand labels. Selecting the prices is one of the most difficult considerations when developing a marketing mix.

Different Pricing Strategies that are Commonly Used Include

(i) **Market Penetration** Charging lower prices for new products to help them enter the market and gain market share quickly.

(ii) **Competitive Pricing** Pricing at a slightly lower prices than competitors.

(iii) **Strategic Pricing** Emphasising the quality of brand positioning of a product to allow a higher price to be charged.

Competitive pricing is a key strategy for Aldi. Aldi is able to offer quality products at low prices as it buys in great volume. The fact that Aldi buys such large quantities of these products allows great leverage for negotiating the best possible prices with its suppliers.

This is called economies of scale. Buying large quantities of each products allows Aldi to pass these savings to its customers.

The place element of the marketing mix involves identifying where the product or service will be sold. Aldi keeps its store layouts simple to limit waste and keeps the costs down. This means Aldi can focus on offering its customers the lowest possible prices for its products. When considering new store locations, Aldi takes into account

(i) the number of people visiting an area as well as the demography of the area, e.g. the population of the area should be more than 30,000 people.

(ii) the position of store Aldi focuses on edge of the town centre locations with good visibility from a main road and not too much competition.

(iii) the accessibility of the store and its public transport links.

(iv) the number of parking spaces available.

Above the Line Promotion

For Aldi to achieve its objective of increasing its market share, it had to ensure its promotional activity demonstrated the balance of its marketing mix, e.g. to increase customer loyalty it had to communicate its key quality and value messages.

Promotion helps to

(i) increase awareness and improve brand recognition

(ii) increase demand for products

(iii) improve brand image

(iv) highlight the superiority of products and services.

Above the line promotions are paid for advertising aimed at a mass audience. These include the media such as television, radio, magazines and newspapers that reach a large number of people. This form of promotion can be costly. It can also be difficult to target specific audiences. Aldi uses a range of above the line methods to reach its customers and potential customers.

These Include

Advertising on TV the 'Like Brands' campaign features 20 second TV adverts which focus on a particular product. The adverts show, a famous brand as a benchmark for quality side-by-side with an Aldi brand product. They use the slogan 'Like Brands, Only Cheaper'.

This reinforces the message that Aldi products are cheaper than leading brands but equal in terms of quality. The adverts provide personality to the Aldi brand use humour which helps to build trust and an emotional connection with target audiences.

Printed leaflets are distributed within stores (1 million copies printed per week) and also to customers living in areas surrounding the stores. These leaflets help to reinforce the 'Like Brands' campaign. They also showcase products with limited availability and seasonal offers available in stores.

Newspaper adverts extend the 'Like Brands' campaign and help to showcase a variety of product categories. They also communicate Aldi's Swap and Save' message. This campaign demonstrates the amount that shoppers could save if they swapped their weekly shop to Aldi. They compare Aldi products to famous brands to demonstrate Aldi's value for money message.

In-store posters are also used to highlight the 'Swap and Save' message. Below the line promotion uses different ways to engage with customers. These methods can be more easily targeted to specific audiences than above the line methods. They offer organisations a greater level of control over their communications.

Aldi Uses a Range of Below the Line Methods

These include

(i) Social media
(ii) Targeted emails to customers
(iii) 3rd party endorsement and awards
(iv) Public relations and media relations

Aldi's Facebook and Twitter pages encourage two-way communication with customers. These social media channels provide a platform through which Aldi can interact with customers. It can then assess their opinions about the brand.

One objective of this form of promotion is to create 'Aldi Advocates'. These are consumers who recommend Aldi to others, through stimulating interactions about the high quality and low prices of Aldi product.

e.g. the 'I love Aldi' campaign asked fans to send a virtual Aldi Valentines card to a Facebook friend. This was encouraged by providing rewards. The campaign gave consumers the chance to win a £10 voucher. They could also win a box of Aldi chocolates for their Valentine. The campaign also encouraged consumers to complete the sentence 'I love Aldi because...' directly onto Aldi's Facebook page to encourage positive brand feedback.

Aldi also uses direct emails. These e-mails allow Aldi to communicate a variety of message to target customers.

e.g. They can convey the 'Swap and Save' message as well as to promote seasonal message such as products associated with Pancake Day. Aldi's website is an integral part of its below the line promotion. It features all of Aldi's key promotional messages as well as additional content to engage consumers. Examples include recipe ideas and weekly offers.

Aldi developed the www.likealdi.co.uk micro-website to further encourage brand engagement with the 'Like Brands' TV campaign. The site provides consumers with the opportunity to upload their ideas for the next Aldi TV campaign.

Aldi also uses a dedicated recruitment website to promote its employer brand message and career opportunities.

A further below-the-line method used to highlight the quality of Aldi's products is positive 3rd party endorsements. Aldi has entered over 1,000 of its products into awards such as Grocer Golds, Pizza And Pasta Awards (PAPA) and the British Frozen Food Federation Awards.

In 2012, Aldi was awarded 'Best Supermarket' by Consumer Watchdog. It beats competition from Marks and Spencer and Waitrose. Further positive endorsements for production on TV and in the press re-affirm the message that Aldi products are of the highest quality and also are great value for money. e.g. Aldi's Christmas pudding was awarded runner up and acknowledged as a 'bargain' in a taste test comparison in Good Housekeeping magazine.

Effective public and media relations help to create positive press exposure. Aldi has secured record coverage through hardworking and innovative media relations.

Journalists from newspapers such as The Grocer, The Financial Times and The Times were invited for exclusive interviews with Aldi's Group of Managing Directors. They discussed record breaking sales results.

Aldi: Creating Value Through the Marketing Mix

Further coverage was gained through targeting key media at specific times with seasonal promotional message. The 'Swap and Save' campaign highlighted the savings available through shopping at Aldi at times when value for money is high on the agenda. This was particularly relevant with its 'Back to School' and Christmas products.

Conclusions

Aldi has a distinct approach to retailing that has given it a competitive advantage in a crowded marketplace. Aldi's unique balance of the marketing mix enables it to provide high quality, own branded products at the lowest possible price.

Aldi's innovative 'Like Brands' and 'Swap and Save' marketing campaigns are improving brand perceptions.

They are aiding the achievement of Aldi's marketing objectives. The campaigns have increased Aldi's sales per store by +100% over 3 years through creating more loyal customer.

Its multi-channel promotional activity is engaging consumers and creating positive feedback.

Courtesy The Times 100 Business Case Studies.

1 Give the definition of marketing, as given by the 'Chartered Institute of Marketing'.

Ans Chartered Institute of Marketing defines marketing as 'The process responsible for identifying, anticipating and satisfying consumers requirements profitably'.

2 What does Aldi's marketing mix focuses on?

Ans Aldi's marketing mix focuses on

(i) **Product** High quality 'Like Brands'.

(ii) **Price** Aldi offers lower prices than its competitors without compromising on quality.

(iii) **Place** Aldi outlets are expanded globally.

(iv) **Promotion** Aldi uses a combination of above the line and below the line promotion techniques.

3 Which pricing strategy is followed by Aldi? Give any one benefit of this method.

Ans Aldi follows 'competitive pricing strategy' which aims at pricing products at a slightly lower prices than competitors. The advantage of this method is that it helps to enhance the demand for the product.

4 What are the factors considered by Aldi, when deciding the location of its store?

Ans The following factors are considered by Aldi

(i) The population of the area should exceed 30,000.

(ii) Aldi focuses on the edge of the town centre locations with good visibility from main road and not much competition.

(iii) The accessibility of the store.

(iv) Parking space available.

5 What is Aldi's goal?

Ans Aldi's goal is to provide our customers with products they buy regularly and ensure that those products are of the highest possible quality of guaranteed low prices.

6 How does Aldi use social media as below the line promotion method?

Ans Aldi uses Facebook and Twitter pages to encourage two-way communication with customers. This type of media promotion helps in building the brand image.

CHAPTER ASSESSMENT

Objective Type Questions (1 Mark)

1 Ingredients or the tools on the variables which the marketer mixes in order to interact with a particular market are called
(a) marketing mix (b) marketing strategy (c) product mix (d) None of these

2 Shortest channel of distribution is
(a) indirect channel (b) one level channel (c) direct channel (d) None of these

3 Plan that positions a company's brand or product to gain a competitive advantage is
(a) marketing strategy (b) sales strategy (c) marketing mix (d) product mix

4 Good brand should be .... and ....

5 .... gives the creator of original work exclusive rights to it, usually for a limited time.

6 Branding, labelling and packaging are the content of price mix. State true or false.

7 Logo is an identifying symbol for a product or business. State true or false.

Short Answer Type I Questions (2 Marks)

8 What do you mean by marketing mix?

9 What is a sales strategy?

10 Why is direct sales strategy referred to as 'negative selling'?

11 A sound sales strategy has certain criteria. What are they?

Short Answer Type II Questions (3 Marks)

12 Give three characteristics of good brand name.

13 What are the functions of labelling?

14 What is cost-plus pricing strategy?

15 What is the significance of sales strategy.

Long Answer Type Questions (5 Marks)

16 What do you mean by personal selling?

17 Explain advantages and disadvantages of Above The Line approach (ATL).

18 Explain advantages and disadvantages of Below The Line approach (BTL).

19 Differentiate between advertising, personal selling, sales promotion and publicity.

20 Write a note on entrepreneur's perspective on brand name.

For explanations scan the given QR Code

CHAPTER 04

Enterprise Growth Strategies

In this Chapter...

- Growth and development of an enterprise
- Franchising
- Growth through mergers and acquisitions
- Reasons for mergers and acquisitions

Growth and Development of an Enterprise

Growth is alwasys essential for the survival of the enterprise. Once a business has started generating adequate profits, growth is the next exciting challenge for an entrepreneur.

A successful entrepreneur is one who makes sure that there is a constant flow of new ideas and is also committed to try out these ideas, so as to ensure the growth of the business.

The decision to expand one's scale of operation must be the result of thoughtful consideration of various factors affecting the business, such as financial viability, level of competition, etc. The rule of thumb is that one should only expand when there are untapped opportunities that can benefit the business.

On the road of growth, an entrepreneur has to play the dual role of a manager as well as a leader.

Also, to ensure the efficiency, profitable functioning and growth of enterprise, extra managerial ability is required.

The expansion of an enterprise may be in the form of diversification of activities or acquition of ownership and control of other business.

Thus, expansion may be in the following forms

1. Internal Expansion

It is a slow and time consuming process which is the result of a gradual increase in the activities of the enterprise.

A firm may expand internally by

- expanding its present production capacity by increasing the number of machines.
- replacing old machines with advanced technological machines.
- entering in new areas of production/marketing or both.
- increasing the output of the enterprise.

Internal expansion is generally financed through long-term sources of finance and also through undistributed profits and reserves.

The net results of internal expansion are

– Increase in business activities.
– Broadening the present capital structure.

2. External Expansion or Business Combination

External expansion occurs when two or more business enterprises come together with a common objective of expanding their business.

A firm may expand externally by
- franchising
- mergers and acquisitions

External expansion is financed through long-term sources of finance.

The net results of external expansion are
- Expansion of capital base as well as business activities.
- Elimination of unnecessary competition.
- Synergy effect is achieved.

Franchising

Franchising can be defined as an arrangement whereby the manufacturer or sole distributor of a trademarked product or service gives exclusive rights of local distribution to independent retailers in return for their payment of royalties and conformance to standardised operating procedures.

According to **Arnold S Goldstein**, "Franchising occurs when the franchisee markets a product or service developed by a franchiser under an agreement and license to do so." Today, franchising is helping thousands of individuals to be their own boss and operate their own business. It allows entrepreneurs to be in business for themselves, but not by themselves.

There is usually a much higher likelihood of success of a franchise opened by an individual as compared to independent business, since a proven business formula is in place. Following terms related to franchising are as follows

1. Franchisor

A franchisor sells the right to open stores and sell products or services using its brand, expertise and intellectual property. Thus, a person or company offering the franchise is known as the franchisor.

2. Franchisee

The person or entity who purchases the franchise and is given the opportunity to enter a new business with a better chance to success, is known as the franchisee.

3. Franchise Agreement

It is a legal document defining the mutual terms and conditions between a franchisor and a franchisee.

The agreement is designed to assure that all the franchisees within an organisation are treated equitably.

The **main ingredients** of a franchise agreement are as follows

(i) **Contract Explanation** It is the part of the agreement that defines the type of relationship, a franchisee is entering into with the franchisor.

(ii) **Operations Manual** This section of the agreement lays forward the guidelines that the franchisee must legally follow while operating the business, as specified by the franchisor.

From time to time, amendments may be made and the franchisee must be prepared to adjust operations accordingly. He should be aware that the contents of the document are confidential.

(iii) **Proprietary Statements** These statements outline, how the franchise name is to be used and also the marketing and advertising procedures required to be followed by the franchisee.

It also states the proportionate share of franchisee towards national advertising campaigns.

(iv) **Ongoing Site Maintenance** This includes the types and time frames regarding various maintenance items and upgrades that must be made to the franchisee's location.

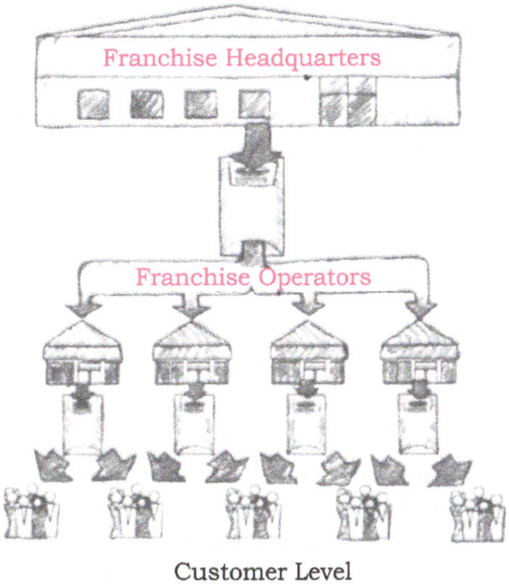

Franchise Chain

Types of Franchising

Following are the four different types of franchising opportunities available

Types of Franchising
- Product franchise business opportunity
- Manufacturing franchise opportunity
- Business franchise opportunity venture
- Business format franchise opportunity

1. **Product Franchise Business Opportunity** Under this model, the manufacturer grants a store owner the authority to distribute goods manufactured by the manufacturer and allows the owner to use the name and trademark owned by the manufacturer. The store owner is either required to pay a fee or purchase a minimum inventory of stock in return for these rights. e.g. tyre stores.
2. **Manufacturing Franchise Opportunity** Under this model, the franchisee is conferred with exclusive rights to manufacture a product and sell it to the public, using the franchisor's name and trademark. This type of franchise is common in food and beverage industry.
3. **Business Franchise Opportunity Venture** This model requires that a business owner purchases and distributes the products for one specific company. The company provides the business with customers and in return, the business owner pays a fee or any other form of compensation to the company. e.g. vending machine routes and distributorship.
4. **Business Format Franchise Opportunity** This is the most popular form of franchising. In this model, the franchisor provides the franchisee a proven method of operating a business using its name and trademark. The franchisor assists the franchisee in starting and managing the business. The franchisee pays a fee or royalty in return. Sometimes, the franchisee may even be required to purchase supplies from the franchisor. This model is operative in the education sector.

CHECK POINT 01

1. Mention net results of internal expansion.
2. Name the source through which external expansion can be financed.
3. What do you mean by franchisee?
4. Name the ingredients of franchise agreement.
5. How many types of franchising are there?

How Franchising Helps Start-ups (New Businesses)

Franchising helps start-ups in the following ways
- Franchising provides the start-ups with a ready market for the product which is the most difficult part of business to establish. For this, the start-ups are required to pay royalty to the franchisor.
- The franchisors impart training to the start-ups, so that they are able to market their products or services. The start-ups are usually granted such training on the payment of a fee.
- The start-ups can grow at a faster rate, without increasing their labour or operating costs.
- The spirit of mutual cooperation and collective gains lead to the success of the start-ups. Franchisors' efforts to boast their franchises are always sincere, so there is no-clash of interest.

Advantages of Franchising

The advantages enjoyed by both franchisee and franchisor are discussed below

Advantages of Franchising

To Franchisee
- Product acceptance
- Management expertise
- Capital requirements
- Knowledge of the market
- Operating and structural controls

To Franchisor
- Quick expansion
- Cost advantages
- Reduced risk

Advantages to the Franchisee

Following are the advantages enjoyed by a franchisee

1. **Product Acceptance** The franchisee usually enters into a business that has an accepted name, product or service. He does not have to spend resources to establish the credibility of the business and create a market for his product. The credibility already exists based on the years the franchise has existed.
2. **Management Expertise** The franchisor provides managerial assistance related to all aspects of operating the franchise, to the franchisee. For this purpose, training programmes are conducted which includes classes in accounting, personnel management, marketing and production.

3. **Capital Requirements** Franchise offers an opportunity to start a new venture with up-front support from franchisor, which saves considerable time and capital of the franchisee.

   In some cases, the franchisor also finances the initial investment to start the franchise operation. Savings in start-ups are also reflected in the pooling of money by individual franchisees for advertising and sales promotion.

   This allows advertising on both local as well as national level to enhance the image and credibility of the business, something that would be impossible for a single operation.

4. **Knowledge of the Market** Franchisors are well aware of the existing market conditions. With their experience and knowledge, they can provide advice and assistance to the franchisees for carving out a market for themselves.

   This is particularly important because of regional and local differences in markets. Also, franchisors constantly evaluate the market conditions and determine the most effective strategies to communicate to the franchisees.

5. **Operating and Structural Controls** Generally, a new venture is faced with the problems of quality control and managerial controls. The franchisor helps the franchisee to combat both the problems.

   Standardisation in supplies and products/ services offered helps to ensure that the entrepreneur will maintain quality standards. It also supports a consistent image on which the franchise business depends for expansion.

Advantages to the Franchisor

The advantages a franchisor gains through franchising are related to expansion risk, capital requirements and cost advantages, which are discussed below

1. **Quick Expansion** The first and foremost advantage of franchising for franchisor is that, it allows a business to expand quickly, using little capital.

   A franchisor can expand a business nationally and even internationally, by authorising and selling franchises in selected locations. Also, operating a franchised business requires fewer employees, thus cutting down an operational cost.

2. **Cost Advantages** The huge size of a franchised company offers many advantages to the franchisor. The franchisor can purchase supplies in large quantities, thus achieving economies of scale.

   Many franchise businesses produce parts, accessories, packaging and raw materials in large quantities and then sell them to franchisees, earning a certain amount of profit in between.

   Also, one of the biggest cost advantage of franchising a business is the ability to commit larger sums of money towards advertising.

3. **Reduced Risk** One of the biggest benefits to the franchisor in a franchise agreement is the ability to expand without an increase in risk.

   Because the franchisee takes on the debt and the liability of opening a unit under the name of the franchise, the franchisor gets all the benefit of an additional location without taking on the risk themselves.

Disadvantages of Franchising

Along with the multiple advantages of growing a business through the franchise mode, certain disadvantages also exist.

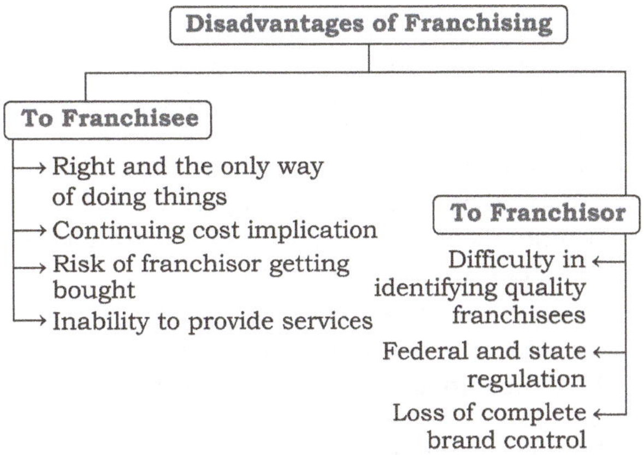

Disadvantages to the Franchisee

Some of the key disadvantages which exist for the franchisee are as follows

1. **Right and the only way of doing Things** Entering into the franchise agreement, limits the degree of freedom for the franchisee. He looses his spirit of innovation.

2. **Continuing Cost Implication** In addition to the original franchise fees and royalties, the franchisors also demand a percentage of revenues. They may also charge extra for providing advertising and training facilities. So, entering into franchise agreements with well-known brands becomes a very expensive proposition.
3. **Risk of Franchisor getting Bought** The franchisee faces serious problems and difficulties when the franchisor either fails or gets bought out by another company.
4. **Inability to provide Services** When promises made in the franchise agreement are not kept, the franchisees may be left without any support in important areas such as advertising, training, quality control, etc. This may be a cause for their failure.

Disadvantages to the Franchisor

The disadvantages which exist for the franchisor are as follows

1. **Difficulty in identifying Quality Franchisees** The franchisor may find it difficult to identify quality franchisees.

   Even after extending all possible support towards training and providing capital, poor management skills of the franchisee may lead to the failure of the franchise and adversely affect the goodwill of the franchisor.
2. **Federal and State Regulation** While not entirely a drawback, dealing with the federal regulations set down by the Federal Trade Commission (FTC) for franchises can be a nuisance for franchisors. These regulations ensure that franchises are operated fairly, but it requires time and effort from the franchisors to meet all of these regulations.
3. **Loss of Complete Brand Control** When a franchisor allows a franchisee to open a business under their brand, they are giving away some of the control over their small business branding.

CHECK POINT 02

1. Mention any one way in which franchising helps start-up.
2. Mention any two advantages of franchising.
3. Mention any two disadvantages of franchising.
4. Write full form of FTC.

Growth through Mergers and Acquisitions (M&As)

Mergers and Acquisitions (M&As) is a strategy that ensures the accelerated growth of a business and also helps a business to expand externally.

Businesses of any size can flourish as a result of merging with another existing company or acquiring a business and absorbing it into its current operations.

The process of growth is accelerated by acquiring a target in a line of business in which the bidding company wants to enlarge when compared with internal expansion, because the company already exists in place, with its own production capacity.

Growing through M&A, may usually turn out to be less expensive compared with internal expansion, particularly, when replacement cost of assets is higher than the market value of target assets.

Mergers

A merger is a combination of two companies into one larger company. In merger, the acquiring company takes over the assets and liabilities of the merged company. All the combining companies are dissolved and only the new entity continues to operate.

Merger commonly takes place in the following two forms

1. **Amalgamation** In amalgamation, two entities combine together and form a new entity, extinguishing both the existing entities.
2. **Absorption** In absorption, one entity gets absorbed into another but the latter does not lose its entity.

For instance, $X + Y = Z$, where Z is a new company (amalgamation) and $X + Y = X$, where company Y is merged into company X (absorption).

e.g. digital computers was absorbed by Compaq after it was acquired in 1997. The merger of TOMCO Limited with HLL is a classic example of absorption.

The term consolidation is used when the two firms involved are of similar size. In a consolidation, a new firm is created after the merger and both the acquiring firm's and the target firm's stockholders receive stock in this new firm.

Citi Group, for instance, was created after the consolidation of Citicorp and Travellers Insurance Group.

Types of Mergers

Various types of mergers are as follows

Types of Mergers
- → Conglomerate mergers
- → Horizontal mergers
- → Market extension mergers
- → Product extension mergers
- → Vertical mergers

1. Conglomerate Mergers

In this type of merger, the firms which are involved in totally unrelated businesses come together. This form of merger can take the following two forms

(i) **Pure Conglomerate Merger** This merger involves firms with nothing in common.

(ii) **Mixed Conglomerate Merger** This merger involves firms that are looking for product extensions or market extensions.

e.g. the merger between the Walt Disney Company and the American Broadcasting Company.

2. Horizontal Mergers

This merger occurs between companies in the same industry. It is generally between competitors' offering the same goods or services. It is generally prevalent in oligopoly market form where few big firms operate in the industry.

Its goal is to create a new, larger organisation with more market share. If the merging companies' business operations are similar, there may be opportunities to join centain operations such as manufacturing and reduce costs.

e.g. a merger between Tata Motors and Hyundai would be horizontal in nature.

3. Market Extension Mergers

This type of merger takes place between companies that deal in the same products but in separate markets. The main purpose is to make sure that merging companies can get access to a bigger market share. e.g. a merger between a company operative in North India with a company operative in South India.

4. Product Extension Mergers

This merger takes place between two business organisations that deal in products which are related to each other and operate in the same market.

This type of merger allows the merging companies to group together their products in order to increase their profitability.

e.g. a merger between a ski-manufacturer with a ski-apparel company. Both companies are selling in the snow skier market but through merger, their offering is extended.

5. Vertical Mergers

A merger between two companies producing different goods or services for one specific finished product is termed as a vertical merger. A vertical merger occurs when two or more firms, operating at different levels within an industry's supply chain, merge operations.

The logic behind the merger is to increase synergies created by merging firms that would be more efficient operating as one.

e.g. an automobile company joining with a parts' supplier. This deal would allow the automobile division to obtain better pricing on parts and the parts division would be guaranteed a steady stream of business.

Acquisitions

An acquisition is a corporate action in which a company purchases most or all of target company's shares to gain control of that company. Acquisition is a general term which includes

- Acquisition of control,
- Acquisition of tangible assets and intangible assets,
- Acquisition of rights and other kinds of obligations.

Acquisitions are made as part of company's growth strategy when it is more economical to take over an existing business as compared to expanding internally.

Types of Acquisitions

There are four types of acquisitions which are as follows

1. **Friendly Acquisition** The companies involved approve the acquisition under friendly terms. There is no forceful acquisition and the process is cordial.
2. **Reverse Acquisition** In this type of acquisition, a private company takes over a public company.

3. **Backflip Acquisition** In this form of acquisition, the purchasing company becomes the subsidiary of the purchased company. It is very rare.
4. **Hostile Acquisition** The whole transaction is carried out through force. The target company is driven to such extreme situations, that it has to agree with the acquisition contrary to its own will. Or in another way, the purchasing company can buy majority of shares of the targeted company, thereby, initiating acquisition.

CHECK POINT 03

1. What do you mean by merger?
2. Define pure conglomerate merger.
3. What do you mean by acquisition?
4. In which type of acquisition, a private company takes over a public company?
5. What is hostile acquisition?

Steps Involved in the Process of Mergers and Acquisitions

Steps to be followed in the process of mergers and acquisitions are as follows

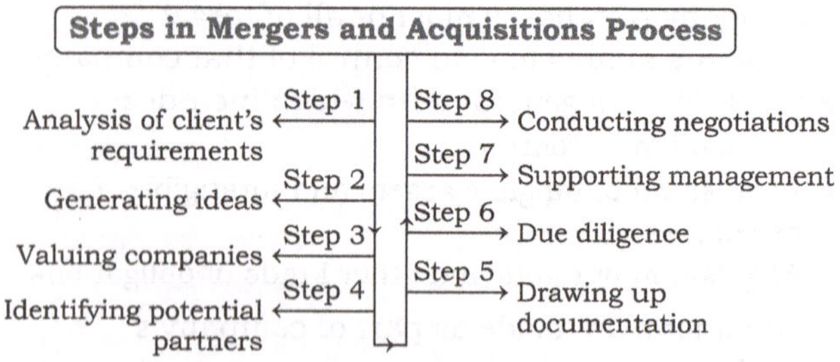

Step 1 **Analysis of Client's Requirements** Under this step, the client's needs requiring mergers and acquisitions are analysed.

Step 2 **Generating Ideas** Keeping in view the client's requirements, ideas are generated to meet his/her objectives. These ideas are based on the study conducted on various companies considered for this purpose.

Step 3 **Valuing Companies** This step puts a monetary value to each company reviewed, so that the purchase price could be negotiated.

Step 4 **Identifying Potential Partners** After the companies are valued, those within the budget are identified, so that future plan of action could be carried on.

Step 5 **Drawing up Documentation** The issues to consider at this stage are drawing up of the letter of intent, confidentiality agreements, etc. between the buyer and the seller companies.

Step 6 **Due Diligence** Accounting and law firms are hired to conduct due diligence. Lawyers review contracts, agreements, leases, pending litigation and all other outstanding or potential liability and obligations, so that the buyer can have a better understanding of the target company's binding agreements as well as overall legal related exposure.

Step 7 **Supporting Management** If after the reports on due diligence, the company wants to continue with the process of merger and acquisition, then the next step is to ensure that managements of both the companies are supportive of the process.

Step 8 **Conducting Negotiations** This is the last step in the process of merger and acquisition wherein the concerned parties negotiate with each other, so that a favourable deal is struck between them.

Reasons for Mergers and Acquisitions

Some of the commonly identified reasons for mergers and acquisitions are given below

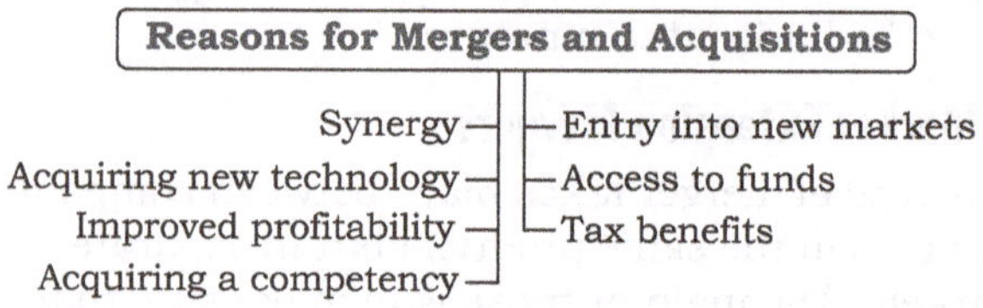

1. Synergy

It implies a condition wherein 2 + 2 = 5, i.e. the combined value of the merging firm exceeds the sum of the individual values of the merged firms.

e.g. if firms X and Y merge, then the value of combined entity V(XY) is expected to be greater than [VX+VY]. Synergy accrues in the form of revenue enhancement and cost savings.

It is the most common reason, why businesses opt for M&A. They aim to reap the benefits of synergy.

Synergy can take the following two forms

(i) **Operating Synergy** This refers to the cost savings that accrue through economies of scale or because of increased turnover leading to increased profits.

(ii) **Financial Synergy** This is the direct result of financial factors such as lower taxes, higher debt capacity or better use of idle resources.

Also, the new firm stands to gain in the form of 'tax shield', i.e. when a firm with accumulated losses merge with a profitable firm and the combined firm can sets off such losses against its profit, a financial synergy occurs, known as 'tax shield'.

2. Acquiring New Technology

To remain competitive, companies need to constantly upgrade their technology. So, by buying a company with unique and modern technology, the buying company upgrades its existing technology and ensures a competitive edge in the market. e.g. a merger between Blackberry and Treo which aims at incorporating cell phone capability and e-mail connectivity in one device.

3. Improved Profitability

Companies indulge in mergers and acquisitions if they feel that it would help to increase their profitability. A study conducted by International Business Owners Survey showed that 34% of businesses use M&A to maintain or improve their profitability. e.g. European Media Group Betelsmann, Pearson and others have driven their growth by expanding into the USA through M&As.

4. Acquiring a Competency

Companies, sometimes opt for mergers and acquisitions to acquire a competency or capability that they do not have and which the other firm does. e.g. IBM merged with Daksh for acquiring competencies that he latter possessed.

5. Entry into New Markets

Mergers help companies to enter into new markets without facing stiff competition from existing companies. It helps to ease the entry route for a company seeking to enter a new market.

e.g. the merger of Orange, Hutch and Vodafone took place to achieve this objective.

6. Access to Funds

If a company is faced with shortage of funds and it also does not have proper access to raise funds from capital market, then it may decide to merge with another company which has surplus funds.

e.g. Tamil Nadu Dadha Pharmaceuticals (TDPL) merged with the Sun Pharma because it did not have funds to launch new products.

7. Tax Benefits

Mergers and acquisitions are also adopted to reduce tax liabilities. By merging with a loss-making entity, a company with high tax liability can set-off accumulated losses of the merging company from its profits, thereby reducing it's tax liability.

e.g. Hinduja Finance acquired Ashok Leyland Information Technology (ALIT), so that the accumulated losses of ALIT could be set-off against its book profits.

The following **examples** show how mergers and acquisitions helped the combining companies

- When Hindustan Unilever Limited Company acquired Lakme, it helped HUL to enter the cosmetics market through an established brand.
- When Glaxo and Smithkline Beecham merged, they not only gained market share but also eliminated competition between each other.
- Tata Tea acquired Tetley to leverage Tetley's international marketing strengths.

Reasons for Failure of Mergers and Acquisitions

The common reasons for the failure of mergers and acquisitions are as follows

Reasons for Failure of Mergers and Acquisitions

- Unrealistic price paid for target company
- Difficulties in cultural integration
- Overstated synergies
- Integration difficulties
- Poor bussiness fit
- Inadequate due diligence
- High leverage
- Boardroom split
- Regulatory issues
- Human resource issues

1. Unrealistic Price Paid for Target Company

If the purchase price paid by acquirer company far exceeds the actual value of the target company, then the burden of the over priced assets will dilute the earning capacity of the resultant company, leading to its failure.

This phenomenon is generally noticed in the later years when the acquirer has to revalue the assets and write-off goodwill booked at the time of M&A.

2. Difficulties in Cultural Integration

If the merging entities have different corporate cultures, styles of leadership, differing employee expectations and functional differences, then the process of merger should be carried out in such a way, so as to be able to accommodate these differences, failing which the merger would be a disaster.

There may be acute contrasts between the attitudes and values of the two companies, especially if the new partnership crosses national boundaries.

3. Overstated Synergies

Mergers and acquisitions are tools for creating synergies through increased revenues, reduced costs and reduction in networking capital. Overestimation of these synergies can lead to failure of mergers.

4. Integration Difficulties

The companies often face the problem of integration. The new company formed has to adapt to a new set of challenges emerging from changed circumstances. To do this, the company prepares plans to integrate the operations of the combining entities.

If the plans are inadequate or are not implemented properly, integration becomes difficult, leading to the failure of merger or acquisition.

5. Poor Business Fit

Mergers and acquisitions also fail when the products or services of the merging entities do not naturally fit into the acquirer's overall plan. This delays efficient and effective integration and causes failure.

6. Inadequate Due Diligence

Due diligence helps in detecting financial and business risks that the acquirer inherits from the target company. Inaccurate estimation of related risk can result in the failure of the merger.

7. High Leverage

To pay the price of acquisition, the acquirer may borrow heavily from the market, which will create a very high leveraged structure and increase the interest burden of the company.

This increased burden would reduce the profitability of the company and may defeat the very purpose of acquisition.

8. Boardroom Split

Specific personality clashes between executives in the two companies can prove to be a major problem causing slowing down or preventing integration of entities and ultimately leading to an unsuccessful merger.

9. Regulatory Issues

The entire process of merger requires legal approvals. If any of the stakeholders are not in the favour of mergers, they might create legal obstacles and slow down the entire process. These delays may adversely affect the process of mergers and acquisitions.

10. Human Resource Issues

A merger or acquisition is identified with job losses, restructuring and the imposition of a new corporate culture and identity. This can create uncertainty, anxiety and resentment among the company's employees. They may also be reluctant to embrace new corporate culture and identity. These factors impact the workers morale and productivity, which are crucial to the success of mergers and acquisitions.

CHECK POINT 04

1. How many steps are there in the process of mergers and acquisitions?
2. In which form synergy occurs?
3. Define operating synergy.
4. Give any one reason for mergers and acquisitions.
5. Give any one reason for the failure of mergers and acquisitions.

EXAM PATTERN EXERCISE

Objective Type Questions (1 Mark)

Multiple Choice Questions

1 Net result of internal expansion can be attributed as
(a) increase in business activities
(b) broadening the present capital structure
(c) Both (a) and (b)
(d) None of the above

Ans (c) Both (a) and (b)

2 Komal Company Ltd. was initially producing crayons. Now, it has decided to produce oil paints and water paints also. The company is attempting to
(a) expand internally (b) expand externally
(c) Both (a) and (b) (d) None of these

Ans (a) expand internally

3 Franchising include
(a) franchisor (b) franchisee
(c) franchise agreement (d) All of these

Ans (d) All of these

4 The advantages of franchising for a franchiser is/are
(a) quick expansion (b) cost advantage
(c) Both (a) and (b) (d) None of these

Ans (c) Both (a) and (b)

5 .... outline how the franchise name is to be used and also the marketing and advertising procedures required to be followed by the franchisee.
(a) Operations manual
(b) Proprietary statements
(c) Ongoing site maintenance
(d) None of the above

Ans (b) Proprietary statements

6 What is common among McDonalds, Goli Vada Pav, Naturals Ice-creams and Ferns-N-Petals? **(CBSE SQP)**
(a) All are multinational corporations working in India.
(b) All have adopted franchising as their growth strategy.
(c) All have merged with big companies.
(d) All of the above

Ans (b) All have adopted franchising as their growth strategy.

7 In which type of acquistion, a private company takes over a public company?
(a) Friendly acquisition (b) Reverse acquistion
(c) Hostile acquisition (d) Backflip acquisition

Ans (b) Reverse acquisition

8 Last step in the process of merger and acquisition is
(a) due diligence
(b) generating ideas
(c) conducting negotiations
(d) valuing companies

Ans (c) conducting negotiations

9 In .... form of acquisitions, the purchasing company becomes the subsidiary of the purchased company.
(a) friendly (b) reverse
(c) backflip (d) hostile

Ans (c) backflip

10 .... synergy refers to the cost savings that accrue through economies of scale.
(a) Operating (b) Financial
(c) Overstated (d) None of these

Ans (a) Operating

11 The goal of a .... merger is to create a new larger organisation with more market share.
(a) conglomerate
(b) horizontal
(c) market extension (d) Both (b) and (c)

Ans (d) Both (b) and (c)

12 When two companies that may not compete with each other but exist in the same supply chain merge, it is known as **(CBSE 2023)**
(a) horizontal merger
(b) vertical merger
(c) market extension merger
(d) product extension merger

Ans (b) vertical merger

13 A merger between Fiat and Tata motors would be an example of
(a) conglomerate merger
(b) vertical merger
(c) horizontal merger (d) market extension

Ans (c) horizontal merger

14 "X + Y = Z, where Z is a new company". It shows
(a) absorption (b) amalgamation
(c) acquisition (d) None of these

Ans (b) amalgamation

15 Ankit Private Limited Company deals in dairy products. The company is quite aware about the importance of growth and believe in the saying. 'You either grow or you die'. Therefore, the company is planning to expand its current production capacity by increasing the number of its livestock. Which form of expansion is the company planning?
(a) Internal expansion (b) External expansion
(c) Both (a) and (b) (d) None of these

Ans (a) It is a slow and time consuming process which is a result of a gradual increase in the activities of the enterprise.

16 Rahul, who is a diploma holder in computers, decides to take franchise of NIIT for his backward town of Katni. Form of franchise decided to be taken by him is
(a) product franchise business opportunity
(b) manufacturing franchise opportunity
(c) business franchise opportunity venture
(d) business format franchise opportunity

Ans (d) business format franchise opportunity

17 After completing his MBA from NIPS, Bangalore, Vivek decided to start his own business by taking the franchise of 'Ferns-N-Petals'. Since, this is Vivek's first venture, advice him about the main clause of a franchise agreement which defines the type of relationship.
(a) Contract explanation
(b) Operations manual
(c) Proprietary statements
(d) Ongoing site maintenance

Ans (a) It is a part of the agreement that defines the type of relationship, a franchisee is entering into with the franchisor.

18 Both mergers and acquisitions are enterprise growth strategies but how they come into existence makes them different from each other. Which of the given statements below justifies the given statement? **(CBSE SQP)**
(a) Merger is always friendly, whereas acquisition is always hostile.
(b) Merger may be friendly, whereas acquisition is always hostile.
(c) Merger is always depending on synergy, whereas acquisition is never based on synergy.
(d) Merger is consensual, whereas acquisition is forced.

Ans (d) Merger is consensual, whereas acquisition is forced.

19 **Assertion** (A) A firm may expand internally by expanding its present production capacity by increasing the number of machines.

Reason (R) Internal expansion is a slow and time consuming process which is a result of a gradual increase in the activities of the enterprise.

Alternatives
(a) Both Assertion (A) and Reason (R) are correct
(b) Assertion (A) is correct, but Reason (R) is incorrect
(c) Assertion (A) is incorrect, but Reason (R) is correct
(d) Both Assertion (A) and Reason (R) are incorrect

Ans (a) Both Assertion (A) and Reason (R) are correct

20 **Assertion** (A) Backflip acquisition is a rare case of acquisition in which the purchasing company becomes a subsidiary of the purchased company.

Reason (R) Both the companies approve of the acquisition but the entire process is done by force. **(CBSE 2023)**

Alternatives
(a) Both Assertion (A) and Reason (R) are true and Reason (R) is the correct explanation of Assertion (A)
(b) Both Assertion (A) and Reason (R) are true, but Reason (R) is not the correct explanation of Assertion (A)
(c) Assertion (A) is true, but Reason (R) is false
(d) Assertion (A) is false, but Reason (R) is true

Ans (a) Both Assertion (A) and Reason (R) are true and Reason (R) is the correct explanation of Assertion (A)

21 **Assertion** (A) Synergy is the primary reason for the mergers to take place between the two companies.

Reason (R) The turnover and output produced by the individual firm would be more than the turnover produced by the firm after merger.

Alternatives

(a) Both Assertion (A) and Reason (R) are correct
(b) Assertion (A) is correct, but Reason (R) is incorrect
(c) Assertion (A) is incorrect, but Reason (R) is correct
(d) Both Assertion (A) and Reason (R) are incorrect

Ans (b) Mergers are most commonly done to gain market share, reduce cost of operations, expand to new territories, unite common products, grow revenues and increase profits.

22 Given below are types of franchising with their meanings. Match them correctly.

Column I (Type of Franchising)		**Column II** (Meaning)
A. Product franchise business opportunity	(i)	A business owner purchases and distributes the products for one specific company.
B. Manufacturing franchise opportunity	(ii)	The franchisor provides the franchisee a proven method of operating a business.
C. Business franchise opportunity venture	(iii)	The manufacturer grants a store owner the authority to distribute goods.
D. Business format franchise opportunity	(iv)	The franchisee is conferred with exclusive rights to manufacture and sell a product.

Codes

	A	B	C	D
(a)	(ii)	(i)	(iii)	(iv)
(b)	(iii)	(iv)	(i)	(ii)
(c)	(iv)	(iii)	(ii)	(i)
(d)	(iii)	(ii)	(iv)	(i)

Ans (b) (iii) (iv) (i) (ii)

23 Given below are the types of acquisitions with their meanings. Match them correctly.

Column I (Type of Acquisitions)		**Column II** (Meaning)
A. Friendly Acquisition	(i)	Purchasing company becomes a subsidiary of the purchased company.
B. Reverse Acquisition	(ii)	Both companies agree to the acquisition mutually.
C. Backflip Acquisition	(iii)	Purchased company forces purchasing company for acquisition and buys all of its shares.
D. Hostile Acquisition	(iv)	Private company takes over public company.

Codes

	A	B	C	D		A	B	C	D
(a)	(ii)	(iv)	(i)	(iii)	(b)	(iv)	(i)	(ii)	(iii)
(c)	(ii)	(i)	(iv)	(iii)	(d)	(ii)	(iv)	(i)	(iii)

Ans (a) (ii) (iv) (i) (iii)

24 Given below are types of mergers with examples of each. Match them correctly. **(CBSE SQP)**

Column I (Types of Mergers)		**Column II** (Examples)
A. Vertical Merger	(i)	A watch manufacturer acquiring a cement manufacturer
B. Market Extension Merger	(ii)	Bank of Madura merged with ICICI Bank
C. Conglomerate	(iii)	A textile company acquires a cotton yarn manufacturer
D. Horizontal Merger	(iv)	Hindustan Unilever Company acquired Lakme, it helped HUL to enter the cosmetics market

Codes

	A	B	C	D		A	B	C	D
(a)	(i)	(ii)	(iii)	(iv)	(b)	(iii)	(iv)	(i)	(ii)
(c)	(i)	(iii)	(ii)	(iv)	(d)	(iii)	(ii)	(i)	(iv)

Ans (b) (iii) (iv) (i) (ii)

25 Which concept is highlighted in the given image?

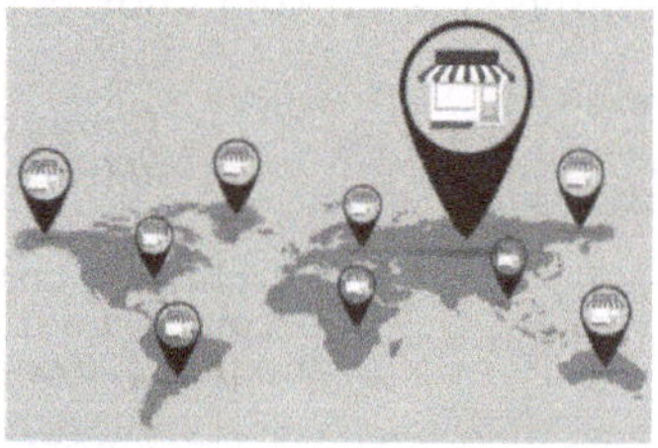

(a) Franchising (b) Merger

(c) Acquisition (d) None of these

Ans (a) It is a joint venture between a franchisor and a franchisee.

26 Which concept is highlighted in the given image?

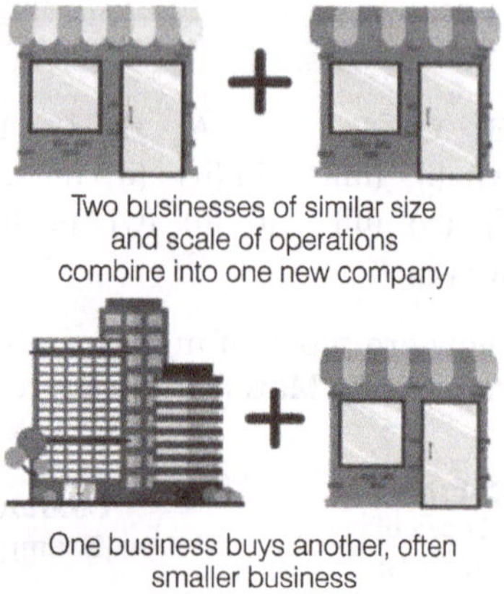

(a) Franchising (b) Merger

(c) Acquisition (d) Both (b) and (c)

Ans (d) A merger is a combination of two companies into one larger company. Acquisition is a corporate action in which a company purchases most or all of target companies' shares to gain control of that company.

Fill in the Blanks

27 While ensuring the growth of his enterprise, an entrepreneur has to play the dual role of a .... as well as a ....

Ans manager, leader

28 Growth is essential for the business as it facilitates ....

Ans survival

29 .... is generally financed through long-term loans, undistributed profits and reserves.

Ans Internal expansion

30 .... is the Indian corporate who has gone through the franchising route.

Ans Raymond Limited

31 Manufacturing franchise opportunity is common in .... industry.

Ans food and beverage

32 Rohit Beverages Ltd. introduced a new fruit juice 'CAPTA'. It contains various refreshing vitamins and minerals. Rohit Beverages Ltd. also designed an attractive packaging for its promotion.

Their sales graph is a clear indication of their success. In order to capture huge market share, they decided to give exclusive rights to retailers to manufacture and sell the product to the public. This concept discussed above is ....

Ans manufacturing franchise opportunity

33 Hiva Ltd. and Mehta Communications provide cable TV network in adjacent areas of Jaipur. After sometime the market was slowly taken over by big cable companies.

Both Hiva Ltd. and Mehta Communications understood the competition and decided to come together so as to increase their market share.

This strategy helped them in cost saving through economies of scale as they could cover more areas now. It led to the overall growth of both the companies. Growth strategy adopted is ....

Ans merger

34 Mergers commonly take the form of .... and ....

Ans amalgamation, absorption

35 The largest Hamburger manufacturer 'Hamber' in India merged with well-known cold drink manufacturer "Soda Pop" and renamed the brand "Ham Pop" to impart a different identity. The type of merger discussed above is ....

Ans product extension merger

36 When a firm with accumulated losses merge with a profitable firm and the combine firm can set-off such losses against its profit, a financial synergy occurs, known as ....

Ans tax shield

State True or False

37 A firm may expand internally by entering new areas of production or marketing or both.

Ans True

38 Business franchise opportunity venture is operative in the education sector.

Ans False. Business format franchise opportunity is operative in the educational sector.

39 McDonald currently has the most franchise units worldwide as any franchise system.

Ans True

40 Contract explanation is the part of the agreement that defines the type of relationship a franchisee is entering into with the franchisor.

Ans True

41 If the merging companies have different corporate cultures or styles of leadership, then this can be a reason for the failure of merger.

Ans True

42 A merger between a ski manufacturer company with a ski apparel company is an example of product extension merger.

Ans True

43 The merger between Orange, Hutch and Vodafone took place to acquire a competency.

Ans False. It took place to gain entry into new markets.

44 Company B produces cricket bats and Company A produces cricket balls. Both the companies decide to merge together and after merger, Company A loses its identity and exists as a part of Company B. The merger being discussed here is absorption.

Ans True

45 In horizontal merger, the firms which are involved in totally unrelated businesses come together.

Ans False. In conglomerate merger, firms engaged in unrelated businesses come together.

46 Synergy effect means that the combined worth of the new enterprise is less than the individual worth of the combining firms.

Ans False. It means that the combined worth of the new enterprise is greater than the individual worth of combining firms.

Case Based Questions

47 Read the following article and answer the questions that follow

A business cannot only aim to succeed only once in its lifetime, therefore, businesses develop and implement various techniques and methods to be constantly profitable. With this mindset, a business can continue to develop and grow for a long time.

Nest Wings was a successful restaurant located in the outer areas of Mumbai serving its customers all the delicacies from the major metropolitan cities of India at affordable prices. But, the business became stagnant at a point and then the owner started to add more products and services to the restaurant, like play area for children, gaming sections, candy store outside, etc. The owner also granted permission to two businessmen to open a branch of Nest Wings in Pune.

With the addition of more facilities and a new store in Pune, the restaurant started to flourish again. The profits started increasing and customers were attracted to the restaurant for its new services. The quick decision making of the owner protected the business from falling apart and the owner decided to open more branches in nearby cities.

(i) What is the next challenge for an entrepreneur after the business has started making adequate profits?

(a) Increased sales

(b) Enhanced customer service

(c) Increased revenue

(d) Growth

Ans (d) Growth

(ii) "But, the business became stagnant at a point and then the owner started to add more products and services to the restaurant, like play area for children, gaming sections, candy store outside, etc."

This is .... type of expansion of business.

(a) internal

(b) external

(c) product

(d) None of the above

Ans (a) internal

(iii) "The owner also granted permission to two businessmen to open a branch of Nest Wings in Pune. "

What are the Pune businessmen be called, to the owner?

(a) Franchisor (b) Franchisee
(c) Agents (d) Partners

Ans (b) Franchisee

(iv) Which of the following advantages did the owner of the restaurant enjoyed by allowing a new branch?

(a) Cost advantage
(b) Quick expansion
(c) Reduced risk
(d) All of the above

Ans (d) All of the above

(v) Which type of external expansion is discussed in the above case?

(a) Mergers (b) Acquisition
(c) Franchising (d) Venture

Ans (c) Franchising

48 Read the following article and answer the questions that follow

"Super Fresh" and "Fresh Fruits" are two different businesses that produce and sell fresh fruit juices in cans, bottles, and their outlets. Both companies are direct competitors and are located in the same city.

The rivalry between the businesses cost loss of sales to both for quite a long time. Therefore, the owners decided to come into an agreement and Fresh Fruits having more profits and valuation than Super Fresh proposed to join and make one company retaining Fresh Fruits as the name of the company.

The former agreed and an agreement was signed by both owners. After this venture, the companies joined their production and other activities. Customers were happy with the quality of the product and sales increased. The costs were saved and revenue was enhanced.

The idea of combining the business resulted in huge profits and both owners were happy. The inadequate competition was erased and the new business emerged with great potential.

(i) The expansion used by the businesses is

(a) internal expansion
(b) external expansion
(c) joint venture (d) None of the above

Ans (b) external expansion

(ii) Which type of external expansion was used by Super Fresh and Fresh Fruits?

(a) Merger (b) Acquisition
(c) Franchising (d) None of these

Ans (a) Merger

(iii) "Therefore, the owners decided to come into an agreement and Fresh Fruits having more profits and valuation than Super Fresh proposed to join and make one company retaining Fresh Fruits as the name of the company."

The above statement highlights which of the following technique of expansion?

(a) Amalgamation (b) Venturing
(c) Renting (d) Absorption

Ans (d) Absorption

(iv) "The costs were saved and revenue was enhanced."

Which of the following terms explains the above sentence?

(a) Synergy (b) Growth
(c) Development (d) Expansion

Ans (a) Synergy

(v) The merger between Super Fresh and Fresh Fruits is an example of which type of merger?

(a) Product extension merger
(b) Vertical merger
(c) Horizontal merger (d) None of the above

Ans (c) Horizontal merger

Short Answer Type I Questions (2 Marks)

1 One of the most important advantages of buying a franchise is that entrepreneur does not have to incur all the risks associated with the new business. Do you agree?

Ans Yes, an entrepreneur when buying a franchise, enters into a business that has an accepted name, product or service. The risks when starting a new business are of product acceptance, management expertise, meeting capital requirements, knowledge of the market and operating and structural controls.

When going through franchising way, these risks are minimised through the franchise relationship.

2 How meeting capital requirements is not difficult, when opting to start a business by buying a franchise?

Ans In some cases, the franchisor finances the initial investment to start the franchise operation.

The initial capital required is to purchase a franchise includes, fee for the franchise, construction costs and purchase of equipments.

Other financial benefits may include

(i) Pooling of money by individual franchisees for advertising and sales promotion.

(ii) The layout facility, control of stock and inventory and potential buying power, of entire franchise operations, save a lot of funds of the entrepreneur.

3 Anil signed a contract with Phelari group to bottle and distribute their soft drink brand 'Kickapo'. The taste of this soft drink was unique and it became the most preferred soft drink consumed by teenagers.

The agreement stated that Anil should use the same ingredients used by Phelari group while bottling the product. Identify and give the meaning of this type of enterprise growth opportunity. **(CBSE SQP Term II)**

Ans The type of franchising highlighted in the case is manufacturing franchise opportunity. These types of franchises provide an organisation with the right to manufacture a product and sell it to the public, using the franchisor's name and trademark.

4 What is a franchise agreement? List out its main components.

Ans Franchise agreement is a legal document, which defines the mutual terms and conditions between a franchisor and a franchisee.

The main components of a franchise agreement are as follows

(i) Contract explanation

(ii) Operations manual

(iii) Ongoing site maintenance

(iv) Proprietary statements

5 Giving any two reasons, explain how franchising is a viable option for the growth of start-up firms. **(CBSE 2020)**

Ans Franchising is a viable option for the growth of start-up firms. This is explained with the help of the following points

(i) Franchising provides the start-ups with a ready market which is the most difficult part of business to establish. For this, the start-ups are required to pay royalty to the franchisor.

(ii) The franchisors impart training to the start-ups, so that they are able to market their products or services. The start-ups are usually granted such training on the payment of a fee.

6 Vimal Company Limited, were earlier producing pencils, now they have decided to further venture into the field of notebooks and paper. What do you think the company is attempting to do? Identify and explain the concept. **(CBSE TBQ)**

Ans Vimal Company Limited is attempting to expand internally. Internal expansion results from the gradual increase in the activities of the concern.

A firm may expand internally by adding more machines, upgrading its technologies, increasing production or entering new fields on the production or marketing sides.

Internal expansion is usually financed through long-term sources of finance or through ploughing back of profits.

Internal expansion leads to an increase in business activities and also broadens the present capital structure.

7 Distinguish between internal expansion and external expansion. **(CBSE 2017)**

Ans Differences between internal expansion and external expansion are

Basis	Internal Expansion	External Expansion
Meaning	Internal expansion is a result of gradual increase in the activities of the enterprise. It is a slow and time consuming process.	External expansion occurs when two or more business enterprises come together with a common objective of expanding their business.

Basis	Internal Expansion	External Expansion
Methods of Expansion	A firm may expand internally by (i) expanding its present production capacity (ii) replacing old machines with new technology machines. (iii) entering new areas of production and marketing.	A firm may expand externally by (i) Franchising (ii) Mergers and acquisitions.

8 Enumerate the importance of franchising. **(CBSE TBQ)**

Ans The importance of franchising are as follows

(i) For the franchisee
(a) Product acceptance
(b) Capital requirements
(c) Operating and structural controls

(ii) For the franchisor
(a) Quick expansion
(b) Cost advantages

9 Explain briefly the advantages of franchising for the franchisor.

Ans The advantages of franchising for the franchisor are as follows

(i) **Quick Expansion** The first and foremost advantage of franchising for the franchisor is that, it allows a business to expand quickly using very little capital.

(ii) **Cost Advantages** The huge size of a franchised company offers many advantages to the franchisor in the form of economies of scale.

10 How can mergers and acquisitions help a firm to enter into new markets?

Ans Mergers and acquisitions ensure hassle free entry into new markets. Under normal conditions, a company can enter a new market but may have to face stiff competition from existing companies. However, if the merger route is adopted, one can enter the market with greater ease and avoid too much competition.

This is achieved by merging with established companies of that market. The merger of Orange, Hutch and Vodafone took place to achieve this objective.

11 Differentiate between consolidation and merger. **(CBSE TBQ)**

Ans In general, when the combination involves firms that are of similar size, the term 'consolidation' is applied whereas, when the two firms differ significantly by size, the term 'merger' is used.

12 Name the two forms that merger can take place. **(CBSE TBQ)**

Ans Merger commonly takes the two forms. In the first form, two entities combine together and form a new entity, extinguishing both the existing entities. This form is termed as 'amalgamation'. In the second form, i.e. 'absorption', one entity gets absorbed into another but the latter does not lose its entity.

13 Differentiate between horizontal merger and vertical merger.

Ans Differences between horizontal and vertical merger are (Any two)

Basis	Horizontal Merger	Vertical Merger
Meaning	This merger is between competitors offering the same goods or services.	This merger is between companies producing different goods or services for one specific finished product.
Motive	To eliminate competition.	To ensure uninterrupted flow of supplies.
Example	A merger between Tata Motors and Hyundai.	A merger between Tata Motors and MRF Tyres.

14 Kamal Ltd. are manufacturers of textiles, having their plant in Surat, a city of Gujarat. Vastra Ltd. are the manufacturers of readymade garments and sell their products throughout the country. They also export their products to America and European countries. Vastra Ltd. source their textiles from Kamal Ltd.

The management of the two companies decided to merge to have economies of large scale production.

(i) Identify the type of merger entered into by Kamal Ltd. and Vastra Ltd.

(ii) Also, explain a type of merger other than the one identified in (i) above. **(CBSE 2019)**

Ans (i) Kamal Ltd. and Vastra Ltd. have entered into a vertical merger.

(ii) Another form of merger is horizontal merger. This merger occurs between companies in the same industry.

It is generally between competitors offering the same goods or services. The goal of a horizontal merger is to create a new larger organisation with more market share.

15 Merger between 'Larsen and Toubro (L and T)' with key business area in construction engineering and manufacturing critical equipments and 'Voltas Limited' an Indian multinational electronics company specialised in manufacturing home appliances, whose business fields are totally unrelated has taken place.

Identify and explain the type of merger between 'Larsen and Toubro (L and T)' and 'Voltas Limited'. **(CBSE 2023)**

Ans The given case highlights the conglomerate mergers.

In this type of merger, the firms which are involved in totally unrelated businesses come together. This form of merger can take the following two forms

(i) Pure conglomerate merger
(ii) Mixed conglomerate merger

16 What is operating synergy? How is it different from financial synergy? **(CBSE SQP Term II)**

Ans Operating synergy refers to the cost savings that come through economies of scale or increased sales and profits. It leads to the overall growth of the firm.

On the other hand, financial synergy is the direct result of financial factors such as lower taxes, higher debt capacity or better use of idle cash.

17 Explain the types of acquisitions. **(CBSE TBQ)**

Ans There are four types of acquisitions

(i) **Friendly Acquisition** Both the companies approve of the acquisition under friendly terms.

(ii) **Reverse Acquisition** A private company takes over a public company.

(iii) **Backflip Acquisition** The purchasing company becomes the subsidiary of the purchased company.

(iv) **Hostile Acquisition** The target company is acquired by force.

18 Explain any two types of acquisition.

Ans (i) **Friendly Acquisition** The companies involved approve the acquisition under friendly terms. There is no forceful acquisition and the process is cordial.

(ii) **Reverse Acquisition** In this type of acquisition, a private company takes over a public company.

19 Ayaan Manufacturing Company, a leading company of housing sector registered a turnover of ₹ 2,000 crore in 2015-16. This spectacular progress prompted the directors of the company to look out for further growth plans. The company has decided to grow externally through the process of mergers and acquisitions.

You are approached by the company, as an expert on mergers and acquisitions. The directors of the company want to know the process of mergers and acquisitions. You are required to give them a brief outline of the process.

Ans As an expert on mergers and acquisitions, I will give the directors of Ayaan Manufacturing Company, the various steps involved in the process, which are as follows

***Step* 1** Analysis of client's requirements.
***Step* 2** Generating ideas.
***Step* 3** Valuing companies.
***Step* 4** Identifying potential partners.
***Step* 5** Drawing up documentation.
***Step* 6** Due diligence.
***Step* 7** Supporting management.
***Step* 8** Conducting negotiations.

20 ABC Company, manufacturing shoes, has taken over XYZ Company which also manufactures shoes at a small scale. What do you think will be the reason for this kind of takeover? **(CBSE TBQ)**

Ans Reasons for this takeover can be (Any two)

(i) **Small Size of XYZ Company** Smaller companies are relatively easy to acquire. Even the shareholders of these companies do not resist takeovers in anticipation of the stock of a large company.

(ii) **Specific Assets** XYZ company may have very specific assets in the form of customer base, employees, intellectual property, that ABC Company can grab through takeover.

(iii) **Increased Market Share** The market share of ABC Company will increase after takeover. This might also be one of the reason for this takeover.

21 "Aggressive entry of Reliance Jio has launched a big price war. With its free services, Jio has upset the bigger players. The Vodafone-Idea merged entity will only add fuel to the fire. Since the merged entity will have more resources, the telecom price war is going to get messier.

Idea-Vodafone merger may lead to more consolidation. Reliance Communications, Tata Teleservices and Aircel are already in talks for merger. Airtel has bought India operations of Telenor. Reliance is surely going to face stiff fight from the new biggies. The consumer will be the king."

Source *Economictimes.indiatimes.com, 20th March, 2017.*

Identify and explain the type of merger stated in the above article.

Ans Horizonal merger is stated in the above article. For explanation, refer to text on page 131.

Short Answer Type II Questions (3 Marks)

1 A business may either grow or die. Elucidate.

Ans Growth is essential for the survival of the business. A business is bound to die, if it does not try to expand its activities. As we know, that business exists in a dynamic environment and it is impossible to hold a business in a steady state.

It should either grow or shrink. So, we can easily conclude that a non-growing business is like a house of cards, easily toppled by the slightest change in the external or internal environment of the business.

2 "The expansion of an enterprise may be in the form of acquisition of ownership and control of other businesses". Identify and explain the form of expansion highlighted in the given statement.

Ans Form of expansion highlighted in the statement is external expansion. External expansion occurs when two or more business enterprises come together with a common objective of expanding their business. A firm may expand externally by

(i) franchising

(ii) mergers and acquisitions

External expansion is financed through long-term sources of finance.

The net results of external expansion are

(i) Expansion of capital base as well as business activities.

(ii) Elimination of unnecessary competition.

(iii) Synergy effect is achieved.

3 How does franchising help start-ups?

Ans Start-ups benefit from franchising in the following ways (Any three)

(i) Franchising provides the start-ups with a ready market of an established product, which is the most difficult part of business to establish.

(ii) The franchisors also impart training to the start-ups, so that they are able to market their products and services.

(iii) The rate of growth of the start-ups is accelerated as they save on their labour and operating costs.

(iv) The spirit of mutual cooperation and collective gains, that exist between the franchisor and franchisee, help the start-ups to be successful.

So, by keeping the above points in view, we can safely conclude that start-ups can resort to franchising for sure success.

4 What are the disadvantages of franchising to the franchisee? **(CBSE TBQ)**

Ans The disadvantages of franchising for the franchisee are as follows (Any three)

(i) **Right and the Only Way of Doing Things** Franchising limits the degree of freedom of the franchisee. He looses his spirit of innovation.

(ii) **Continuing Cost Implication** In addition to the original franchise fees and royalties, the franchisors also demand a percentage of revenues and may also charge extra for providing advertising and training facilities. All this escalates the cost of operation for the franchisee.

(iii) **Risk of Franchisor getting Bought** The franchisee faces serious problems and difficulties when the franchisor either fails or gets bought out by another company.

(iv) **Inability to Provide Services** When promises made in the franchise agreement are not kept, the franchisees may be left without any support in key operational areas leading to their failure.

5 'Pretty You' is an established brand in the salon and makeover industry. It is currently operating in Delhi with a network of 5 branches.

It now wants to make its presence known in different cities of North India and gradually would be establishing its identity throughout the country. For this, the company decides to give exclusive rights to independent retailers to take advantage of the brand 'Pretty you' in return for their payment of royalties and conformance to standardised operating procedures.

Identify and explain the form of expansion discussed above. **(CBSE 2023)**

Ans The form of expansion discussed is franchising.

Franchising can be defined as an arrangement whereby the manufacturer or sole distributor of a trademarked product or service gives exclusive rights of local distribution to independent retailers in return for their payment of royalties and conformance to standardised operating procedures.

According to Arnold S Goldstein, "Franchising occurs when the franchisee markets a product or service developed by a franchiser under an agreement and license to do so."

Today, franchising is helping thousands of individuals to be their own boss and operate their own business. It allows entrepreneurs to be in business for themselves, but not by themselves.

6 Alpha Ltd., a multinational restaurant chain company, gives an exclusive right to four Indian companies to set up the restaurants in metropolitan cities in India in return for their payment of royalties and conformance to standardised operating procedures.

Indian companies decided to employ local workers and to distribute left-over food amongst the needy as a provision in the agreement with Alpha Ltd.

(i) Identify and give the meaning of the concept discussed in the above para.

(ii) List the main ingredients of the agreement that Alpha Ltd. will enter into with the Indian companies. **(CBSE 2017 Modified)**

Ans (i) The concept discussed in the above para is 'Franchising'. It can be defined as "an agreement whereby the manufacturer or sole distributor of a trademarked product or service gives exclusive rights of local distribution to independent retailers in return for their payment of royalties and conformance to standardised operating procedures".

(ii) The main ingredients of a franchise agreement are listed below

(a) Contract explanation
(b) Operations manual
(c) Proprietary statements
(d) Ongoing site maintenance

7 Differentiate between product franchise and manufacturing franchise.

Ans Difference between product franchise and manufacturing franchise are

Basis	Product Franchise	Manufacturing Franchise
Mode of Operation	Under this form, the manufacturer grants a store owner the authority to distribute goods manufactured under their brand name.	Under this form, the franchisee is conferred with exclusive rights to manufacture and sell a product, using the franchisor's name and trademark.
Operative in	This form of franchising is common in automobile sector and its related goods.	This form of franchising is prevalent in the food and beverage industry.
Used	It is used in petroleum and automobile industry.	It is used in soft drink industries.

8 Explain meaning, advantages and limitations of horizontal integration.

Ans Horizontal integration is a long-term strategy of the firm which is based on growth throughout acquisition or merger of one or more similar business operating at the same stage of production and marketing.

Advantages of horizontal integration are as follows

(i) It eliminates cut throat competition.
(ii) Economies of scale reduces the cost per unit.
(iii) Larger control over market.

Disadvantages of horizontal integration are as follows

(i) May lead to monopoly power and exploitation of customers.

(ii) Does not control supply of raw material.

9 'Healthy Juice India Limited' and 'Asli Juice Limited' are engaged in the production of fruit juice. Both the companies sell the juice in 1,000 ml tetra packs and are in direct competition. To avoid competition, the management of both the companies decided to merge and formed a new company 'Asli Healthy Juice India Limited'.

The new company decided to sell the fruit juice through the company owned outlets throughout the country.

(i) Name and explain the 'enterprise growth strategy'.

(ii) Also identify the channel of distribution decided by 'Asli Healthy Juice India Limited'. **(CBSE 2015)**

Ans (i) The enterprise growth strategy being discussed is 'Mergers and Acquisitions'. Mergers and Acquisitions are a form of external growth strategy that ensures the accelerated growth of a business and also helps a business to expand.

The example given above is specifically of 'Merger'. A merger is a combination of two companies into one larger company. So, in this case, Healthy Juice India Limited and Asli Juice Limited merge to form Asli Healthy Juice India Limited. Also, since a new company is formed, therefore this type of merger is referred to as 'amalgamation'.

(ii) The company is opting for direct channel or zero channel of distribution.

10 'Sultan Trucks Limited' are the manufacturers of commercial trucks for the last 20 years. The company had been doing good business, but recently due to irregular supply of parts by its suppliers, the company could not make timely delivery of trucks to the parties, who had booked their trucks.

The customers cancelled their bookings and there were very few new bookings. The sales of the company started declining that resulted into losses. The management of the company analysed the problem and decided to takeover those two firms because of whom the problem arose, one of them was supplying tyres for its trucks and another axles to the company.

The company also extended credit facilities to the customers and started booking the trucks without charging any booking amount.

It also decided to employ 100 unemployed youth, with 50% reservation for females to take up the cleaning operations, using the imported machines, inside the factories as well as the surrounding areas.

Identify and state the concepts of 'enterprise marketing and growth strategies' discussed in the above paragraph. **(CBSE 2015 Modified)**

Ans The 'enterprise growth strategies' discussed in the question is 'vertical merger'. Vertical merger is between two or more companies producing different goods or services for one specific finished good. So, here an automobile company has taken over the companies producing tyres and axles. This will help the automobile company to cut down on its expenses and also ensure uninterrupted supply of parts.

The marketing strategy discussed in the question relates to the promotion-mix used by the company to increase its sales.

By offering sales promotion incentives to the customers in the form of credit facilities and zero booking amount, the company aims to increase its sales.

11 Beta Ltd. is a steel manufacturing company having its headquarters at Mumbai. It is the tenth largest steel manufacturing company of the world. Gama Ltd. are also steel manufactures with their headquarters in Rangoon, the capital of Myanmar.

For a long poriod the company (Gama Ltd.) had been facing workers unrest and it decided to sell its business to an international bidder. The highest bid for this was made by Beta Ltd. for ₹ 10 lakh crore.

Afterwards Beta Ltd. realised that the assets of Gama Ltd. were overvalued and liabilities were under-assessed and hence the price paid by them was higher. The employees of the two entities have different corporate cultures and styles of leadership which led to the problem of co-ordination. Ultimately Beta Ltd. had to close its business.

(i) Identify the growth strategy adopted by Beta Ltd.

(ii) Quoting lines from the above paragraph, explain any two reasons for the failure of Beta Ltd. after it took over the business of Gama Ltd. **(CBSE 2019)**

Ans (i) The growth strategy adopted by Beta Ltd. is acquisition. A corporate action in which a company buys most of the target company's ownership stakes in order to assume control of the target firm is termed an acquisition.

(ii) Two reasons for the failure of Beta Ltd. after it look over the business of Gama Ltd. are as follows

(a) Unrealistic price paid for the target company. The following lines are indicative of this reason

"Afterwards Beta Ltd. realised .... was higher".

(b) Difficulties in cultural integration. The following lines are indicative of this reason

"The employees of the two .... problem of co-ordination".

12 Elaborate on any three types of mergers. **(CBSE SQP Term II)**

Ans Refer to topic 'types of mergers' on page 131.

13 What is synergy? In what forms can it take place? **(CBSE TBQ)**

Ans Synergy implies a condition wherein $2 + 2 = 5$, i.e. the combined value of the resulting firm exceeds the individual value of the merging firms. So, $V(xy) > V(x) + V(y)$.

Synergy is the most common reason, why companies opt for mergers and acquisitions.

Synergy can take the following forms

(i) **Operating Synergy** These accrue in the form of cost savings through economies of scale or because of increased turnover leading to increased profits.

(ii) **Financial Synergy** This is the direct result of financial factors such as lower taxes, higher debt capacity or better use of idle resources.

14 Apart from synergy, explain any three reasons, why companies opt for mergers and acquisitions?

Ans Apart from synergy, the four reasons why companies opt for mergers and acquisitions are as follows (Any three)

(i) **Acquiring New Technology** Many a times, companies merge or buy another company to upgrade its technology and ensure a competitive edge in the market.

(ii) **Acquiring a Competency** Companies also opt for mergers and acquisitions to acquire a competency or capability that they do not have and which the other firm does.

(iii) **Access to Funds** If a company is faced with shortage of funds and it also does not have proper access to raise funds from capital market, then it may decide to merge with another company which has surplus funds.

(iv) **Tax Benefits** By merging with a loss-making entity, a company with high tax liability can set-off accumulated losses of the merging company from its profits, thereby reducing their tax liability.

Long Answer Type Questions (5 Marks)

1 What is a franchise agreement? Explain the main ingredients of a franchise agreement.

Ans Franchise agreement is the legal document that binds the franchisor and franchisee. This document explains what the franchisor expects from the franchisee in running the business. Main ingredients of a franchise agreement are

(i) **Contract Explanation** It outlines the type of relationship between the franchisee and franchisor.

(ii) **Operations Manual** It is the section of the agreement that details the guidelines that the franchisee must legally follow while operating a business.

(iii) **Proprietary Statements** It outlines how franchise name is to be used and also the marketing and advertising procedures to be followed by the franchisee.

(iv) **Ongoing Site Maintenance** It states the types and time frames regarding various maintenance items and upgrades that must be made to the franchisee's location.

2 Explain the different types of franchising. **(CBSE 2019, TBQ)**

Ans The different types of franchising available are as follows

(i) **Product Franchise Business Opportunity** Manufacturers use this method of franchising to govern, how a retailer distributes their products. The manufacturer grants a store owner the authority to distribute goods manufactured by him, under his name and trademark.

The store owner is either required to pay a fee or purchase a minimum inventory of stock in return for these rights. e.g. tyre stores.

(ii) **Manufacturing Franchise Opportunity** Under this type of franchise arrangement, the franchisee is granted the right to manufacture a product and sell it to the public, using the franchisor's name and trademark. This type of franchise is common in the food and beverage industry.

(iii) **Business Franchise Opportunity Ventures** This type of franchise arrangement provides that the franchisee purchases and distributes the products of only the franchisor's company. The franchisor in return, provides a ready clientele to the franchisee. The franchisee is required to pay a fee or any other form of compensation, as stipulated in the franchise agreement. This form is prevalent in specialised goods industry catering to a selected few.

(iv) **Business Format Franchise Opportunity** This is the most popular form of franchising. In this form, the franchisor provides the franchisee a proven method of operating a business under his name and trademark. He also provides him with managerial assistance to start-up the business. The franchisee is required to pay franchise fees and may also be called upon to purchase supplies from the franchisor.

3 Explain any four advantages of franchising to a franchisee. **(CBSE 2019)**

Ans Following are the advantages enjoyed by a franchisee

(i) **Product Acceptance** The franchisee usually enters into a business that has an accepted name, product or service. He does not have to spend resources to establish the credibility of the business and create a market for his product. The credibility already exists based on the years the franchise has existed.

(ii) **Management Expertise** The franchisor provides managerial assistance related to all aspects of operating the franchise, to the franchisee. For this purpose, training programmes are conducted which includes classes in accounting, personnel management, marketing and production.

(iii) **Capital Requirements** Franchise offers an opportunity to start a new venture with up-front support from franchisor, which saves considerable time and capital of the franchisee. In some cases, the franchisor also finances the initial investment to start the franchise operation. Savings in start-ups are also reflected in the pooling of money by individual franchisees for advertising and sales promotion.

This allows advertising on both local as well as national level to enhance the image and credibility of the business, something that would be impossible for a single operation.

(iv) **Knowledge of the Market** Franchisors are well aware of the existing market conditions. With their experience and knowledge, they can provide advice and assistance to the franchisees for carving out a market for themselves.

Also, franchisors constantly evaluate the market conditions and determine the most effective strategies to communicate to the franchisees.

4 Explain the advantages of franchising, both for the franchisor and franchisee. **(CBSE TBQ)**

Ans The advantages of franchising are as follows

(i) **For the Franchisee** Refer to Q.No. 3 of long answer type questions (5 Marks).

(ii) **For the Franchisor** Refer to text on page 129.

5 Being a foodie himself, Rahul decided to venture into the food sector and started an outlet, taking the franchise of 'Amrit Pav Corner', market leaders in this segment. He had to convince his parents regarding his choice and he did so by quoting the importance of franchise. List six benefits which he would have shared with his parents. He also decides to distribute any leftover food to roadside dwellers.

Ans Refer to text on page 128 and 129.

6 Kamal started a gym named as 'Strong Muscles Gym'. He installed large number of machines and equipments of different types and appointed trained trainers to help the customers in the use of machines.

Initially he kept a low fee per hour so that the boys and girls belonging to poor families may also avail the facilities of the gym.

Very soon his gym became popular and he started operating in three shifts. For this, he appointed additional trainers. He also installed extra machines so that more customers could be enrolled. In two years, he started earning good profits.

He took a nearby building on rent and started a 'Recreation and Health Club' for the senior citizens of the locality on very nominal charges.

He also encouraged young boys and girls to participate in the cleanliness drive started by the Prime Minister.

They agreed and started giving one hour daily for the cleanliness of the nearby areas, before the opening of the 'Strong Muscles Gym' and the 'Recreation and Health Club'.

Identify and explain the type of business expansion that took place under the entrepreneurship of Kamal.

(CBSE 2017 Modified)

Ans The business expansion that took place under the entrepreneurship of Kamal is 'internal expansion'. It is a slow and time consuming process which is a result of a gradual increase in the activities of the enterprise.

Internal expansion is generally financed through long-term sources of finance and also through undistributed profits and reserves.

Internal expansion results in increase in the business activities of the firm and also broadens the capital structure of the firm.
A firm expands internally by

(i) Expanding its present production capacity by increasing the number of machines.
(ii) Replacing old machines with advanced technological machines.
(iii) Entering new areas of production and marketing.
(iv) Increasing the output of the enterprise.

7 Rahul, who is a diploma holder in computers, decides to take franchise of NIIT for his backward town of Katni.

Which form of franchise will he take? Give any four advantages of franchising that will accrue to Rahul.

Ans The form of franchise that Rahul will have to take is 'Business format franchise opportunity'. Under this model, the franchisor provides the franchisee a proven method of operating a business using its name and trademark. This model is operative in the education sector.

For advantages of franchising that will accrue to Rahul, refer to Q. No. 3 of long answer type questions (5 Marks).

8 Explain in detail the types of mergers.

(CBSE TBQ)

Or In the following cases, identify the types of merger.

(i) A merger between firms that are involved in totally unrelated business activities.
(ii) A merger occurring between companies in the same industry.
(iii) It takes place between two companies that deal in the same products but in separate markets.
(iv) It takes place between two business organisations that deal in products that are related to each other and operate in the same market.
(v) It is between two companies producing different goods or services for one specific finished product. **(CBSE TBQ)**

Ans (i) Conglomerate merger.
(ii) Horizontal merger.
(iii) Market extension merger.
(iv) Product extension merger.
(v) Vertical merger.

For detailed explanation of all these mergers refer to text on page 131.

9 Read the following article from a Business Newspaper and answer

"Fone India Ltd. is the second largest mobile network operator in India by subscriber base, after Virel. Huber Evel Ltd. (HEL) was another leading mobile operator in India. In the year 2007, Fone India Ltd., acquired a 52 % stake in HEL.

Fone India's main motive in going in for the deal was its strategy of expanding into emerging and high growth markets which will lead to improved profitability in the business."

(i) Quoting the lines from the passage identify and explain reasons for taking up a stake by Fone India Ltd.,
(ii) Also explain any three reasons apart from the one identified in part (i).

(CBSE SQP Term II)

Ans (i) (a) **Entry into New Markets** A company can enter the market avoiding too much competition.

Line "Deal was its strategy of expanding into emerging and high growth markets".

(b) **Improved Profitability** The acquisition will lead to increased profits for the firm.

Line "Lead to improved profitability in the business."

(ii) Three reasons other than the one identified in part (i) are as follows

(a) **Synergy** Synergy between the participating firms determines the increase in value of the combined entity.

(b) **Acquiring New Technology** By buying another company with unique technology, the buying company can maintain or develop a competitive edge.

(c) **Acquiring a Competency** Companies also opt for mergers and acquisitions to acquire a competency or capability that they do not have and which the other firm does.

10 Explain briefly the steps involved in the process of mergers and acquisitions.

Ans The steps involved in the process of mergers and acquisitions are as follows

***Step* 1 Analysis of Client's Requirements** First and foremost, the client's requirements for M&As are analysed.

***Step* 2 Generating Ideas** Ideas are generated to meet the requirements of the client.

***Step* 3 Valuing Companies** A monetary value is put on each company reviewed, so that purchase price could be negotiated.

***Step* 4 Identifying Potential Partners** The companies within budget are identified, so that future plan of action can be initiated.

***Step* 5 Drawing up Documentation** Letter of intent, confidentiality agreements, etc are drawn up.

***Step* 6 Due Diligence** The process of due diligence is carried out, so that the buyer can have a better understanding of the target company's binding agreements as well as overall legal related exposure.

***Step* 7 Supporting Management** The next step is to ensure the support of management of both the companies.

***Step* 8 Conducting Negotiations** The concerned parties negotiate with each other, so that a favourable deal is struck between them.

11 One of the steps of the process of mergers and acquisitions is 'Due diligence'. What is meant by it and what purpose does it serve?

Ans 'Due diligence' means a comprehensive appraisal of a business undertaken by a prospective buyer with a view to establish its assets and liabilities and evaluate its commercial potential. Generally, accounting and law firms are hired to conduct due diligence.

Lawyers review contracts, agreements, leases, pending litigation and all other outstanding or potential liability obligations, so that the buyer can have a better understanding of the target company's binding agreements, as well as, overall legal related exposure.

The purpose of 'due diligence' are

(i) It helps the buyer to have a correct and reliable assessment of the business to be purchased.

(ii) Due diligence serves to confirm all material facts in regards to a sale.

12 Explain any four reasons for failure of mergers and acquisitions. **(CBSE 2020)**

Ans Reasons for failure of mergers and acquisitions are as follows

(i) **Overstated Synergies** Mergers and acquisitions are tools for creating synergies through increased revenues, reduced costs and reduction in networking capital. Overestimation of these synergies can lead to failure of mergers.

(ii) **Poor Business Fit** Mergers and acquisitions also fail when the products or services of the merging entities do not naturally fit into the acquirer's overall plan. This delays efficient and effective integration and causes failure.

(iii) **Inadequate Due Diligence** Due diligence helps in detecting financial and business risks that the acquirer inherits from the target company. Inaccurate estimation of related risk can result in the failure of the merger.

(iv) **Boardroom Split** Specific personality clashes between executives in the two companies can prove to be a major problem causing slowing down or preventing integration of entities and ultimately leading to an unsuccessful merger.

13 Mohan Steel Limited merged with Surya Iron Limited to form Surya Mohan Limited. But only after 2 years, Surya Mohan Limited company failed. Is this an exceptional case? What according to you can be the reason for this failure?

Ans No, it is not an exceptional case. Many a times, mergers and acquisitions fail due to many reasons. According to me, the reasons for the failure of the above merger can be

(i) Unrealistic price paid for target company.
(ii) Difficulties in cultural integration.
(iii) Overstated synergies.
(iv) Integration difficulties.
(v) Inadequate due diligence.
(vi) High leverage. (vii) Boardroom split.
(viii) Regulatory issues.
(ix) Human resource issues.

14 Merger and Acquisition (M&A) have become a foremost strategic alliance for business, product and geographic tactics in global market. Using meta-literature review, we conduct a synthesis analysis on M&A to assess motives, methods, financing sources, announcement effects, cross-border competitions, success-failure, valuation issues and business strategies. We review 155 recent and relevant papers preferably published during 2015-2020 in 58 leading business journals of ISI-WOS through bibliometric study coupled with content analysis.

We show influential aspects of journals, authors, articles, topics, thematic areas, findings, contributions, research gaps, suggestions and current landscape of M&A. We recommend that firms having constraints might consolidate energies by resorting to productive M&A. Finally, we identify future research questions to extend the research avenues.

Overall, this academic novelty significantly contributes to enhancing our knowledge in dynamic managerial capabilities, outlines further study agenda and eventually provides business strategy and investment implications in global context.

Source *Journal of Economics and Business Volume 116, July-August 2021,106004.*

(i) Which concept is highlighted in the above paragraph?
(ii) Explain any five reasons for it.

Or 'Mergers and Acquisitions' are inspired by a desire to diversify or achieve higher growth rate due to varied reasons. Explain any five such reasons of mergers and acquisitions. **(CBSE 2023)**

Ans (i) Concept discussed in the given paragraph is 'Growth through mergers and acquisitions'.
(ii) Refer to topic 'Reasons for mergers and acquisitions' on page 132 and 133.

15 From the last few decades, maximum studies focused to understand the importance of going into the deal of Mergers & Acquisitions (M&A). The current study examined the motivation to recognise either the assumed benefits of the deal of Mergers and Acquisitions have posted increase or not.

The current study calculated whether the deal is beneficial or harmful for the organisations who want to enter into the deal of M&A. The study scrutinises the issues by using theperspective of history, waves, motives and methods to determine merger and acquisition value.

The study focuses on the current literature available on M&A from the recent past to portray unlike the methods used to gauge performance of M&A.

Although field of M&A research is far too broad and more complex to be covered in a review paper, therefore, the study attempts to start covering some historical and background issues such as history, waves in M&A, methods of measuring deals and M&A motives.

Source *https://www.researchgate.net/publication/312104015_Mergers_and_Acquisitions_A_Conceptual_ Review.*

(i) Which concept is highlighted in the above paragraph?
(ii) Explain various reasons for its failure.

Ans (i) The concept highlighted in the paragraph is mergers and acquisitions.
(ii) For reasons for failure of mergers and acquisitions, refer to text on page 134.

CASE STUDIES

Case 1

Goli Vada Pav

Launched in 2004, Goli Vada Pav repackaged 'Vada Pav', a humble street-food popular in Mumbai, into a branded fast food concept. It follows franchise business model and today is uniquely positioned in Indian Quick Service Restaurant (QSR) segment. Read on to discover more about the brand's success and growth journey.

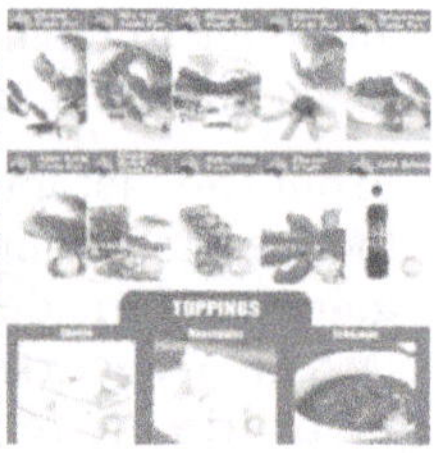

Origin and Concept

Goli Vada Pav, a quick serve food concept with authentic Indian touch, originated in Mumbai in 2004. The brand's founders, Venkatesh Iyer and Shiv Menon, realised the huge scope of business in tapping the adult and lower income customers by selling widely popular local street food 'Vada Pav' to them, in an organised way. Thus, the idea of Indian finger food Goli Vada Pav Private Limited was born that retailed the humble mouth watering spicy ethnic delicacy, which was pocket friendly as well as prepared and served in hygienic conditions. Indian QSR market is flooded with brands like McDonald's, Subway and Quiznos but the success of brand 'Goli Vada Pav No. 1 reaffirms the fact that a strong home grown concept cannot only thrive but also compete with international brands.

What Makes Concept So Special?

Vada Pav is basically a spicy vegetable patty in bun sold by street food vendors. The brand Goli Vada Pav No. 1, has pioneered the concept of selling Vada Pav through retail outlet. The brand's stores offer quality and hygienic fast food which is quite affordable. It has successfully branded the traditional street food. It sells hygienically prepared food items made in fully automated 'HACCP' certified handsfree plant with an authentic touch.

'Goli Vada Pav' is a typical finger food made of spices, vegetables and mashed potatoes packed in 'Vada Pav'. Today, it is known to be an established, reputed and popular Indian fast food brand that offers a clean and ethnic finger food for those who have less money and time.

Popular Products

The brand offers wide assortment of items to cater to varied taste buds and preferences of customers. Its outlets serve different finger dishes like sweet chutney, dry chutney and fried green chilly. Its famous dishes include Goli Schezwan Vada Pav, Goli Cheese Vada Pav, Goli Sabudana Vada, Goli Mix Veg Vada Pav, Goli Tikki Vada Pav, Goli Palak Makkai Tikki, Goli Cheese Ungli, and Goli Masala Vada Pav.

As the name suggests vada is a common thing, which is mixed with other things for different taste. The company's food offerings not only entice the taste buds of consumers, but they are also touted to be nutritional.

Success Journey Till Now

The brand has opted for franchise business models to grab a quick bite into the Indian quick serve business. Today, Goli Vada Pav has extensive presence across 40 Indian cities in 6 states. Goli Vada Pav No. 1 outlets are spread across the length and breadth of the country.

Its stores can be found in cities like Aurangabad, Ahmednagar, Bengaluru, Belgaum, Chandrapur, Chennai, Coimbatore, Dhulia, Hubli, Hyderabad, Jalgaon, Kolhapur, Mumbai, Pune and many more. It operates about 150 stores, of which over 140 are *via* franchise route.

Lucrative Business Opportunity

The brand's concept offers lucrative business opportunity for aspiring franchisees. The factors that make this concept a money spinner are

Vada Pavs are popular, all-time favourite and convenient fast food. The product is hygienic and less oil fried snack having universal appeal. It's a standard tasty food that can be consumed 365 days of the year. The store format and operations are relatively less cumbersome.

The product is easy to make and it being a finger food, one doesn't require plates, spoons, tables and chairs to eat it.

It is a mobile food that can be consumed while walking, talking, standing or travelling, and is therefore, preferred by people on the move. Therefore, the franchisee store owner would not require huge investments like infrastructure, kitchen and restaurant, etc., which substantially cut the input costs.

Franchising Facts

The company is looking to strengthen its pan Indian franchise network. It is targeting especially tier I, tier II, tier III cities and small towns for expansion and opening more number of stores. It would like to partnership with potential franchise partners who can invest ₹ 10-20 lakh.

For opening a Goli Vada Pav No. 1 store, area requirement is about 350 sq ft. The preferred location for opening an outlet is a high street traffic areas like market, colleges, business areas and residential catchments.

Franchisee Training and Support

The franchisee will get the 8 years old well established brand name with standard operating procedures in all aspects of business. The company will provide initial and refresher training for business owners and store staff and end-to-end logistics support and regular replenishment of stocks and operational support to monitor and drive business.

Franchising Adds Flavour to Further Growth

The brand's offerings are economical and for the masses, therefore it has access to a large customer base. It is committed to take Vada Pav from the Mumbai streets to a brand which will be known all over the world.

Growing popularity of the concept has encouraged Goli Vada Pav No. 1 to continue with its expansion plans. The brand encourages entrepreneurship and offers lucrative franchise opportunities across India. The company plans to have 500 outlets by the end of the year 2015.

1 Name some international brands operating in India as Quick Service Restaurants (QSRs).

Ans McDonald's, Subway, Quiznos are some international brands operating as QSRs in India.

2 What according to you, is the reason for the tremendous success of 'Goli Vada Pav'?

Ans The reasons attributable to the success of 'Goli Vada Pav' is that, it is mouth watering, pocket friendly and also prepared and served in hygienic conditions.

3 What makes this concept lucrative for the investors?

Ans This concept is lucrative for the investors because the product is hygienic and less oil fried snack having universal appeal. The store format and operations are relatively less cumbersome.

The product is easy to make and being a finger food, one does not require plates, spoons, tables or chairs to eat it. Therefore, infrastructure costs will also be scaled down.

4 In the chapter, we have discussed the advantages of franchising, as enjoyed by the franchisee. Quote lines from the passage indicating the advantages as enjoyed by the franchisees of Goli Vada Pav.

Ans (i) **Product Acceptance** The lines which convey that the product is widely acceptable are "Vada Pavs are popular, all-time favourite and convenient fast food. The product is hygienic and less oil fried snack having universal appeal".

(ii) **Management Expertise** The lines which convey that assistance is provided by the franchisor for smooth management is "the company will provide initial and refresher training for business owners and store staff and end-to-end logistics support and regular replenishment of stocks and operational support to monitor and drive business".

Case 2

It's Natural. It's Yummy: It's Natural Ice-cream

It's natural. It's yummy. Those who have tasted it, swear by it. The unique feature of the ice-creams manufactured by Natural Ice-cream is that, they contain no artificial flavours, preservatives or stabilisers, only fresh fruit pulp or dry fruits.

Started as a 300 sq ft ice-cream parlour at Juhu, a North-West Mumbai suburb, in 1984, the brand is a runaway success. It now has 89 franchise outlets across West and South India: 47 in Mumbai, 29 in the neighbouring urban clusters of Navi Mumbai, Thane and Pune and the rest scattered across selected cities of Maharashtra and neighbouring states.

Ten more will be opened in the current financial year. Natural's revenues have risen from ₹ 14 lakh in 1986 to ₹ 40 crore in 2010-11. The franchises may be many, but the manufacturing hub is just one, located in another Mumbai suburb, Kandivali. Every morning, a fleet of trucks rolls out from the factory carrying the ice-cream to all the Natural outlets, thus ensuring quality is not compromised.

The store at Juhu has been renovated and expanded repeatedly and is now more than 3 times its original size. 'It is a landmark in the area', says a beaming Kamath. It all began after Kamath broke away from his elder brother's ice-cream business, Gokul Ice-cream, in 1983. 'I took my share of the inheritance and set-up Natural', says Kamath.

From the start, he was at enormous pains to keep to quality– a trait he maintains to this day. Seasonal fruits are bought in bulk daily from the market, with only the best quality ones being chosen. The extracted pulp is heated, to get rid of unwanted bacteria and then stored in aluminium sealed packages.

Kamath, who from the start involved himself in every aspect of manufacture and distribution, says, he has experimented with 60 different kinds of fruit. (In case of non-seasonal fruits, however, Kamath has no choice but to buy pulp and get it machine processed).

The means, Natural uses to enforce quality control, however, impose their own limits on the brand's expansion. All the temperature control in the world cannot preserve the taste and more importantly, the freshness of ice-cream beyond a specified number of hours, during which Natural's trucks can cover only a finite distance. This explains why Natural's outlets are largely in Western India and it has no outlet yet in the national capital, despite the obvious business opportunity Delhi presents. 'The National Capital Region has remained an elusive destination', admits Pai.

But the scenario may soon change. Though, Natural officials are reluctant to share details of their financial relationship with the franchises, they do reveal that plans are a foot for a major change in operational strategy.

The man responsible is Kamath's son, Srinivas, who was inducted into the business in 2009. Srinivas, 27, believes that since it is dealing in perishable products such as ice-cream, Natural has to set-up manufacturing units in other locations, if it wants to keep expanding.

Srinivas wants to set-up 'mega shops' in far away cities and towns, which will both manufacture natural ice-creams and sell it. 'Raw materials will be supplied from here, as well as trained workers who will make the ice-cream at the mega shops', says Srinivas.

'Frozen, non-perishable fruit pulp and processed milk can be stored for a maximum of 4 days without harm. That is enough time to transport them to wherever the mega shops are opened.

Again, in a change of strategy, Natural intends to open only one shop in these far away areas. 'Instead of investing in multiple franchises, Natural will have just one mega shop per town', Srinivas adds.

Natural will also impose its conditions: the outlet must have atleast 2000 sq ft floor space and must be located in a central area. The first such outlet is set to open shortly in Chandigarh, depending on its success, more such shops will follow.

Natural is in no hurry to get to Delhi, but it has big plans when it does. 'Delhi is very big market. To meet its demand, we'll have to double our existing capacity', says Pai. Natural's ambitions go even further.

'Our founder wants Delhi to be the launch pad for Natural's global ventures, especially in West Asia', he adds.

1 Why has quality control became a deterrent to Natural's expansion plans?

Ans Quality control has become a deterrent for Natural's expansion plans because the freshness of the ice-cream cannot be maintained beyond a specified number of hours, during which natural's trucks can cover only a finite distance.

2 How do they plan to overcome the above deterrent?

Ans To overcome the above problem, they should plan to set-up their manufacturing units in other locations.

3 What are their future plans?

Ans Their future plans are that they want to expand nationally as well as internationally.

4 'Instead of investing in multiple franchises, Natural will have just one mega shop per town,' says Srinivas. What do you understand by 'multiple franchises'?

Ans 'Multiple franchises' means more than one outlet of the franchisor in a particular geographical area.

Case 3

Indian Franchise Boom

For small and first time entrepreneurs in India, taking up franchise of a well-established brand is a good proposition. Buying a franchise of an established brand is a good alternative to starting on a new idea from scratch or could offer a faster way to take an existing business to the next level.

To list a few

Gift a flower...and a cake...and a candle...

Ferns N Petals, founded by Vikas Gutgutia, a Delhi based company and the leading brand of floral boutiques in India is marked as a one-stop-shop for all flower requirements, whether it is for daily or occasional gifting, for floral decoration in weddings, corporate events or for an individual parties. Floral boutiques are aesthetically designed and its air-conditioned outlets reflect style and high taste to cater to elite customers.

FNP's floral boutique offers a vast variety of fresh cut flowers and unique flower arrangements, artificial and dry flower and an exclusive range of object d'art such as scented candles, candle stands, imported Italian glass vases, wooden gift accessories with intricate carving, photo-frames, miniature exportable gift items, fragrance items based on aromatherapy and potpourris, etc.

These boutiques offer a vast variety of exquisite flower arrangements and displays to match the distinct needs and tastes of the customers. Growth of FNP, too, is attributable to franchising.

Food Courts Work Well with Franchising Models

Haldiram Franchise—A Profitable Business Opportunity

The food and beverage industry has not experienced any crunch, mainly because the people are spending money in a big way on eating out, together with entertainment. The Indian economy is growing rapidly, automatically creating more room for the growth of this industry.

The Haldiram Marketing franchise is associated with sweets and namkeens for the discerning consumers for the past six decades in India and across the world. The food and beverage franchise made a modest start in the beginning of 1941 in Bikaner in the state of Rajasthan in India. According to the sweet and savoury products franchise, sweet and salt are opposite to each other, but they perform wonders on the taste buds.

The Haldiram Marketing franchise uses both sweet and salt in its foods, with mithais (sweets) and namkeens (salty snacks). This unique concept of the food and beverage franchise has made it to be a leader in the sweet industry and it has also maintained this position for many years.

The sweet and savoury products franchise has been synonymous with sweets, similar as Cadbury is to chocolates.

The Haldiram Marketing franchise can by default be termed as taste of tradition of India. The sweet and savoury products franchise has certain prospective markets, such as those in China, Russia, the United Kingdom, Madagascar and Ukraine, for promoting and marketing the brand of Haldirams.

Among various food joints from domestic sector, Haldiram franchise has carved a separate niche for themselves. Haldiram made a humble beginning, when it commenced its business in Bikaner, in the State of Rajasthan. Since then, the food and beverage franchise has witnessed phenomenal growth and is currently a renowned manufacturer of sweets across the globe. The sweet and savoury products franchise has a chain of restaurants and is also anticipated to start amusement parks.

The Haldiram franchise is the flag bearer of the traditional Indian sweet. This food and beverage franchise was started by Shri Ganga Bisanji Agarwal alias Haldiram Agarwal.

He is the grandfather of Shri Shivkisan Agarwal, who was responsible for the fame and success of the sweet and savoury products franchise. Moreover, he made the brand of Haldirams a household name in the Indian subcontinent.

Hotel Saravana Bhavan

Hotel Saravana Bhavan is the largest vegetarian restaurant chain in the world, founded in 1981 by Rajagopal, offers South Indian cuisine. They have more than 20 outlets in Chennai, 33 in India and 47 around the world (including USA, Canada, United Kingdom, France, Germany, Singapore, Malaysia and the Middle East.

There are plans to open 5 star vegetarian hotels. This chain is also an example of successful model of franchising.

Jumboking

Jumboking began its journey to brand the Vada Pav on 23rd August, 2001. Jumboking in its 12th year of operations is a pioneer in the food retail company in India in the Quick Service Restaurants (QSRs) segment.

Inspired by western models and applying it to Indian food, Jumboking believes that the common man has the constitutional right to get hygienic food at an affordable price!

Jumboking has been founded by Dheeraj Gupta. Jumboking has a team of people spanning the functional areas of operations, business development, franchisee relations and marketing.

They have 51 operational outlets across India. It plans to put up a total of 500 stores by December 2018. Says Dheeraj Gupta, Founder and MD Jumboking, 'We feel the Indian market can support more than 1000 Jumboking stores'.

The company has appointed City Master Franchisees/single unit franchisees in Aurangabad, Mumbai, Bengaluru, Delhi, Indore, Raipur, Amravati, Goa and Mysore.

Examples of other franchises which are taking India and the world by storm include Chi Kitchen and Bar (cuisine), Mahindra First Choice Wheels (used cars), Van Heusen (clothing), EduKart.com (education), Koutons Retail (fashion), The Yellow Chilli (restaurant chain) and VLCC (beauty and wellness).

1. Who are the target customers of 'Ferns N Petals'?

Ans The target customers of 'Ferns N Petals' are the elite class.

2. Which factor attributes to the success of Ferns N Petals?

Ans Ferns N Petals owe its success to franchising.

3. Who is responsible for the fame and success of Haldiram?

Ans Shri Shivkisan Agarwal is responsible for the fame and success of Haldiram.

4. Which type of franchise does Haldiram offer?

Ans Haldiram offers product based franchise.

5. Which is the largest vegetarian restaurant chain in the world?

Ans Hotel Saravana Bhavan is the largest vegetarian restaurant chain in the world offering South Indian cuisine.

6. What does 'Jumboking' believe in?

Ans 'Jumboking' believes that the common man has the constitutional right to get hygienic food at an affordable price.

7. Which is the common factor linking the above four examples?

Ans The common factor is that all the four ventures achieved phenomenal success through franchising.

Case 4

Kraft's Takeover of Cadbury-By Scott Moeller

The Story In 2009, the US food company Kraft Foods launched a hostile bid for Cadbury, the UK-listed chocolate maker. It became clear almost exactly two years later in August 2011, Cadbury was the final acquisition necessary to allow Kraft to be restructured and indeed split into two companies by the end of 2012: a grocery business worth approximately, $16bn and a $32bn; global snacks business.

Kraft needed Cadbury to provide scale for the snacks business, especially in emerging markets such as India.

The challenge for Kraft was how to buy Cadbury when it was not for sale.

The History

Kraft itself was the product of acquisitions that started in 1916 with the purchase of a Canadian cheese company. By the time of the offer for Cadbury, it was the world's second largest food conglomerate, with seven brands that each generated annual revenues of more than $1bn.

Cadbury, founded by John Cadbury in 1824 in Birmingham, England had also grown through mergers and demurrers. It too had recently embarked on a strategy that was just beginning to show results.

Ownership of the company was 49% from the US, despite its UK listing and headquarters. Only 5% of its shares were owned by short-term traders at the time of the Kraft's bid.

The Challenge

Not only was Cadbury not for sale, but it actively resisted the Kraft's takeover.

Sir Roger Carr, the Chairman of Cadbury was experienced in takeover defences and immediately put together a strong defensive advisory team.

Its first act was to brand the 745 pence per share offer 'unattractive', saying that it 'fundamentally undervalued the company'.

The team made clear that even if the company had to succumb to an unwanted takeover, almost any other confectionery company (Nestle, Ferrero and Hershey were all mentioned) would be preferred as the buyer.

In addition, Lord Mandelson, then the UK's business secretary, publicly declared that the government would oppose any buyer who failed to 'respect' the historic confectioner.

The Response

Cadbury's own defence documents stated that shareholders should reject Kraft's offer because the chocolate company would be 'absorbed into Kraft's low growth conglomerate business model-an unappealing prospect that sharply contrasts with the Cadbury strategy of a pure play confectionery company'.

Little did Cadbury's management know that Kraft's plan was to split it into two to eliminate its conglomerate nature and become two more focused businesses, thereby creating more value for its shareholders.

The Result

The Cadbury team determined that a majority of shareholders would sell at a price of roughly 830 pence a share. A deal was struck between the two Chairmen on 18th January, 2010 at 840 pence per share plus a special 10 pence per share dividend. This was approved by 72% of Cadbury shareholders, two weeks later.

The Key Lessons

In any takeover, especially a cross-border deal in which the acquired company is as well known as Cadbury was in the UK, the transaction will be front-page news. In this case, it was the lead business story for at least four months. Fortunately, this deal had no monopoly or competition issues, otherwise those regulators could also have been involved.

But aside from any regulators, most other commentators will largely be distractions. It is important for the acquiring company's management and advisers to stay focused on the deal itself and the real decision-makers the shareholders of the target company.

As this deal demonstrates, these shareholders may not (and often will not) be the long-term traditional owners of the target company stock, but rather very rational hedge funds and other arbitragers (in Cadbury's case, owning 31% of the shares at the end), who are swayed only by the offer price and how quickly the deal can be completed.

Other stakeholders may have legitimate concerns that need to be addressed but this can usually be done after the deal is completed, as Kraft did.

1 Which form of acquisition is discussed above? Quote the lines indicating the form.

Ans Hostile acquisition is being discussed above. The lines from which it can be inferred "Not only was cadbury not for sale, but it actively resisted the Kraft's takeover".

2 What was Kraft's motive behind acquisition of Cadbury?

Ans Kraft's objective was to split itself into two segments as
(i) Grocery business
(ii) Global snacks business

Kraft needed Cadbury to provide scale for snacks business.

CHAPTER ASSESSMENT

Objective Type Questions (1 Mark)

1 A firm may expand externally by
(a) franchising
(b) mergers and acquisitions
(c) Both (a) and (b)
(d) None of these

2 A legal document defining the mutual terms and conditions between a franchisor and a franchisee is called
(a) franchise agreement
(b) charter
(c) deed
(d) All of these

3 Strategy that ensures the accelerated growth of a business and also helps a business to expand externally is called
(a) mergers
(b) acquisitions
(c) Both (a) and (b)
(d) franchising

4 In .... acquisition, whole transaction is carried out through force.

5 Synergy accrues in the form of revenue enhancement and ....

6 External expansion is financed through long-term sources of finance. State true or false.

7 Vending machine routes and distributorship is an example of manufacturing franchise opportunity. State true or false.

Short Answer Type I Questions (2 Marks)

8 Mention two ways in which an organisation can expand externally.

9 Write a short note on franchising.

10 What do you understand by franchisor and franchisee?

11 Mention any two disadvantages of franchising to franchisor.

12 Define mergers and also state its two forms.

Short Answer Type II Questions (3 Marks)

13 Write a short note on internal expansion.

14 Mention the net results of internal and external expansion.

15 "Along with the multiple advantages of growing a business through the franchise mode, certain disadvantages also exist." Comment.

16 Explain horizontal mergers and market extension mergers.

Long Answer Type Questions (5 Marks)

17 Explain different types of acquisitions.

18 Explain in detail about 'Synergy'.

19 Explain different steps involved in the process of mergers and acquisitions.

For explanations scan the given QR Code

CHAPTER 05

Business Arithmetic

In this Chapter...

- Unit of sale
- Break-even analysis
- Working capital
- Inventory control
- EOQ
- Return on Investment (RoI)
- Return on Equity (RoE)
- EBITDA

Every business person needs some quick and easy way of checking the progress of the business or to plan corrective action.

He can do so by calculating unit of sale, unit price and unit cost which will provide the gross profit as a result.

Unit of Sale

This can be defined as the measure of unit in which the products are sold. Unit of sale is a management tool that is required to understand the economics of the business in an easy and standardised way and for tracking progress over a number of years and taking corrective actions, when necessary.

e.g. unit of sale for apples will be kilograms.

To understand this further, a list of businesses with their respective unit of sale is given below

Business	Item being Sold/Serviced	Unit of Sale
Grocer	Rice	Kilogram
Dairy	Milk	Litre
Grocer	Oil	Litre
Garment Shop	T-shirt	Piece
Textile Shop	Fabric	Metre
Coaching Class	Tution	Time: Hour

The table hold goods if the business is dealing in one product only. But, for a business dealing in multiple products, say for example, 'Big-Bazaar' where one can buy rice, oil, milk, t-shirts, etc., and suppose a customer buys 2 kg of rice, 5 litres of oil and 2 t-shirts, then in such an instance, the unit of sale for Big Bazaar will be **number of customers** and not individual unit of sale. Similarly, for a restaurant, the unit of sale will be 'diner' and for a beauty parlour, it will again be a 'customer'.

Unit Price

It is the price at which one unit of sale is sold. e.g. if 100 litre of milk is sold for ₹ 5,000, then unit price will be ₹ 50 (5,000 ÷ 100).

For a business dealing in multiple products, unit price is the **average amount** billed per customer. e.g. if the 50 customers paid ₹ 1,75,000 for various items purchased by them from 'Big-Bazaar', then unit price will be ₹ 3,500 (1,75,000 ÷ 50).

Example 1 Following are the details from the sales register of Big Bazaar, Jabalpur on a particular day. What will be the unit of sale and the unit price?

Number of Customers	Per Customer Billed (₹)	Total Billed (₹)
7	1,500	10,500
8	2,000	16,000
12	2,200	26,400
13	2,550	33,150

Number of Customers	Per Customer Billed (₹)	Total Billed (₹)
20	3,000	60,000
10	3,500	35,000
5	4,200	21,000
7	5,000	35,000
18	6,000	1,08,000
Total 100		3,45,050

Sol. Since, the customers purchased multiple items from the retail store, therefore, the unit of sale will be 'customer' and the average purchase made by one customer is the 'unit price' i.e.

$$\text{Unit Price} = \frac{\text{Total Billed Amount}}{\text{Number of Customers}}$$

$$= \frac{3{,}45{,}050}{100} = ₹\ 3450.5$$

Unit Cost

This can be defined as the cost incurred by a company to produce, store and sell one unit of sale of a particular product or service. But, it should be remembered that unit cost refers to the variable cost like raw material, packing material, sales commission, freight, etc.

Variable costs are directly proportional to the level of output. For a business dealing in multiple products, unit cost is the **average cost** of the products.

e.g. if during a day, Big-Bazaar sells various products to 100 customers being the total billed amount as ₹ 2,10,000 and the cost of the goods sold is ₹ 1,70,000, then the unit cost will be ₹ 1,700 (₹ 1,70,000 ÷ 100). Unit cost is also referred to as cost of goods sold.

In some cases, unit cost can be calculated in another way.

e.g. for every item, if the purchase price is 80% of selling price and the selling price is ₹ 2,100 per customer, then in such case, the unit cost would be ₹ 1,680 (80% of ₹ 2,100).

Now, if in the first instance, the selling price is ₹ 2,100 and unit cost comes out to be ₹ 1,700, then **gross profit** will be ₹ 400/per unit of sale (2,100 – 1,700) and the gross profit in second instance will be ₹ 420/per unit of sale (2,100 – 1,680). This will depend on the industry specifics.

Example 2 A stationery store sold in one day, the following items at the prices indicated.

Products	Price per Unit (₹)	Quantity Sold
Student Notebook	40	35
Reynolds Pens	40	40
Erasers	5	5
Scale (12″ plastic)	15	10
Flip Chart	10	5
Sketch Pens (One dozen)	25	3

The shopkeeper also found out, based on the number of bills issued by him, that there were in all 50 customers. If customer is the unit of sale, what is the unit price in this case?

If the cost of each stationery item is 75% of its selling price, calculate the unit cost and the gross margin per unit of sale.

Sol.

Products	Price per Unit (P) (₹)	Quantity Sold (Q)	Billed Amt (P × Q) (₹)
Student Notebook	40	35	1,400
Reynolds Pens	40	40	1,600
Erasers	5	5	25
Scale (12′ plastic)	15	10	150
Flip Chart	10	5	50
Sketch Pens (One dozen)	25	3	75
Total Billed Amount			3,300

$$\text{Unit Price} = \frac{\text{Total Billed Amount}}{\text{Number of Customers}} = \frac{3{,}300}{50} = ₹\ 66$$

Unit Cost = 75% of 66 = ₹ 49.5

Gross Margin Per Unit = Unit Price – Unit Cost
= 66 – 49.5 = ₹ 16.5

Formulae at a Glance

- $\text{Unit Price Per Customer} = \frac{\text{Total Billed Amount}}{\text{Number of Customers}}$
- $\text{Unit Cost Per Product} = \frac{\text{Total Cost of Goods Sold}}{\text{Unit of Sales}}$
- Gross Profit Per Unit = Unit Price – Unit Cost

Break-even Analysis

This analysis refers to a system of determination of that level of activity where total cost equals total selling price. It portrays the relationship between cost of production, volume of production and the sales value.

In other words, break-even point is the level of sales that equals all the expenses required for generating that revenue. It is not more than the expenses (i.e. no profit) nor is it less than the expenses (i.e. no loss).

So, at the break-even level,

Total Revenue = Total Expenses

i.e. (Quantity Sold × Unit Price) = (Quantity Sold × Unit Cost) + Fixed Expenses

or Quantity Sold × (Unit Price − Unit Cost) = Fixed Expenses

or Quantity Sold × Gross Profit Per Unit = Fixed Expenses

The benefit of break-even analysis is same for single product as well as multiple product business.

Sales Mix Break-even Point Calculation

Sales mix is the proportion in which two or more products are sold. For sales mix break-even point calculation, following assumptions are made

- The proportion of sales mix must be pre-determined.
- The sales mix must not change within the relevant time period.
- All cost can be categorised as variable or fixed.
- Sales price per unit, variable cost per unit and total fixed cost are constant.
- All units produced are sold.

The calculation method for the break-even point of sales mix is based on the contribution approach method. Since, sales mix includes multiple products, there arises a problem of dealing with different contribution margin per unit and contribution margin ratios.

This problem is overcome by calculating weighted average contribution margin per unit and contribution margin ratio, which are then used to calculate the break-even point for sales mix. The procedure is explained with the help of the following example

Example 3 Following information is related to sales mix of product A, B and C.

Product	A	B	C
Sales Price Per Unit	₹ 15	₹ 21	₹ 36
Variable Cost Per Unit	₹ 9	₹ 14	₹ 19
Sales Mix Percentage	20%	20%	60%
Total Fixed Cost	₹ 40,000		

Calculate the break-even point in units and in rupees.

Sol. ***Step 1*** Calculate the contribution margin per unit for each product.

Product	A (₹)	B (₹)	C (₹)
Sales Price Per Unit	15	21	36
(−) Variable Cost Per Unit	(9)	(14)	(19)
Contribution Margin Per Unit	6	7	17

Step 2 Calculate the weighted average contribution margin per unit for the sales mix using the following formula

Weighted Average Unit Contribution Margin = Product A CM (Contribution Mix) Per Unit × Product A Sales Mix Percentage + Product B CM Per Unit × Product B Sales Mix Percentage + Product C CM Per Unit × Product C Sales Mix Percentage

Product	A	B	C
Sales Price Per Unit	₹ 15	₹ 21	₹ 36
(−) Variable Cost Per Unit	₹ (9)	₹ (14)	₹ (19)
Contribution Margin Per Unit	₹ 6	₹ 7	₹ 17
(×) Sales Mix Percentage	20%	20%	60%
	₹ 1.2	₹ 1.4	₹ 10.2

∴ Weighted Average CM Per Unit = 1.2 + 1.4 + 10.2 = ₹ 12.80

Step 3 Calculate total units of sales mix required to break-even using the following formula

Break-even Point in Units of Sales Mix = Total Fixed Cost (÷) Weighted Average CM Per Unit

Total Fixed Cost	₹ 40,000
(÷) Weighted Average CM Per Unit	₹ 12.80
Break-even Point in Units of Sales Mix	₹ 3,125

Step 4 Calculate number of units of product A, B and C at break-even point.

Product	A	B	C
Sales Mix Ratio	20%	20%	60%
(×) Total Break-even Units	₹ 3,125	₹ 3,125	₹ 3,125
Product Units at Break-even Point	625	625	1,875

Step 5 Calculate break-even point in rupees as follows

Product	A (₹)	B (₹)	C (₹)
Product Units at Break-even Point	625	625	1,875
(×) Price Per Unit	15	21	36
Product Sales in Rupees	9,375	13,125	67,500

∴ Break-even Point (in Rupees)

= 9,375 + 13,125 + 67,500 = ₹ 90,000

Multi-product Break-even Analysis

This approach finds break-even point for each individual product in a multi-product company.

The calculation procedure is explained with the help of the following example

Example 4 Toy Craft produces toy alligators and toy dolphins. Fixed costs are ₹ 12,90,000 per year. Sales revenue and variable costs per unit are as follows

	Alligators (₹)	Dolphins (₹)
Sales Price	20	25
Variable Costs	8	10

(i) Suppose the company currently sells 1,40,000 alligators per year and 60,000 dolphins per year (Sales mix percentage 14 : 6). Assuming the sales mix stays constant, how many alligators and dolphins must the company sell to break-even?

(ii) Suppose the company currently sells 60,000 alligators per year and 1,40,000 dolphins per year (Sales mix percentage 6: 14).
Assuming the sales mix stays constant, how many alligators and dolphins must the company sell to break-even per year?

(iii) Explain why the total number of toys needed to break-even in (i) is the same and/or different from the number in (ii).

Sol. (i)

Units	Alligators 1,40,000 (₹)	Dolphins 60,000 (₹)	Total 2,00,000 (₹)
Sales Price per Unit	20	25	—
Variable Cost per Unit	8	10	—
Sales (A)	28,00,000	15,00,000	43,00,000
(–) Variable Cost (B)	(11,20,000)	(6,00,000)	(17,20,000)
Contribution Margin (A – B)	16,80,000	9,00,000	25,80,000
(–) Fixed Cost	—	—	(12,90,000)
Net Income	—	—	12,90,000

Weighted Average Contribution Margin

= Total Contribution /Total Units

= 25,80,000/2,00,000 = ₹ 12.90

Break-even Point

= Fixed Cost/Weighted Average Contribution

= 12,90,000/12.90 = 1,00,000 units

Allocating total units to each product based on expected units proportion = 14 : 6

Alligators to be produced for break-even

$$= 1,00,000 \times \frac{14}{20} = 70,000 \text{ units}$$

Dolphins to be produced for break-even

$$= 1,00,000 \times \frac{6}{20} = 30,000 \text{ units}$$

So, toy crafts has to produce 70,000 toy alligators and 30,000 toy dolphins for break-even.

(ii)

Units	Alligators 60,000 (₹)	Dolphins 1,40,000 (₹)	Total 2,00,000 (₹)
Sales Price per Unit	20	25	—
Variable Cost per Unit	8	10	—
Sales (A)	12,00,000	35,00,000	47,00,000
(–) Variable Cost (B)	(4,80,000)	(14,00,000)	(18,80,000)
Contribution Margin (A – B)	7,20,000	21,00,000	28,20,000
(–) Fixed Cost	—	—	(12,90,000)
Net Income	—	—	15,30,000

Weighted Average Contribution Margin

= Total Contribution/Total Units

= 28,20,000/2,00,000 = ₹ 14.10

Break-even Point

= Fixed Cost/Weighted Average Contribution

= 12,90,000/14.10 = 91,489 units

Allocating total units to each product based on expected units proportion = 6 : 14

Alligators to be produced for break-even

$= 91,489 \times \frac{6}{20} = 27,447$ units

Dolphins to be produced for break-even

$= 91,489 \times \frac{14}{20} = 64,042$ units

So, toy crafts has to produce 27,447 toy alligators and 64,042 toy dolphins for break-even.

(iii) The number of toys to break-even in both the examples (i) and (ii) are different because of different weighted average contribution margin.

Revise your Formulae

Quantity × (Unit Price – Unit Cost) = Fixed Expenses

Weighted Average Contribution Margin $= \frac{\text{Total Contribution}}{\text{Total Units}}$

Total Revenue = Total Expenses

(Quantity × Unit Price) = (Quantity × Unit Cost) + Fixed Expenses

Quantity × Gross Margin (or Profit) per Unit = Fixed Expenses

Break-even Point $= \frac{\text{Fixed Expenses}}{\text{Weighted Average Contribution}}$

CHECK POINT 01

1. Define unit of sale.
2. What do you mean by break-even analysis?
3. What is sales mix?
4. State any one assumption of sales mix break-even point analysis.
5. What is meant by 'multi-product break-even analysis?

Working Capital

Money needed to fund the normal day-to-day operations of the business is known as working capital. It refers to that part of total capital, which is required for holding current assets or it may also be defined as excess of current assets over current liabilities.

Working capital indicates the liquidity levels of businesses for managing day-to-day expenses and covers inventory, cash, accounts payable, accounts receivable and short-term debt. It is an indicator of the short-term financial position of an organisation and is also a measure of its overall efficiency.

It can be calculated as

Working Capital = Current Assets – Current Liabilities

1. **Current Assets** These are the assets which are expected to get converted into cash or cash equivalents within a period of one year.

   Examples of current assets in order of liquidity are
   - Cash in hand/Cash at bank
   - Marketable securities
   - Bills receivables
   - Debtors
   - Finished goods inventory
   - Work-in-progress
   - Raw materials
   - Prepaid expenses
2. **Current Liabilities** These refer to those liabilities which are payable within a period of one year.

   Examples of current liabilities are
   - Bills payable
   - Creditors
   - Outstanding expenses
   - Advances received from customers, etc.

Types of Working Capital

There are two types of working capital which are as follows

1. **Gross Working Capital** (GWC) It refers to investment in all the current assets taken together, i.e. Gross Working Capital = Sum Total of all Current Assets

   It is also known as current capital or circulating capital.
2. **Net Working Capital** (NWC) It refers to excess of current assets over current liabilities, i.e. Net Working Capital = Current Assets (CA) – Current Liabilities (CL)

   NWC can either be positive or negative.

   If CA > CL, then NWC is positive and if CA < CL, then NWC is negative.

Need for Working Capital : Operating Cycle

The duration between buying the raw material and receiving cash from the customer is known as operating cycle or Cash Conversion Cycle (CCC). During the time required to convert raw material into end product, various expenses like wages, rent, salary, etc are to be paid. Once the end product is ready, it has to be sold and money to be received from customers.

The Cash Conversion Cycle is the length of time between a firm's purchase of inventory and the receipt of cash from accounts receivables. CCC represents the number of days a firm's cash remains tied up in the operations of the business.

Different products will have different operating cycles. "Longer the operating cycle, requirement of working capital will be more, while shorter the cycle, less working capital is needed."

For instance, the operating cycles of a trading concern and a manufacturing concern are explained below

1. **In a Trading Concern** Since, there is no manufacturing, the operating cycle will be shorter. Here, the operating cycle will include the length of time taken for
   - Procurement of goods, and
   - Realisation of sales revenue

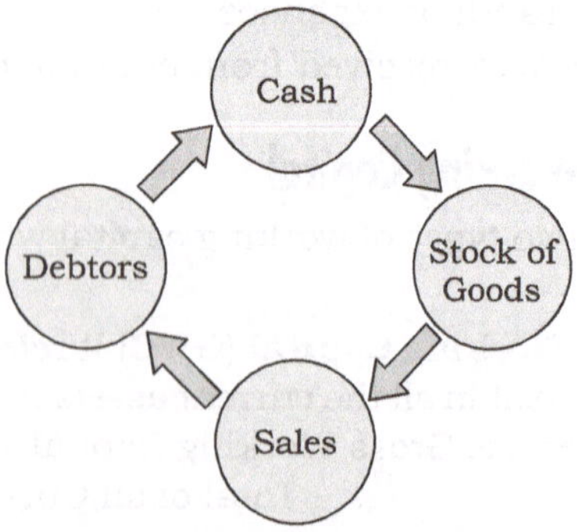

Operating Cycle or Cash Conversion Cycle for Trading

2. **In a Manufacturing Company** It includes manufacturing, thus operating cycle will be longer. Here, operating cycle is the length of time needed to complete the following
   - Conversion of cash into raw materials.
   - Conversion of raw materials into work-in-progress.
   - Conversion of work-in-progress into finished goods.
   - Conversion of finished goods into accounts receivable.
   - Conversion of accounts receivable into cash.

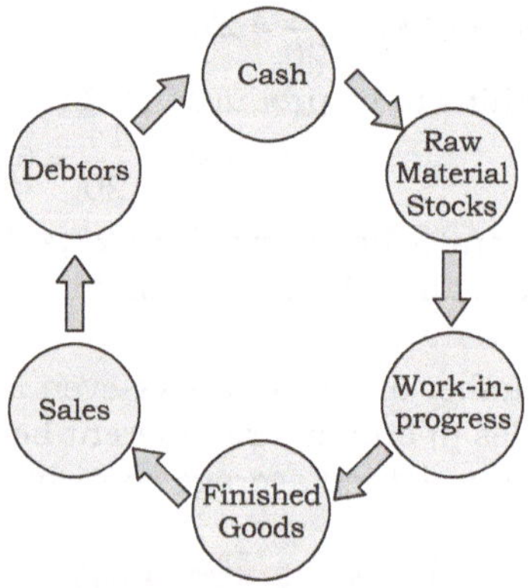

Operating Cycle or Cash Conversion Cycle for Manufacturing Business

Factors Affecting Working Capital

The finance manager must keep in mind following factors before estimating the amount of working capital

Factors Affecting Working Capital

Nature of business	Credit availed
Scale of operation	Operating efficiency
Business cycle fluctuation	Availability of raw materials
Seasonal factors	Level of competition
Operating cycle	Inflation
Credit allowed	Growth prospects

1. **Nature of Business** In case of trading concern or retail shop the requirement of working capital is less because length of operating cycle is small.

   The manufacturing company requires huge amount of working capital because they have to convert raw material into finished goods before any sale become possible.
2. **Scale of Operation** The firms operating at large scale need to maintain more inventory, debtors, etc.

   So they generally require large working capital whereas firms operating at small scale require less working capital.
3. **Business Cycle Fluctuation** During boom period, the sales as well as production are likely to be larger, thus more amount of working capital is required.

Whereas during depression period, less working capital will be required, since the sales as well as production will be less.

4. **Seasonal Factors** The working capital requirement is constant for the companies which are selling goods throughout the season whereas the companies which are selling seasonal goods require huge amount during peak season due to higher level of activity whereas during lean season, demand is very low, so less working capital is needed.
5. **Operating Cycle** The amount of working capital directly depends upon the length of operating cycle. If operating cycle is long then more working capital is required whereas for companies having short operating cycle, the working capital requirement is less.
6. **Credit Allowed** Credit policy refers to average period for collection of sale proceeds. It depends on number of factors such as creditworthiness of clients, industry norms etc. A company following liberal credit policy requires more working capital due to higher amount of debtors, whereas company following strict credit policy require less working capital.
7. **Credit Availed** Just as firm allows credit to its customers, it also may get credit from its suppliers. To the extent, it avails the credit on purchases, the working capital requirement is reduced and *vice-versa.*
8. **Operating Efficiency** The firm which have high degree of operating efficiency will require less amount of working capital as compared to firm which have low degree of efficiency and require more working capital.
9. **Availability of Raw Materials** If raw materials are easily and readily available, lower stock levels can be maintained, thus require less working capital. Whereas, when the raw materials are scarce or not readily available, higher stock levels will have to be maintained, thus requiring high working capital.
10. **Level of Competition** Higher level of competitiveness may necessitate company to maintain larger stock of finished goods which will increase the working capital requirement. Whereas, a business having less competition will require less working capital.
11. **Inflation** Price level changes also affect the working capital requirement. With rising prices, larger amount is required even to maintain a constant volume of production and sales.

    Thus, working capital requirement becomes higher with the higher rate of inflation. But if company can increase the price of its own goods also, then there will be less problem of working capital.
12. **Growth Prospects** Companies which have a possibility of growth potential or are planning to expand, will require more amount of working capital to meet higher production and sales target whenever required.

CHECK POINT 02

1. What is working capital?
2. State any two examples of current liabilities.
3. Write the name of any three factors affecting working capital.
4. State the formula to calculate net working capital.
5. What is cash conversion cycle?

Inventory Control

Inventory means the stock of raw materials, semi-finished goods, consumables, spare parts and finished goods or we can also say that inventory is required directly or indirectly to make a sale (of the finished goods) and may also represent different stages in the process of getting the finished goods (i.e. the stock of raw materials and work-in-progress). In accounting terms, inventory refers to the value of all the items, in the inventory list that is owned by the business.

Inventory control refers to the process of deciding what and how much of various items to be kept in stock. It is a system which is expected to help achieve desirable behaviour of the inventory items.

An effective inventory control system aims at

- Providing stock as and when the need arises.
- Stock should be procured at minimum possible price.

Inventory control has many facets as monetary, physical, safety and many others. It is crucial to understand these aspects in designing an inventory control system.

Various Aspects to be Considered in the Process of Inventory Control

The key terms related to inventory control system and various aspects to be considered are as follows

Various Aspects related to Inventory Control System

- Stock keeping unit code
- Motley crowd
- Space
- Value
- Lead time
- Standard Vs made to order
- Seasonality of supply
- Demand not uniform or not predictable
- Shelf life
- Safety aspects
- Obsolescence

1. **Stock Keeping Unit** (SKU) **Code** Each and every item in the inventory is to be identified with a unique code which signifies certain aspects of the item. This code is termed as SKU code.

   The aspects specified may be colour, weight, size, or any other important characteristic. The SKU code can be a combination of alpha and/ or numeric symbols.

   SKU is the very basic unit for data collection, helps in deriving meaningful information and decision-making. Bar codes and Radio Frequency Identification (RFID) tags are used in tracking, using SKU code.
2. **Motley Crowd** Inventory is basically a motley mix of heterogeneous (different) assemblage of raw materials, packing materials, spare parts, semi-finished goods, finished goods, etc. Collectively, it is termed as motley crowd.
3. **Space** Space requirements for all items of inventory will not be identical and neither will it have any binding on the cost of the product.

   There can be many bulky items with low cost e.g. straw, as well as high value items with low volume, like diamonds. A good inventory control system should keep in mind the space requirements for various inventories needed by the business.
4. **Value** All the items of an inventory are differently priced. So, the value of the inventory should also be an important consideration for an effective control system.
5. **Lead Time** It is the time taken by manufacturer to procure or manufacture an item and is dependent upon a number of factors, *viz.* processing time, scheduling of machines, distance between source and point of use, etc. Inventory control system has to consider the above factors before formulating an effective plan.
6. **Standard vs Made to Order** Some of the items of the inventory may be standard and could be sourced from a number of suppliers. Other items may be specific and can be sourced from certain suppliers only. An effective control system considers this aspect also.
7. **Seasonality of Supply** If the item is an agricultural product (grains, vegetables, fruits, etc.), then its supply would be seasonal. This can play a key role in designing the inventory control system.
8. **Demand not Uniform or not Predictable** Demand for an item could be seasonal, i.e. it may depend on weather conditions, festival seasons, school opening dates, etc. So, demand for umbrellas, crackers, sweets, school uniforms, etc., are easy to predict. But for other items it may not be easy to predict demand, e.g. requirement of a spare part.

   So, an effective inventory control system has to formulate an effective plan for forecasting demand, so that it is able to meet the demand successfully.
9. **Shelf Life** Items like vegetables, fruits, flowers, fish, etc., are perishable in nature. This calls for special storage conditions and equipments such as cold storage, freezers, etc. These involve huge establishing costs.

   Similarly, some of the manufactured food or medicines have expiry dates, beyond which they are not fit for consumption. The above factors impose certain constraints on inventory management.
10. **Safety Aspects** Some of the items are hazardous in nature and special precautions have to be taken in their storage. e.g. gasoline and hazardous chemicals like phosphorus and potassium chlorate. Inventory control system should ensure safety of men, material and machines while deriving a plan for their storage.
11. **Obsolescence** Due to advancement of technology, certain items may not be used and their value and demand both falls. So, this aspect of inventory management should also be kept in view by an effective control system.

When to Order Inventory

In a scientific system of inventory control, the following levels of quantities are fixed

1. Minimum Stock Level

A minimum stock level is a threshold value that indicates the level below which the quantity actual material should not normally be allowed to fall.

In other words, a minimum stock level is a minimum quantity of a particular item that must be kept at all times. The main objective of fixing the minimum stock level is to ensure that the required quantity of each item is available at all times.

The main factors to be considered while fixing the minimum stock level are

- Average rate of consumption of materials.
- Time needed to procure fresh supplies under top priority conditions.
- Reorder level.
- Production requirements in terms of materials.
- Minimum quantity of materials that can be procured advantageously.

2. Maximum Level

It is the quantity of materials beyond which a firm should not exceed its stocks. If the quantity exceeds maximum level limit, then it will be termed as overstocking. A firm avoids overstocking because it will result in high material costs.

Maximum stock level will depend upon the following factors

- Availability of capital for the purchase of materials.
- Maximum requirement of materials at any point of time.
- Availability of space for storing the material.
- Rate of consumption of materials.
- Cost of maintaining the stores.
- Possibility of fluctuations in prices of various material.
- Nature of material.
- Availability of material.
- Restrictions imposed by the government.
- Possibility of changes in fashions.

3. Danger Level

It is the level below which stocks should not fall in any case. If danger level approaches, then immediate steps should be taken to replenish the stocks even if more cost is incurred in arranging the material.

4. Reorder Level

In management accounting, reorder level (or reorder point) is the inventory level at which a company should place a new order or start a new manufacturing run. Reorder level depends on a company's work order lead time and its demand during that time as well as the availablility of safety stock.

Pareto's Principle

This principle was propounded by Vilfredo Pareto, an Italian economist, who studied land ownership in Italy in the early 1900's and found that roughly 20% of the population held title to about 80% of the land. For this reason, Pareto's Principle is often referred to as the '80/20' rule.

So, Pareto's principle basically states that 'A relatively handful of things will generate the bulk of the results' or 'vital few, trivial many'. The value of Pareto's Principle in inventory management is in reminding us to stay focused on the 20% that matters.

ABC Analysis of Inventory Control

ABC (Always Better Control) analysis can help in better inventory control. It is based on Pareto's Principle.

In ABC analysis, a company reviews its inventory and sorts all SKUs in three categories, called 'A', 'B' and 'C' items.

A typical breakdown might look like this

- **'A' Inventory** 10-20% of the items in terms of quantity account for 70-80% of the total value of items.
- **'B' Inventory** 15-25% of the items in terms of quantity account for 10-20% of the total value of inventory.
- **'C' Inventory** 65-75% of the items in terms of quantity account for 5-10% of the total value of inventory.

Based on the above information it can be concluded that, inventory 'A' is outstandingly important, inventory 'B' is average important and inventory 'C' is relatively unimportant.

So, more attention should be devoted to inventory 'A' less to 'B' and still less to 'C'. ABC analysis helps in an efficient and effective inventory control.

Suggested Policy Guidelines for 'A', 'B', and 'C' Classes of Inventory

(A) **Items** (High Consumption Value)	(B) **Items** (Moderate Consumption Value)	(C) **Items** (Low Consumption Value)
Very strict consumption control	Moderate control	Loose control
No/very low safety stock	Low safety stock	High safety stock
Phased delivery (Weekly)	Once in three months	Once in 6 months
Weekly control report	Monthly control report	Quarterly report
Maximum follow-up	Periodic follow-up	Exceptional
As many sources as possible	Two or more reliable	Two reliable
Accurate forecasts	Estimates on past data	Rough estimate
Central purchasing/storage	Combination purchasing	Decentralised
Maximum efforts to control lead time	Moderate	Minimum clerical efforts
To be handled by Sr. officers	Middle level	Can be delegated

Economic Order Quantity (EOQ)

Economic Order Quantity is the quantity which is most economical to order. It is the quantity for which order should be placed when the stock reaches re-order level.

Assuming that the future demand is known, one needs to determine **when** to place an order (Reorder point) and **how much** to order (order quantity). Also, to avoid zero stock status before the supply arrives, the concept of **safety stock** is used.

Safety stock is a term used by logisticians to describe a level of extra stock that is maintained to mitigate risk of stock outs (short fall in raw material or packaging) caused by uncertainties in supply and demand.

EOQ is determined after considering the following factors

1. **Ordering Costs** These costs refer to the cost incurred for acquiring stock. These costs include
   - Cost of placing an order
   - Cost of transportation
   - Cost of receiving goods – Cost of inspecting goods

There is an inverse relationship between order size and ordering cost.

Larger the order size	Lower the ordering costs because of fewer orders.
Smaller the order size	Higher the ordering costs because of more orders.

2. **Carrying Costs** The term carrying costs refer to the costs incurred in maintaining a given level of inventory. These costs include
   - Cost of storage space,
   - Cost of handling materials,
   - Cost of insurance,
   - Cost of deterioration or obsolescence,
   - Cost of store staff, and
   - Interest on funds invested in purchasing the stock.

Assumptions of EOQ

The computation of EOQ is based on the following assumptions
- Prior knowledge of annual usage of inventory
- Constant rate of usage
- Constant ordering costs
- Constant carrying costs
- Zero lead-time/delivery period

Determination of EOQ

EOQ can be determined with the help of the following formula $EOQ = \sqrt{\frac{2PD}{C}}$, where

P = Cost of placing one order or ordering cost per order

D = Annual demand for the inventory

C = Inventory carrying cost per unit

At EOQ level, ordering costs are equal to carrying costs and their sum is the least possible cost likely to be incurred on placing an order.

Example 5 Annual quantity of jeans sold by a shop is 1,200 at the rate of ₹ 100 per piece. Cost of placing an order and receiving goods is ₹ 500/ per order. Inventory holding cost is ₹ 30 per annum. What is the Economic Order Quantity (EOQ) for the shopkeeper?

Sol. Here, D = 1,200; P = ₹ 500 and C = ₹ 30

So, $2 \times P \times D = 12{,}00{,}000$

This divided by 30 = 40,000

Square root of which is = 200

So, the EOQ is 200 jeans.

$$\text{Number of Orders Placed} = \frac{\text{Annual Consumption}}{\text{EOQ}}$$

Also find the number of orders placed, ordering cost and carrying cost at the level of EOQ

$$= \frac{1{,}200}{200} = 6 \text{ orders}$$

$\therefore$ Ordering cost = 6×500 = ₹ 3,000

Average inventory = $200 \times \frac{1}{2} = 100$ units

$\therefore$ Carrying cost = 100×30 = ₹ 3,000

So, it can be observed that at EOQ, ordering cost and carrying cost are the same.

Re-order Quantity (ROQ) or Re-order Level

After understanding how much units to order, one should also know when to place a order. Re-order level helps to determine the same. Re-order level is that level of stock at which fresh order should be placed for replenishment of stock. It is computed with the help of following formula

$$\text{Re-order Quantity} = \text{Average Daily Usage} \times \text{Average Lead Time}$$

Example 6 The following information is taken from the cost records of Blue Chip Ltd.

Monthly consumption of component 'x' = 100 – 120 units.

Lead time or re-order period = 4 – 6 days. Find the re-order level.

Sol. Re-order Level = Maximum Consumption × Maximum Lead Time

Accordingly, $= 120 \times 6 = 720$ units

So, new order should be placed when stock reaches 720 units.

CHECK POINT 03

1. Define inventory.
2. What do you mean by SKU?
3. Who propounded Pareto's principle?
4. Why is it important to identify re-order level?
5. What is EOQ?

Profitability Ratios

Profitable business means earning more than what one spends. Profitability is an indication of the efficiency with which the operations of the business are carried on. Poor operational performance may indicate poor sales and hence, poor profits. A lower profitability may also arise due to lack of control over expenses.

Entrepreneurs are interested in knowing about the profitability of their ventures over different time periods and also as compared to competing firms. Profitability ratios help to facilitate such comparisons.

Two important profitability ratios are as follows

1. Return on Investment (RoI)

It is a measure of overall profitability of the business. It indicates the percentage of return on total capital employed in the business, irrespective of the fact whether it is self-owned or debt capital. It is also referred to as 'Return on Capital Employed' (RoCE).

It is calculated with the help of the following formula

$$\text{Return on Investment (RoI)} = \frac{\text{Net Profit}}{\text{Total Capital Invested}} \times 100$$

where, Total Capital Invested = Equity + Debt

e.g. if you spend ₹ 1,00,000 to open a grocery shop and make a net profit of ₹ 20,000 in 1 year, your annual RoI equals $(20{,}000/1{,}00{,}000) \times 100 = 20\%$.

When calculating RoI, the investment will include not only what the investor spent out of his/her pocket, but also all borrowed funds. In the example, the owner might have invested ₹ 40,000 of his own money (equity) and secured a loan for ₹ 60,000 but this ratio will consider the total investment of ₹ 1,00,000.

2. Return on Equity (RoE)

It is a measure of profitability, calculated as a percentage of equity only. RoE can be calculated by dividing the net income by the equity of the investor and multiplying the result by 100.

The net income would be determined after deducting interest from net profit. The following formula helps in the computation of RoE

$$\text{Return on Equity (RoE)} = \frac{\text{Net Income}}{\text{Equity}} \times 100$$

where, Net Income = Operating Profit – Interest Expenses

In the example taken above, where the grocery owner had invested ₹ 40,000 and the interest payable by him on borrowed amount is ₹ 6,000, then

$$\text{RoE} = \frac{(20{,}000 - 6{,}000)}{40{,}000} \times 100$$

$$= 35\%$$

The below examples will help you to understand the above two ratios

Example 7 Calculate Return on Investment (RoI) and Return on Equity (RoE) on the basis of given information.

You have newly started a beauty parlour business, you spend ₹ 1,50,000 to open the parlour of which you invested ₹ 70,000 of your own money and borrowed a loan for ₹ 80,000.

Interest rate per annum is 7%. Sales revenue per month is ₹ 80,000. Cost of goods sold is ₹ 30,000 per month. Fixed expenses is ₹ 30,000 (salary ₹ 20,000, rent and utility ₹10,000), depreciation ₹ 3,000 and tax @ 14%. **CBSE TBQ**

Sol.

Total Capital Invested	= ₹ 1,50,000
Equity (Own money)	= ₹ 70,000
Debt	= ₹ 80,000
Income statement of beauty parlour for 1st month	
Sales Revenue	= ₹ 80,000
(–) Cost of Goods Sold	= ₹ (30,000)
Gross Margin	= ₹ 50,000
(–) Fixed Expenses	
Salary	₹ 20,000
Rent and Utility	₹ 10,000
Interest @ 7% $\left(80{,}000 \times \frac{7}{100} \times \frac{1}{12}\right)$	₹ 467
Depreciation (3,000/12)	₹ 250
Profit Before Tax	₹ 19,283
(–) Tax @ 14%	₹ (2,700)
Profit After Tax	= ₹ 16,583

Return on Investment (RoI)

$$= \frac{\text{Net Profit (Profit after tax)}}{\text{Total Capital Invested}} \times 100$$

$$= \frac{16{,}583}{1{,}50{,}000} \times 100 = 11.05\%$$

$$\text{Return on Equity (RoE)} = \frac{\text{Net Profit}}{\text{Equity}} \times 100$$

$$= \frac{16{,}583}{70{,}000} \times 100 = 23.69\%$$

Note *Depreciation and fixed expenses are assumed to be calculated on monthly basis. The profitability ratios are an average.*

Example 8 Let us take the case of two people, A and B starting identical business and performing identically in terms of sales, variable cost, fixed cost, etc. The only difference is A did not borrow any money and B did. Interest rate is 10% per annum. Here are some figures for both A and B.

Items	A (₹)	B (₹)
Total Investment = x	10,00,000	10,00,000
Source of Funds		
Equity = y	10,00,000	4,00,000
Loan = z	—	6,00,000
Total	10,00,000	10,00,000
Interest Rate per annum		10%
Income Statement for 1 Year		
Sales Revenue (a)	7,00,000	7,00,000
(–) Cost of Goods Sold (b)	(3,00,000)	(3,00,000)
Gross Margin (c) = (a – b)	4,00,000	4,00,000
Fixed Expenses		
Salary, etc	2,00,000	2,00,000
Rent, Utility, etc	50,000	50,000
Interest	—	60,000
Depreciation and Amortisation	10,000	10,000
Total Fixed Expenses = (d)	2,60,000	3,20,000

Items	A (₹)	B (₹)
Profit before tax = (g) = (c – d)	1,40,000	80,000
Tax @20% = (e)	28,000	16,000
Profit after tax = f = (g – e)	1,12,000	64,000
Some Ratios		
RoI = (f/x)	11.2%	6.4%
RoE = (f/y)	11.2%	16%
EBITDA = (PBT + Int. + Dep. and Amrt.)	1,50,000	1,50,000
(EBITDA / Investment) × 100	15%	15%
(EBITDA / Equity) × 100	15%	37.5%

EBITDA stands for Earnings Before Interest, Tax, Depreciation and Amortisation. This is arrived at by adding interest, depreciation and amortisation to PBT.

In the given example, B makes less profit than A in terms of RoI. But, if we compare RoE, then B is ahead from A.

So, for a true measure of how 'own money' or 'equity' is being used, RoE is a good indicator. RoI, on the other hand, gives an indication of how the 'total money' or 'total investment' is being used.

EBITDA

The acronym EBITDA stands for Earnings Before Interest, Taxes, Depreciation and Amortisation.

Its utility lies in normalising the extraneous factors to be able to measure and compare true effectiveness of one operation and the managerial decisions with another operation.

It is one of the most widely used measures for evaluating a business for acquisition.

The various components of EBITDA are discussed below

1. **Interest** Interest is a financial expense, paid to the owner of the fund to compensate him for parting with his funds.

   The interest paid is not an operational expense but it is a cost incurred due to 'funding decision'. Adding back the interest to Profit before Tax (PBT), takes away the effect of this funding decision.
2. **Taxes** Taxes are levied by the government. If you are comparing profits of one period to another, the rates might have changed. Two companies may have different tax treatments due to difference in state taxes or special duties.

   The business owner or manager has no control over these taxes. So, to avoid distortion in the profit, tax component is added back to the profit.
3. **Depreciation and Amortisation** There are different options available to depreciate (tangible assets) or amortise (intangible assets).

   One company may use a particular method and another one a totally different one. So, to avoid distortion due to differing practices being followed, depreciation and amortisation are added back.

   Price for a business is often quoted in terms of a multiple of its EBITDA — say (M) × (EBITDA), where M has a numeric value that varies from industry to industry.

   Basic philosophy in this thought process is when someone buys a business, he or she buys the 'future cash flows' from that business. Hence, they are willing to pay a multiple of EBITDA.

CHECK POINT 04

1. Define ROQ.
2. What are the two profitability ratios?
3. Total Capital Invested = ... + Debit.
4. What is EBITDA?
5. Mention various components of EBITDA.

EXAM PATTERN EXERCISE

Objective Type Questions (1 Mark)

Multiple Choice Questions

1 Measure of unit in which the products are sold, is called
(a) unit cost (b) unit of sale
(c) unit price (d) None of these

Ans (b) unit of sale

2 The price at which one unit of sale is sold, is called
(a) unit of sale (b) unit cost
(c) unit price (d) None of these

Ans (c) unit price

3 Break-even point is the level where **(CBSE 2023)**
(a) the revenue generated is equal to all the expenses required for generating the revenue.
(b) the revenue generated is less than all the expenses required for generating the revenue.
(c) the revenue generated is more than all the expenses required for generating the revenue.
(d) Both (a) and (b)

Ans (a) the revenue generated is equal to all the expenses required for generating the revenue.

4 Contribution =
(a) Cost Price + Variable Cost
(b) Selling Price – Variable Cost
(c) Fixed Cost + Profit (d) Both (b) and (c)

Ans (d) Both (b) and (c)

5 .... costs are directly proportional to the level of output.
(a) Fixed (b) Variable
(c) Both (a) and (b) (d) None of these

Ans (b) Variable

6 What does total cost include?
(a) Variable cost (b) Fixed cost
(c) Both (a) and (b) (d) None of these

Ans (c) Total cost is the sum of all costs incurred by a firm in producing a certain level of output i.e. variable cost and fixed cost.

7 Investment in all the current assets taken together is called
(a) net working capital
(b) gross working capital
(c) Both (a) and (b) (d) None of these

Ans (b) gross working capital

8 Which of the following is a factor affecting working capital?
(a) Scale of operation (b) Seasonal factors
(c) Credit allowed (d) All of these

Ans (d) All of these

9 Pareto's principle is referred to as the
(a) '80/20' rule (b) '70/20' rule
(c) '60/10' rule (d) '50/50' rule

Ans (a) '80/20' rule

10 A business needs capital for
(a) procuring fixed assets
(b) meeting day-to-day expenses
(c) growth and diversification
(d) All of the above

Ans (d) All of the above

11 Which amongst the following is/are example(s) of current liabilities?
(a) Debtors (b) Creditors
(c) Bills receivables (d) Prepaid expenses

Ans (b) Current liabilities are a company's debts or obligations that are due to be paid to creditors within one year.

12 According to ABC analysis, 'B' inventory accounts for .... of the items in terms of quantity.
(a) 10-20% (b) 15-25%
(c) 40-50% (d) 65-75%

Ans (b) 15-25%

13 XYZ Company uses 500 units of an item per day and the order lead time is 7 days. Re-order level will be
(a) 1,000 units (b) 500 units
(c) 3,500 units (d) None of these

Ans (c) RoL = Usage per Day × Lead Time
$= 500 \times 7 = 3,500$

14 When total current assets exceed total current liabilities, it refers to **(CBSE SQP)**

(a) gross working capital

(b) temporary working capital

(c) Both (a) and (b)

(d) net working capital

Ans (d) net working capital

15 The average monthly output of a sugar mill is 50,000 tons. Sales price per kg is ₹40 and variable cost per kg is ₹20. If the fixed expenses are ₹50,000, the break-even point in units will be **(CBSE Term I 2021)**

(a) 25,000 units (b) 2,500 units

(c) 250 units (d) 5,000 units

Ans (b) Break-even Point $= \frac{50,000}{40-20} = \frac{50,000}{20}$

$= 2,500$ units

16 Annual consumption of units in Aahaar Limited = 2,000 units,
Buying cost per order = ₹ 12,
Price per unit = ₹ 1,000,
Storage cost as percentage of price per unit = 12%,
EOQ = ?

(a) 400 units (b) 20 units

(c) 200 units (d) 100 units

Ans (b) EOQ $= \sqrt{\frac{2AP}{C}} = \sqrt{\frac{2 \times 2,000 \times 12}{120}} = 20$

17 A firm has capital of ₹ 10,00,000; sales of ₹ 5,00,000; gross profit of ₹ 2,00,000 and expenses of ₹ 1,00,000. Return on investment for the firm will be **(CBSE SQP)**

(a) 50% (b) 20% (c) 10% (d) 30%

Ans (c) Return on Investment

$$= \frac{\text{Net Profit}}{\text{Total Capital Invested}} \times 100$$

$$= \frac{2,00,000 - 1,00,000}{10,00,000} \times 100$$

$$= \frac{1,00,000}{10,00,000} \times 100 = 10\%$$

18 A firm has capital of ₹ 10,00,000 of which ₹ 6,00,000 is debt fund; sales of ₹ 5,00,000; gross profit of ₹ 2,00,000 and expenses of ₹ 1,00,000. Return on equity for the firm will be **(CBSE SQP)**

(a) 50% (b) 25%

(c) 150% (d) 30%

Ans (b) Return on Equity $= \frac{\text{Net Income}}{\text{Equity}} \times 100$

$$= \frac{2,00,000 - 1,00,000}{10,00,000 - 6,00,000} \times 100$$

$$= \frac{1,00,000}{4,00,000} \times 100 = 25\%$$

19 Sahiba has a boutique in Nagpur, which she started in 2020. She has invested ₹ 2,00,000 from her savings and borrowed ₹ 3,00,000 from the bank @ 10% per annum. She made a net profit of ₹ 50,000 in the year 2021-2022. In the above case the 'return on equity' is **(CBSE 2023)**

(a) 10%

(b) 20%

(c) 25%

(d) 40%

Ans (b) In this case, the total equity is the sum of Sahiba's initial investment and any profits reinvested in the business, which is 2,00,000 + 50,000 = ₹ 2,50,000.

The net income is ₹ 50,000.

Therefore, the RoE is (50,000/2, 50,000) × 100 = 20%.

20 Electronics India Ltd. manufactures three products X, Y and Z. The total fixed cost is ₹80,000 and the weighted average contributions per unit is ₹20. The break-even point of sales mix will be **(CBSE Term I 2021)**

(a) ₹4,000 (b) ₹6,000

(c) ₹8,000 (d) ₹2,000

Ans (a) Break-even Point

$$= \frac{\text{Fixed Cost}}{\text{Contribution Margin}}$$

$$= \frac{80,000}{20} = ₹\ 4,000$$

21 Sushant has opened a grocery shop with an investment of ₹ 3 lakh. Out of this, ₹ 1 lakh was his own and the rest he borrowed from friends and relatives. At the end of the year, he earned a net profit of ₹ 40,000. Which ratio will be higher?

(a) RoI

(b) RoE

(c) Both will be the same

(d) None of the above

Ans (b) RoE will be higher because it is calculated on equity only, whereas RoI is calculated on the sum of equity and debt.

22 Ramandeep is a technical entrepreneur who started developing interactive website of businesses. Due to lot of competition in this field he is experiencing a decline in the demand. He wishes to understand his revenue position as compared to his investment. Which one of the following combinations would help him in assessing the profitability of his business? **(CBSE 2023)**

I. Economic order quantity
II. Return on investment
III. Return on equity
IV. Break-even analysis

Codes

(a) I and III (b) III and IV
(c) II and III (d) I and IV

Ans (c) II and III

23 During the last month, a total of 450 people took meals in a restaurant and the total billed amount was ₹ 90,000. The unit price per person will be **(CBSE Term I 2021)**

(a) ₹ 200 (b) ₹ 475
(c) ₹ 325 (d) ₹ 210

Ans (a) Unit Price per Person $= \frac{90,000}{450} =$ ₹ 200

24 Harshdeep is the stock keeper of Neha Textiles Ltd. The company is into converting cotton yarn into fabric and then further computerised printing on the same to add value to the fabric. He wants to know the ideal quantity of yarn to be ordered so that the production process does not stop. How can he know the correct time to place an order? **(CBSE SQP)**

(a) By calculating break-even point
(b) By calculating re-order point
(c) By calculating economic order quantity
(d) By calculating lead time

Ans (b) By calculating re-order point

25 A grocery store sold the following items at the price per unit mentioned against each

Item	Price Per Unit (₹)	Quantity Sold
Edible Oil	100	5
Bathing Soap	50	4
Cereals	75	10
Broom	10	1

The above items were sold to 10 customers. The 'Unit Price' would be **(CBSE Term I 2021)**

(a) ₹ 1,460 (b) ₹ 146
(c) ₹ 100 (d) ₹ 75

Ans (b) Unit Price

$$= \frac{(100 \times 5) + (50 \times 4) + (75 \times 10) + (10 \times 1)}{10}$$

$$= \frac{500 + 200 + 750 + 10}{10} = \frac{1,460}{10} = ₹\ 146$$

26 From the information given below, calculate the circulating capital of a company **(CBSE 2023)**

Assets	Amt (₹)	Liabilities	Amt (₹)
Stock	60,000	Trade Payables	20,000
Debtors	55,000	Short-term Loans	10,000
Cash	65,000	Outstanding Expenses	5,000
Short-term Investments	20,000		

(a) ₹ 35,000
(b) ₹ 1,65,000
(c) ₹ 2,00,000
(d) ₹ 2,35,000

Ans (c) Sum total of all current assets (60,000 + 55,000 + 65,000 + 20,000 = ₹ 200,000)

27 Calculation of break-even point is useful for the entrepreneur as it helps in assessing **(CBSE SQP Term I)**

(a) The maximum level of output to be produced
(b) The effect of change in quantity of input upon the production.
(c) The cost price of the product.
(d) The profitable options in line of production.

Ans (d) The profitable options in line of production.

28 Aloma Ayurvedic Limited is a well-established name in the market for ayurvedic medicine. It has entered into the market of immunity booster drinks and has introduced immunity shots in special packaging, in two flavours. Total fixed cost incurred in the entire operation is ₹ 5,60,000. Based on the break-even point analysis, will it be economically viable for Aloma Ayurvedic Limited to continue with the production of these immunity shots? **(CBSE SQP Term I)**

	AloTurm (50ml/ shot) (Aloevera and Turmeric)	**AloAm** (50ml/ shot) (Aloevera and Amla)
Selling Price Per Shot (in ₹)	50	75
Variable Cost Per Shot (in ₹)	25	45
Sales Mix in the Year	4,000 shots	6,000 shots

(a) Yes, as there is a big market for immunity boosting products.
(b) No, because there is a limited variety of immunity boosting shots being introduced by the company.
(c) No, because the break-even point is very greater than the combined sale of the two varieties
(d) Yes, because the break-even point is smaller than the combined sale of the two varieties.

Ans (c) No, because the breakeven point is very greater than the combined sale of the two varieties

29 **Assertion** (A) A transport service provider needs less working capital.

Reason (R) A service firm sells more on a cash basis and does not have to maintain inventory.

Alternatives
(a) Both Assertion (A) and Reason (R) are correct
(b) Assertion (A) is correct, but Reason (R) is incorrect
(c) Assertion (A) is incorrect, but Reason (R) is correct
(d) Both Assertion (A) and Reason (R) are incorrect

Ans (a) Both Assertion (A) and Reason (R) are correct

30 **Assertion** (A) Higher the lead time, the lower is the amount of working capital required.
Reason (R) If the raw material is available freely and continuously, then less working capital is needed as less inventory has to be maintained.

Alternatives
(a) Both Assertion (A) and Reason (R) are correct
(b) Assertion (A) is correct, but Reason (R) is incorrect
(c) Assertion (A) is incorrect, but Reason (R) is correct
(d) Both Assertion (A) and Reason (R) are incorrect

Ans (c) Higher the lead time, higher is the amount of working capital required.

31 Given below are the arithmetic skills in Column I. Match them with their correct formula in Column II.

Column I (Arithmetic Skills)		**Column II** (Formula)	
A.	Working Capital	(i)	Fixed Costs/(Average Price – Variable Costs)
B.	Break-even Analysis	(ii)	Current Value of Investment – Cost of Investment/Cost on Investment
C.	Return on Equity	(iii)	Current Assets – Current Liabilities
D.	Return on Investment	(iv)	Net Income/ Shareholder's Equity

Codes

	A	B	C	D		A	B	C	D
(a)	(iii)	(i)	(iv)	(ii)	(b)	(iv)	(ii)	(i)	(iii)
(c)	(ii)	(iv)	(i)	(iii)	(d)	(iii)	(ii)	(i)	(iv)

Ans (a) (iii) (i) (iv) (ii)

32 Given below are the arithmetic skills in Column I. Match them with their correct definition in Column II.

Column I (Arithmetic Skills)		**Column II** (Definition)	
A.	Break-even Analysis	(i)	Refers to that part of total capital, which is required for holding current assets.
B.	Inventory Control	(ii)	Refers to a system of determination of that level of activity where total cost equals total selling price.
C.	Working Capital	(iii)	Quantity for which order should be placed when the stock reaches re-order level.

Column I (Arithmetic Skills)	Column II (Definition)
D. Economic Order Quantity	(iv) Aims at providing stock as and when the need arises.

Codes

	A	B	C	D		A	B	C	D
(a)	(ii)	(iii)	(iv)	(i)	(b)	(iv)	(i)	(ii)	(iii)
(c)	(ii)	(iv)	(i)	(iii)	(d)	(iv)	(ii)	(i)	(iii)

Ans (c) (ii) (iv) (i) (iii)

33 Match the following **(CBSE SQP Term I)**

Column I	Column II
A. Break-even point	(i) A summary of projected assets, liabilities
B. Proforma income statement	(ii) Actual payments are received or made
C. Cash flow	(iii) Total revenue is equal to total cost of a firm
D. Proforma balance sheet	(iv) Net profit calculated from projected revenue minus projected costs and expenses

Codes

	A	B	C	D		A	B	C	D
(a)	(iii)	(iv)	(ii)	(i)	(b)	(iii)	(ii)	(iv)	(i)
(c)	(ii)	(iii)	(i)	(iv)	(d)	(iv)	(iii)	(ii)	(i)

Ans (a) (iii) (iv) (ii) (i)

34 Which concept is highlighted by the given picture?

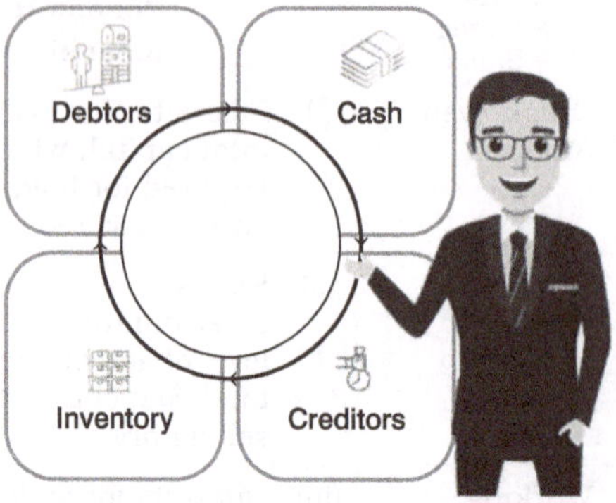

(a) Working capital (b) Fixed capital
(c) Inventory control (d) All of these

Ans (a) Working capital indicates the liquidity levels of businesses for managing day-to-day expenses and covers inventory, cash, accounts payable etc.

35 Which concept is higlighted by the given picture?

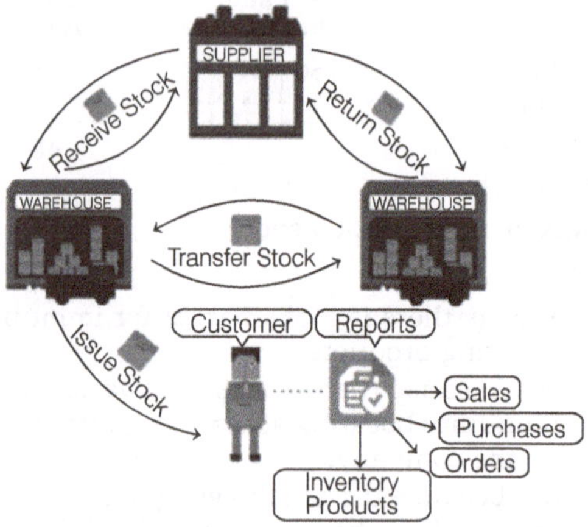

(a) Working capital
(b) Fixed capital
(c) Inventory control (d) None of these

Ans (c) It refers to the process of deciding what and how much of various items to be kept in stock.

Fill in the Blanks

36 .... can be defined as the measure of unit in which products are sold.

Ans Unit of sale

37 For a coaching class, the unit of sale will be an .... and for a restaurant, the unit of sale will be a ....

Ans hour, diner

38 .... can be defined as the cost incurred by a company to produce, store and sell one unit of sale of a particular product or service.

Ans Unit cost

39 Tangible assets are .... whereas intangible assets are ....

Ans depreciated, amortised

40 Inventory is collectively termed as ....

Ans motley crowd

41 Ordering cost and carrying cost are .... related to each other.

Ans inversely

42 .... indicates the percentage of return on total capital employed in the business.

Ans Return on investment

43 .... is an indication of the efficiency with which the operations of the business are carried on.

Ans Profitability

44 .... is the length of time between the firms purchase of inventory and the receipt of cash from account receivable.

Ans Cash conversion cycle

45 Amit is running an 'Advertising agency' and earning a lot by providing this service to big industries. The working capital requirement of the firm will be ....

Ans less

46 The fixed expenses of Toys Craft Limited is ₹ 5,50,000. The selling price of its toy is ₹ 100 and the variable cost is ₹ 60 per unit. The break-even quantity will be .... units.

Ans $\frac{5,50,000}{(100-60)} = 13,750$

47 Yogesh, a businessman, is engaged in the purchase and sale of ice creams. Now, he is keen to start his own ice cream factory. Factors that will affect his fixed capital requirements are .... and ....

Ans level of collaboration, financial alternatives available

State True or False

48 Interest paid is an operational expense.

Ans False. Interest paid is a financial expense.

49 If 100 litre of milk is sold for ₹ 5,000, then unit price will be ₹ 50.

Ans True. Unit Price = 5,000 ÷ 100 = ₹ 50

50 At break-even point, a firm is able to recover all its expenses.

Ans False. At break-even point, a firm is able to recover only its fixed expenses.

51 Fixed Expenses = Quantity × (Unit Price – Unit Cost)

Ans True

52 The alphabet 'T' in the acronym EBITDA stands for Tax.

Ans True

53 Gross margin and gross profit are one and the same. **(CBSE SQP)**

Ans True

54 Each and every item of inventory is identified by a unique code, referred to as stock keeping code.

Ans True

55 When total current assets exceed total current liabilities, if refers to gross working capital. **(CBSE 2020)**

Ans False. It refers to net working capital.

56 If current liabilities exceed current assets, then net working capital will be positive.

Ans False. It will be negative because NWC = CA – CL.

57 Current assets provide liquidity to the business and help in day-to-day operation of the business.

Ans True

58 Gross profit represents the business' profit from selling a product before deducting overheads or fixed expenses.

Ans True

59 In an outlet of Reliance Fresh in Noida, on a particular day, 120 customers visited and paid ₹ 2,40,000 for various items purchased. The unit price is ₹ 1,500.

Ans False. The unit price will be ₹ 2,000. i.e. 2,40,000 ÷ 120.

60 Vilfredo Pareto studied land ownership in Italy and found that roughly 30% of the population held 70% of the land.

Ans False. He found that 20% population held 80% of the land.

61 Amit is running an 'Advertising agency' and earning a lot by providing this service to big industries. The working capital requirement of the firm will be less.

Ans True

62 Ranjan and Rajneesh are friends. Ranjan has a readymade garments shop whereas Rajneesh manufactures readymade garments.

Their common friend. Revansh, thinks that the Cash Conversion Cycle (CCC) for both of them will be the same as they deal in same business. Revansh's view is correct.

Ans False. CCC of a manufacturing firm is lengthier than that of a trading firm.

63 After pursuing a course in event management, Kajal and her brother Kamal promoted an event management company under the name KK Entertainment Private Limited. They strive together as dedicated and dynamic professionals managing different kinds of formal and informal events across all major cities in India and abroad.

They design the event idea and co-ordinate the different aspects of the event to make it a grand success. As a policy, they take fifty percent of the payment as advance from the client before the start of an event and receive the balance charges after the successful completion of the event. In context of the above case, the working capital requirements of KK Entertainment Private Limited will be relatively more.

Ans False. It is less as they are engaged in providing event management services, wherein there is no need to maintain inventory.

Case Based Questions

64 Read the following article and answer the questions that follow

Seema has opened a restaurant by investing ₹ 15,00,000 in which ₹ 5,00,000 were her own savings and ₹ 10,00,000 were borrowings from a bank in the type of loan. During the first month of opening, only 30 people took a meal at the restaurant and the billed amount came to ₹ 39,000.

Rita is the stock manager for the restaurant and keeps a record of all the raw material used in the daily activities. Rita wants to be sure of the inventory or stock level that they should keep in the store and wants to be efficient in ordering the materials from the supplier. After completing first three months of business, Seema estimated that the fixed costs of the restaurant were ₹ 20,00,000 and the variable costs were ₹ 10,00,000. The current assets amounted to ₹ 5,00,000 and current liabilities were ₹ 3,00,000.

After seeing a decline and loss in business, Seema took some ideas from friends and relatives and came up with an interior that provided a cozy space for students to study and socialise with affordable fast foods and snacks served by the restaurant.

With this idea implemented, the restaurant reported ₹ 25,00,000 of profit in the first year and became a famous space for quality time.

(i) Identify the unit price of the restaurant in the first month?

(a) ₹ 1,400 (b) ₹ 1,300
(c) ₹ 1,200 (d) ₹ 1,500

Ans (b) Unit Price = Order Value /No. of Customers
= 39,000/30 = ₹ 1,300

(ii) The loan taken by Seema is a .... liability.

(a) non-current
(b) current
(c) Both (a) and (b)
(d) None of the above

Ans (a) non-current

(iii) "Rita wants to be sure of the inventory or stock level that they should keep in the store and wants to be efficient in ordering the materials from the supplier."

Which of the following methods can be used by Rita to become efficient in stock ordering?

(a) Calculating break-even point
(b) Calculating daily sales
(c) Calculating profits
(d) Calculating re-order point

Ans (d) Calculating re-order point

(iv) What was the working capital at the end of three years?

(a) ₹ 8,00,000 (b) ₹ 2,00,000
(c) ₹ 1,00,000 (d) ₹ 4,00,000

Ans (b) Working Capital = Current Assets − Current Liabilities
= 5,00,000 − 3,00,000
= ₹ 2,00,000

(v) What is the return on investment that Seema made in the restaurant?

(a) 1.78 (b) 1.90
(c) 1.87 (d) 1.67

Ans (d) Return on Investment = Net Profit/ Investment
= 25,00,000/15,00,000
= 1.67

65 Read the following article and answer the questions that follow

Stencils Limited is a stationary business that sells made-in- India stationary products to its customers. Stencils Limited has 7 stores in Hyderabad and also sells products through various online websites and pages. Gurmeet, the owner of Stencils Limited is an ex-army officer and runs his business with proper discipline and rules.

He calculates the unit price unit cost and unit of sale at the end of every month to ascertain the health of the business. The business deals in hundreds of different stationary products and has become a prominent stop for customers to get purely domestically made products.

The business was going very well, until one of the stores reported a problem in the short-term financial position of the company and poorly dealt inventory and cash. Gurmeet ordered a probe into the matter and it was revealed that the problem was due to a lack of operational efficiency.

The manager of another store advised Gurmeet to look after the inventory control with a flexible approach rather than the old fixed way of ordering materials.

After thinking for some time, Gurmeet agreed to shift to flexible inventory order system, which is, ordering inventory as and when needed. This showed a positive effect on the operational efficiency of the store.

(i) "He calculates the unit price, unit cost and unit of sale at the end of every month to ascertain the health of the business." What do we get after calculating the above mentioned figures?

(a) Net profit (b) Gross profit
(c) Net margin (d) Gross margin

Ans (b) Gross profit

(ii) For a business like Stencils Limited, the unit price is the .... billed per customer.

(a) total amount
(b) gross amount
(c) average amount
(d) aggregate amount

Ans (c) average amount

(iii) "The business was going very well, until one of the stores reported a problem in the short-term financial position of the company and poorly dealt inventory and cash."

Which of the following is an indicator of such problem?

(a) Units sold
(b) Inventory level
(c) Break-even point
(d) Working capital

Ans (d) Working capital

(iv) What will be the length of operating cycle for Stencils Limited?

(a) Short
(b) Medium
(c) Long
(d) Very long

Ans (a) Short

(v) What else could have done to deal with the operational efficiency problem?

(a) Procurement of material at minimum possible cost
(b) Identifying bottlenecks in the processes
(c) Optimum utilisation of resources
(d) All of the above

Ans (d) All of the above

Short Answer Type I Questions (2 Marks)

1 Explain the importance of unit of sale as a management tool.

Ans Unit of sale is a management tool that is required to understand the economics of the business in an easy and standardised way. It helps a business in tracking progress over a number of years and taking corrective actions, when necessary.

2 Give the 'Unit of sale' for the following businesses.
Mall, Restaurant, Cricket Match, Theatre.

Ans

Business	Unit of Sale
Mall	Customer
Restaurant	Diner
Cricket Match	Spectator
Theatre	Audience

3 'Ayush Generic Medicines', a chemist shop sells generic medicines. On 15th February, 2016 medicines as per the details given below were sold

No. of Customers	Per Customer Billed (₹)
15	370
20	430
45	500
25	1,000
95	1,200

Calculate the average amount of medicines sold per customer. **(CBSE 2017)**

Ans

No. of Customers	Per Customer Billed (₹)	Total Billed (₹)
15	370	5,550
20	430	8,600
45	500	22,500
25	1,000	25,000
95	1,200	1,14,000
Total = 200 customers		Total = ₹ 1,75,650

Average amount of medicines sold per customer

$= \frac{\text{Total Billed Amount}}{\text{Total Number of Customers}} = \frac{1,75,650}{200}$

= ₹ 878.25

4 Number of people who took their meals and the total billing for each of the 5 weeks is in the following table. What are the 'unit of sale' and the 'unit price' in this case? If the variable cost is 50% of the sale price, calculate the 'unit cost' and the 'gross margin' per unit of sale. **(CBSE TBQ)**

Weeks	Number of People taking Meals	Total Amount Billed (₹)	Average Amount Billed (₹)
Week 1	120	18,000	150
Week 2	60	12,300	205
Week 3	70	10,220	146
Week 4	80	17,680	221
Week 5	90	21,600	240
Total	420	79,800	—

Ans Unit of sale in the above example will be 'diners', i.e. people buying the meals.

Unit Price $= \frac{\text{Total Billed Amount}}{\text{Number of Diners}} = \frac{79,800}{420}$ = ₹ 190

Unit Cost = 50% of Unit Price = 50% of 190
= ₹ 95

Gross Profit Per Unit = Unit Price – Unit Cost
= 190 – 95
= ₹ 95

5 A beauty parlour had varying number of customers during 5 weeks. This information and the total weekly billing are in the following table. What are the 'unit of sale' and the 'unit price' in this case?

If the cost of goods sold or variable cost is 60% of the sale price, calculate the 'unit cost' and the 'gross margin' per unit of sales. **(CBSE TBQ)**

Weeks	Number of Customers	Total Amount Billed (₹)	Average Amount Billed (₹) per Customer
Week 1	10	1,000	100
Week 2	17	1,445	85
Week 3	13	923	71
Week 4	22	5,082	231
Week 5	18	3,150	175
Total	80	11,600	—

Ans Unit of sale in this case is 'customer'.

Unit Price $= \frac{\text{Total Billed Amount}}{\text{Number of Customers}}$

$= \frac{11,600}{80}$

= ₹ 145

Unit Cost = 60% of Unit Price = 60% of 145
= ₹ 87

Gross Margin Per Unit of Sale = Unit Price – Unit Cost
= 145 – 87
= ₹ 58

6 Fixed Expenses = Quantity Sold × Gross Profit per Unit. How?

Ans We know that at break-even level,
Total Revenue = Total Cost.

i.e. (Quantity Sold × Unit Price)
= (Quantity Sold × Unit Cost) + Fixed Expenses

Or Quantity Sold × (Unit Price – Unit Cost) + Fixed Expenses

Or Quantity Sold × Gross Profit per Unit
= Fixed Expenses

7 Explain the concept of 'Break-even point' with the help of an example. **(Delhi 2014)**

Ans 'Break-even point' is the point of production at which total sales equals total cost. It is the condition of 'no profit, no loss' for an enterprise.

Suppose, a shirt manufacturer sells 100 shirts for ₹ 50,000 and his total cost also amounts to ₹ 50,000, then the production of 100 shirts is his break-even point.

8 What is referred to as the excess of selling price over variable cost?

Ans Contribution refers to the excess of selling price over the variable cost. It is also referred to as gross margin. It can be expressed by the following formula

Contribution = Selling Price − Variable Cost

or Contribution = Fixed Cost + Profit

9 At zero level of output, total expenses are also zero. Do you agree? Why or why not?

Ans At zero level of output, total cost is not zero as the business has to bear certain fixed cost even at this level, such as salary of the administrative staff, rent of premises, etc.

10 The fixed expenses of 'Wick and Wack' Limited is ₹ 2,75,000. The selling price of the toy 'Wick and Wack' is ₹ 50 and the variable cost is ₹ 30 per unit. Find the break-even quantity and sales at break-even level.

Ans Fixed expenses = ₹ 2,75,000

Contribution Per Unit = Selling Price − Variable Cost

= 50 − 30 = ₹ 20

$$\therefore \text{ Break-even Quantity} = \frac{\text{Fixed Expenses}}{\text{Contribution Per Unit}} = \frac{2,75,000}{20}$$

= 13,750 units

Sales at Break-even Level

= Break-even Quantity × Selling Price Per Unit

= 13,750 × 50 = ₹ 6,87,500

11 What kind of items are included in working capital?

Ans All items of recurring nature are included in working capital which are either due for payment or recovery in the course of one year. e.g. arrears of rent to be collected from tenant or arrears of rent to be paid to landlord.

12 Net working capital can be negative or positive, but gross working capital is always positive. Why?

Ans Net working capital is basically the difference between current assets and current liabilities. If current assets are more than current liabilities, net working capital will be positive. If on the other hand, current liabilities are more than current assets, working capital will be negative. But, gross working capital is the sum of current assets only, therefore it is always positive.

13 Ramu is buying and selling ice-cream. Explain his working capital requirements. **(CBSE TBQ)**

Ans Ramu is engaged in a trading business. Working capital requirement of a trading business is less as compared to a manufacturing business because of a shorter cash conversion cycle. So, his working capital needs will comprise of

(i) Cash for purchasing ice-creams.

(ii) Cash for payment of various operating expenses and meeting short-term liabilities, ex-payment to creditors for credit purchase of ice-creams, etc.

14 Nitin is a young entrepreneur who has decided to venture into the business of manufacturing cycles for children.

He wants to have an assessment that in how many days, his investment will start generating cash flows. So, give him the operating cycle of a manufacturing company.

Ans For a manufacturing company, operating cycle is the length of time needed to complete the following

(i) Conversion of cash into raw materials.

(ii) Conversion of raw materials into work-in-progress.

(iii) Conversion of work-in-progress into finished goods.

(iv) Conversion of finished goods into accounts receivables.

(v) Conversion of accounts receivables into cash.

15 Rahul wants to open a retail outlet dealing in men's wear. Give his operating cycle.

Ans Rahul is engaged in a trading business. In a trading concern, the operating cycle will include the length of time taken for

(i) Procurement of goods

(ii) Realisation of sales revenue

16 Working capital is of two types. Explain them.

Ans There are two types of working capital

(i) **Gross Working Capital** It refers to investment in all the current assets taken together.

(ii) **Net working Capital** It refers to the excess of current assets over current liabilities.

17 Give reasons for the following situations in business. **(CBSE SQP)**

(i) Operating cycle is shorter in trading business than in manufacturing business.

(ii) Shelf life has an impact on the inventory.

Ans (i) In manufacturing activity, the entrepreneur starts with buying raw materials and packing materials etc. These materials are then converted into the end product. During the time required to convert raw material to the end product, various expenses like wages, rent, salary, utility bill, insurance etc are to be paid. Once the end product is ready, it has to be sold and money is received from the customer. Whereas in trading business, entrepreneur buys finished products and then sells them to customers. So, operating cycle is shorter in trading business.

(ii) Items like vegetables, fruits, flowers and fish are perishable in nature. This calls for special storage conditions and equipment such cold storage, freezers etc. These have financial implications.

Similarly, some of the manufactured food or medicinal products have expiry dates, beyond which they are not fit for consumption. This imposes certain constraints on inventory management. These products are therefore bought in limited quantity as compared to those goods which are non-perishable.

18 Why is inventory control essential for an entrepreneur? Give any two reasons.

Or State any four advantages of 'inventory control'.

Ans Inventory control is essential for the following reasons

(i) To know whether materials are readily available for production use.

(ii) To ensure prompt delivery of materials to consumers.

(iii) To stabilise fluctuations of demand.

(iv) To control carrying and holding costs.

19 What is Pareto's Principle? **(CBSE TBQ)**

Ans Pareto's Principle basically states that a relatively handful of things will generate the bulk of the results. It is also referred to as '80/20' rule.

20 What is ABC analysis? **(CBSE TBQ)**

Ans In ABC (Always Better Control) analysis, a company classifies all its inventory in three groups- 'A', 'B' and 'C'.

'A' group contains inventory which is 70-80% in terms of value, but only 10-20% in terms of quantity. 'B' group contains inventory which is 10-20% in terms of value and 15-25% in terms of quantity. 'C' group contains inventory which is 5-10% in terms of value and 65-75% in terms of quantity.

21 A company uses 300 units of an item per day and the order lead time in 5 days. What should be the level of inventory when a new order is being placed?

Ans Re-order Level = Maximum Rate of Consumption × Maximum Re-order Period

Accordingly, Re-order Level = 300 × 5

= 1,500 units

So, the level of inventory should be 1,500 units when a new order is being placed.

22 There is a positive relationship between order size and carrying cost. Why?

Ans Larger the order size, higher the carrying cost because of high average inventory. Smaller the order size, lower the carrying cost because of low average inventory.

23 There is an inverse relationship between order size and ordering cost. Why?

Ans Larger the order size, lower the ordering costs because of fewer orders. Smaller the order size, higher the ordering costs because of more orders.

24 What is the basic difference between 'depreciation' and 'amortisation' ? Give any two methods of charging depreciation.

Ans The basic difference between 'depreciation' and 'amortisation' is that depreciation is charged on tangible assets and amortisation is an act of writing-off intangible assets.

Two methods of charging depreciation are as follows

(i) Fixed instalment method

(ii) Reducing balance method

25 Interest is an operational expense or a financial expense? Give reason.

Ans Interest is paid to the owner of the fund to compensate him for parting with his funds. So, it is a financial expense and not an operational one.

26 A book shop sells pens 30,000 quantity per year. Demand is uniform. Purchase cost is ₹ 6 per pen. Holding cost per annum is 20% of purchase cost. Ordering cost is ₹ 500 per order. What should be the EOQ for the shopkeeper? **(CBSE TBQ)**

Ans Here, D = ₹ 30,000; P = ₹ 500 and C = 1.2 (20% of 6). So, $2\times P\times D = 3{,}00{,}00{,}000$. This divided by 1.2 = 2,50,00,000.

Square root of which is 5,000. So, the EOQ is 5,000 pens.

27 Pankaj an entrepreneur started a new website 'SAVO ELECTRICITY' to sell LED bulbs. In the first year he sold 2,400 bulbs at the rate of ₹ 100 each. His cost of placing an order and receiving the bulbs is ₹ 500 per order. If the economic order quantity is 200 bulbs, find out the inventory holding cost per year. **(CBSE 2016)**

Ans Given, Annual Requirement of Inventory or Annual Sales in units (A) = 2,400 bulbs,

Cost of Placing Order (P) = ₹ 500 and

Economic Order Quantity (EOQ) = 200 bulbs.

We know that, $EOQ=\sqrt{\dfrac{2AP}{C}}$,

where C is the inventory holding cost per unit.

So, on substituting the variables, we get

$$200=\sqrt{\frac{2\times 2{,}400\times 500}{C}}$$

On squaring both the sides, we get

$$40{,}000=\frac{24{,}00{,}000}{C}$$

$$\Rightarrow \quad C=\frac{24{,}00{,}000}{40{,}000}=₹\,60$$

So, inventory holding cost per year = Inventory Cost per Unit × Average Inventory

$$=60\times\frac{200}{2}=60\times 100$$

$$=₹\,6{,}000$$

Note *Average Inventory* = EOQ/2

28 The annual quantity of Jackets sold by Meghana Wool Mart is 12,000 at the rate of ₹ 1,000/per jacket.

The cost of placing an order and receiving goods is ₹ 500/per order. Inventory holding cost is ₹ 300/per annum. What is the economic order quantity for Meghana Wool Mart? **(CBSE SQP Term II)**

Ans Here, D = 12,000; P = ₹ 500 and C = ₹ 300

$$\text{Now, EOQ}=\sqrt{\frac{2PD}{C}}=\sqrt{\frac{2\times 500\times 12{,}000}{300}}$$

$$=\sqrt{\frac{1{,}20{,}00{,}000}{300}}$$

= 200 Jackets

29 Write a short note on 'Return on investment'.

Ans Return on Investment (RoI) indicates the percentage of return on total capital invested in the business.

Return on Investment (RoI)

$$=\frac{\text{Net Profit}}{\text{Total Capital Invested}}\times 100$$

where, Total Capital Invested = Equity + Debt.

30 What do you understand by 'Return on equity'?

Ans Return on Equity (RoE) is a measure of profitability, calculated as a percentage of equity only.

$$\text{Return on Equity (RoE)}=\frac{\text{Net Income}}{\text{Equity}}\times 100$$

where, Equity = Money invested by the owner himself.

31 Companies may have their level of optimal working capital that maximises their values through the effective management of current liabilities and assets.

Previously, many studies were made on the impact of working capital management on the company's performance in different sectors; however, its impact on the performance of firms that are engaged in export activities was not given any consideration and this particular study has attempted to investigate the fundamental impact of working capital management on the export firm's performance in Ethiopia.

To analyse this particular study, a total of 164 exporters operating in Ethiopia have been taken as a sample and both primary and secondary data collection methods were used.

The data gathered from the sample of the study were analysed using a multiple linear regression model and the result reveals that working capital management which was measured by account receivables period, cash conversion cycle and accounts payable period has a statistically significant and positive correlation with the performance of exporting firms in Ethiopia which was measured by both return on assets and return on investment.

However, working capital management which was measured by the inventory conversion period has a statistically significant and positive impact on return on investment, but it has an insignificant impact on the performance of sampled export firms in Ethiopia which was measured by return on assets.

Based on the result of the study, firms may need to extend credit terms for customers, may prolong their cash conversion cycle, may need an extended payment period and may or may not hold a high volume of inventory. All extending periods and cycles shall be made up to the extent of attaining an optimal level of working capital and better to implement a conservative policy of working capital management.

Thus, it is advisable to consider the result of this study while making decisions regarding their working capital management to support their performance.

Source *Volume 2021 |Article ID 6681572.*

Which concept is highlighted in the given paragraph?

Ans Importance of working capital. Working capital refers to the money needed to fund the normal day-to-day operations of the business. It is that part of total capital, which is required for holding current assets or it may also be defined as excess of current assets over current liabilities.

Short Answer Type II Questions (3 Marks)

1 Name and explain the concept which states that at a particular volume of production, a firm neither makes a profit nor a loss.

Ans Break-even point is the concept which states that at a particular level of production a firm is neither making any profit nor sustaining a loss.

At break-even point, revenue equals the total cost.

In the above graph, 'B' is the break-even point at which sales equals costs.

2 Break-even analysis has a major impact on the business decision-making. Comment. **(CBSE SQP)**

Ans Break-even analysis impacts business decision-making in the following manner

(i) It helps in setting profit goal and sales target.

(ii) In a manufacturing environment, it helps in determining the products that are not contributing to meet the fixed expenses and thus brings up the item for discussion in management meetings about its continuity.

(iii) Break-even point is the level of sales (or revenue generated) that equals all the expenses required for generating that revenue.

There is neither loss nor profit. It helps the organisation to determine the level when will it turn profitable.

3 Following information is related to sales mix of Pen, Sketch pen and Geometry box.

Product	Pen	Sketch Pen	Geometry Box
Sales Price Per Unit (in ₹)	40	45	75
Variable Cost Per Unit (in ₹)	22	30	40
Sales Mix-Percentage	20%	20%	60%

Total fixed cost is ₹ 90,000. Calculate the weighted average contribution per unit for the sales mix. **(CBSE 2016)**

Ans

Product	Pen	Sketch Pen	Geometry Box
Sales Price per Unit (₹)	40	45	75
(–) Variable Cost per Unit (₹)	(22)	(30)	(40)
Contribution per Unit (₹)	18	15	35
(×) Sale Mix Percentage	20%	20%	60%
	3.6	3	21
Weighted Average Contribution per Unit	3.6+ 3+ 21= 27.6		

4 Bigul Chaturvedi started a school bag business with his brother. Both were very excited about the new venture. With meticulous planning and a lot of hard work they were able to sell 1,000 bags in the first year. But they did not earn any profit.

Both were happy because they were not at loss and revenue generated was equal to the cost. Now they were moving towards earning profit in the second year. **(CBSE 2016)**

(i) Identify the component of financial plan discussed above.

(ii) By giving any four points state how this component is useful for the entrepreneur.

Ans (i) The component of financial plan discussed above is 'Break-even point'.

The break-even point is that level of volume of production at which firm neither makes a profit nor a loss. Here, the total revenue is equal to the total cost of a firm at a given level of capacity.

(ii) Calculation of Break-even Point (BEP) is quite useful for the entrepreneur as it helps in assessing

(a) the minimum level of output to be produced.

(b) the effect of change in quantity of output upon the profits.

(c) the selling price of the product.

(d) the profitable options of the line of production.

5 How is working capital calculated? Illustrate with an example.

Ans Working capital refers to that part of capital which is required for holding current assets. It is calculated with reference to the operating cycle of a business.

e.g. X Company Limited is planning to produce 1,000 units of component 'Y' per week. The raw material costs ₹ 2 per unit and labour cost is ₹ 1 per unit.

Raw material is stored for 2 weeks, work-in-progress duration is 1 week, finished goods are kept for a period of 3 weeks and debtors are allowed a credit period of 2 weeks.

Working capital will be calculated as follows

= Raw Material + Work-in-progress (Material + Labour) + Finished Goods + Debtors

$= (1,000 \times 2 \times 2) + (1,000 \times 2 \times 1) + (1,000 \times 1 \times 1) + (1,000 \times 3 \times 3) + (1,000 \times 3 \times 2)$

$= 4,000 + 2,000 + 1,000 + 9,000 + 6,000$

= ₹ 22,000

6 What are current assets and current liabilities? Explain by giving examples.

Ans Current assets are those assets which are expected to get converted into cash or cash equivalents within a period of one year. Examples of current assets are

(i) Cash in hand/Cash at bank

(ii) Marketable securities

(iii) Bills receivables

(iv) Debtors, etc.

Current liabilities refer to those liabilities which are payable within a period of one year. Examples of current liabilities are

(i) Bills payable

(ii) Creditors

(iii) Outstanding expenses

(iv) Advances received from customers, etc.

7 Calculate working capital of Raja and Co who has the following items in its balance sheet.

Stock ₹ 50,000; trade creditors ₹ 32,000; debtors ₹ 75,000; cash ₹ 1,00,000; dividend payable ₹ 50,000; tax ₹ 44,000; short-term loan ₹ 61,000; short-term investments ₹ 76,000. Calculate gross and net working capital. **(CBSE TBQ)**

Ans Gross Working Capital

= Sum Total of all Current Assets

= Stock + Debtors + Cash + Short-term Investments

= 50,000 + 75,000 + 1,00,000 + 76,000

= ₹ 3,01,000

Net Working Capital = Total Current Assets – Total Current Liabilities

= (Stock + Debtors + Cash + Short-term Investments) – (Trade Creditors + Dividend Payable + Tax + Short-term Loan)

= (50,000 + 75,000 + 1,00,000 + 76,000) – (32,000 + 50,000 + 44,000 + 61,000)

= 3,01,000 – 1,87,000 = ₹ 1,14,000

8 Current assets of a firm are cash = ₹ 50,000, debtors = ₹ 75,000, inventory = ₹ 1,00,500. Its current liabilities are bills payable = ₹ 35,000, Creditors = ₹ 80,000.

On the basis of the given information, compute gross working capital and net working capital.

Ans Gross Working Capital (GWC)

= Sum Total of all Current Assets

= Cash + Debtors + Inventory

= 50,000 + 75,000 + 1,00,500 = ₹ 2,25,500

Net Working Capital (NWC)

= Total Current Assets – Total Current Liabilities

= (Cash + Debtors + Inventory) – (Bills Payable + Creditors)

= (50,000 + 75,000 + 1,00,500) – (35,000 + 80,000)

= ₹ 1,10,500

9

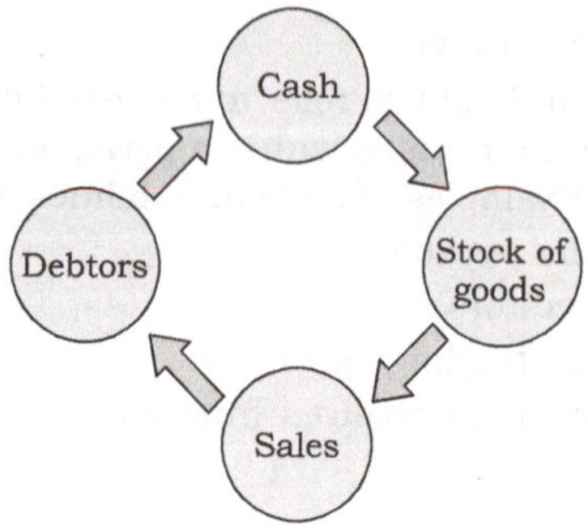

(i) Identify the type of business whose operating cycle is represented above?

(ii) Analyse the working capital requirement for the type of business identified in (i) **(CBSE SQP Term II)**

Ans (i) Trading business

(ii) For trading business, where there is no manufacturing (or conversion), the operating cycle will be shorter, so the working capital requirement would also be less.

10 Give the meaning of 'cash conversion cycle'. How does the nature of business influence its cash conversion cycle? Explain with the help of a diagram. **(CBSE 2023)**

Ans The amount of time (measured in days) it takes for a business to convert its investments in inventory and other resources into cash flows from sales is known as the Cash Conversion Cycle (CCC).

The cash conversion cycle is the length of time between a firm's purchase of inventory and the receipt of cash from accounts receivables. CCC represents the number of days a firm's cash remains tied up in the operations of the business.

Different products will have different operating cycles. "Longer the operating cycle, requirement of working capital will be more, while shorter the cycle, less working capital is needed."

For instance, the operating cycles of a trading concern and a manufacturing concern are explained below

(i) **In a Trading Concern** Refer to Q.No. 9 of short answer type II questions (3 Marks).

(ii) **In a Manufacturing Company** Refer to text on page 164.

11 Calculate the operating cycle of Vijay Enterprises, if working capital requirement per week is ₹ 12,000 and production cycle is one week.

Number of soaps to be produced per week = 200 units

Labour charges per week = ₹ 2,000

Cost of raw materials per week = ₹ 4,000 **(Delhi 2014)**

Ans Operating cycle is the length of time between buying of raw material and receiving cash from customer.

Working capital requirement = ₹ 12,000

Labour charges per week = ₹ 2,000

Cost of raw material per week = ₹ 4,000

Combined cost of labour and raw materials = ₹ 6,000

Operating Cycle

$$= \frac{\text{Working Capital Requirements}}{\text{Combined Cost of Labour and Raw Materials}}$$

$$= \frac{12,000}{6,000} = 2 \text{ weeks}$$

12 Janata Foods Ltd.' is a restaurant situated on a national highway near Hyderabad. The following figures have been extracted from the books of Janata Foods Ltd. **(CBSE 2017)**

Particulars	Amt (₹)
Stock of Raw Material	1,50,000
Short-term Loans	1,83,000
Trade Creditors	96,000
Trade Debtors	2,25,000
Dividend Payable	1,50,000
Tax Payable	1,32,000
Short-term Investments	2,28,000

From the above information, calculate the following

(i) Gross working capital (ii) Net working capital

Ans (i) Gross Working Capital

= Sum Total of All Current Assets

= Stock of Raw Material + Trade Debtors + Short-termInvestments

= 1,50,000 + 2,25,000 + 2,28,000 = ₹ 6,03,000

(ii) Net Working Capital = Current Assets − Current Liabilities,

where,

Current Assets = Stock of Raw Material + Trade Debtors + Short-term Investments

= 1,50,000 + 2,25,000 + 2,28,000

= ₹ 6,03,000

Current Liabilities = Short-term Loans + Trade Creditors + Dividend Payable + Tax Payable

= 1,83,000 + 96,000 + 1,50,000 + 1,32,000

= ₹ 5,61,000

∴ Net Working Capital = 6,03,000 − 5,61,000

= ₹ 42,000

13 Explain inventory control and state its objectives. **(CBSE TBQ)**

Ans Inventory control involves the planning, organising and controlling the procurement, storage and usage of stock so as to achieve the objectives of efficiency and economy.

The various objectives of inventory control are as follows

(i) To avoid the situation of understocking and overstocking.

(ii) To ensure the procurement of good quality material at minimum cost.

(iii) To minimise ordering and carrying cost.

(iv) To avoid wastages and losses during storage and usage.

(v) To maintain proper and upto date records of inventory.

14 Explain 'Stock keeping unit code', 'Lead time' and 'Safety aspects' as items that make up the inventory. **(CBSE 2020)**

Ans Refer to text on page 166.

15 Find out EOQ and number of orders to be placed during the year from the following information.

Annual consumption = 120 units

Buying cost per order = ₹ 20

Price per unit = ₹ 100

Storage cost as percentage of inventory = 12%.

Ans Given Annual usage (D) = 120 units

Buying cost per order (P) = ₹ 20

$$\text{Storage Cost (C)} = 100 \times \frac{12}{100} = 12$$

$$\text{EOQ} = \sqrt{\frac{2PD}{C}} = \sqrt{\frac{2 \times 20 \times 120}{12}}$$

$$= \sqrt{400} = 20 \text{ units}$$

$$\text{Number of orders} = \frac{120}{20} = 6 \text{ orders}$$

16 Paramveer Singh runs an online business for gym equipments. The annual demand for the Waist Flexors sold by him is 16,000 units.

The annual holding cost of Waist Flexors per unit is ₹ 48 and the cost of placing an order is ₹ 1,500. Calculate the Economic Order Quantity of Waist Flexors. **(CBSE 2018)**

Ans Annual Demand (A) = 16,000 units.

Annual Holding Cost (C) = ₹ 48 per unit.

Cost of Placing an Order (P) = ₹ 1,500

$$\text{Economic Order Quantity} = \sqrt{\frac{2AP}{C}}$$

$$= \sqrt{\frac{2 \times 16{,}000 \times 1{,}500}{48}}$$

$$= \sqrt{10{,}00{,}000} = 1{,}000 \text{ units}$$

17 Aditya Bearings Ltd. are the manufacturers and suppliers of ball bearings to fan manufacturing companies. The company requires 900 kg of wrought iron for its production process. The cost of placing each order is ₹ 50 and carrying cost is ₹ 100. Calculate economic order quantity. **(CBSE 2019)**

Ans Economic Order Quantity (EOQ) = $\sqrt{\frac{2AP}{C}}$, where

A = Annual usage = 900 kg

P = Cost of placing order = ₹ 50

C = Carrying cost = ₹ 100

On substituting we get, EOQ

$$= \sqrt{\frac{2 \times 900 \times 50}{100}} = \sqrt{900} = 30 \text{ kg}$$

18 'The shop', a readymade garments retail shop, sold 5,000 shirts at ₹ 200 per shirt during the year ended 31st March, 2014. Cost of placing an order and receiving goods is ₹ 1,000 per order. Inventory holding cost is ₹ 250 per year. Calculate the 'Economic order quantity' for 'the shop'. **(CBSE 2015)**

Ans Annual sales (in units) = 5,000 shirts

Cost of placing an order (P) = ₹ 1,000

Inventory holding cost per unit (C) = ₹ 250

$$\text{Economic Order Quantity} = \sqrt{\frac{2AP}{C}}$$

Where, A = Annual sales in units

P = Cost of placing an order

C = Carrying cost per unit

On substituting the above variables, we get

$$\text{EOQ} = \sqrt{\frac{2 \times 5{,}000 \times 1{,}000}{250}}$$

$$= \sqrt{40{,}000} = 200 \text{ shirts}$$

19 'Meow Milk Center' sells 3,000 bottles of flavoured milk per year. Cost of one milk bottle is ₹ 60. Holding cost per annum is ₹ 12. Ordering cost is ₹ 500 per order. Calculate the 'Economic order quantity'. **(CBSE 2020)**

Ans Economic Order Quantity (EOQ) = $\sqrt{\frac{2PD}{C}}$,

where, P = Cost of placing an order = ₹ 500

D = Annual demand = 3,000 bottles

C = Inventory carrying cost per unit = ₹ 12

On substituting, we get,

$$\text{EOQ} = \sqrt{\frac{2 \times 500 \times 3{,}000}{12}}$$

$$= \sqrt{2{,}50{,}000}$$

$$= 500 \text{ bottles}$$

20 Arjun owns a factory which manufactures glass products. Some of his products are also patented.

During the last 3 years of operating business, he has failed to provide for depreciation and amortisation.

Now, some of the assets need replacement and he is facing shortage of funds. Advise him, as to why he should charge depreciation and amortisation?

Ans When an asset is purchased, it is nothing more than a payment in advance for the use of the asset. Depreciation or amortisation is the cost of using that asset per year and should, therefore, be debited to profit and loss account of the business. If depreciation is not provided, the profits of the concern will be overstated. It is also possible that owners have withdrawn such profits.

So, at the end of the working life of the asset, there will be no funds to purchase the assets, as in the given instance. So, depreciation and amortisation should be charged to business as an expense.

21 Differentiate between RoE and RoI.

Ans Return on Equity (RoE) and Return on Investment (RoI), both are profitability ratios.

Yet, they differ on the following aspects Difference between return on equity and return on investment are

Basis	Return on Equity (RoE)	Return on Investment (RoI)
Measure of Profitability	Return on equity is a measure of profitability calculated as a percentage of equity only.	It is a measure of overall profitability of the business.
Concept	It is a narrow concept.	It is a broader concept.
Components	There are two components (i) Net income (ii) Shareholders' funds of equity	There are two components (i) Net profit (ii) Total capital employed
Formula	$\text{RoE} = \frac{\text{Net Income}}{\text{Equity}} \times 100$	$\text{RoI} = \frac{\text{Net Profit}}{\text{Capital Employed}} \times 100$

22 From the following information, calculate the return on investment.
Net profit (After tax) ratio 12%, Tax rate 50%

Revenue from Operations	₹ 10,00,000
15% Long-term Borrowings	₹ 4,00,000
Equity Share Capital	₹ 1,50,000
Reserves and Surplus	₹ 1,50,000
20% Preference Share Capital	₹ 50,000

Ans Net Profit after Tax = Revenue from Operations × Net Profit Ratio

$$= 10,00,000 \times \frac{12}{100}$$

$$= ₹\ 1,20,000$$

Net Profit before Tax

= Net Profit after Tax + $\left(\text{Net Proft after Tax} \times \frac{50}{100}\right)$

$$= 1,20,000 + \left(1,20,000 \times \frac{50}{100}\right)$$

$$= ₹\ 1,80,000$$

Net Profit before Interest and Tax

$$= \text{Net Profit before Tax} + \left(4,00,000 \times \frac{15}{100}\right)$$

$$= 1,80,000 + \left(4,00,000 \times \frac{15}{100}\right)$$

$$= 1,80,000 + 60,000 = ₹\ 2,40,000$$

Capital Employed = Equity Share Capital + Long-term Borrowings + Reserves and Surplus + Preference Share Capital

$$= 1,50,000 + 4,00,000 + 1,50,000 + 50,000$$

$$= ₹\ 7,50,000$$

Return on Investment (RoI)

$$= \frac{\text{Net Profit before Interest and Tax}}{\text{Capital Employed}} \times 100$$

$$= \frac{2,40,000}{7,50,000} \times 100 = 32\%$$

23 Calculate the Return on Equity (RoE) for Malti International Limited manufacturing pre mix for instant shakes and smoothies from the details given below **(CBSE SQP Term II)**

(i) Investment ₹ 10,00,000
(ii) Borrowed funds ₹ 6,00,000
(iii) Interest rate per annum is 10%.
(iv) Monthly sales revenue is ₹ 6,00,000 and cost of goods sold is ₹ 3,00,000.
(v) Fixed expenses per month ₹ 2,00,000 (salary ₹ 1,50,000, rent and utility ₹ 50,000)
(vi) Depreciation ₹ 10,000
(vii) Tax @ 20%.

If Malti International Limited wishes to know how their own money is being used, which parameter for performance evaluation, RoE or RoI, should be used?

Ans **Calculation of RoE**

Particulars		Amt (₹)
Sales Revenue for the Year (6,00,000 × 12)		72,00,000
(–) Cost of Goods Sold (CoGS) for the Year (3,00,000 × 12)		(36,00,000)
Gross Revenue		36,00,000
(–) Fixed Expenses	(24,00,000)	
Depreciation	(10,000)	(24,10,000)
Gross Profit		11,90,000
(–) Interest on Borrowed Capital		(60,000)
Profit after Interest Before Tax		11,30,000
(–) Tax @ 20%		(2,26,000)
Net Earnings after Interest and Tax		9,04,000
RoE (Net Income/Equity × 100)		9,04,000/ 4,00,000 × 100 = 226%

∴ RoE for Malti Enterprises is 226%
RoE is a good indicator for performance evaluation.

24 Harsha started her herbal beauty products shop in Chandigarh with a capital of ₹ 9,00,000. She took a loan of ₹ 5,00,000 from the State Bank of India at 9% per annum interest. During the year ended 31st March, 2016 her sales were ₹ 20,90,000 and the cost of goods sold was ₹ 15,30,000. She paid monthly rent of the shop ₹ 11,000 and a monthly salary of ₹ 25,000 to the employees. The tax rate is 30%.
Calculate the return on equity. **(CBSE 2017)**

Ans Return on Equity (RoE)

$$= \frac{\text{Net Income or Profit after Tax}}{\text{Equity}} \times 100$$

Where,

Net Income = Sales – Cost of Goods Sold – Rent – Salary – Interest – Tax

$= 20,90,000 - 15,30,000 - (11,000 \times 12) - (25,000 \times 12) - (5,00,000 \times 9\%) - 24,900$ (WN)

= ₹ 58,100

Equity = ₹ 9,00,000

$$\therefore \text{ Return on Equity (RoE)} = \frac{58,100}{9,00,000} \times 100 = 6.46\%$$

Working Note

Profit before Tax

$= 20,90,000 - 15,30,000 - 1,32,000 - 3,00,000 - 45,000$

= ₹ 83,000

Tax = 83,000 × 30% = ₹ 24,900

25 Price for a business is often quoted as a multiple of EBITDA. Why?

Ans Price for a business is often quoted in terms of a multiple of its EBITDA, say e.g. (M) × EBITDA, where M has a numeric value that varies from industry to industry. Basic philosophy in this thought process is that when someone buys a business, he or she buys the 'future cash flows' from that business. Hence, they are willing to pay a multiple of EBITDA.

Long Answer Type Questions (5 Marks)

1 A factory is engaged in manufacturing washing machines. The following information is available to you

Sales = ₹ 4,00,000
Direct labour cost (2,000 units) = ₹ 40,000
Direct material cost (2,000 units) = ₹ 1,00,000
Direct expenses (2,000 units) = ₹ 20,000
Fixed cost = ₹ 1,20,000
Find out
(i) Variable cost per unit
(ii) Total cost
(iii) Quantity to be sold at break-even point
(CBSE 2014 C)

Ans (i) Total Variable Cost = Direct Labour Cost + Direct Material Cost + Direct Expenses

$= 40,000 + 1,00,000 + 20,000$

= ₹ 1,60,000

$$\text{Variable Cost Per Unit} = \frac{\text{Total Variable Cost}}{\text{Number of Units}} = \frac{1,60,000}{2,000} = ₹\ 80$$

(ii) Total Cost = Total Variable Cost + Fixed Cost

$= 1,60,000 + 1,20,000 =$ ₹ 2,80,000

$$\text{(iii) Break-even Point} = \frac{\text{Fixed Cost}}{\text{P/V Ratio}}$$

$$\text{P/V Ratio} = \frac{\text{Sales} - \text{Total Variable Cost}}{\text{Sales}} = \frac{4,00,000 - 1,60,000}{4,00,000} = 0.6$$

$$\text{Break-even Point} = \frac{1,20,000}{0.6} = 2,00,000$$

$$\because \text{ Selling Price Per Unit} = \frac{4,00,000}{2,000} = ₹200$$

Quantity to be Sold at Break-even Point

$$= \frac{2,00,000}{200} = 1,000 \text{ units}$$

2 A factory is engaged in manufacturing coolers. The following information is available to you

Sales = ₹ 2,50,000
Direct labour cost (for 100 units) = ₹ 25,000
Direct material cost (for 100 units) = ₹ 62,500
Direct expenses (for 100 units) = ₹ 12,500
Fixed cost = ₹ 75,000
Calculate
(i) Variable cost per unit (ii) Total cost
(iii) Break-even point
Are actual sales exceeding the sales required to break-even? **(CBSE 2013)**

Ans (i) Variable Cost = Direct Labour Cost + Direct Material Cost + Direct Expense

$= 25,000 + 62,500 + 12,500 =$ ₹ 1,00,000

$$\text{Variable Cost Per Unit} = \frac{\text{Variable Cost}}{\text{Number of Units}} = \frac{1,00,000}{100} = ₹\ 1,000 \text{ per unit}$$

(ii) Total Cost = Fixed Cost + Variable Cost
$= 75{,}000 + 1{,}00{,}000 = ₹\ 1{,}75{,}000$

(iii) Break-even Point $= \dfrac{\text{Fixed Cost}}{\text{P/V Ratio}}$

P/V Ratio $= \dfrac{\text{Sales} - \text{Variable Cost}}{\text{Sales}}$

$= \dfrac{2{,}50{,}000 - 1{,}00{,}000}{2{,}50{,}000} = 0.6$

Break-even Point $= \dfrac{75{,}000}{0.6} = ₹\ 1{,}25{,}000$

Yes, actual sales are more than the sales required to break-even.

3 Bright Lights Pvt. Ltd. started a business of making three varieties of bulbs. From the following information, calculate break-even for the three varieties of bulbs for the company in units

Particulars	LED Bulb Zero Watt	LED Bulb 10 Watts	LED Bulb 20 Watts
Sales Price (₹)	80	45	60
Variable Cost (₹)	40	15	20
Sales Mix	50%	20%	30%

Fixed costs for the production process is ₹ 76,000. **(CBSE 2020)**

Ans

Particulars	LED Bulb Zero Watt	LED Bulb 10 Watts	LED Bulb 20 Watts
Sales Price per Unit (₹)	80	45	60
(–) Variable Cost per Unit (₹)	(40)	(15)	(20)
Contribution Margin per Unit (₹)	40	30	40
(×) Sales Mix Percentage	50%	20%	30%
Contribution Mix (₹)	20	6	12

∴ Weighted Average Contribution Mix (WACM)
$= 20 + 6 + 12$
$= ₹\ 38$

Now, break-even point in units

$= \dfrac{\text{Fixed Cost}}{\text{WACM}} = \dfrac{76{,}000}{38}$

$= 2{,}000$ units

Break-even Point of LED Bulbs

Particulars	LED Bulb Zero Watt	LED Bulb 10 Watts	LED Bulb 20 Watts
Sales Mix Ratio	50%	20%	30%
(×) Total Break-even Units (₹)	2,000	2,000	2,000
Product Units at Break-even Point	1,000	400	600
(×) Price per Unit (₹)	80	45	60
Product Sales (in ₹)	80,000	18,000	36,000

4 A manufacturing plant produces four different types of machinery tools and their variable costs and price are given below. The fixed costs are allocated – taking into consideration the utilisation of common resources for different products and they are also given separately for each product. Here, is the basic data

Products A, B, C and D
Selling Price ₹ 1,00,000; ₹ 50,000; ₹ 70,000 and ₹ 2,00,000 respectively.

Variable Cost ₹ 30,000; ₹ 25,000; ₹ 30,000 and ₹ 1,00,000 respectively.

Allocated fixed expenses per month ₹ 3,50,000; ₹ 2,50,000; ₹ 10,00,000 and ₹ 15,00,000 respectively. Compute break-even level for each of the product. **(CBSE TBQ)**

Ans

Products	A (₹)	B (₹)	C (₹)	D (₹)
Unit Selling Price	1,00,000	50,000	70,000	2,00,000
Unit Variable Cost	30,000	25,000	30,000	1,00,000
Contribution per Unit (Unit Selling Price – Unit Variable Cost)	70,000	25,000	40,000	1,00,000
Fixed Expenses per Month	3,50,000	2,50,000	10,00,000	15,00,000

Break-even Quantity $= \dfrac{\text{Fixed Expenses}}{\text{Contribution Per Unit}}$

So, Break-even Quantity for 'A'

$= \dfrac{3{,}50{,}000}{70{,}000} = 5$ units

Break-even Quantity for 'B'

$$= \frac{2,50,000}{25,000} = 10 \text{ units}$$

Break-even Quantity for 'C'

$$= \frac{10,00,000}{40,000} = 25 \text{ units}$$

Break-even Quantity for 'D'

$$= \frac{15,00,000}{1,00,000} = 15 \text{ units}$$

5 What is break-even point? Why should entrepreneurs know about break-even point? **(CBSE 2010 C)**

Or Why is it important for an entrepreneur to do break-even analysis? **(CBSE 2019)**

Ans **Break-even Point** Refer to to text on page 161.

Entrepreneurs should know about the break-even point of their enterprise as it helps them to take strategic decisions by providing them with the following information

(i) **Profitability of Products Business can be Known** The profitability of different products can be known with the help of break-even point.

The problem of managerial decision regarding temporary or permanent shut down of business or continuation at a loss can be solved by analysing break-even point.

(ii) **Effect of Changes in Cost and Selling Price can be Demonstrated** The effect of changes in fixed and variable costs at different levels of production is conveyed to the management through break-even point analysis.

So, it helps the management to provide for the requisites for the survival of the enterprise.

(iii) **Cost Control can be Exercised** The break-even point analysis shows the relative importance of fixed cost in the total cost of a product. If the costs are high, it induces the entrepreneur to take measures to control such costs.

Thus, it is a managerial tool for control and reduction of costs, elimination of wastage and achieving better efficiency.

(iv) **Forecasting and Planning Possible** Break-even point analysis is very helpful for forecasting, long-term planning, growth and stability.

6 A hotel had varying number of guests during five weeks. The information regarding the number of guests and the average weekly billing is presented in the following table

Week	No. of Guests	Average Billed (₹)
1	240	300
2	120	410
3	140	292
4	160	442
5	180	480

(i) What is the 'Unit of sale' and 'Unit price' in this case?

(ii) If the cost of goods sold or variable cost is 60% of the sales price, calculate the 'Unit cost' and the 'Gross profit'. **(CBSE 2019)**

Ans (i) The unit of sale is 'guest'. The unit price will be computed as follows

No. of Guests	Average Billed (₹)	Total Billed (₹)
240	300	72,000
120	410	49,200
140	292	40,880
160	442	70,720
180	480	86,400
840		3,19,200

$$\text{Unit Price} = \frac{\text{Total Billed Amount}}{\text{Total Guest}}$$

$$= \frac{3,19,200}{840} = ₹\ 380$$

(ii) Unit Cost = 60% of 380 = ₹ 228

Gross Profit = Unit Price − Unit Cost

= 380 − 228 = ₹ 152

7 Calculate break-even point for a textile shop on the basis of the given information.

Garments sold are silk sarees, cotton sarees, suit materials, kids wear.

Selling prices (in ₹)

Silk sarees = ₹ 3,500/ saree, Cotton sarees = ₹ 900/ saree, Suit materials = ₹ 1,800/ suit, Kids wear = ₹ 450/wear

Variable cost Silk sarees = 1,050 pieces, Cotton sarees = 270 pieces, Suit materials = 540 pieces, Kids wear = 135 pieces

Allocated fixed expenses

Silk sarees = ₹ 2,45,000, Cotton sarees = ₹ 1,57,500, Suit material = ₹ 63,000, Kids wear = ₹ 70,875

Ans Contribution per Unit of Silk Sarees

= Selling Price per Saree – Variable Cost per Saree

= 3,500 – 1,050 = ₹ 2,450

Contribution per Unit of Cotton Sarees

= Selling Price per Saree – Variable Cost per Saree

= 900 – 270 = ₹ 630

Contribution per Unit of Suit Material = Selling Price per Unit – Variable Cost per Unit

= 1,800 – 540 = ₹ 1,260

Contribution per Unit of Kids Wear = Selling Price per Unit – Variable Cost per Unit

= 450 – 135 = ₹ 315

Break-even Point (in terms of quantity)

$$= \frac{\text{Fixed Expenses}}{\text{Contribution per Unit}}$$

Accordingly, Break-even Point

$$\text{For silk sarees} = \frac{2{,}45{,}000}{2{,}450} = 100 \text{ sarees}$$

$$\text{For cotton sarees} = \frac{1{,}57{,}500}{630} = 250 \text{ sarees}$$

$$\text{For suit material} = \frac{63{,}000}{1{,}260} = 50 \text{ pieces}$$

$$\text{For kids wear} = \frac{70{,}875}{315} = 225 \text{ pieces}$$

Combined Break-even Sale (in ₹)

= (100 × 3,500 + 250 × 900 + 50 × 1,800 + 225 × 450)

= 3,50,000 + 2,25,000 + 90,000 + 1,01,250

= ₹ 7, 66, 250

8 'Good Wash Limited' are the manufacturers of different sizes of fully automatic washing machines marked as 'small', 'medium', 'large' and 'industrial'. From the information given below, calculate the 'break-even quantity' of the machines manufactured per month. **(CBSE 2015)**

Machine	Unit Selling Price (₹)	Unit Variable Cost (₹)	Fixed Expenditure per Month (₹)
Small	10,000	3,000	35,000
Medium	15,000	8,000	35,000
Large	20,000	13,000	70,000
Industrial	35,000	20,000	1,50,000

Ans **Break-even Quantity of 'Small Machine'**

Unit selling price = ₹ 10,000

Unit variable cost = ₹ 3,000

Contribution Per Unit

= Unit Selling Price – Unit Variable Cost

= 10,000 – 3,000 = ₹ 7,000

Fixed Expenses = ₹ 35,000

$$\text{Break-even Quantity} = \frac{\text{Fixed Expenses}}{\text{Contribution Per Unit}}$$

$$= \frac{35{,}000}{7{,}000} = 5 \text{ units of machines}$$

Break-even Quantity of 'Medium Machine'

Unit selling price = ₹ 15,000

Unit variable cost = ₹ 8,000

Contribution Per Unit

= Unit Selling Price – Unit Variable Cost

= 15,000 – 8,000 = ₹ 7,000

Fixed expenses = ₹ 35,000

$$\text{Break-even Quantity} = \frac{\text{Fixed Expenses}}{\text{Contribution Per Unit}}$$

$$= \frac{35{,}000}{7{,}000}$$

= 5 units of machine

Break-even Quantity of 'Large Machine'

Unit selling price = ₹ 20,000

Unit variable cost = ₹ 13,000

Contribution Per Unit

= Unit Selling Price – Unit Variable Cost

= 20,000 – 13,000 = ₹ 7,000

Fixed expenses = ₹ 70,000

$$\text{Break-even Quantity} = \frac{\text{Fixed Expenses}}{\text{Contribution Per Unit}}$$

$$= \frac{70{,}000}{7{,}000} = 10 \text{ units of machines}$$

Break-even Quantity of 'Industrial Machine'

Unit selling price = ₹ 35,000

Unit variable cost = ₹ 20,000

Contribution Per Unit

= Unit Selling Price – Unit Variable Cost

= 35,000 – 20,000 = ₹ 15,000

Fixed expenses = ₹ 1,50,000

$$\text{Break-even Quantity} = \frac{\text{Fixed Expenses}}{\text{Contribution Per Unit}}$$

$$= \frac{1{,}50{,}000}{15{,}000} = 10 \text{ units of machines}$$

9 'Baked Delight Ltd' is a well known name in breads and bakery products. It has diversified into flavoured fox nuts and popcorn.

The two were introduced as smart snacking options for health and diet conscious people. To start with, both will be sold in a standard packing of 50 gm each. Fixed cost for these will be ₹ 1,00,000. Sale price and variable cost per unit is as follows

Particulars	Classic Salted Fox Nuts	Caramel Salted Popcorn
Sale price per unit(₹)	120	80
Variable cost per unit (₹)	70	30
Sales mix percentage (%)	40	60

Form the information calculate break-even point in units and rupees. **(CBSE 2023)**

Ans To calculate the break-even point, we need to find out how many units of each product (classic salted fox nuts and caramel salted popcorn) we need to sell to cover the fixed cost of ₹ 1,00,000.

Let's assume the number of units of classic salted fox nuts sold be 'x', and the number of units of caramel salted popcorn sold be 'y'.

We know the sales mix percentage, which means 40% of the total units sold will be classic salted fox nuts and 60% will be caramel salted popcorn.

Hence, we can write

$x + y$ = total units sold

$\Rightarrow \quad 0.4x + 0.6y = 1$

(since sales mix percentage equals 100%) where 1 represents the total sales mix percentage.

Now, let's calculate the contribution margin per unit for each product

Contribution margin per unit for classic salted fox nuts

= Sale price per unit – Variable cost per unit

= 120 – 70 = ₹ 50

Contribution margin per unit for caramel salted popcorn = Sale price per unit – Variable cost per unit

= 80 – 30 = ₹ 50

Since both products have the same contribution margin per unit, we can use the weighted average of the sale price and variable cost per unit for the break-even calculation.

Now, weighted average sale price

$= (0.4 \times 120) + (0.6 \times 80) =$ ₹ 96

Weighted average variable cost per unit

$= (0.4 \times 70) + (0.6 \times 30) =$ ₹ 46

Now, we can calculate the break-even point in units

Fixed cost/Contribution margin per unit

= 1,00,000/50

= 2,000 units

So, to break-even, 'Baked Delight Ltd.' needs to sell a total of 2,000 units of classic salted fox nuts and caramel salted popcorn.

To calculate the break-even point in rupees, we can multiply the break-even point in units by the weighted average sale price

Break-even point in rupees = Break-even point in units × Weighted average sale price

$= 2{,}000 \times 96 =$ ₹ 1,92,000

Therefore, 'Baked Delight Ltd.' needs to sell 2,000 units of the products or generate a revenue of ₹ 1,92,000 to break-even.

10 What is working capital? What is the need for working capital? **(CBSE TBQ)**

Ans Working capital refers to that part of total capital which is required for holding current assets. It may also be defined as the excess of current assets over current liabilities.

A business needs working capital for a number of uses. Some of them are as follows (Any three)

(i) **Ensures Solvency of the Business** Working capital helps a business to operate smoothly without any financial problem for making the payment of short-term liabilities.

(ii) **Enhances Goodwill** Sufficient working capital enables a business concern to make prompt payments and hence helps in creating and maintaining goodwill. Goodwill is enhanced because all current liabilities and operating expenses are paid on time.

(iii) **Ensures Easy availability of Loans** A firm having adequate working capital can arrange loans from banks and financial institutions in easy and favourable terms.

(iv) **Regular Supply of Raw Material** Prompt payment to creditors of raw materials ensures regular supply of inventory and uninterrupted production.

11 What is meant by 'working capital'? Why is working capital called the 'circulating capital'? Illustrate with an example, how working capital is calculated? **(CBSE 2013)**

Ans Working capital is that part of total capital that is needed for holding the current assets of the business. It can also be defined as the excess of current assets over current liabilities, i.e.
Working Capital = Current Assets − Current Liabilities

Working capital is called the 'changing' or 'circulating capital', since the money circulates in various forms of current assets in a continued manner. e.g. funds once tied-up in the form of raw material are later converted into the form of finished goods which are then ultimately sold.

Working capital can be calculated using the following steps

(i) Estimate the number of units to be produced in a specified period.

(ii) Estimate the cost of variable inputs i.e. labour cost, raw material, direct overheads, etc.

(iii) Estimate the credit period to be extended to debtors.

On the basis of the above estimates, working capital requirement can be computed.

For Working Capital Calculation Refer to Q. No. 12 of short answer type II questions (3 Marks).

12 Calculate Return on Investment (RoI) and Return on Equity (RoE) on the basis of given information. You have newly started a beauty parlour business, you spend ₹ 1,50,000 to open the parlour of which you invested ₹ 70,000 of your own money and borrowed a loan for ₹ 80,000. Interest rate per annum is 7%. Sales revenue per month is ₹ 80,000. Cost of goods sold is ₹ 30,000 per month. Fixed expenses is ₹ 30,000 (salary ₹ 20,000, rent and utility ₹ 10,000), depreciation ₹ 3,000 and tax @ 14%.

Ans

Total Capital Invested	= ₹ 1,50,000
Equity (Own money)	= ₹ 70,000
Debt	= ₹ 80,000

Income statement of beauty parlour for 1st month

Sales Revenue	= ₹ 80,000
(−) Cost of Goods Sold	= ₹ (30,000)
Gross Margin	= ₹ 50,000
(−) Fixed Expenses	
Salary	= ₹ (20,000)
Rent and Utility	= ₹ (10,000)
Interest @ 7% $\left(80{,}000 \times \frac{7}{100} \times \frac{1}{12}\right)$	= ₹ (467)
Depreciation $\left(\frac{3{,}000}{12}\right)$	= ₹ (250)
Profit before Tax	= ₹ 19,283
(−) Tax @ 14%	= ₹ (2,700)
Profit after Tax	= ₹ 16,583

Return on Investment (RoI)

$$= \frac{\text{Net Profit (Profit after tax)}}{\text{Total Capital Invested}} \times 100$$

$$= \frac{16{,}583}{1{,}50{,}000} \times 100 = 11.05\%$$

$$\text{Return on Equity (RoE)} = \frac{\text{Net Profit}}{\text{Equity}} \times 100$$

$$= \frac{16{,}583}{70{,}000} \times 100$$

$$= 23.69\%$$

Note *Depreciation and fixed expenses are assumed to be calculated on monthly basis. The profitability ratios are an average.*

13 Calculate Return on Investment (RoI) and Return on Equity (RoE). Total investment ₹ 10,00,000 out of it ₹ 4,00,000 is owner's own money and he borrowed a loan for ₹ 6,00,000. Interest rate per annum is 10%.

Monthly sales revenue is ₹ 6,00,000 and cost of goods sold is ₹ 3,00,000, fixed expenses per month ₹ 2,00,000 (salary ₹1,50,000, rent and utility ₹ 50,000), depreciation ₹ 10,000 and tax @ 20%.

Ans

Capital Invested	= ₹ 10,00,000
Equity (Own money)	= ₹ 4,00,000
Debt	= ₹ 6,00,000

Income statement of restaurant for the 1st month

Sales Revenue	= ₹ 6,00,000
(−) Cost of Goods Sold	= ₹ (3,00,000)
Gross Margin	= ₹ 3,00,000

(–) Fixed Expenses

Salary	= ₹ (1,50,000)
Rent and Utility	= ₹ (50,000)
Interest @10% $\left(6,00,000 \times \frac{10}{100} \times \frac{1}{12}\right)$	= ₹ (5,000)
Depreciation $\left(\frac{10,000}{12}\right)$	= ₹ (833)
Profit before Tax	=₹ 94,167
(–) Tax @ 20%	=₹ (17,000)
Profit after Tax	= ₹ 77,167

Return on Investment (RoI)

$$= \frac{\text{Net Profit}}{\text{Capital Invested}} \times 100$$

$$= \frac{77,167}{10,00,000} \times 100 = 7.7\%$$

Return on Equity (RoE)

$$= \frac{\text{Net Profit}}{\text{Equity}} \times 100 = \frac{77,167}{4,00,000} \times 100 = 19.29\%$$

Note *Depreciation is assumed to be calculated on monthly basis.*

14 State whether the working capital requirements of a business manufacturing the following items are big or small. Justify your answer.

(i) Air coolers (ii) Bread
(iii) Sugar
(iv) Locomotives
(v) Furniture manufactured against order

Ans Working capital requirements can be made only after assessing the various components of current assets and current liabilities.

(i) **Air Coolers** The companies manufacturing air coolers need more working capital.
Reasons
(a) The industry is of seasonal in nature in which the coolers are sold only in the summer season.
(b) Being a durable good, it can be stocked for a longer period.

(ii) **Bread** The companies manufacturing bread need less working capital.
Reasons
(a) The nature of bread is perishable. It cannot be stocked for a longer period and therefore it has to be sold quickly.
(b) Mostly, bread is sold for cash and even if it is sold on credit, then the period of credit is short.

(iii) **Sugar** Sugar manufacturing companies require large working capital.
Reasons
(a) Sugar industries produce sugar generally between December and April because of the seasonal nature of sugarcane the key raw material.
(b) Material cost is high as a percentage of total cost.
(c) Work-in-progress is huge.

(iv) **Locomotives** Locomotives manufacturing companies require large working capital.
Reasons
(a) Gestation period is quite large.
(b) Material and labour costs are also quite high.

(v) **Furniture Manufactured against Order** It requires small amount of working capital.
Reasons Furniture is being manufactured against order, therefore, some advance must have been received. Also after goods are ready, the balance payment is immediately received.

15 Illustrate how an entrepreneur assesses the working capital requirements of an enterprise taking into consideration the operating cycle? **(CBSE 2011)**

Ans To assess the working capital requirements of an enterprise taking operating cycle into consideration, an entrepreneur should know the following

(i) **Purchase of Raw Materials and Consumable Stores** Fund requirement for holding raw materials depends upon
(a) Average consumption of raw material.
(b) Fluctuations in raw material consumption.
(c) Fluctuations in raw material availability.
(d) Minimum order size supplied by the vendors.
(e) Storage facilities available.

(ii) **Expenses** It is generally a common practice that cash equivalent to one month's cash expenses should be kept for meeting contingencies like fluctuation in material prices, delay in realisation from debtors, etc.

The quantum of such cash retention for meeting working capital requirements depends upon the process time also.

For activities having long process time like ship building, higher quantum of cash balance has to be maintained.

(iii) **Work-in-progress** The funds locked up in work-in cash progress depends on the following factors

(a) Time required for conversion of raw material.

(b) Number of products handled at a time in the process.

(c) The steps in the process.

(d) Value of raw material in semi-finished products.

(e) Value added at each stage.

(iv) **Finished Goods** Goods may be manufactured against firm orders or against anticipated orders. In the former case, the quantum of finished goods held depends on

(a) Delay due to inspection of finished goods especially where an external agency is involved.

(b) Delay in preparation of despatch documents.

(c) Delay in shipment.

In the latter case, i.e. in case of goods manufactured against anticipated orders, the quantity of finished goods held depends upon

(a) Average despatch quantity of finished goods.

(b) Minimum and maximum quantity that can be despatched.

So, after the above factors are assessed and analysed, then only the working capital requirements can be computed.

16 Explain briefty the various aspects to be considered in the process of inventory control.

Ans Refer to text on page 166.

17 Why is Return on Investment (RoI) deemed as a yardstick for the performance of an enterprise?

Ans An entrepreneur, when starts an enterprise either arranges funds from his own sources or from the market, these funds have certain cost. As in case of own funds, the expected market rate can be applied when investing these funds and when these funds are borrowed from the market, there is certainly a cost involvement. No businessman is going to pay interest from his own pocket.

So, calculating return on investment helps an entrepreneur to take decision regarding the investment in any specific project with the help of return on investment, he may judge the exact position of the returns. It is obvious from the discussion that return on investment should be higher than the highest rate of interest paid on any debt or loan.

The ultimate test of efficiency is the return on investment. It is the most important yardstick by which the performance of an enterprise can be judged.

The formula for calculating return on investment is given below

Return on Investment

$$= \frac{\text{Net Profit Before Interest and Tax}}{\text{Total Investment}} \times 100$$

As we know that all the funds required, are not introduced in the beginning of the operation. In such a case, we calculate average return on investment. The formula for calculating average return on investment is as given below

Average Return on Investment

$$= \frac{\text{Net Profit Before Interest and Tax}}{\text{Average Investment}}$$

where, Average Investment

$$= \frac{\text{Initial Investment} + \text{Final Investment}}{2}$$

18 Karan has started a restaurant on National Highway No. 1 in the name of 'Apna Dhaba' by spending ₹ 20,00,000. He invested ₹ 8,00,000 of his own and took a loan of ₹ 12,00,000 from SBI at the rate of 6% per annum.
His monthly sales revenue is ₹ 12,00,000 and the cost of goods sold is ₹ 7,00,000. He pays monthly salaries of ₹ 2,00,000 to his employees. The rate of tax is 25%. You are required to calculate the following for Karan **(CBSE 2015)**

(i) Return on investment

(ii) Return on equity

Ans (i) Return on Investment

$$= \frac{\text{Net Profit}}{\text{Total Capital Invested}} \times 100$$

Sales = ₹ 12,00,000

Cost of Goods Sold (COGS) = ₹ 7,00,000

∴ Gross Profit = Sales − CoGS

= 12,00,000 − 7,00,000 = ₹ 5,00,000

Salaries = ₹ 2,00,000

Interest = ₹ 6,000 $\left(12,00,000 \times \frac{6}{100} \times \frac{1}{12}\right)$

So, profit before tax

= 5,00,000 – 2,00,000 – 6,000

= ₹ 2,94,000

Tax Rate = 25%

∴ Tax = 2,94,000 × $\frac{25}{100}$ = ₹ 73,500

Profit after Tax/Net Profit

= (2,94,000 – 73,500) = ₹ 2,20,500

Total Capital Invested = Equity + Debt

= 8,00,000 + 12,00,000

= ₹ 20,00,000

∴ RoI = $\frac{2,20,500}{20,00,000}$ × 100 = 11.025%

(ii) Return on Equity (RoE) = $\frac{\text{Net Income}}{\text{Equity}} \times 100$

Net Income/Net Profit (as calculated above)
= ₹ 2,20,500

Equity = ₹ 8,00,000

∴ Return on Equity

= $\frac{2,20,500}{8,00,000}$ × 100 = 27.56%

19 Parvesh has started a restaurant in a small town by the name of 'Spices of India' by spending ₹ 50,00,000. He invested ₹ 10,00,000 of his own and took a loan of ₹ 40,00,000 from State Bank of India @ 6% per annum. His monthly sales revenue is ₹ 20,00,000 and monthly cost of goods sold is ₹ 10,00,000. He pays a monthly salary of ₹ 2,00,000 to his employees. The GST rate is 18%.

Calculate (i) Return on investment (ii) Return on equity. **(CBSE 2019)**

Ans (i) Return of Investment (RoI)

= $\frac{\text{Net Profit}}{\text{Total Capital Invested}} \times 100$

Here, Net Profit = Sales – Cost of Goods Sold – Salary

= 20,00,000 – 10,00,000 – 2,00,000

= ₹ 8,00,000

Total Capital Invested = Equity + Debt

= 10,00,000 + 40,00,000 = ₹ 50,00,000

On substituting, RoI

= $\frac{8,00,000}{50,00,000}$ × 100 = 16%

(ii) Return of Equity (RoE) = $\frac{\text{Net Profit}}{\text{Equity}} \times 100$

= $\frac{8,00,000}{10,00,000}$ × 100

= 80%

Note *GST is an indirect tax therefore it will not affect RoI and RoE.*

20 Raman is a potential investor who wishes to be a part of Equity Linked Saving Scheme (ELSS). He has given the particulars of two companies to seek your advice for investment. Compare the return on equity of the two companies and suggest to Raman where he should invest. **(CBSE 2018)**

Particulars	Alpha Ltd. (₹)	Beta Ltd. (₹)
Total Capital Invested	20,00,000	20,00,000
Owned Funds	10,00,000	10,00,000
Interest on Borrowings from Bank	60,000	50,000
Cost of Goods Sold per Month	7,00,000	8,50,000
Monthly Sales Revenue	10,00,000	15,00,000
Salaries	2,40,000	3,60,000
Utilities	75,000	1,00,000
Depreciation	5,500	6,000
Tax Rate	20%	25%

Ans

Particulars	Alpha Ltd. (₹)	Beta Ltd. (₹)
Monthly Sales Revenue	10,00,000	15,00,000
(–) Cost of Goods Sold per Month	(7,00,000)	(8,50,000)
Gross Margin	3,00,000	6,50,000
(–) Fixed Expenses		
Salaries	(2,40,000)	(3,60,000)
Utilities	(75,000)	(1,00,000)
Depreciation	(5,500)	(6,000)
Interest on Borrowings from Bank	(60,000)	(50,000)
Profit/Loss before Tax	(80,500)	1,34,000
(–) Tax	–	(33,500)
Profit/Loss after Tax	(80,500)	1,00,500

$$\text{Return of Equity} = \frac{\text{Net Income}}{\text{Equity}} \times 100$$

Net Income of Alpha Ltd. = 0%

(Because Alpha Ltd. has incurred loss)

Net Income of Beta Ltd.

$$= \frac{1,00,500}{10,00,000} \times 100 = 10.05\%$$

∴ Raman should invest in Beta Ltd.

21 There are all sorts of ways in which investors measure the financial health of a company. They'll look at sales and cash flow. They'll consider various assets and any outstanding debt. Beyond these traditional tools, one of the most common measurements in determining a company's value is EBITDA.

EBITDA is an acronym that stands for "earnings before interest, taxes, depreciation and amortisation." This all sounds impressive, but how do you understand EBITDA and why it's used as a valuation metric for your business?

I've worked closely with middle-market businesses in many sectors during my time as the managing partner of a middle-market investment bank. This experience has given me the knowledge necessary to pull back the curtain on EBITDA and explain how it affects the way people see their businesses.

(i) Which concept is highlighted in the given paragraph?

(ii) Explain its various components.

Ans (i) EBITDA

(ii) Refer to text on page 171.

22 Inventory is the supply of raw materials, partially finished goods called work-in-progress and finished goods, an organisation maintains to meet its operational needs. It represents a sizeable investment and a potential source of waste that needs to be carefully controlled. Inventory is defined as a stock of goods that is maintained by a business in anticipation of some future demand.

The quantity to which inventory must fall in order to signal that an order must be placed to replenish an item.

Using an extension of a standard inventory-dependent demand model provide a convenient characterisation of products that require early replenishment. The optimal cycle time is largely governed by the conventional trade-off between ordering and holding costs, whereas the reorder point relates to a promotions-oriented cost-benefit perspective.

The optimal policy yields significantly higher profits than cost-based inventory policies, underscoring the importance of profit-driven inventory management.

To work towards perfect order metrics, there has to be aggressive inventory management, restructuring supply chain operations, and updating standards to the perfect standard. When updating the metrics, this would include the cases shipped vs. the orders on-time delivery, data synchronisation, damages and unusable products, days in supply, the ordering time cycle, and shelf level of service.

Inventory problems of too great or too small quantities on hand can cause business failures. If an organisation experiences stock-out of a critical inventory item, production halts could result. Inventory management indicates the broad frame work of managing inventory.

The inventory management technique is more useful in determining the optimum level of inventory and finding answers to problem of safety stock and lead time.

Inventory management has become highly developed to meet the rising challenges in most corporate entities and this is in response to the fact that inventory is an asset of distinct feature.

Source *Jour of Adv Research in Dynamical & Control Systems, Vol. 10, 10-Special Issue, 2018.*

(i) Which concept is highlighted in the given paragraph?

(ii) Explain Pareto's principle and ABC analysis of inventory control.

Ans (i) Inventory control

(ii) **Pareto's Principle** This principle was propounded by Vilfredo Pareto, an Italian economist, who studied land ownership in Italy in the early 1900's and found that roughly 20% of the population held title to about 80% of the land. For this reason, Pareto's Principle is often referred to as the '80/20' rule.

So, Pareto's principle basically states that 'A relatively handful of things will generate the bulk of the results' or 'vital few, trivial many'.

The value of Pareto's Principle in inventory management is in reminding us to stay focused on the 20% that matters.

ABC Analysis of Inventory Control This analysis can help in better inventory control. It is based on Pareto's Principle.

In ABC analysis, a company reviews its inventory and sorts all SKUs in three categories, called 'A', 'B' and 'C' items. A typical breakdown might look like this

(a) **'A' Inventory** 10-20% of the items in terms of quantity account for 70-80% of the total value of items.

(b) **'B' Inventory** 15-25% of the items in terms of quantity account for 10-20% of the total value of inventory.

(c) **'C' Inventory** 65-75% of the items in terms of quantity account for 5-10% of the total value of inventory.

Based on the above information it can be concluded that, inventory 'A' is outstandingly important, inventory 'B' is average important and inventory 'C' is relatively unimportant. So, more attention should be devoted to inventory 'A' less to 'B' and still less to 'C'.

CHAPTER ASSESSMENT

Objective Type Questions (1 Mark)

1 Gross profit per unit is calculated by using the formula
(a) Selling Price per Unit + Cost Price per Unit (b) Selling Price per Unit– Cost Price per Unit
(c) Selling Price per Unit – Contribution (d) None of these

2 Variable cost include
(a) packing material (b) raw material (c) commission on sales (d) All of these

3 Proportion in which two or more products are sold is called
(a) sales mix (b) product mix (c) price mix (d) place mix

4 Longer the operating cycle, working capital quantum required will be ....

5 Current liabilities represent .... source of funds.

6 Working capital is called the circulating capital. State true or false.

7 The SKU code can be a combination of alpha and/or beta symbols. State true or false.

Short Answer Type I Questions (2 Marks)

8 Write a short note on unit cost.

9 What do you mean by break-even analysis?

10 State all the assumptions for calculation of sales mix break-even point.

11 State any two examples of each current assets and current liabilities.

12 What do you mean by working capital?

Short Answer Type II Questions (3 Marks)

13 Explain different types of working capital.

14 Explain briefly CCC.

15 Write a short note on operating cycle of a trading concern.

16 Discuss operating cycle of a manufacturing company.

Long Answer Type Questions (5 Marks)

17 Write a short note on Pareto's principle.

18 How can EOQ be calculated? Explain.

19 Explain the factors affecting working capital.

20 Explain in detail ABC analysis of inventory control.

For explanations scan the given QR Code

CHAPTER 06

Resource Mobilisation

In this Chapter...

- Finance
- Capital Market
- Primary Market
- Angel Investors
- Venture Capital

Finance

Finance refers to funds or monetary resources needed by individuals, business houses and the government. It is one of the most important pre-requisite to start an enterprise. Basically, it represents money management and the process of acquiring needed funds.

In other words, finance is defined as the management of money and includes activities such as investing, borrowing, lending, budgeting, saving and forecasting.

Need of Finance

Right from the very beginning, i.e. conceiving an idea, finance is required to

- Promote or establish the business
- Acquire fixed assets
- Make market investigations
- Develop product
- Keep men and machines at work
- Encourage management to make progress and create value
- Expand, diversify, improve and grow
- Be enough to meet unexpected/unplanned expenses

So, we can say that finance is the elixir that assists in the formation of new businesses and also allows businesses to take advantage of opportunities to grow and expand.

Sources of Finance

An enterprise can raise finance through various sources.

These sources can be broadly classified as

1. **Internal Sources** It includes all those sources which are generated from within the business. The various sources of this form of financing are
   - Equity shares
   - Preference shares
   - Retained earnings
   - Global Depository Receipts (GDRs)
   - American Depository Receipts (ADRs)
   - Indian Depository Receipts (IDRs)
2. **External Sources** It includes those sources of financing, which are raised from outside the business. The various external sources are
   - Debentures and bonds
   - Loan from financial institutions
   - Loan from commercial banks
   - Public deposits
   - Trade credit
   - Inter-corporate deposits

A business is always in need for additional funds. But, before choosing from among the above sources, an entrepreneur should be aware of the fact that not all of them are equally appropriate for all enterprises at all times as these different sources carry different

- Obligations
- Responsibilities
- Opportunities

Capital Market

It may be defined as an organised mechanism meant for effective and smooth transfer of money capital or financial resources from the investors to the entrepreneurs.

The role of transferring financial resources from the surplus units to the deficit units is known as **financial intermediation**.

Capital market plays a very vital role of financial intermediatory. Here, productive capital is raised and made available for industrial purposes.

In other words, capital market refers to the whole network of all organisations, institutions and instruments that provide medium and long-term funds to the government as well as industrial sector. Funds are raised in this market through both debt and equity.

Importance of Capital Market

Capital markets are the most important source of raising finance for the entrepreneurs as this market can

- mobilise the financial resources on a nationwide scale.
- secure the required foreign capital and know-how to promote economic growth at a faster rate.
- ensure the most effective allocation of mobilised financial resources by investing in projects capable of generating highest returns or by investing in underdeveloped priority areas so as to promote balanced industrialisation.

Types of Capital Market

The capital market can be classified as

– Primary market (New issues market)
– Secondary market

Note *Secondary market is out of the scope of syllabus. Thus, only meaning is discussed for knowledge purpose.*

Primary Market

It is also known as the new issues market, as this market deals with the new securities being issued for the first time. By issue of new securities, primary market facilitate the transfer of investible funds from savers to entrepreneurs seeking funds for

– setting new enterprises
– expanding
– diversifying

The 'new issues' may be issued by

– new companies, also called initial issues.
– old companies, also called further issues.

Initial Issues

When for the first time, entrepreneur for the purpose of obtaining capital funds decides to issue securities to the public, then such issue of securities is termed as an 'initial issue' or 'new money issues'.

Methods of Floatation of New Issues

An entrepreneur can raise the required capital through 'initial issue' by the following methods

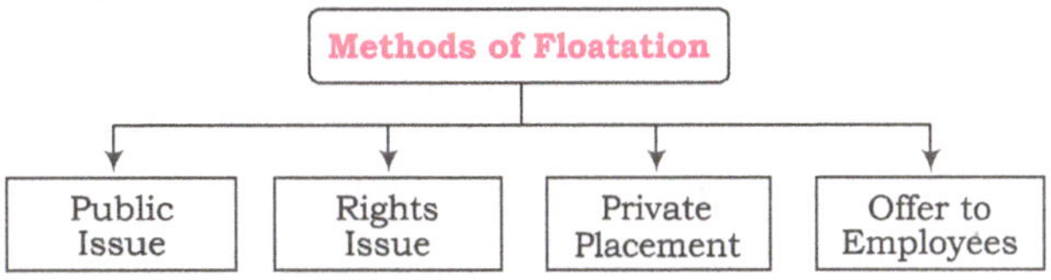

1. **Public Issue**

   Public issue involves raising of funds directly from the public through the issue of prospectus. It is the most popular method of raising finance.

   This method requires compliance to various statutory laws relating to prospectus drafting, listing agreements, etc.

   The **advantages** of raising finance through public issue are

   (i) **Access to Capital** The first and foremost advantage that an entrepreneur stands to gain by going public is access to capital. In addition, the capital does not have to be repaid and does not involve an interest charge.
   Entrepreneur can use the capital, thus raised, for
   – growth and expansion.
   – retiring existing debt.
   – corporate marketing and development.
   – as a source of acquisition capital.

   (ii) **Other Advantages** Other advantages of raising finance through this source are
   - **Mergers and Acquisitions** Public stock of a company can be used for an enterprise to grow through acquisitions.
   - **Higher Valuations** Public companies are valued more than private companies.
   - **Benchmark Trading Prices** The trading prices of a public company's stock serves as a standard of the offer price of other securities.

- **Capital** Raising capital to meet additional requirements later on is typically easier because of extra liquidity for the investors.
- **Incentives** Stock options and stock incentives can be very helpful in attracting employees.
- **Reduced Business Requirements** While an underwritten initial public offering requires significant earnings, this however does not prevent a private company from going public.
- **Liquidity** A public company provides liquidity for management, minority shareholders and investors.
- **Prestige** Raising capital through this source increases the visibility of the company among customers, investors and suppliers and add prestige to its name.

Inspite of the advantages, this source suffers from some **disadvantages** also which are stated below

- Going public raises the obligations and reporting requirements of a company, such as
  - (a) Increasing accountability to public shareholders.
  - (b) Need to maintain dividend and profit growth trends.
  - (c) Need to observe and adhere strictly to the rules and regulations of governing bodies.
- A company becomes more vulnerable to an unwelcome takeover.
- Increased costs in complying with higher level of reporting requirements.
- Relinquishing some control of the company following the public offering.
- Suffering a loss of privacy as a result of media interest.

Overall, going public is a complex decision that requires careful consideration and planning.

2. **Rights Issue**

Rights issue is a method of raising additional finance from existing shareholders by offering securities to them on pro-rata basis, i.e. giving them a right to purchase certain number of shares in proportion to the shares they are holding.

In case the existing shareholders are not willing to purchase, then they can renounce their right in favour of another person. This method is comparatively inexpensive as it does not require any brokers, agents, underwriters, prospectus or enlistment, etc.

3. **Private Placement**

Private placement means the direct sale by a company of its securities to a limited number of institutional investors like

- Unit Trust of India
- Life Insurance Corporation of India
- General Insurance Corporation of India
- Army Group Insurance
- State Level Finance Corporations, etc.

This is an effective source of raising capital if the company do not wish to disclose information in the open market.

4. **Offer to Employees**

Stock options or offering shares to employees enables employees to become shareholders of the company and subsequently be able to share the profits of the company, leading to

- higher efficiency
- low employee turnover
- cordial relations
- low flotation cost
- wider/higher generation of funds

So, a company can choose from either of the methods or a combination of them to raise finance through primary market.

IPO (Initial Public Offer)

A company proposing to raise resources by a public issue should first select the type of securities, i.e. shares and/or debentures to be issued by it. The decision regarding the issue of shares to be made at par or premium should be decided keeping in view the SEBI guidelines.

The whole process of issue of shares can be divided into two parts

- Pre-issue activities
- Post-issue activities

All activities beginning with the planning of capital issues, till the opening of the subscription list are pre-issue activities, while all activities subsequent to the opening of the subscription list may be called post-issue activities.

The various **steps** involved in public issue of shares are enumerated below

Steps involved in IPO

- Compliance with the SEBI guidelines
- Holding of general meeting
- Intimation to stock exchange
- Appointment
- Drafting of prospectus
- Approval of prospectus
- Approval of board of directors
- Registration of prospectus with RoC
- Application to stock exchange to list shares
- Printing and distribution of prospectus and application forms
- Announcements and advertisements
- Subscription list
- Separate bank account
- Minimum subscription
- Allotment of shares
- Oversubscription
- Compliance report

(i) **Compliance with the SEBI Guidelines** Before making any issue of capital, it is to be ensured that the proposed issue complies with the provision of the SEBI guidelines for disclosure and investor protection with regards to pricing of issue, promoters contribution, lock in period, reservation, etc.

(ii) **Holding of General Meeting** If it is required by the articles of association, that consent of shareholder is to be obtained, then meeting of the shareholders will be called.

(iii) **Intimation to Stock Exchange** A copy of the memorandum and articles of association of the company is to be sent to the stock exchanges where the shares are to be listed, for approval.

(iv) **Appointment** A company, which issues shares, has to appoint one or more merchant bankers, who act as lead managers to the public issues. The company may also appoint registrars, underwriters, brokers, etc.

(v) **Drafting of Prospectus** Apart from the notice of offer to issue shares to public, prospectus should also disclose

- justification of premium, if called.
- Net Assets Value (NAV).
- high and low price of the shares of the company for the last two years.
- a clause that company shall refund the entire application money if minimum subscription is not received.
- a statement by the lead managers that in their opinion, the assets of the underwriters are adequate to meet their obligations.

(vi) **Approval of Prospectus** The draft prospectus along with the application from the issue of shares should be approved by the solicitors/legal advisors/stock exchange (where application has been made seeking permission for shares to be draft in) of the company to ensure that it contains all disclosures and information as required by various statues, rules, notification, etc.

(vii) **Approval of Board of Directors** After the concerned parties/agencies have approved the draft prospectus and the application form, the Board of Directors of the company should approve the final draft, before filing it with Registrar of Companies.

(viii) **Registration of Prospectus with RoC** Before the prospectus is issued to the public, it must be filed with the Registrar of Companies, duly signed thereon by every director or proposed director of the company. The prospectus must be registered with RoC within 3 months of vetting of SEBI.

(ix) **Application to Stock Exchange to List Shares** Before filing prospectus with the Registrar of Companies, the company should submit on application to the stock exchange(s) for enlistment of securities offered to the public by the said issue.

The fact that an application has/have been made to the stock exchange must be stated in the prospectus.

(x) **Printing and Distribution of Prospectus and Application Forms** After receipt of acknowledgement card from the SEBI and the intimation from Registrar of Companies regarding registration of prospectus, the company should take steps to issue the prospectus within 90 days of its registration with RoC.

For this compliance, requisite steps for printing and distribution amongst banker, underwriter, public, etc should be made.

(xi) **Announcements and Advertisements** Announcement regarding the proposed issue should be made atleast ten (10) days before the subscription list opens.

No advertisement should include brand names for the issue except the normal commercial name of the company or commercial brand names of the company or commercial brand names of its products already in use.

(xii) **Subscription List** As stipulated by SEBI guidelines, the subscription list for public issue is to be kept open for atleast three working days and for a total period of not exceeding ten working days, which is to be disclosed in prospectus as well.

(xiii) **Separate Bank Account** A separate bank account is opened for the purpose of collecting the proceeds of the issue. Further, the date of opening and closing of the subscription list should be intimated to all the collecting and controlling branches of the bank with whom the company has entered into an agreement for the collection of application forms.

(xiv) **Minimum Subscription** As per the SEBI guidelines, if the company does not receive 90% of the issue amount from the public subscription including development from underwriters within 120 days from the date of the issue, the amount of subscription received is required to be refunded to the applicants.

In case of disputed development also, subscription is required to be refunded if 90% of the issued amount plus accepted. Development from underwriters, if any, is not received within 120 days of the issue of prospectus, all the money received from the applicants is required to be repaid forthwith without interest.

If any such money is not so repaid in the next 10 days (after the expiry of 120 days), the directors of the company are jointly and severally liable to repay that money, with interest from the expiry of the 130 days.

The company should refund the amount within 10 weeks of the closing of the subscription list and pay interest, if refunds are delayed by more than 8 days after this period.

(xv) **Allotment of Shares** A return of allotment inform no. 2 of the Companies (Central Government's) General Rules and Form, 1956 should be filed with Registrar of Companies within 30 days of the date of allotment along with the fees payable, as prescribed in Schedule X of the Act.

In case, the issue is oversubscribed, the basis of allotment has to be decided in consultation with the stock exchange authorities as per the guidelines laid down by the stock exchange.

(xvi) **Oversubscription** The oversubscribed amount after the finalisation of allotment, should be refunded to the applicants within 10 weeks of the closure of subscription list. If the money is not so refunded, the company is liable to refund the money with interest as specified from the expiry of the 8 days after 10 weeks of the closure of subscription list.

(xvii) **Compliance Report** As stipulated by SEBI guidelines within 45 days of the closure of issue, a report in the prescribed form along with a compliance certificates from statutory auditor/ practicing chartered accountant or by a company secretary in practice is to be forwarded to SEBI by the lead managers.

Secondary Market

It is a market where purchase and sale of existing securities takes place. It is also known as old securities market or stock exchange.

In this market, securities are not directly issued by the company to investors but are sold by existing investors to other investors.

This market enhances the marketability of securities and thereby provides liquidity to investments.

From the investor's view point, this market imparts liquidity to the long-term securities held by them by providing an auction market for these securities.

Secondary market operates through the medium of stock exchanges which regulate the trading activities in this market and ensures a measure of safety and fair dealings to the investors.

CHECK POINT 01

1. Name the most important pre-requisite to start an enterprise.
2. Mention any two external sources of finance.
3. What is primary market?
4. What is right issue?
5. What is IPO?

Angel Investors

The term 'angel' originally comes from broadway, where it was used to describe wealthy individual who provide money for theatrical productions.

In 1978, **William Wetzel**, a professor at the University of New Hampshire and founder of its center for venture research, completed a pioneering study on how entrepreneurs raised seed capital in the USA and he began using the term 'angel' to describe the investors who supported them.

An angel investor or angel, also known as a business angel or informal investor or angel funder, is an affluent individual who provides capital for a business start-up, usually in exchange for convertible debt or ownership equity. Angel investors, generally provide capital for a business start-up and early stage companies having a high-risk, high-return matrix.

Features of Angel Investors

The service provided by angel investors is invaluable. They provide seed funding and formal venture capital. Humorously, they were initially given the acronym FFF, i.e. Friends, Family and Fools. But, it is usually difficult to raise more than a few thousands from friends and family, thus, angel investment is a common second round of financing for high-growth start-ups or early stage companies.

They are willing to take on the risk of a brand new firm and enjoy the benefits of its success later on.

The various features exhibited by angel investors are as follows

- Most angel investors are current or retired executives, business owners or high net worth individuals, who have the knowledge, expertise and funds that help start-ups match up to industry standards.
- As angel investors bear extremely high risk and their share is subjected to dilution after second round of funding, therefore they expect a high return on their investment.
- Apart from investing funds, they also provide proactive advice, guidance, industry connections and mentoring start-ups in its early stage.
- Their objective is to create great companies by providing value creation, and simultaneously helping investors to earn a high return on their investments.
- They have a keen desire to keep themselves acquainted with current developments and mentoring another generation of entrepreneurs by making use of their vast experience.

Venture Capital

Venture capital is a type of private equity capital provided as seed funding to early stage, high-potential, high-risk, growth-up companies and entrepreneurs who lack the necessary experience and funds to give shape to their ideas. It is also known as risk-capital.

Development of entrepreneurship demands combination of three vital factors

- Innovative ideas
- Competency in project preparation and implementation
- Project financing

There may be many people with good project ideas. These ideas however, do not get translated into commercially viable practical projects in the absence of the other two factors. Many young entrepreneurs with innovative ideas suffer because of this.

It is in this context that the venture capital can play a crucial role in entrepreneurship development by providing the two missing links.

Venture capital, thus is an equity-based investment in a growth-oriented small to medium business enterprises, which in most cases would not qualify for bank loans, in return for minority shareholding in the business or the irrevocable right to acquire. It is a professionally managed pool of equity capital.

Features of Venture Capital

Venture capital is characterised as a long-term investment discipline, usually occurring over a five-years period, that helps in the creation of

- early stage companies
- expansion and revitalisation of existing businesses
- financing of leveraged buyouts of existing divisions of major or privately owned enterprises

So, keeping in view the above usage of venture capital, the various features exhibited by it are

- It is basically a equity finance in relatively new companies.
- It is long-term investment in growth oriented small or medium firms.
- Venture capitalist not only provides capital but also business skills to investee firms.
- It involves high risk-return spectrum.
- It is a subset of private equity.
- The venture capital institutions have a continuous involvement in the business after making the investment.
- Venture capital institutions disinvest the holdings either to the promoters or in the market.

Funding : Venture Capital vs Loans

Obtaining venture capital is substantially different from raising debt. With a loan, a lender gives a business money and the business has a contractual obligation to pay back that amount plus interest over some period of time.

Many a times, the loan is backed by assets. This backing allows the lender to recoup some of its investment in case the lendee defaults.

With venture capital, the start-up business issues shares in exchange for money. The venture capitalist's partnership fund actually becomes a partial owner of the start-up.

Also, venture capital is usually only used with high growth industries, where risk is much higher.

In these cases, there are little or no assets to back the loan in the event of default, therefore, the potential payouts must be drastically higher to result in a successful investment.

Investment Criteria for Venture Capitalists

Venture capitalists are very selective in deciding what to invest in and as a rule of thumb

- They may invest in one in four hundred opportunities presented to them.
- Looks for the extremely rare, yet sought after qualities, such as
  - (a) Innovative technology
  - (b) Potential for rapid growth
  - (c) A well-developed business model
  - (d) An impressive management team
- Looks for an 'exit' in the time frame of typically 3-7 years.
- Are inclined towards ventures with exceptionally high growth potential.

So, entrepreneurs are expected to carry out detailed due diligence prior to seeking venture capital as a source of financing.

When to Seek Venture Capital Finance

As venture capitalists investments are illiquid, requiring extended time frame to harvest, an entrepreneur should carefully evaluate and analyse the stage at which he/she would require venture capitalist to assist in.

They can typically seek venture capital to assist in any of the following stages in the company's development

I. Early Stage Financing

This stage includes

1. **Seed Capital Finance** It refers to the capital required by an entrepreneur for conducting research at pre-commercialisation stage.

   During this stage, the entrepreneur has to convince the venture capitalist, why his idea/ product is worthwhile.

   The venture capitalist will then investigate into the technical and economical feasibility of the idea. Entrepreneur's ability, technological skills and competencies are closely scrutinised by the venture capitalist. He may deny to assist if the findings and investigations are not upto his satisfaction.

2. **Start-up Finance** If the idea/product/process is qualified for further investigation and/or investment, the process will go to the second stage, i.e. the start-up stage. A business plan is presented by the entrepreneur to the venture capitalist firm. A management team is then formed to run the venture. If the company has a board of directors, then a person or persons from the venture capitalist firm will take seats at the board.

   The management team establishes a feasible production line to produce the product.

   The venture capitalist firm monitors the feasibility of the product and the capability of the management team from the board of directors.

3. **Second-round Financing** At this stage, the idea has been transformed into a product and is being produced and sold. The entrepreneur at this stage, needs assistance from the venture capitalist for expansion, modernisation and diversification, so that economies of scale and stability could be attained.

   Venture capitalist firm will be interested in financing this stage only if he is convinced about the capability of the management team to triumph against competition.

II. Last Stage Financing/Bridge/Pre-public Stage

This is the last stage of the venture capital financing process. The main goal of this stage is for the venture to go public, so that investors can exit the venture with a profit matching with the risk that they have taken.

At this stage, the venture achieves a certain amount of market share and has opportunities to
- Merge with other companies.
- keep competitors away from the market.
- eliminate competition.
- develop and grow.

Entrepreneur at this stage, should introduce a follow-up product/services to attract new client and markets, as only through this, he can create interest as venture capitalist firms to get further financial assistance.

Venture Capital Institutions in India

At present, many venture capital companies/funds have been set-up in India, in both the public and the private sectors, e.g.

- Industrial Development Bank of India's Venture Capital Fund.
- Technology Development and Information Company of India Limited (TDICIL).
- Risk Capital and Technology Finance Corporation Limited.
- Gujarat Venture Finance Limited (GVFL).
- Andhra Pradesh Industrial Development Corporation (APIDC) Venture Capital Fund.
- National Venture Fund for Software and IT Industry.
- The Canbank Venture Capital Fund, the Credit Capital Venture Fund Limited, etc.

Entrepreneurs should be careful about sharing their business plans with venture capital firms.

They are advised to protect their proprietary intellectual property by entering into non-disclosure agreements with them.

CHECK POINT 02

1. Define angel investors.
2. Mention any two features of angel investors.
3. Mention any two features of venture capital.
4. Mention the stages in which an entrepreneur can seek a venture capitalists.
5. Give any two examples of venture capital institutions in India.

EXAM PATTERN EXERCISE

Objective Type Questions (1 Mark)

Multiple Choice Questions

1 Internal sources of finance include

(a) trade credit (b) equity shares
(c) public deposit (d) All of these

Ans (b) equity shares

2 In the capital market, funds are raised through

(a) debt (b) equity
(c) Both (a) and (b) (d) None of these

Ans (c) Both (a) and (b)

3 Full form of IPO is

(a) Initial Public Offer
(b) Innovative Public Offer
(c) Internal Public Offer (d) None of these

Ans (a) Initial Public Offer

4 Which amongst the following is/are the feature(s) exhibited by angel investors?

(a) They bear extremely high risk
(b) They provide proactive advice and guidance
(c) They are generally current or retired executives
(d) All of the above

Ans (d) All of the above

5 Karma Limited needs finance to fund its expansion plans. However, it does not wants to issue its shares publicly, as it involves a number of legal formalities. What other options(s) are available for the company?

(a) Rights issue
(b) Private placement
(c) Offer to employees
(d) All of the above

Ans (d) All of the above

6 At the .... stage of financing, the venture achieves a certain amount of market share and has opportunities to develop and grow.

(a) seed capital (b) pre-start-up
(c) second (d) bridge

Ans (d) bridge

7 Which amongst the following is/are venture capital institutions in India?

(a) Gujarat Venture Finance Limited
(b) Technology Development and Information Company of India Limited
(c) Risk Capital and Technology Finance Corporation Limited
(d) All of the above

Ans (d) All of the above

8 Deepak Ltd., has been manufacturing cycles since 2015. Their market share in this field is 35%.

They decided to introduce new cycles with advanced gear systems in 2022. For the same they estimated their financial requirements to be ₹ 15 crore. They decided to raise the same through a limited number of sophisticated investors. Identify this kind of issue.

(a) Right issue (b) Public issue
(c) Private placement (d) None of these

Ans (c) Private placement

9 Karuna is studying in Kanpur University. She got an idea to make a safety gadget for college going girls which will give alert message to the registered numbers as well as nearest policy stations, if the wearer is in any kind of danger. To execute her idea she requires finance.

She convinced one of her teacher who has the knowledge of making such gadget to provide her finance for feasibility studies. Identify the source of funding used by Karuna.

(a) Right issue (b) Funding
(c) Angel investors (d) None of these

Ans (c) Angel investors

10 ABC Ltd., decided to raise funds by issuing shares. The finance department felt that the company should offer the shares to existing shareholders on a pro-rata basis. Out of the following, identify the method of raising the funds beings suggested by the finance department.

(a) public issue (b) right issue
(c) private placement (d) offer to employees

Ans (b) right issue

11 Ganga Dhar was working as the production manager in a German company. The company was producing remote operated high-end kitchen equipments. He resigned from his job and returned to his hometown, Patna.

In Patna, he met his old friend Aditya, who has been managing his factory producing steel utensils with old technology. Ganga Dhar encouraged Aditya to help him by providing funds and expertise so that the production unit run by Aditya can develop into a big production house and its investors may get high returns on investment.

Identify the kind of 'source of capital' provided by Ganga Dhar to Aditya.

(a) Angel investors
(b) Venture capital
(c) Financing
(d) None of the above

Ans (a) Angel investors

12 Which among the following is not a feature of venture capital?

(a) It is a equity finance in relatively new companies
(b) Venture capitalist also provides business skills to investee firms
(c) Venture capital is a subset of government equity
(d) Venture capital involves high-risk return spectrum

Ans (c) Venture capital is a subset of government equity

13 **Assertion** (A) Capital market plays a very vital role of financial intermediatory.

Reason (R) In capital market, productive capital is raised and made available for industrial purposes.

Alternatives

(a) Both Assertion (A) and Reason (R) are correct
(b) Assertion (A) is correct, but Reason (R) is incorrect
(c) Assertion (A) is incorrect, but Reason (R) is correct
(d) Both Assertion (A) and Reason (R) are incorrect

Ans (a) Both Assertion (A) and Reason (R) are correct

14 **Assertion** (A) Offer to employees means sale of its securities by a company to a limited number of sophisticated investors.

Reason (R) Offer to employees enables employees to become shareholders and share the profits of the company. **(CBSE 2023)**

Alternatives

(a) Both Assertion (A) and Reason (R) are true and Reason (R) is the correct explanation of Assertion (A)
(b) Both Assertion (A) and Reason (R) are true, but Reason (R) is not the correct explanation of Assertion (A)
(c) Assertion (A) is true, but Reason (R) is false
(d) Assertion (A) is false, but Reason (R) is true

Ans (d) Private placement is the offer of shares to a group of limited institutional shareholders.

15 **Assertion** (A) Venture capital is characterised as a long-term investment discipline, usually occurring over a five-years period.

Reason (R) Venture capital is long-term investment in growth oriented large firms only.

Alternatives

(a) Both Assertion (A) and Reason (R) are correct
(b) Assertion (A) is correct, but Reason (R) is incorrect
(c) Assertion (A) is incorrect, but Reason (R) is correct
(d) Both Assertion (A) and Reason (R) are incorrect

Ans (b) Venture capital is long-term investment in growth oriented small or medium firms.

16 Given below are the methods of floatation of new issues in Column I and their features in Column II. Match them accordingly.

Column I		Column II	
A.	Public issue	(i)	It does not require any brokers, agents, underwriters etc.
B.	Right issue	(ii)	It requires compliance to various statutory laws.
C.	Private placement	(iii)	It enables employees to become shareholders of the company.
D.	Offer to employees	(iv)	Direct sale by a company if its securities.

Codes

	A	B	C	D		A	B	C	D
(a)	(ii)	(i)	(iv)	(iii)	(b)	(i)	(iii)	(ii)	(iv)
(c)	(iii)	(iv)	(i)	(ii)	(d)	(iv)	(iii)	(i)	(ii)

Ans (a) (ii) (i) (iv) (iii)

17 Given below are stages of venture capital finance in Column I and their features in Column II. Match them correctly.

Column I	Column II
A. Seed capital finance	(i) Idea has been transformed into a product.
B. Start-up finance	(ii) Last stage of venture capital financing process.
C. Second-round financing	(iii) The entrepreneur has to convince the venture capitalist about the reliability of his product.
D. Pre-public stage	(iv) A business plan is presented by the entrepreneur to the venture capitalist firm.

Codes

	A	B	C	D		A	B	C	D
(a)	(iii)	(iv)	(i)	(ii)	(b)	(iii)	(ii)	(i)	(iv)
(c)	(ii)	(i)	(iv)	(iii)	(d)	(ii)	(iii)	(i)	(iv)

Ans (a) (iii) (iv) (i) (ii)

18 Which concept is indicated in the given figure?

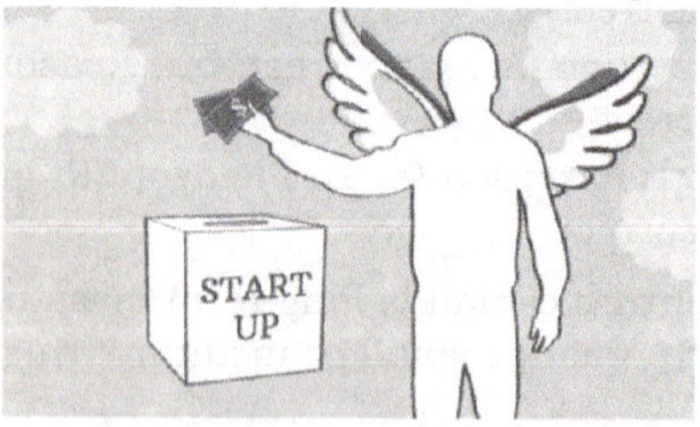

(a) Angel investors (b) Source of finance
(c) Venture capital (d) None of these

Ans (a) An angel investor is an affluent individual who provides capital for a business start-up, usually in exchange for convertible debt or ownership equity.

Fill in the Blanks

19 Finance raised by issue of ADRs and GDRs is said to be raised from ....

Ans internal sources

20 .... means the direct sale by a company of its securities to a limited number of institutional investors.

Ans Private placement

21 As per SEBI guidelines, if the company does not receive 90% of the issue amount from public subscription within .... from the date of issue, the amount received is required to be refunded.

Ans 120 days

22 Angel investors provide .... finance for product development and initial marketing but with no commercial sales.

Ans start-up

23 As an industry, venture capital has originated in the ....

Ans USA

24 A viable venture is born when knowledge, skills, ... and ...... is strategically applied. **(CBSE 2020)**

Ans experience, creativity

25 .... refers to the whole network of all organisations, institutions and instruments that provide medium and long-term funds to the government and industrial sector.

Ans Capital market

26 Divakar limited issued 20,000 equity shares of ₹ 10 each. Public applied for 31,500 shares. The oversubscribed amount, after the finalisation of allotment, should be refunded to the applicants within .... of the closure of subscription list.

Ans 10 weeks

27 The word 'angel' was originally coined by ...... in 1978 to describe the investors who supported entrepreneurs to raise seed capital.

Ans William Wetzel

28 .... is an equity based investment in a growth-oriented, small to medium sized business, which in most cases would not qualify for receiving bank loans. **(CBSE 2020)**

Ans Venture capital

29 Divij is an innovative entrepreneur. He has decided to open an online portal which helps people to order groceries 24 × 7. But before launching his portal, he wants to investigate the marketability of his idea. He approached Tech Marts, a venture capital firm, to fund his investigation. Divij is looking for .... finance.

Ans seed capital

State True or False

30 Primary market is also referred to as 'new issues market'.

Ans True

31 Primary market enhances the marketability and liquidity of securities by providing a platform where existing shareholders can sell their securities.

Ans False. Secondary market enhances the marketability and liquidity of securities.

32 Rights issue is a method of raising additional finance from existing shareholders by offering securities to them on pro-rata basis.

Ans True

33 Direct sale of its securities by a company to a limited number of sophisticated investors is known as right issue. **(CBSE 2020)**

Ans False. It is known as private placement.

34 Announcement regarding the proposed issue should be made atleast 20 days before the subscription list opens.

Ans False. It should be made 10 days before the subscription list opens.

35 Venture capital is basically equity finance in relatively new companies.

Ans True

36 Angel investors generally invest in a business involving low risk and high return.

Ans False. They invest in business involving high risk and high return.

37 The secondary market offers opportunity to an entrepreneur to issue additional capital as and when required. **(CBSE 2020)**

Ans False. The primary market offers this advantage.

38 George Doriot, the founder of American Research and Development Corporation (ARDC), is known as the father of venture capitalism.

Ans True

39 Venture capitalist firms will be interested in providing start-up finance only if they are convinced about the capability of the management team to triumph against competition.

Ans True

40 Devidayal Ltd. is into manufacturing of stainless steel and copper utensils from last 20 years and has a good reputation in the market. The company needs funds for expansion. It decided to bring a new issue of shares worth ₹ 1 crore.

Through a circular, these shares will be proposed to the existing shareholders and in case they are not willing to subscribe, they can renounce the same in favour of another person. Devidayal Ltd. is raising capital through private placement. **(CBSE 2020)**

Ans False. Devidayal is raising capital through right issue.

Case Based Questions

41 Read the following article and answer the questions that follow

Zyler Corp. is an established business manufacturing steel tools and products. The top-management of the company decided to expand its business in two new areas and held a meeting of all the senior and divisional managers for insights upon the idea. The management was trying to decide the sources of finance to generate funds to be spent on the expansion.

Mohan, a senior manager stated that the company should take loan from ABY Bank, whereas, Reenu, a divisional manager suggested that the company should use its retained earnings for the expansion.

The management was not ready to take borrowed funds as well as to reduce its retained earnings.

Therefore, it was decided that the funding will be made with the help of issue of shares to the existing shareholders on a pro-rata basis. The shares were allotted to the shareholders and the company got its funding for the expansion.

The management was happy with the funding choice because they thought that it was inexpensive comparatively to other sources of funding.

(i) Which source of finance was suggested by Reenu?

(a) Internal (b) External
(c) Both (a) and (b) (d) None of these

Ans (a) Internal

(ii) Which of the following is the benefit of Reenu's suggestion over Mohan's?
(a) No dilution of ownership
(b) Less burden of payment
(c) Easier to obtain funds
(d) All of the above

Ans (d) All of the above

(iii) "Therefore, it was decided that the funding will be made with the help of issue of shares to the existing shareholders on a pro-rata basis."

Which of the following share issue is highlighted in the above text?
(a) Private placement
(b) Public issue
(c) Right issue
(d) None of the above

Ans (c) Right issue

(iv) A company seeking funds for expansion can resort to the .... market.
(a) primary
(b) secondary
(c) Both (a) and (b)
(d) None of the above

Ans (a) primary

(v) Which values were depicted by the company by inviting the ideas of divisional manager along with the senior management?
(a) Belongingness
(b) Motivation
(c) Both (a) and (b)
(d) None of the above

Ans (c) Both (a) and (b)

42 Read the following article and answer the questions that follow

Alpha Limited and Beta Limited are two competitor firms operating in the trading industry. Both firms operate various shops that are indulged in selling various grocery items to the customers. Alpha Limited wants to become a public company and for this, the management has decided to enter the capital market.

Alpha Limited entered the capital market by issuing its shares for the first time and invited investors to invest in the company. After seeing this, Beta Limited decided to expand and revitalise into a grand business to compete with Alpha. The management of Beta Limited was not as skilled as Alpha limited; therefore, they ended up losing money by taking borrowed funds from family and friends.

On the other hand, Alpha Limited utilised the funds captured from the share issue for expansion and achieved the goal that Beta wanted to achieve. Therefore, without proper planning and knowledge about the capital markets and sources of finance, no business can flourish.

(i) The capital market plays the role of ....
(a) financial investor (b) financial agent
(c) financial intermediary
(d) None of the above

Ans (c) financial intermediary

(ii) The issue made by Alpha Limited is called
(a) initial issue (b) new money issue
(c) Both (a) and (b) (d) None of these

Ans (c) Both (a) and (b)

(iii) "After seeing this, Beta Limited decided to expand and revitalise into a grand business to compete with Alpha."

Which of the following sources of finance should be opted by Beta Limited?
(a) Venture capital (b) Angel investor
(c) Borrowing/Loans (d) All of these

Ans (a) Venture capital

(iv) Which of the following is the advantage that Alpha Limited got from shares issue?
(a) Less debt than borrowings
(b) Provide liquidity
(c) Growth and development
(d) All of the above

Ans (d) All of the above

(v) Before making a public issue of shares, the company needs to make sure that
(a) shares are inexpensive
(b) shares are diluted
(c) the issue is as per the SEBI guidelines
(d) All of the above

Ans (c) the issue is as per the SEBI guidelines

Short Answer Type I Questions (2 Marks)

1 Why does an entrepreneur needs 'second-round financing'?

Ans At this stage, the idea has been transformed into a product and is being produced and sold. The entrepreneur, at this stage, needs assistance from venture capitalist for expansion, modernisation and diversification.

2 What is the need of finance? **(CBSE TBQ)**

Ans Finance is needed for the following reasons
(i) Meeting fixed capital requirement.
(ii) Meeting working capital requirement.
(iii) For growth and expansion.
(iv) For diversification.
(v) For technology upgradation.

3 An entrepreneur is a person who bears the risks, unites various factors of production and carries out a creative innovation and for all these, what is the basic requirement to be reached to this extent? **(CBSE TBQ)**

Ans Finance is the basic requirement. Whether running a home based business or a mid-sized venture, the first and foremost requirement is that of finance.

Finance is the elixir that assits in the formation of new businesses and allows businesses to take advantage of opportunities to grow and expand.

4 State some mushrooming sources of raising finance in the business. **(CBSE TBQ)**

Ans Some mushrooming sources available to an entrepreneur for raising finance are as follows
(i) Capital markets
(ii) Angel investors
(iii) Venture capital
(iv) Specialised financial institutions

5 For what purpose is finance required right from the very beginning, i.e. conceiving an idea? **(CBSE TBQ)**

Ans Right from the very beginning, i.e. conceiving an idea, finance is required to
(i) promote or establish the business.
(ii) acquire fixed assets.
(iii) make market investigations.
(iv) develop product.
(v) keep men and machines at work.
(vi) encourage management to make progress and create value.
(vii) expand, diversify, improve and grow.
(viii) to be able to meet unexpected business expenses.

6 Why are capital markets regarded as 'financial intermediaries' ? State. **(CBSE 2023)**

Ans Capital market may be defined as an organised mechanism meant for effective and smooth transfer of money capital or financial resources from the investors to the entrepreneurs. The role of transferring financial resources from the surplus units to the deficit units is known as financial intermediation.

Capital market plays a very vital role of financial intermediatory. Here, productive capital is raised and made available for industrial purposes.

7 Which sources provide the supply for long-term funds? **(CBSE TBQ)**

Ans Long-term funds are those funds which will be kept in business for a period exceeding five years. These funds can be raised both from internal as well as external sources.

Internal sources of long-term funds are
(i) Equity shares (ii) Preference shares
(iii) Retained earnings

External sources of long-term funds are
(i) Debentures
(ii) Long-term loans from banks and financial institutions

8 Ketan won a cash prize of ₹ 50,000 in the National Level Robotics Competition. On the advise of his father, he visits a nearby bank to open a fixed deposit account in his name with the prize money.

His sister Suhasini accompanied him to the bank. On reaching the bank, he notice big banners which are placed within the premises containing information about the various arrangements through which corporates may raise their capital through the bank.

Being a finance graduate, Suhasini explains to Ketan that banks play the role of the financial intermediary by helping in the process of channelising the savings of the households into the most profitable business ventures.

In context of the above case

(i) Name another financial intermediary that helps in the process of channelising the savings of the households into the most productive use.

(ii) Also, outline any one advantage of financial intermediary as identified in part (i).

Ans (i) Financial market is the other financial intermediary that helps in the process of channelising the savings of the households into the most productive use.

(ii) Financial market helps to secure the required foreign capital and know how to promote economic growth at a faster rate.

9 Madhav's is one of the India's most trusted brands in Indian sweets and snacks segment. The company has manufacturing plants in Kota, Kanpur, New Delhi and Mumbai. Madhav's has its own retail chain stores and a range of restaurants in these cities.

Now, the company plans to extend its business in 12 more cities in India. In order to raise the funds, its directors have decided to float a public issue through prospectus.

Besides, it intends to raise money to meet the floatation cost in terms of brokerage, underwriting commission, advertising etc.

In context of the above case

(i) What is the other name used for the funds required to meet floatation costs?

(ii) State the two types of financial market that the company intends to approach to meets its financial needs.

Ans (i) Bridge financing is the other name used for the funds required to meet floatation costs.

(ii) Two types of financial markets are

(a) Capital market

(b) Money market

10 How stock options lead to enable employees to become shareholders and share the profits of the company? **(CBSE TBQ)**

Ans Employee Stock Option Scheme (ESOS) is an option provided to the employees to buy company's share, mostly as a preferential price which is less than the market price.

By opting to buy the stock option, the employees become shareholders of the company and become entitled to share the future profits of the company.

ESOS is offered to employees to increase their motivation level and to retain them in the company.

11 Give the various sources of raising finance through new issue.

Ans The various sources are as follows

(i) Public issue

(ii) Right issue

(iii) Private placement

(iv) Offer to employees

12 Name the sources of demand for capital. **(CBSE TBQ)**

Ans The demand for capital arises due to the undermentioned reasons

(i) Meeting fixed capital requirements.

(ii) Meeting working capital requirements.

(iii) For growth and expansion.

(iv) For diversification.

(v) For technology upgradation.

13 Entrepreneur can use the capital raised for a variety of purposes. What are they? **(CBSE TBQ)**

Ans The capital raised may be used for

(i) Setting new enterprises

(ii) Expanding

(iii) Diversifying

14 How can an entrepreneur raises funds by selling the issue mainly to the institutional investors? **(CBSE TBQ)**

Ans Private placement is a mode of financing through which entrepreneur raise funds by selling the issue mainly to institutional investors like

(i) Unit Trust of India

(ii) Life Insurance Corporation of India

(iii) General Insurance Corporation of India, etc.

15 Incorporated in 1990, Kuku Diary Ltd., is one of the leading manufacturers and marketers of dairy-based branded foods in India. In the initial years, its operations were restricted only to collection and distribution of milk.

But, over the years it has gained a reasonable market share by offering a diverse range of dairy based products including fresh milk, flavoured yogurt, ice creams, butter milk, cheese, ghee, milk powders etc.

In order to raise capital to finance its expansion plans, Kuku Dairy Ltd. has decided to approach capital market through a mix of offer for sale of ₹ 3 crore shares and a public issue of ₹ 5 crore shares.

(i) Name the segment of capital market being approached by the company.

(ii) Identify the two methods of floatation used by the company to raise the required capital.

Ans (i) Primary market is the segment of capital market being approached by the company.

(ii) The two methods of floatation used by the company to raise the required capital are

(a) Issue through prospectus

(b) Offer for sale

16 The decision of 'going public' by a company is considered to be a complex decision that requires careful consideration and planning as it requires additional obligations and reporting requirements. State any two such obligations and reporting requirements. **(CBSE 2023)**

Ans Public issue involves raising of funds directly from the public through the issue of prospectus. It is the most popular method of raising finance. This method requires compliance to various statutory laws relating to prospectus drafting, listing agreements, etc.

Going public raises the obligations and reporting requirements of a company, such as (any two)

(i) Increasing accountability to public shareholders.

(ii) Need to maintain dividend and profit growth trends.

(iii) Need to observe and adhere strictly to the rules and regulations of governing bodies.

17 'Apart from investing funds, they also provide proactive advice'. Who are 'they' in the above sentence? In which business do 'they' invest funds?

Ans 'They' are angel investors. Angel investors generally provide capital for a business start up and early stage companies having a high-risk, high-return matrix.

18 What are the demerits of availing venture capital for an entrepreneur?

Ans Venture capital investors more or less become the non-working partners and obtain many times the returns for the investments they have made.

Also, they may sometimes interfere in the day-to-day working of the enterprise.

19 Enlist several categories of financing possibilities in which smaller ventures sometimes rely on. **(CBSE TBQ)**

Ans The categories of financing possibilities are as follows

(i) Early stage financing, which comprises of

(a) seed capital

(b) start-up capital

(ii) Expansion or development financing, which comprises of

(a) working capital requirements

(b) funding for expansion plans

(c) bridge financing

(iii) Acquisitions and leveraged buyout financing.

20 Why are venture capitalists typically very selective in deciding while doing the investment? **(CBSE TBQ)**

Ans Venture capitalists are typically very selective in deciding while doing the investment due to the following reasons

(i) High-risk associated with ventures.

(ii) No asset backing for investment made.

(iii) Highly illiquid investments.

(iv) Long gestation period.

21 Give any two differences between angel investors and venture capitalists.

Ans Two points of distinction between angel investors and venture capitalists are as follows

(i) Angel investors invest their own money, whereas venture capitalists invest other people money.

(ii) The investment made by angel investors is as small as compared to venture capitalists.

22 State how obtaining venture capital is different from raising loan from a lender. Also state any two areas where venture capitalists decide to invest. **(CBSE 2020)**

Ans Difference between venture capital and loan

Basis	Venture Capital	Loan
Meaning	Venture capital is a type of private equity capital provided as seed funding to high potential, high-risk companies.	With a loan, a lender gives a business money and the business has a contractual obligation to pay back that amount plus interest over some period of time.
Form of Returns	Dividends.	Interest.
Security	No security is offered.	Security is generally offered.

Two areas where venture capitalists decide to invest are as follows

(i) Innovative technology.

(ii) Potential for rapid growth.

23 At present, many venture capital companies have been set-up in India, in both the public and the private sector. Name any two such institutions.

Ans Two such institutions are

(i) Gujarat Venture Finance Limited.

(ii) National Venture Fund for Software and IT industry.

24 What do you understand by venture capital? **(CBSE TBQ)**

Ans Venture capital is an equity based investment in small and medium enterprises in return for minority shareholding in the business or an irrevocable right to acquire. It is a professionally managed pool of equity capital.

25 Research so far have indicated that start-ups in early stage of development encounter with the financial gap which limits companies' ability both to innovate and to commercialise its products (valley of death) (Hudson & Khazragui, 2013).

Moreover, limited human capital, high uncertainty in terms of product and market, volatile development process, weak partnership ties are the utmost impediments for successful start-ups development (Fielden, Davidson and Makin, 2000).

It has been finalised that venture capitalists are valuable contributors in both filling the financial gap (1), and providing value added services (2) like financial, technological, managerial support, and contacts (Hellmann, Puri 2002; Dubocage, Rivaud-Danset & Redi, 2012; Caselli et al., 2009, Bertoni and Tykvova, 2012).

Still the research on venture capital role on the start-ups performance has fragmented the impact on the companies' performance indicators which is revealed in some extent (Peneder, 2010).

Having all mentioned the scientific problem emerges: what is the role of venture capital in start-ups development specifically on the performance indicators (turnover, number of employees) Research is carried out by combining qualitative and quantitative research techniques including analysis and synthesis of the scientific literature, case studies and statistical data as well.

The literature research has identified the characteristics of venture capital financing, specifically there are evidences that venture capital funds trigger the growth of company, product development, inspire entrepreneurship and thus enhancing the competitiveness of start-ups.

Source *Procedia Economics and Finance Volume 26, 2015.*

Which concept is highlighted in the above paragraph? Explain.

Ans **Venture Capital** It is a type of private equity capital provided as seed funding to early stage, high-potential, high-risk, growth-up companies and entrepreneurs who lack the necessary experience and funds to give shape to their ideas.

Short Answer Type II Questions (3 Marks)

1 What do you understand by capital market? How can the capital market in India be broadly classified into different categories? **(CBSE TBQ)**

Ans A capital market may be defined as an organised mechanism meant for effective and smooth transfer of money capital or financial resources from the investors to the entrepreneurs. Capital market deals in medium- term and long-term funds.

The capital market can be divided into two parts

(i) **Primary Market** It refers to the market where securities are sold for the first time. Therefore, it is also known as 'new issues' market. The common instruments of this market are equity shares, preference shares, debentures, etc.

Primary market accelerates the rate of capital formation in the economy, as it facilitates the transfer of surplus funds from investors to the entrepreneurs. The major participants of this market are banks, financial institutions, insurance companies, mutual funds and individuals.

(ii) **Secondary Market** It refers to market for sale and purchase of previously issued securities. It is also known as stock market or stock exchange. Trading can be done nationwide through terminals, but the transactions have to be carried out within the regulatory framework prescribed by SEBI.

2 Explain how capital markets are the most important source of raising finance for an entrepreneur? **(CBSE TBQ, SQP Term II)**

Ans Capital market refers to whole network of all organisations, institutions and instruments that fulfil the medium-term and long-term financial needs of the government and the industrial sector.

They are an important source of raising finance for an entrepreneur because of the below mentioned reasons

(i) **Investment Outlay** Capital market instruments require less investment as the securities are generally low priced. So, investors from all income group can invest in capital market instruments. The broad investor base makes it easier for an entrepreneur to raise finance.

(ii) **Participants** Both individual as well as institutional investors can participate in the capital market. This also facilitates in easy raising of finance.

(iii) **Duration** Capital market deals in medium and long-term funds. So, it provides an entrepreneur with capital requiring no immediate repayment. This helps him to make plans for growth and diversification.

3 This is a market where there is an option to sell and buy new and old financial instruments. It facilitates the transferring of financial resources from surplus units to deficit units.

(i) Identify and define the market.

(ii) Name the function of transferring of financial resources from surplus units to deficit units. **(CBSE 2018)**

Ans (i) The market discussed is capital market. The capital market facilitates the buying and selling of securities.

It refers to the whole network of all organisations, institutions and instruments that provide medium and long-term funds to the government as well as industrial sector.

(ii) The function referred is 'Access to capital'.

4 What is meant by primary market? Briefly explain the concept of 'Right issue for existing companies'. **(CBSE TBQ)**

Ans Primary market is basically to facilitate transfer of resources from the savers to the entrepreneurs seeking funds for

(i) setting new enterprises

(ii) expanding

(iii) diversifying

An entrepreneur can raise the required capital in the primary market by the following methods

(i) Public issue

(ii) Rights issue

(iii) Private placement

(iv) Offer to employees

Rights Issue for Existing Companies

Rights issue is a method of raising additional finance from existing shareholders by offering securities to them on pro-rata basis, i.e. giving them a right, to a certain number of shares in proportion to the shares, they are already holding.

5 Explain some important sources of raising finance in business. **(CBSE TBQ)**

Ans Some of the important sources of raising finance in business are

(i) **Public Issue** It involves raising of funds directly from the public through the issue of prospectus. It is the most popular method of raising finance, but it requires compliances of various statutory laws.

(ii) **Rights Issue** It is a method of raising additional finance from existing shareholders by offering securities to them on pro-rata basis.

(iii) **Private Placement** It means the direct sale by a company of its securities to a limited number of institutional investors.

(iv) **Offer to Employees** Stock options or offering shares to employees enables them to become shareholders of the company and entitles them to a company.

6 Company 'A' goes for public issue of 10,000 shares @ ₹ 10 each. Application were received for only 5,000 shares. Can the company proceed with the process of issuing shares? **(CBSE TBQ)**

Ans No, the company cannot proceed with the process of issuing shares. As per SEBI guidelines, if the company does not receive 90% of the issue amount from the public subscription, then it cannot proceed with the process of issuing shares.

The amount of subscription received is required to be refunded to the applicants. In the given instance, since only 50% of the issue has been subscribed for, therefore, the company cannot proceed with the process of issuing shares.

7 The directors of a company want to modernise its plant and machinery by making a public issue of shares. They wish to approach the stock exchange, while the finance manager prefers to approach a consultant for the new public issue of shares.

Advise the directors whether to approach the stock exchange or a consultant for new public issue of shares and why. Also advise them about any two different methods which the company may adopt for the new public issue of shares.

Ans The directors should approach to the consultant for new public issue of shares as this is the case of primary market. The stock exchange is only meant for securities already issued.

Following are the methods which the company may adopt for the new public issue of shares (Any two)

(i) **Public Issue** Under this method, the company issues a prospectus and invites the general public to purchase shares or debentures.

(ii) **Offer for Sale** Under this method, firstly the new securities are offered to an intermediary (generally firms of stock brokers) at a fixed price. They further resell the same to the general public at a higher price. The advantage of doing this is that the issuing company feels free from the tedious work of making a public issue.

(iii) **Private Placement** Under this method, the company sells securities to the big financial institutions or brokers instead of selling them to the general public. They, in turn, sell these securities to the selected clients at a higher price. This method is preferred as it is a cheaper method of raising funds as compared to a public issue.

8 Explain SEBI's guidelines related to minimum subscription.

Ans As per the SEBI guidelines, if the company does not receive 90% of the issue amount from the public subscription including development from underwriters within 120 days from the date of the issue, the amount of subscription received is required to be refunded to the applicants.

In case of disputed development also, subscription is required to be refunded, if 90% of the issued amount plus accepted development from underwriters, if any, is not received within 120 days of the issue of prospectus.

9 Enumerate the disclosures required to be made in the prospectus of a company.

Ans Apart from notice of offer, to issue shares to public, prospectus should also disclose

(i) justification of premium, if called.

(ii) Net Assets Value (NAV).

(iii) high and low price of the shares of the company for the last 2 years.

(iv) a clause that company shall refund the entire application money, if minimum subscription is not received.

(v) a statement by the leading managers that in their opinion, the assets of the underwriters are adequate to meet their requirements.

10 'Angel investors' and 'venture capital' are the two sources of raising finance for an entrepreneur. Explain the concept of both the sources stating one distinguishing feature of each. **(CBSE 2015)**

Ans **Angel Investors**

Angel investors, also known as 'business angels' or 'angel funders' are affluent individuals, who provide capital for a business start-ups, usually in exchange for convertible debt or ownership equity. They generally provide capital for a business belonging to a high-risk, high-return matrix.

One distinguishing feature of angel investors is

Most angel investors are current or retired executives, business owners or high net worth individuals, who have the knowledge, expertise and funds that help start-ups to match upto industry standards.

Venture Capital

Venture capital is a type of private equity capital provided as seed funding to early stage, high-potential, high-risk, growth-up companies and entrepreneurs who lack the necessary experience and funds to give shape to their ideas. It is also known as risk-capital.

One distinguishing feature of venture capital is

It is a professionally managed pool of equity capital.

11 Why is it said 'A venture capitalists investments are illiquid'? Give reason. **(CBSE TBQ)**

Ans It is rightly said that 'A venture capitalists investments are illiquid'. The reasons for this are as follows

(i) Venture capitalists generally invest in equity of a new company.

(ii) This company has yet to make a standing in the secondary market.

(iii) Because of this, the company's shares are not demanded in stock exchanges, giving it poor liquidity.

Therefore, a venture capitalists holdings are illiquid.

Long Answer Type Questions (5 Marks)

1 What is meant by capital market? Why is it considered as the most important source of raising finance? **(CBSE 2019)**

Ans Refer to topic 'Capital market' and 'Importance of capital market' on page 203.

2 Explain the following as methods of new issues

(i) Public issue (ii) Rights issue **(CBSE 2019)**

Ans (i) Refer to topic 'Public issue' on page 203.

(ii) Refer to topic 'Rights issue' on page 204.

3 Differentiate between primary market and secondary market.

Ans Differences between primary market and secondary market are

Basis	Primary Market	Secondary Market
Meaning	Primary market deals with the trading of newly issued securities.	Secondary market is that part of capital market which deals in already issued securities.
Role of the Issuing Company	Issuing company plays an active role as shares are sold directly to the investors.	The company has no role to play as securities are traded between investors only.
Determination of Price	Price is determined by the company.	Price is determined by the market forces of demand and supply.
Type of Purchasing	Shares are purchased directly from company	Shares are purchased indirectly, i.e. from investors.

4 Evaluate the different options available for an entrepreneur to raise funds from the primary markets. **(CBSE SQP)**

Ans The following options are available

(i) **Public Issue/Going Public** Public issue is the most popular method of raising capital these days by the entrepreneurs. This involves raising of funds directly from the public through the issue of prospectus.

An enterprise organising itself as a public limited company can raise the required funds commonly by preparing a prospectus.

When an entrepreneur offers shares to the public for subscription, he/she is required to comply with all the restrictions and formalities pertaining to the initial issues, prospectus drafting and launch.

(ii) **Rights Issue** It is a method of raising additional finance from existing shareholders by offering securities to them on a pro-rata basis i.e. giving them a right to a certain number of shares in proportion to the shares they are holding.

This method of issuing securities is considered to be inexpensive as it does not require any brokers, agents, underwriters, prospectus or enlistment.

(iii) **Private Placement** It means the direct sale by a company of its securities to a limited number of sophisticated investors. Entrepreneurs, herein, raise funds by selling the issues mainly to the institutional investors like Unit Trust of India, Life Insurance Corporation of India, etc.

Entrepreneurs both from public limited and private limited sector, bank heavily upon raising funds through the issue of varied financial instruments under this segment as at times they do not wish to disclose information to the open market.

(iv) **Offer to Employees** Stock options or offering shares to the employees has gained much popularity in many countries of the world. This method enables employees to become shareholders and share the profits of the company leading to higher efficiency, low labour turnover and low floatation cost.

5 'Ganpati Steel Ltd.' is a large and credit-worthy company manufacturing steel for the Indian market. It now wants to cater to the Asian market and decides to invest in new hi-tech machines. Since the investment is large, it requires long-term finance.

The company decided to raise funds through the capital market. 40% of the funds will be raised directly from the public through the issue of prospectus. 40% of the shares will be directly sold to a limited number of sophisticated investors. 20% of the shares will be offered to the employees.

Identify the methods of flotation of new issues used by the company. Also state one benefit of each method.

The issue was very well accepted by the investors. Mr. Raman, an investor could not get shares allotted when the offer was made to the public.

He wishes to invest in the company. State the option available to him now and how will it benefit Raman? **(CBSE SQP Term II)**

Ans (i) 40% of the funds will be raised directly from the public through the issue of prospectus-IPO.

The primary advantage an entrepreneur stands to gain by going public is access to capital.

(ii) 40% of the shares will be directly sold to a limited number of sophisticated investors – Private placement.
This method is useful at times when the company does not wish to disclose information to the open market.

(iii) 20% of the shares will be offered to the employees – Offer to employees.
This method enables employees to become shareholders and share the profit of the company leading to low labour turnover.

(iv) Raman can go to the secondary market/stock exchange and buy shares.
This market imparts liquidity to the long-term securities held by investors by providing an auction market for these securities.

6 Geeta has completed her B.Tech in Chemical Engineering from a famous Indian Institute of Technology. She wants to start a chemical production unit wherein such chemicals will be produced which are used in automobile colouring and are being imported from other countries now-a-days.

The technology to be used by Geeta is new and untried involving high risk factors along with high growth potential. She wants to raise funds for her project from such a source that provides private equity capital as seed funding to early stage, to give shape to her ideas.

(i) Suggest Geeta the source of finance from where she can fund her project.

(ii) Give the meaning of the source suggested in (i) above and state any four features of this source. **(CBSE 2017)**

Ans (i) The source of finance from where Geeta can fund her project is 'Venture capital'.

(ii) Venture capital is a type of private equity capital provided as seed funding to early stage, high-potential, high-risk growth companies and entrepreneurs who lack the necessary experience and funds to give shape to their ideas. It is also know as risk-capital. Four features of this source are stated below

(a) It is basically equity finance in relatively new companies.

(b) It is long-term investment in growth oriented small or medium firms.

(c) It involves high risk-return spectrum.

(d) Venture capitatlists not only provide capital but also business skills to the new firms.

7 Venture capital is different from loan. How?

Ans Differences between venture capital and loan are

Basis	Venture Capital	Loan
Meaning	Venture capital is a type of private equity capital provided as seed funding to high potential, high-risk companies.	With a loan, a lender gives a business money and the business has a contractual obligation to pay back that amount plus interest over some period of time.
Form of Returns	Dividends.	Interest.
Security	No security is offered.	Security is generally offered.
Paying Back	It make money from selling equity.	It is paid back overtime with interest.

8 What is meant by venture capital? State any five features of venture capital. **(CBSE 2013)**

Ans Venture capital is defined in the journal of central bank, UK as 'an equity by which an investor supports an entrepreneurial talent with finance and business skills to exploit market opportunities and thus, obtain long-term market gains'. The main features of venture capital are as follows

(i) Investor's return is taxed as capital gain rather than ordinary income.

(ii) Investments are made in those enterprises which are new and using new technology of production to produce new products having an expectation of higher profits.

(iii) The venture capital investors cannot interfere in the day-to-day management of the enterprise but they can keep close contact with the promoters to protect and enhance their investment.

(iv) The venture capital investment is highly illiquid. In other words, it is not subject to repayment on demand.

(v) Venture capitalists aim at long-term benefits by funding start-ups.

9 Neeraj, an entrepreneur, is living in a beautiful village of Himachal Pradesh. This village was very famous for its natural beauty but very few people knew about it.

Due to his entrepreneurial inclination he always tried to find out the opportunities.

People of the village are very poor as they are mostly dependent on farming. Neeraj thought of starting a 'Holiday Resort' with cultural centre, restaurant and other facilities in the village.

All the villagers agreed and supported Neeraj for this project. They agreed to co-operate to make this project a success. Neeraj needed capital of ₹ 3 crores for this project.

Is the above paragraph highlighted the concept of venture capital? Clarify.

Ans No. Venture capitalists are very selective in deciding what to invest in and as a rule of thumb

(i) They may invest in one in four hundred opportunities presented to them.

(ii) Looks for the extremely rare, yet sought after qualities, such as

(a) Innovative technology

(b) Potential for rapid growth

(c) A well-developed business model

(d) An impressive management team

(iii) Looks for an 'exit' in the time frame of typically 3-7 years.

(iv) Are inclined towards ventures with exceptionally high growth potential.

So, entrepreneurs are expected to carry out detailed due diligence prior to seeking venture capital as a source of financing.

10 Financing is a very critical issue for the survival and development of Small and Medium Sized Enterprises. Angel investors play a key role in financing small and medium sized enterprises, especially those which are innovative and with high growth potential.

SMEs in their development pass through several stages. Few of the basic stages through which these enterprises pass are

(i) **Seed Stage** The entrepreneur has an idea or concept for potential profitable business, which needs to be developed and proven. In this stage as financing sources can be used savings of founders, family and friends (also called as 3F Money);

(ii) **Start-up Stage** The idea has been already developed up to the level which allows commercialisation preparations. This stage lasts for less than a year.
In this phase as financing sources can be used the angel investors means;

(iii) **Early Stage** In this stage, production and distribution of a specific product or service takes place. This stage lasts up to five years, and business can be still unprofitable. Usually, in this stage, formal venture capital can be used as financing sources

(a) Mention the concept highlighted in the given case.
(b) Explain its two features.

Ans (a) Angel investors
(b) The various features exhibited by angel investors are as follows

- Most angel investors are current or retired executives, business owners or high net worth individuals, who have the knowledge, expertise and funds that help start-ups match up to industry standards.
- As angel investors bear extremely high risk and their share is subjected to dilution after second round of funding, therefore they expect a high return on their investment.
- Apart from investing funds, they also provide proactive advice, guidance, industry connections and mentoring start-ups in its early stage.
- Their objective is to create great companies by providing value creation, and simultaneously helping investors to earn a high return on their investments.

11 'Angel investment' not only brings in funds but also an invaluable mentor to the business.

In the light of this statement, state any three features of angel investors. **(CBSE 2023)**

Or Who are angel investors? State any four features of angel investors. **(CBSE SQP Term II)**

Ans **Angel Investors** Angel investors, also known as 'business angels' or 'angel funders' are affluent individuals, who provide capital for a business start-ups, usually in exchange for convertible debt or ownership equity.

They generally provide capital for a business belonging to a high-risk, high-return matrix.

Features of Angel Investors Refer to Q. No. 10 of long answer type questions (5 Marks).

12 Give the meaning of 'venture capital'. Entrepreneurs can seek venture capital to assist various stages in the company's development.

Explain 'seed capital state' and 'pre-start-up and start-up stage' of financing by venture capitalists. **(CBSE 2023)**

Ans **Venture Capital** Refer to Q. No. 8 of long answer type questions (5 Marks).

Seed Capital Finance It refers to the capital required by an entrepreneur for conducting research at pre-commercialisation stage. During this stage, the entrepreneur has to convince the venture capitalist, why his idea/product is worthwhile. The venture capitalist will then investigate into the technical and economical feasibility of the idea. Entrepreneur's ability, technological skills and competencies are closely scrutinised by the venture capitalist. He may deny assisting if the findings and investigations are not up to his satisfaction.

Pre-start-up and Start-up Finance If the idea/product/process is qualified for further investigation and/or investment; the process will go to the second stage, i.e. the start-up stage. A business plan is presented by the entrepreneur to the venture capitalist firm.

A management team is then formed to run the venture. If the company has a board of directors, then a person or persons from the venture capitalist firm will take seats at the board. The management team establishes a feasible production line to produce the product.

The venture capitalist firm monitors the feasibility of the product and the capability of the management team from the board of directors.

CASE STUDIES

Case 1

Twitter Tweets

Twitter-named after the sound of chirping birds in 2006, has today established itself as a cultural touchstone, growing from a few thousand geeky users to more than 200 million today.

Most of twitter's revenue comes from advertising. Research firm marketer estimates that Twitter will generate $ 582.8 million in worldwide ad revenue for 2013, up from $ 288.3 million in 2012.

Twitter's money making potential has minted the company with an estimated market value of $ 10 billion, based on the appraisals of venture capitalists and other early investors who have been helping to fund the business so far.

Aiming for a sustainable future, Twitter, as has been long expected, tweets 'It will go public'. The law that allowed Twitter to file its initial IPO documents confidentially is called the Jumpstart Our Business Start ups Act (JOBS) President Barack Obama signed the law in 2012.

It is designed to make it easier for small businesses and start ups to grow and create jobs. Do you understand the significance of all this........???

Going public could give Twitter the muscle to become the next facebook or Apple-says one analyst. The capital gains from going public will likely allow the company to make solid investments across the board in hiring, operations and acquisition-that's the power of finance.

1 What is the full form of JOBS?

Ans The acronym JOBS stands for Jumpstart Our Business Start ups Act. It was signed by Barack Obama in 2012.

2 Which source of raising finance has been opted for, by Twitter?

Ans 'Twitter has opted for public issue as a source for raising finance.

3 Where will the company invest the funds so generated?

Ans The company will invest the funds so raised in hiring, operations and acquisitions.

Case 2

Source of Finance

Money is Always a Problem

'Air India has defaulted on working capital loan interest payment of ₹ 200 crores due to the financial crisis that the airlines is facing' confirms Air India sources on 21st May, 2011.

Air India has high-cost loans worth about ₹ 40,000 crores.

Air India is facing a tight financial situation and is in talks with lenders to restructure its debt of ₹ 40,000 crores.

The lenders have agreed to reduce interest rates on part of the debt that is linked to overseas borrowings. The future of the remaining debt is still uncertain, especially because lenders are seeking a conversion of their debt into equity or equity like instruments.

This is perhaps the first time that the national carrier has defaulted on its payments to banks. Sources said the airline had approached banks for more loans but they have declined to help because of the airlines' poor financial health.

And they say 'finance is difficult for new entrepreneurs ....'. Its always a major concern.

1 'Air India' has high cost loans worth about ₹ 40,000 crores. From the above statement, identify the source of finance Air India.

Ans Air India has sourced its funds from external sources.

2 Give one advantage and one disadvantage of raising finance through this source.

Ans Advantage is that control is not diluted. Disadvantage is that fixed expenses in the form of interest, prove to be a burden.

3 What will be the effect of conversion of debt into equity on the financial health of the company?

Ans The conversion would reduce interest payments for the airline, thereby reducing its burden.

Case 3

Interesting History

Before World War II, development capital were primarily the domain of wealthy individuals and families. It was not until after World War II, that what is considered today to be true private equity investments began to emerge by the founding of the first two venture capital firms in 1946

(i) American Research and Development Corporation (ARDC)

(ii) JH Whitney Company

ARDC was founded by George's Doriot, the 'father of venture capitalism' (former dean of Harvard Business School and founder of INSEAD), with Ralph Flanders and Karl Compton (former President of MIT), to encourage private sector investments in businesses run by soldiers who were returning from World War II.

ARDC's significance was primarily that it was the first institutional private equity investment firm that raised capital from sources other than wealthy families. ARDC continued investing until 1971 with the retirement of Doriot. In 1972, Doriot merged ARDC with Textron after having invested in our 150 companies.

1 Name the first two venture capital firms.

Ans The first two venture capital firms, established in 1946, were as follows

(i) American Research and Development Corporation (ARDC)

(ii) JH Whitney Company

2 Who is known as the 'father of venture capitalism'?

Ans George Doriot, the founder of ARDC is known as the father of venture capitalism.

3 What was ARDC's significance?

Ans Before World War II, development capital was primarily the domain of wealthy individuals and families. ARDC's significance was primarily that it was the first institutional private equity investment firm that raised capital from sources other than wealthy families.

CHAPTER ASSESSMENT

Objective Type Questions (1 Mark)

1 External sources of finance include
(a) debentures and bonds
(b) public deposits
(c) trade credit
(d) All of these

2 The role of transferring financial resources from the surplus units to the deficit units is known as
(a) financial intermediation
(b) funding
(c) financing
(d) None of these

3 Key aspects of financial decision-making include
(a) investment
(b) financing
(c) dividends
(d) All of these

4 The market place for new shares is called ....

5 .... include all those sources which are generated from within the business.

6 The only reward the initial public offer investors seek is capital appreciation of their investment. State true or false.

7 Other name of an angle investor is formal investor. State true or false.

Short Answer Type I Questions (2 Marks)

8 Write a short note on finance.

9 Explain briefly internal sources of finance.

10 How is capital market important?

11 State any two advantages of raising finance through public issue.

12 Write a short note on 'Drafting of prospectus'.

Short Answer Type II Questions (3 Marks)

13 Explain right issue and private placement.

14 Elaborate the need of finance briefly.

15 Write any three disadvantages of raising finance through public issue.

16 What is the investment criteria for venture capitalists?

Long Answer Type Questions (5 Marks)

17 Write a short note on 'IPO'

18 Highlight any four steps involved in public issue of shares.

19 Explain in detail 'Angel investors'.

20 Explain venture capital institutions in India.

For explanations scan the given QR Code

PROJECT WORK

Title of the project	Project Report on Market Survey
Product chosen for the project	Fitness Equipments
Name	....
School	....
Year	....
Class	XII
Submitted to	....

PROJECT REPORT

Contents

Acknowledgment

Every project, big or small, is successful largely due to the effort of a number of wonderful people, who have always given their valuable advice or lent a helping hand. I sincerely appreciate and I am thankful for the inspiration, support and guidance of all those people, who have been instrumental in making this project a success.

I would start by expressing my profound gratitude to those who support me with their exemplary guidance, monitoring and constant encouragement throughout the course of this thesis. Also, this opportunity given by them helped me come face-to-face with my hidden talents.

I would also take this opportunity to express my deep regards to my subject teacher Mr/Mrs................. for his/her cordial support, valuable information and guidance which helped me in completing this project through various stages.

Lastly, I thank my family and friends for their constant encouragement and unending patience without which this assignment would not be completed within the limited time frame.

Introduction

Market Survey

A market survey is a tool used to gather information about existing or potential customers in a certain market or a segment of the population. Researchers select a sample of customers from the population. The information from the survey is then used to assess attitudes and beliefs, and in turn, predict market behaviour, such as buying intentions.

The following methods can be used while conducting a survey:

(i) **Personal interview/Direct personal investigation** This method is used when the surveyor has access to all the members.

(ii) **Mailing questionnaire** Under this method, the data in a survey are collected by mail.

(iii) **Telephone interview** In this method, the investigator asks questions over the telephone.

This project has adopted the personal interview method while conducting the survey.

Product Chosen for Market Survey

Product Fitness Equipments

Industry Health and Fitness

Brand name Full-On Fitness Equipments

Tag line Stay Fit, Stay Healthy

Nature of the product Consumer : Durable

Competing brands Cosco and Fitness World

Types of equipments Tread mill, Ellipticals, Bikes and Multi-gym

Innovation offered A trainer will be provided free of cost for 15 days to help a customer devise a fitness plan suited to his way of life.

Reasons, why personal trainer will be helpful are:

⇒ They will teach their trainees new things.

⇒ They push your limits.

⇒ They make you stick to a schedule.

And no doubt, that they are definitely eye-candy!

Social message "A healthy India is a productive India"

The Difference Exercise Makes

Only about 20% of American adults meet their recommended amount of exercise, but skimping on regular sweat sessions has some pretty profound effects. Here are a few of the major differences between an average, 40-year-old exerciser and someone getting little to no physical activity.

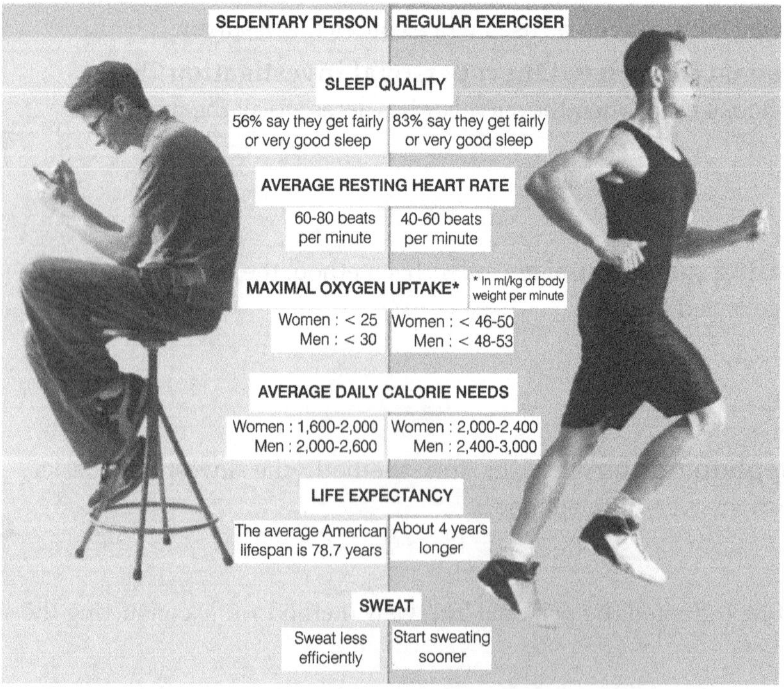

Market Survey on Fitness Equipment

Purpose of Survey

To collect primary data for the preparation of class XII entrepreneurship Market Survey Report, the product being researched is 'Fitness Equipments'. The idea of providing a free trainer for 15 days to help a customer familiarise with the equipments and devise his own fitness regime, is also being researched here.

General Instructions

1. Filling personal details is optional.
2. All the questions are compulsory.
3. Only one or more alternative (where specified) to be choosen.
4. Answer by ticking the most appropriate option.

Disclaimer

All information provided will be treated as confidential.

Market Survey Questionnaire Personal Details

Name .... **Age** ....

Occupation .... **Email** ....

Gender ....

1. Are you and your family health conscious?

   ☐ Yes ☐ No

2. What type of gymming do you preter?

   ☐ Home gymming ☐ Professional gymming ☐ Neither

3. If the respondent's response to the above questions indicates preference towards gymming, then which equipments does he use ?

   ☐ Tread mill ☐ Ellipticals ☐ Bikes

   ☐ Multigym ☐ Othters

4. Which brand do you prefer?

   ☐ Yes ☐ No

5. Are you satisfied with the quality of the equipments that you are using?

   ☐ Yes ☐ No

6. What is/are the problems which you faced while using the equipments?

   ☐ Not aware of the proper usage of the equipment (Can be more than one answer)

   ☐ Not familiar with the functions of the equipment

   ☐ Constant breakdown

   ☐ Others

7. Would you consider changing your brand, if you are provided with a free personal trainer for 15 days?

   ☐ Yes ☐ No

8. If the answer to the above question is in negative, then what are your reasons for brand loyalty?

   ☐ Good quality ☐ Adequate customer support ☐ Others (Please specify)

9. If you are currently not using any home gymming equipments, then what are your reasons for not using it?

   ☐ Lack of professional support ☐ Lack of space

   ☐ Equipment too expensive ☐ Others (please specify)

10. If you are provided with a free personal trainer for 15 days, then would you start using home gymming equipments?

    ☐ Yes ☐ No

Thank you for your cooperation and precious time

Analysis of Market Survey

1. **Are you and your family health conscious?**

Ans The questionnaire was surveyed from 50 respondents. Out of the 50 respondents, 20 agreed that they were health conscious, whereas 30 respondents answered in negative. In terms of percentage, 40% of the respondents answered in affirmative, acknowledging the importance of a healthy life.

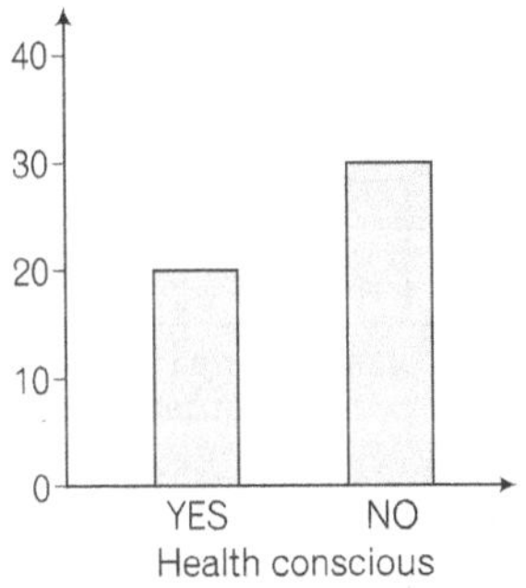

2. **Would you prefer home gymming or professional gymming?**

Ans According to the survey conducted, 15 respondents said that they would prefer home gymming, 20 said that they would prefer professional gymming while the remaining 15 said that they prefer neither of the two. In terms of percentage, 30 % of the respondents said that they prefer home gymming.

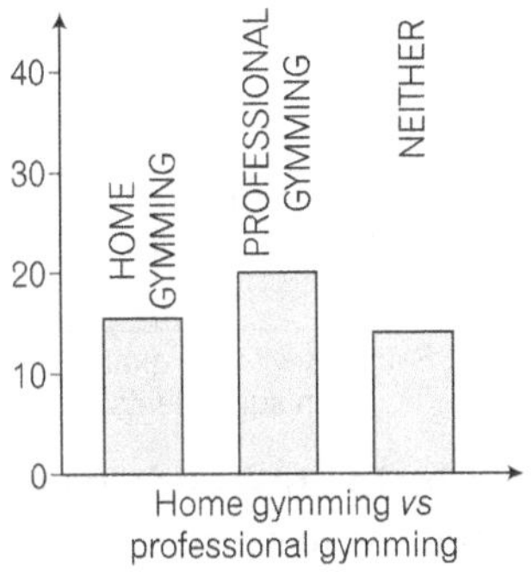

3. **Which equipments does the respondent use?**

Ans 15 respondents prefer home gymming and 20 respondents prefer professional gymming. So in all, 35 respondents use gym equipments. Out of these 35, many of the respondents use more than one equipment. Almost all of them use tread mill, with 33 of the respondents answering that they use it. 15 respondents use ellipticals, 10 use bikes, 5 use multi-gym and other 5 use other equipments such as weights, bench press, etc.

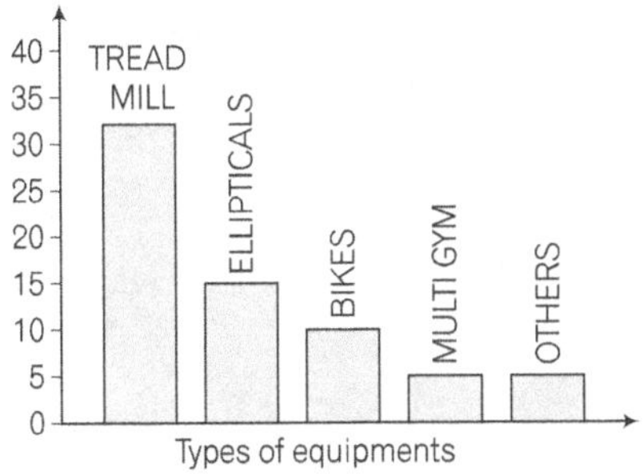

4. Brand preferred by the respondents.

Ans Out of the 35 respondents who use some sort of gymming equipments, 10 preferred Cosco, 15 preferred Fitness World, whereas, the remaining 10 preferred others such as Energie, Physique, etc. This indicates that our main competitor will be Fitness World.

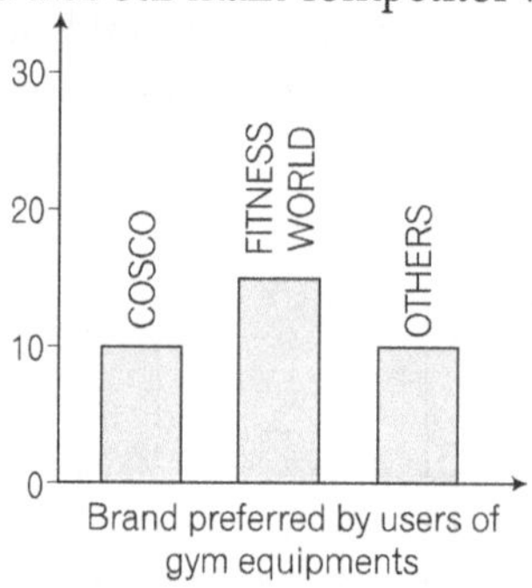

5. Are you satisfied with the quality of the equipments that you are using?

Ans Out of the 35 respondents who use gym equipments, a staggering 30 replied that they were not satisfied with the quality of the gym equipments that they were using. Only 5 of the respondents said that they had no complaints about the quality of their gym equipments.

This response indicates that there is a scope in the market for good quality gym equipments.

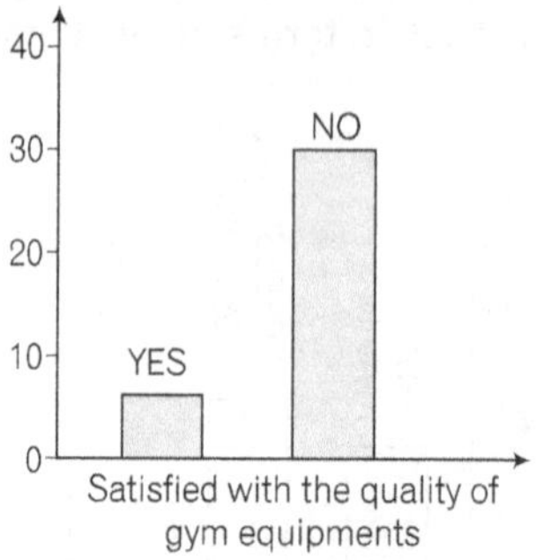

6. What is/are problem(s) faced by the respondents while using the equipments?

Ans All the respondents, whether they were satisfied with the quality of the equipments or not, had faced some or the other problems while using the gym equipments. 20 respondents said that they were not aware of the proper usage of the equipments, 28 said that they were not familiar with the functions of the equipments, 8 had faced the problem of constant breakdown and 6 had faced other problems such as those relating to customer relation, guarantee and warrantee issues, etc. Most of the respondents faced more than one problem.

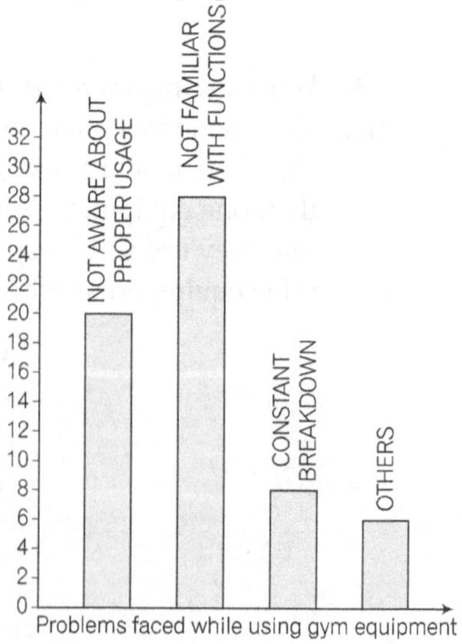

7. **Would you consider changing your brand, if you are provided with a personal trainer for 15 days?**

Ans The answer to this question was to decide the future of our product and out of the 35 respondents, 26 replied that they would definitely consider about changing their brand if provided with a personal trainer, whereas 9 respondents were satisfied with their brands that they were using. So, this means that our venture could be successful. Three cheers to that!

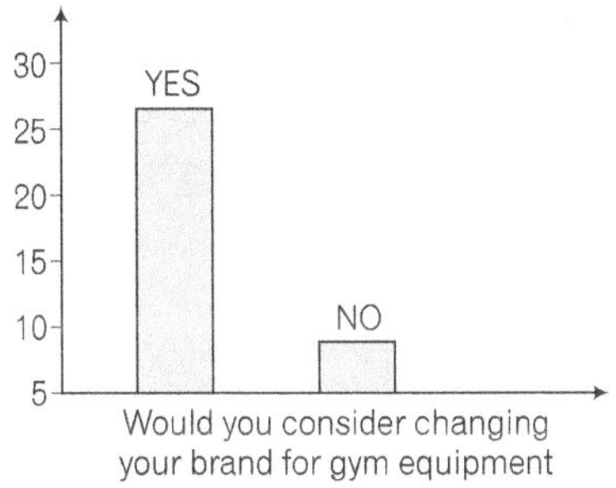

8. **Reasons for brand loyalty, if respondent chooses to stay with his brand.**

Ans Out of the 9 respondents, who replied that they will not change their brand inspite of being provided with a personal trainer, 6 cited good quality as their reason for brand loyalty and the remaining 3 said good customer support was the reason.

9. **Reasons for not using any gymming equipment.**

Ans 15 respondents had said that they were not using any gymming equipment either at home or at a gym. Out of the 15 respondents, 8 said that it was due to a lack of professional support. 3 said that it was due to lack of space and 2 said that it was because the equipment was expensive and the remaining 2 said that they did not use gymming equipments due to health concerns.

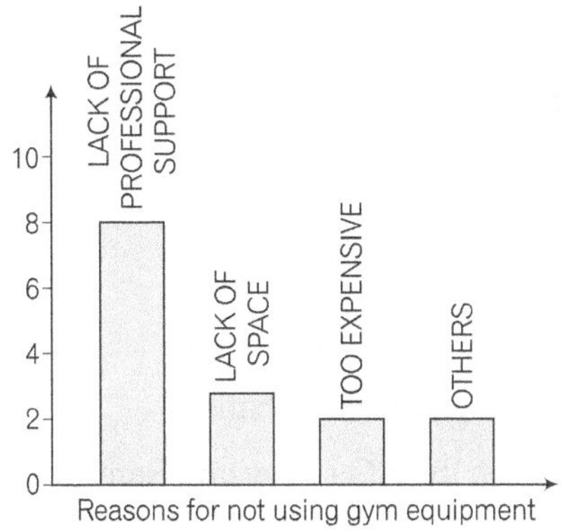

10. If provided with a personal trainer, would you start using home gymming equipment.

Ans This question aims at assessing the market for our product among non-users and also checks the viability of our innovation. 7 out of the 8 respondents gave lack of professional support as their reason for not using gymming equipments, said that they will start using home gymming equipments if provided with a personal trainer. This statistic again confirms that our venture is relevant and has the potential of creating a niche for itself in the market.

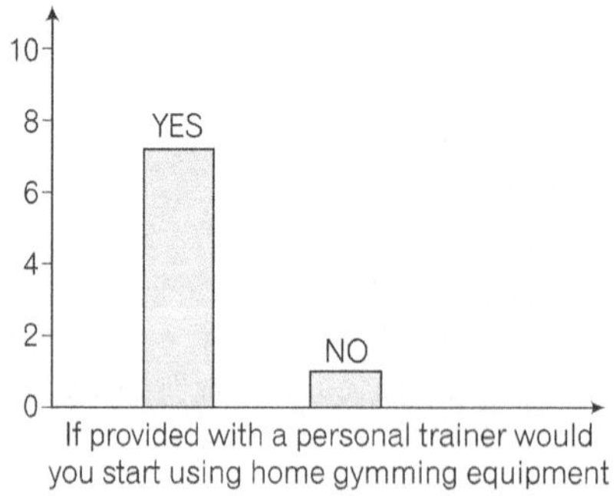

Findings of Market Survey

The findings of the market survey conducted are summarised below :

(i) The market for this product is in its formative years due to lack of health consciousness among people.

(ii) The quality of the products of our competitors is not upto the mark. Because of this, brand loyalty is low. This can be a positive sign for us.

(iii) Majority of the respondents agreed that the innovation offered by us is a great motivator for them to start gymming.

(iv) Price is not a determining factor in this segment, with only 2 respondents saying that they did not use home gymming equipment because it was too expensive.

(v) The findings are in general indicative that there is plenty of scope for our products in this segment. So, what are we waiting for? Lets get ahead with our venture.

Bibliography

- Market Your Way to Growth : By Kotler, Kotler (Times Group Books)
- Entrepreneurship in Action : By Mary Coulter /PHI Learning
- The Journal of Private Enterprise/What Business Ethics can Learn from Entrepreneurship : By Stephen, R C Hicks, Rockford College Illionois.
- Entrepreneurship Class XII : By CBSE
- Entrepreneurship : New Venture Creation : By Holt (EEE)
- http://en.wikipedia.org/

Recommended Readings

1. Men of Steel : By Vir Sanghvi
2. Stay Hungry Stay Foolish : By Rashmi Bansal
3. Follow Every Rainbow : By Rashmi Bansal
4. The Game Changers : By AG Lafley and Ram Charan

Appendix

Important Defined Terms

Population

It is defined as the sum total of all the units unde rconsideration.

Sample

It is defined as a part of population, selected with a view to represent the population in all its characteristics.

Consumer Durable Product

These products are bought by consumers for the act of final consumption and are usable for a number of years.

Primary Data

This data is collected for the very first time by the enumerator for a pre-specified purpose.

Market Survey Evaluation Proforma (For teacher's use)

Student's name : ....

Roll no : ....

Class : ....

Section: ....

Teacher's Assessment

	Basis	Maximum marks	Marks obtained
1.	Initiative, cooperativeness and participation	2	2
2.	Creativity in presentation	2	2
3.	Content, observation and research work	3	3
4.	Analysis of situation	3	3

Overall Remarks

....

Internal teacher's signature
Date ....

....

External teacher's signature
Date ....

PROJECT WORK

	Title of the project	Entrepreneurship
....	Name	....
....	School	....
....	Year	....
	Class	XII
....	Submitted to	....

E N T R E P R E N E U R S H I P

PROJECT REPORT

Contents

Introduction to Business Plan

A business plan is a written representation of an entrepreneur's vision for his business. It is the story of his venture as told by him. Business plans are used by entrepreneurs for various purposes. It can be used to get debt from banks or equity funding from angel investors. But, the most important use of the business plan is to clarify the exact nature of the business to the entrepreneur. Often, many shortcomings in business planning come to fore only after the plan has been put down on paper. So, a business plan gives the entrepreneur an opportunity to think through and come up with answers to questions, he had not considered previously.

A business plan describes the company, its product and its entrepreneurial team. Also, it states the money needed by the business and how it will be spent, as well as the objectives of the business and how they will be achieved. At the end, the business plan must help the entrepreneur to understand the business and make him/her confident that the venture's objectives could be achieved.

My Business Idea

"If, at any time, it comes into my head that a present is due from me to somebody, I am puzzled what to give, until the opportunity is gone" Ralph Waldo Emerson, the famous essayist once said, and this is not only Ralph's dilemna. Most people still have trouble purchasing gifts for their loved ones and when in confusion, what better way to express your love and concern than through flowers. So, sensing this opportunity, I plan to enter into the flower trading business.

The proposed name for my business venture is **Awesome Flowers**.

The name is trendy, catchy and as they say it 'Jara Hatke'.

My Logo

The logo of my business venture will be:

A Tulip flower along with two leaves. Tulip is the most enchanting flower of the spring season. It is versatile, easy to identify and adds a class to whatever arrangement it is used in. The two leaves signify the beauty and character that leaves add to a flower. This logo is simple, yet appealing and will be easy to incorporate in print stationery and signage and also in advertisement media.

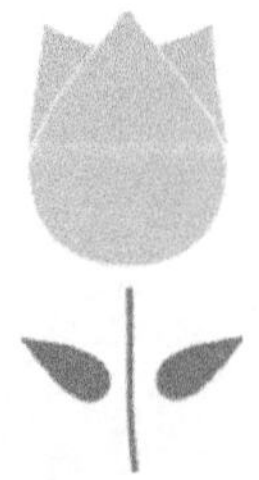

A single orchid with two leaves

My Tagline

The tagline for my business will be :

"From simple to elegant to extraordinary, we make your floral dreams come true".

The tagline is indicative of the variety offered by us, is catchy and sure to add to our appeal.

My Competitive Advantage

I plan to open my flower shop in the upmarket 'Khan Market' of Delhi. According to a survey conducted by me, my main competitors will generally be the franchisees of the following brands :

- Ferns and Petals
- Florista
- Floraindia
- Spring Blossom

In addition to them, there are also local vendors selling flowers and bouquets on the roadside. To give competition to them.
My competitive advantage will be focused on two points:

Same Hour Flower Delivery

Same day is out. Some hour is in. Stuck in a last minute dilemma or just remembered that it is your wife's Birthday. No need to fret. Delivery is guaranteed within hour.

Awesome Flowers Florist

How Sweet it is Bouquet

Spring Waltz Bouquet

Custom Make Your Bouquet

Not satisfied by our wide array of arrangements and bouquets. So, why not give us your requirements. We will custom make your bouquet, based on your specifications. Wouldn't that be a unique gift.

MAKE YOUR OWN
CUSTOM
FLOWER
BOUQUET

My USP

My Unique Selling Proposition (USP) is **'Flower shop at your doorstep'**.

In addition to opening a shop, I have planned to remodel a truck in the form of a flower shop. So, for our discerning and valued customers, we are willing to go an extra mile by enabling them to have their pick of fresh flowers and exotic arrangements at their doorstep. So, step out from the comfort of your home into the beautiful world of flowers.

Also, this mobile flower shop will help me to access target areas such as colleges and university campus. It will definitely enhance my operating horizon.

Marketing Plan

A marketing plan helps to assess the current market scenario, tap the opportunities and helps us to prepare for the threats. It comprises of:

Market Research Plan

As stated above, a market survey conducted by me helped me to identify my competitors, who are mainly franchisees of the leading brands. Amongst the various brands, 'Ferns and Petals' is clearly the market leader with a share of around 30%. Also, the local vendors operating on the streetside command an astounding share of 35% due to their reduced price structure, which can be traced to reduced operating costs. But, a market survey conducted by me on the following grounds helped me to reach to certain conclusions :

- Income of the consumer.
- How old are they?
- What do they do for a living?
- Where do they live?
- Are they professionals, families, college students, seniors, etc ?
- Are they likely to buy by phone, in person or over the internet?
- How often do target customers buy flowers?
- On what occasions ?
- How much do they spend in each case?
- Are flowers a status symbol in their community?
- What role do flowers play in various social ceremonies such as marriages, anniversaries, birthday parties, etc ?
- What role do flowers play in promoting business?
- Do they send flowers to their employees, clients and partners? Do they use flowers in their offices?
- Are they satisfied with the current players of the market?

Findings of the Survey

About 50 respondents were surveyed and the following conclusions drawn from their responses : 48 respondents said that they bought flowers alteast once or twice in a month.

- The income of the consumer was found to be highly correlated to the number of purchases made for flowers.
- Young professionals and college students were the primary buyers of flowers.
- Average spending on flowers for a month amounted to ₹200.
- Even business firms are great consumers in this market.
- Around 60% respondents said that they were not satisfied by the current market players. While some cited high price as the reason, others were not satisfied with the quality of flowers, level of service or the variety on offer.

The above conclusions point out that there is a huge potential in this market, just waiting to be tapped.

My target customers, according to the research conducted by me are college students, young professionals and business firms.

I plan to woo my target customers by cultivating personal relationships through the use of technology and marketing, offering a gift programme that makes purchasing flowers easy and delivering exceptional customer service.

The tools of promotion mix that I would be using are:

Advertising

I would be using this tool of promotion mix quite extensively. The competitive advantage offered by me and my USP are truly unique. To propagate them, I would use print media.

Sales Promotion

In the initial stages, to attract customers towards my shop, I would be using this technique. I will offer discounts to customers, sent samples to business meetings and offer free gifts.

Public Relation

This can be indulged in at a later stage in the business to promote brand consciousness. I would like to conduct a seminar for promoting my business.

Channel of Distribution

The channel of distribution opted for by me is the direct channel.

MANUFACTURER —— CUSTOMER

This channel is most suitable for my business as 'freshness' is the key word.

Quality Specification

Although, there are no quality specifications for this product, but still, I would like to promote organic flowers.

Cost Structure

The cost structure can be inferred only on an average basis, since the products that we are offering are not standardised.

The fixed costs for my venture will be:

(i) Rent of the shop ₹35,000 per month.

(ii) Salary of the staff ₹50,000 per month.

(iii) Electricity and maintenance expenses ₹7,500 per month.

(iv) Interest charges ₹10,000 per month.

(v) Insurance premium ₹1,500 per month.

(vi) Depreciation on equipment ₹ 1,500 per month.

Total fixed expenses per month amount to ₹1,05,500.

The variable cost per unit cannot be ascertained due to the absence of a standardised product. However, the various components of the variable expenses will comprise of :

(i) Cost of flowers

(ii) Packing cost (ribbons, cellophone wraps, cellotape, etc.)

In addition to the above cost, we have to consider loss due to spoilage also, because of the highly perishable nature of our raw material, *viz* flowers.

The range of our products is ₹50-₹5,000. But we will be catering maximum to medium priced bouquets in the range of ₹500-₹750.

So, let us take the average cost of a bouquet to be ₹400.

The average mark-up in this business is 30%. So, a bouquet costing ₹ 400 will be sold for ₹520 plus taxes.

Start-up Costs

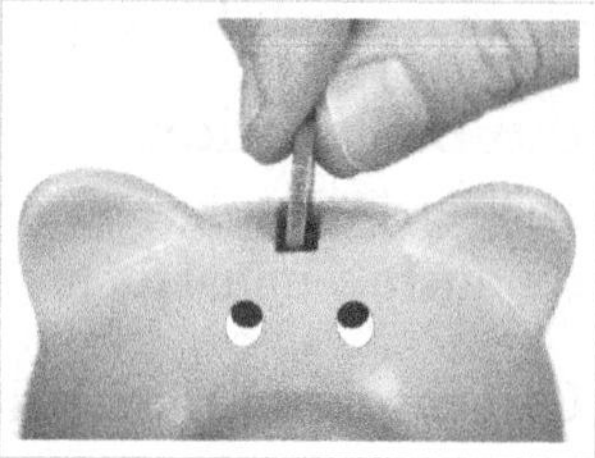

The start-up costs of this project are given below:

- **Cost of the shop** In addition to a monthly rent of ₹35,000, I will be paying ₹5,00,000 as security deposit.
- **Cost of equipment** I will be needing refrigerated display cases to increase the shelf life of my products. The cost of these cases is ₹1,50,000 per case.

Initially, I will be buying 3 cases. In addition, the remodelled truck will cost about ₹12,00,000. Total expenses in this head will amount to ₹16,50,000.

- **Cost of furniture and fixtures** The cost of renovation, along with furniture, fixtures and lightning is estimated to be ₹3,00,000.
- **Computer and point of sale system** A computer to check E-mails, process bills and order supplies is a must. A point of sale system will help to keep a tap on sales and manage inventory. The estimated cost under this head is ₹60,000.

Supplies The various supplies needed for a flower shop are:

- Containers
- Floral Foam
- Preservatives
- Wire
- Tape-Green Waterproof
- Cards
- Delivery Tags
- Wrapping Paper
- Ribbons
- Glue
- Knife
- Scissors
- Staplers
- Trash Can /Boxes
- Floor Mats, etc.

In addition, stationery items and general household items for cleaning are also required.

The cost of purchasing above supplies would be around ₹20,000.

- **Fresh cut flowers and plants** I have found a local supplier, who is willing to sell in small quantities and also has a wide variety and promises good quality. Initially, I would be needing ₹1,50,000 for this head.
- **Advertising costs** Costs related to advertising, making sign boards and glow signs, etc., are estimated to be ₹1,00,000.

So, in all, I will be needing ₹27,80,000 to start my flower shop.

Out of the above ₹27,80,000, ₹7,80,000 will be invested by me, ₹15,00,000 will be raised through a bank loan and the balance ₹5,00,000 will be raised as loan from friends and families

The various risk factors associated with this business are:

- Highly perishable nature of the product.
- Presence of strong competitors.
- Not a popular gift item among middle income group consumers.

I plan to mitigate these risk factors by adopting the following measures:

- Sourcing in raw material in small quantities.
- Promoting the benefits offered by me to gain an edge over my competitors.
- The middle in comed group can be targeted through specific campaigns and offering discounts.

Profit and Loss Statement for the Month of January 2016
(One Year after Starting Business)

S. No.	Particulars	Units	₹
(a)	Sales	227	3,25,500
(b)	Cost of Sales		1,05,250
(c)	Gross profit = a – b		2,20,250
	Fixed expenses (cash)		
	Salaries		50,000
	Rent		35,000
	Utilities		10,000
	Monthly interest only on the loan taken		5,000
	Miscellaneous		4,000
(d)	Total fixed expenses (cash)		1,04,000
(e)	Depreciation (non-cash)		1,500
(f)	Total fixed expenses (cash and non-cash) = d + e		1,05,500
(g)	Operating profit or loss = c – f		11,4,750
(h)	Taxes = use 25% on profits only		28,687.5
(i)	Net profit or loss = g – h		86,062.5

Break-up Point

BEP is the point of No Profit No Loss for the business.

The formula for computing BEP for a business is $\text{BEP} = \dfrac{\text{Fixed Expenses}}{\text{Profit Volume Ratio}}$

Where, $\text{Profit Volume Ratio} = \dfrac{\text{Sales} - \text{Variable Cost}}{\text{Sales}} \times 100$

So, Profit Volume Ratio for the month of January is worked out as:

$$= \frac{3{,}25{,}500 - 1{,}05{,}250}{3{,}25{,}500} \times 100 = \frac{2{,}20{,}250}{3{,}25{,}500} \times 100 = 67\% \text{ approx}$$

$$\text{BEP (in ₹)} = \frac{1{,}05{,}500}{0.67} = ₹\ 1{,}57{,}463 \text{ approx.}$$

If average price of a bouquet is assumed to be ₹ 1,000, then no. of bouquets to be sold to break even are : $\dfrac{1{,}57{,}463}{1{,}000} = 158$ approx.

Proforma for Evaluation (For Teacher's use)

Business plan evaluation proforma

Student's name : ....

Roll no. : ....

Class : ....

Section : ....

Teacher's Assessment

	Basis	**Maximum marks**	**Marks obtained**
1.	Product selection and details	1	
2.	Profit and loss statement	2	
3.	Fixed and variable cost details	2	
4.	Start-up cost calculation	2	
5.	Computation of break-even	3	

Overall remarks

....

....

....

....

....

Internal Teacher's Signature External Teacher's Signature

Date .... SCHOOL STAMP Date ....

III. External Practical Written Paper

Teachers who will be conducting the external practical examination should frame their questions for 5 marks from any one OR a combination of the following topics :

1. Calculation of EOQ.
2. Calculation of working capital requirements.
3. Calculation of break-even point.
4. Identification and calculation of start-up costs/fixed cost/variable cost.

Permission Letter

In an attempt to facilitate better understanding of the subject "Entrepreneurship", CBSE has made it mandatory for the student opting for the subject, to undertake an "Industrial visit/Survey" as a part of the curriculum.

This is to certify that .... of class .... section .... is a bonafide student of .... and has been permitted within the framework of CBSE to undertake this visit.

Looking forward to your cooperation in making this activity a success and a great learning experience for the student.

Thanking you.

....

Principal Teacher Incharge

Latest CBSE SAMPLE PAPER

A Sample Question Paper for CBSE Class XII Issued by CBSE

Entrepreneurship

General Instructions

1. This question paper contains 34 questions. All questions are compulsory.
2. The question paper is divided into four sections – Section A, B, C and D.
3. In Section A : Questions number 1 to 18 are Multiple Choice Questions carrying 1 mark each.
4. In Section B : Questions number 19 to 24 are Short Answer Type-I Questions carrying 2 marks each.
5. In Section C : Questions number 25 to 29 are Short Answer Type-II Questions carrying 3 marks each.
6. In Section D : Questions number 30 to 34 are Long Answer Type Questions carrying 5 marks each.
7. There is no overall choice. However, an internal choice has been provided in Section B, C and D of question paper.

Time : 3 hours **Max. Marks : 70**

Section-A

1. "In a partnership form of business, each partner can bind the firm and other partners by his/her acts."

In the light of the given statement, identify the essential feature of partnership form of business organisation referred to and choose the correct option. (1)

(a) Implied authority (b) Utmost good faith
(c) Mutual agency (d) Separate legal entity

2. Fraggy is a restaurant aggregator and food delivery company. The customers can order food from listed food joints through the 'Fraggy App'. It started when the founders noticed that people were unaware of the functional restaurants in their neighbourhood and were searching for a variety of food options. The founders thought that it would be a great idea to list all the competing restaurants on the 'Fraggy App' and provide their menus as well. .... is the source that led to the emergence of the business idea. (1)

(a) Competition
(b) Change
(c) Problem
(d) Innovation

3. .... is a sophisticated positive sales approach where the salespersons compare the features of their product without mentioning the competition. (1)

(a) Direct sales strategy
(b) Indirect sales strategy
(c) Comparative sales approach
(d) Customer testimonials

4. Refer to the logo of the coffee brand Del Coffee carefully.

® in the given image represents. (1)

(a) Brand mark (b) Brand name
(c) Trademark (d) Tagline

5. Anita, a tech entrepreneur, wants to start her automation consultancy business that will develop AI-based customised solutions for different service providers. She cannot do it all by herself so she has approached her friend Supriya, who is an IIT graduate.

Together they plan to commence the business in a form where their liability is limited and the business is regulated by law.

.... form of business organisation meets the requirements of Anita and Supriya. (1)

(a) Sole proprietor
(b) Partnership
(c) Private limited company
(d) Public limited company

6. Innovation involves translation of a useful idea into an application which has .... (1)

(a) utility
(b) commercial value
(c) creative solution
(d) better performance

7. From the given elements of operational plan in Column I and the objectives given in Column II, choose the correct pair (1)

Column I	Column II
A. Routing	(i) Comparing materials, product or performance with established standards.
B. Dispatching	(ii) Determining exact path a product/service has to follow right from raw material to finished good.
C. Inspection	(iii) Initiating production as per the pre-conceived production plan.
D. Follow-up	(iv) Expediting function that relates to evaluation and appraisal of work performed.

Codes

(a) A-(i)
(b) B-(ii)
(c) C-(iii)
(d) D-(iv)

8. Nirmala dairy farms have been in the business of processing pure ghee using the 'Bilona technique'. The cost per kilo of ghee comes out to be ₹ 2,000. The owners have estimated that a reasonable profit margin will be 25%. So they have decided to sell the product at ₹ 2,500 per kilo.

On the basis of the given text, identify which of the following is the drawback of the indicated pricing strategy and choose the correct option. (1)

(a) It attracts only the bargain hunters who switch to other brands if the price rises
(b) Is not a viable option if there are strict legal and government regulations
(c) It does not take into account the competitor's pricing and actions
(d) It leads to a series of counteroffers that sometimes result in no sale

9. Logo of a company .... (1)

(i) is the key visual component of an enterprise's overall brand identity.
(ii) provides essential information about the company through a set colour combination, fonts, images and impressions
(iii) is a memorable dramatic phrase that will sum up the product
(iv) can be a graphic mark or emblem used to promote instant public recognition

Codes

(a) (ii) and (iii)
(b) (i) and (iv)
(c) (iii), (iv) and (v)
(d) (i), (ii) and (iv)

10. Identify, which of the following intellectual property is not patentable? (1)

(a) Process of manufacturing
(b) Machine used for manufacturing
(c) Designs or patterns used for manufacturing
(d) Substances used for manufacturing

11. .... is the ingredient of a franchise agreement which outlines the marketing and advertising procedures to be used by franchisee. (1)

(a) Contract explanation
(b) Operations manual
(c) Ongoing site maintenance
(d) Proprietary statements

12. .... element of the financial plan describes how the enterprise funds will be dedicated to different assets so that the enterprise can earn the highest possible return. (1)

(a) Investment decision
(b) Financing decision
(c) Income statements
(d) Cash flow statement

13. **Assertion** (A) New companies (start-ups) find it difficult to go public.

Reason (R) A new company needs to maintain dividend and profit growth trends. (1)

Alternatives

(a) Both Assertion (A) and Reason (R) are true and Reason (R) is the correct explanation of Assertion (A)
(b) Both Assertion (A) and Reason (R) are true, but Reason (R) is not the correct explanation of Assertion (A)
(c) Assertion (A) is true, but Reason (R) is false
(d) Assertion (A) is false, but Reason (R) is true

14. Given below are assumptions that are made by an entrepreneur in the break-even point analysis for a multi-product business. (1)

(i) The proportion of the sales mix must be predetermined.
(ii) The sales mix must change within the relevant period.
(iii) All costs can be categorised as variable or fixed.
(iv) Sales price per unit, variable cost per unit and total fixed cost are calculated as per the forces of demand and supply.
(v) All units produced are not sold.

Codes

(a) (i) and (iii) (b) (ii) and (iii)
(c) (iv) and (v) (d) (i) and (iv)

15. Identify, which of the following is not a current asset for a furniture manufacturing unit? (1)

(a) Debtors
(b) Outstanding expenses
(c) Stock of table and chairs
(d) Short-term investment

16. Identify, which of the following is an advantage of issuing shares through 'rights issue'. (1)

(a) It is an inexpensive method of issuing shares
(b) It leads to higher employee motivation and lower labour turnover
(c) It results in higher valuations of companies and better prestige
(d) This method helps in maintaining confidentiality

17. In .... acquisition, the purchasing company becomes a subsidiary of the purchased company. (1)

(a) friendly (b) reverse
(c) backflip (d) hostile

18. Suvidha Store is a grocery store that retails fast moving consumer goods. The store buys its supplies on credit and sells them on cash basis. With growing competition, it has also started selling goods on credit. The above step taken by Suvidha store may lead to .... in its working capital requirement and its cash conversion cycle will be .... (1)

(a) increase, longer (b) decrease, longer
(c) no change, longer (d) increase, shorter

Section-B

19. Explain 'product identification' as the first step in idea and opportunity assessment. (2)

Or Differentiate between a basic idea and post scanning idea.

20. Rohit is a trained plumber and has worked for a hardware shop for more than 3 years. He is very popular in the area and people generally request his employer to send Rohit for their repair and maintenance tasks.

Rohit is planning to start a business of his own where he will directly reach his clients upon a phone call. He will provide services instantaneously within 15 minutes of the request received. His present clients may put in a positive word for him among their friends and neighbours which can help his business grow.

On the basis of the given text identify, giving reasons, any two elements of business opportunity. (2)

21. Refer to the images given below.

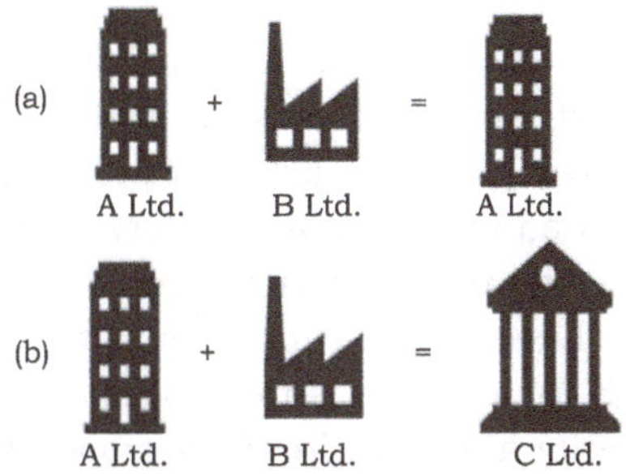

(i) Identify the type of enterprise growth strategy adopted in the two scenarios indicated in the aforesaid image. (1)

(ii) List the two forms of the growth strategy indicated. (1)

Or

Discuss briefly the two forms of 'synergy' that accrue to the merging firms. (2)

22. Zakir is keen on giving up his job and starting a new fitness industry business. He has to choose among fitness drinks, gym equipment and fitness gear.

Zakir decided to spend more time in the gym inside his apartment complex and in nearby localities, especially on weekends and late evenings, to observe the people and understand their requirements.

He took the membership of Gym Community Trade Association through which he got the advantage of their social networking tools like Instagram page, gym websites and community Whatsapp groups. He conducted an online survey to ascertain the viable product for his business idea. The response so collected gave him the clarity that he should go with fitness gear.

By quoting lines from the above passage, identify the ways of trend spotting used by Zakir. (2)

23. Describe the 'elevator pitch' format of business plan used by entrepreneurs. How is it different from an 'internal operational' plan? (2)

24. Tic Tac Electricals Ltd. manufactures switches and plugs in an industrial area in the state of Haryana. On an average, they manufacture 2,500 switches per day. Their raw material supplier is based in Punjab and takes 5 days to deliver the requirement once the order is received. Estimate the reorder level for Tic Tac Electricals Ltd. (2)

Or The following information relates to the newly established Boutique – 'The Pearl'

(i) Total capital invested ₹ 40,00,000 out of which ₹ 20,00,000 is a bank loan at 15% per annum.

(ii) Net profit after tax is ₹ 6,00,000.

Calculate return on equity for 'The Pearl Boutique'.

Section-C

25. Prudent Pharma has been a well-established manufacturer of curative medicines in India for the past 15 years. The company is planning to enter a new line of products known as 'nutraceuticals' which has both nutritional and medicinal benefits. With rising awareness levels and easy access to information, people are keen to try nutraceuticals as these health supplements claim to delay or reduce the impact of chronic diseases.

As income levels of the population have improved, nutraceuticals promise to emerge as a growing niche market in the country. It is governed by health and safety regulations and the company needs to acquire the required licenses to venture into this field. Though the concept is new to India, internationally it is already a growing market with multiple international brands.

Prudent Pharma is in talks for a potential international tie-up for research and development. On the basis of the given text, identify by quoting lines, any three macro environment factors that may affect the future of Prudent Pharma. (3)

26. "An entrepreneur must pay attention to the quantity and quality of the manpower for his business as it directly impacts the performance and resulting productivity of the organisation."

(i) In the light of the aforesaid statement, identify the component of a business plan that helps an entrepreneur fulfill the stated purpose. (1)

(ii) State the objective and importance of the identified component. (2)

Or

"One of the components of a business plan effectively establishes how the entrepreneur will compete and operate in the market place.

It acts as a guideline regarding the marketing objectives, strategies and activities to be followed by any new enterprise."

(i) Identify the component of the business plan discussed above.

(ii) Explain the steps described in the plan that help an entrepreneur find the group of customers whose needs the enterprise aims to fulfil.

27. In 2022, a popular snacking brand 'Pom-Pom' completed 25 years in India. They were one of the first such brands in the country and wanted to start a campaign that allowed the brand to connect with the consumers directly.

The marketing team created the idea of 'Me and Mera Pom-Pom' where people were encouraged to share their stories woven around their experiences with the product. Such a campaign enabled the consumers to send their message to the company rather than receiving it from them.

People shared some of the most poignant and private moments of their lives. Some uploaded their viral films too.

(i) Identify the promotional approach used by 'Pom-Pom' to reach its customers. (1)

(ii) Explain any two important features of this approach. (2)

28. Explain any three market related considerations to be used by an entrepreneur while selecting the channel for distribution. (3)

Or "A channel of distribution consists of three types of flows." Explain the three flows.

29. Tutu Pump Co. uses about 7,500 valves per year, which is constant throughout the year. The valve costs ₹ 15 per unit and the carrying cost is estimated to be ₹ 3 per unit.

The cost of placing an order and its processing is ₹ 18.

Calculate the Economic Order Quantity (EOQ). Give any one benefit that Tutu Pump Co. derives after calculating the EOQ. (3)

Section-D

30. As the world is drowned in the rubble of plastic it has become a now or never situation to protect the world. Indian entrepreneurs, Mrs. and Mr. Smith launched 'Green India' in 2021 with the aim to provide a simple replacement for harmful plastic with bamboo based products. Using technology for processing of the bamboo plant, the brand has developed around 22 products, with manufacturing around 30 lakh Bamboo toothbrushes which have been delivered across India and 18 countries in the world.

"India is the second largest bamboo grower in the world and also one of the biggest bamboo importers. It made me think about how we are underutilising our bamboo resources," comments Mr. Smith. This agripreneur has since engaged 4,000 farmers from villages of Nanded in Maharashtra to manufacture products.

After completing his masters degree from the University of Maharashtra, he joined the IT industry in France.

It was there that the idea of starting a sustainable business struck him.

He was supported by his wife who helps with human resources and accounts.

He gives credit to social media platforms for the boost to sales and growing popularity of eco-friendly products. Green India is now looking to add another 1,000 families to completely depend on their products. Their major aim is to reduce 1 million kilogram of plastic waste every year from next year onwards.

On the basis of the given text and common understanding, answer the following questions

(i) Identify the idea field used by Mr. Smith to launch the business. (1)

(ii) Explain any two more idea fields, other than the one identified above. (2)

(iii) Giving reasons, mention any two socio-economic benefits that the above business has. (2)

31. Elaborate the advantages of a franchise form of business to a franchisee. (5)

Or "Pricing can also be used as a demarcation, to differentiate and enhance the image of a product."

(i) In the light of the above statement, explain penetration and skimming as two important pricing strategies that can be used by an entrepreneur. (1)

(ii) Give any two advantages of both penetration and skimming strategies. (4)

32. Mr. Prasad started a cakes and confectionery business in 2010 by the name of 'Happiness to Order'. In no time his bakery became the talk of the town for customised cakes as per the occasion. He used high quality liquid glucose and icing sugar to make the fondants for his cakes. Seeing the popularity, he opened 4 more outlets in different localities. Over the years people have become cautious of what they eat and are cutting down on sugar. The fondants that were once the USP of his bakery were now losing market to the competitors as they introduced a healthier version of bakery products, especially cakes without gluten or sugar but almond flour, oats flour, etc.

His cooks advised him to experiment with healthier options which Mr. Prasad was reluctant to try. He could not adapt to the changing environment and all 5 outlets started running into loss. Eventually, he decided to close the business.

He owes ₹ 15,00,000 to his supplier firm whom he had taken goods on credit in the past year. On the basis of the given text and common understanding, answer the following questions

(i) Mr. Prasad's business funds are insufficient to repay the debts, can the supplier claim Mr. Prasad's assets? Give valid reasons in support of your answer. (2)

(ii) "Environment scanning is important for an entrepreneur." Justify the statement, giving valid reasons in support of your answer. (3)

33. Zoke Ltd. manufactures eco-friendly furnishing and upholstery products. The fixed cost for the production process is ₹ 22,56,000.

The following information is available about its range of products

Variety	**Cushion Covers** (per pair)	**Curtains** (set of two pairs)	**Bed covers** (Standard king size)
Selling Price (in ₹)	555	1,150	1,550
Variable Cost (in ₹)	275	550	750
Sales Mix	30%	40%	30%

From the given data, calculate the following

(i) Total weighted average contribution margin. (1)

(ii) Break-even quantity for each product. (3)

(iii) Break-even point (in ₹) for a pair of cushion covers. (1)

34. (i) "The highly anticipated Initial Public Offer (IPO) of Life Insurance Corporation of India (LIC), emerged as the largest turnout in terms of public participation in the nation's history." Identify the type of capital market LIC of India has approached. (1)

(ii) Distinguish between the two types of capital markets. (2)

(iii) "Capital markets are an important source of raising finance for entrepreneurs." (2)

Justify the statement, giving valid reasons in support of your answer.

Or (i) Distinguish between angel investors and venture capitalists. (2)

(ii) Describe the role of an angel investor in an entrepreneurial venture. (3)

Answers

1. (c) Mutual agency 2. (c) Problem
3. (b) Indirect sales strategy
4. (c) Trademark
5. (c) Private limited company
6. (b) commercial value
7. (d) D-(iv)
8. (c) It does not take into account the competitor's pricing and actions
9. (d) (i), (ii) and (iv)
10. (c) Designs or patterns used for manufacturing
11. (d) Proprietary statements
12. (a) Investment decision
13. (b) Both Assertion (A) and Reason (R) are true, but Reason (R) is not the correct explanation of Assertion (A)
14. (a) (i) and (iii)
15. (b) Outstanding expenses
16. (a) It is an inexpensive method of issuing shares
17. (c) backflip
18. (a) increase, longer
19. **Product Identification** The ideas should lead to a definite product/service, which an entrepreneur can sell. The proposed product should be such that it can be marketed at a reasonable cost.

    Also, it should be analysed in the light of possible product substitutes, preferences of customers, modifications suggested, etc.

    If the product is already available in the market, identify the reason for introducing the same product or service.

    Or

    The initial spotting of ideas i.e. basic idea is of a random nature, whereas, the development of ideas after scanning the environment i.e. post scanning idea is a more purposeful activity. The former is an experiential process while the latter is a strategic process.
20. Two elements of business opportunity are
    (i) **Assured Market Scope** He is very popular in the area and people generally request his employer to send Rohit for their repair and maintenance tasks.
    (ii) **Practicability of Idea** He will provide services instantaneously within 15 minutes of the request received.
21. (i) Merger is the type of enterprise growth strategy adopted in the two scenarios.
    (ii) Two forms of the growth strategy indicated are
    (a) Absorption (b) Amalgamation

    Or The two forms of 'synergy' that accrue to the marging firms are as follows
    (i) **Operating Synergy** This refers to the cost savings that accrue through economies of scale or because of increased turnover leading to increased profits.
    (ii) **Financial Synergy** This is the direct result of financial factors such as lower taxes, higher debt capacity or better use of idle resources.

    Also, the new firm stands to gain in the form of 'tax shield', i.e. when a firm with accumulated losses merge with a profitable firm and the combined firm can sets-off such losses against its profit, a financial synergy occurs, known as 'tax shield'.
22. The ways of trend spotting used by Zakir are
    (i) **Watch Trends** 'Zakir decided to spend more time in the gym inside his apartment complex and in nearby localities. He simply observed the people.'
    (ii) **Talk Trends** 'He conducted an online survey to ascertain the viable product for his business idea.'
23. **Elevator Pitch** It is basically a 3 minute summary of the business plan's executive summary. This format is often used as a teaser to awaken the interest of the potential investors, customers or strategic partners.

    Elevator pitch is different from an internal operational plan as it is a 3 minute summary while an internal operational plan is a detailed plan describing planning details that are needed by management, but may not be of interest to external stakeholders.
24. Reorder Level = Lead Time × Daily Requirement
    $= 5 \times 2{,}500 = 12{,}500$ units

    Or $\text{Return on Equity} = \dfrac{\text{Net Profit after Tax}}{\text{Total Equity}} \times 100$

    $$= \frac{6{,}00{,}000}{20{,}00{,}000} \times 100 = 30\%$$

25. Macroenvironment factors that may affect the future of Prudent Pharma are

(i) 'Governed by health and safety regulations and the company needs to acquire the required licenses' – Legal factor.

(ii) 'Rising awareness levels and easy access to information of people' – Social factor.

(iii) 'As income levels of the population have improved' – Economic factor.

26. (i) The component of a business plan that helps an entrepreneur fulfill the stated purpose is 'manpower plan'.

(ii) **Objective** of manpower plan is to determine the number and type of employees required, along with their roles, responsibilities and recruitment strategy, to ensure the smooth functioning of the business.

Manpower plan is **important** as it helps in assessing what kind of people are required, how many people are required, how the people will be selected and how to procure the people.

Or (i) The component of the business plan discussed is 'marketing plan'.

(ii) Steps in identification of the 'target market' are

(a) Deciding what the entrepreneur wishes to pursue is based on market research or industry analysis done and complied with by competent people or the entrepreneurs.

(b) Divide the market into smaller groups based on

- Consumer's characteristics *viz.* Geographic (State, country, etc.), Demographic (Sex, age, etc.), Psychographics (Personality, lifestyle, etc.)
- Buying situations *viz.* Buying conditions (time available, etc.), Usage, desired benefits (Features of product).

27. (i) Below the line approach is the approach used by 'Pom-Pom' to reach its customers.

(ii) Features of below the line approach are

(a) The purpose of the activities is to develop the brand by creating awareness and building a brand profile.

(b) It can lead to an actual sale which is easy to measure.

28. Three market related considerations to be used by an entrepreneur while selecting the channel for distribution are as follows

(i) **Number of Buyers** If the number of buyers is large, then long chain of distribution should be opted, but if the number of buyers is small, then smaller channels should be considered.

(ii) **Types of Buyers** Buyers are commonly classified as

(a) General buyers

(b) Industrial buyers

For general buyers, long chain of distribution should be used and short-chain for industrial buyers.

(iii) **Buying Habits** A manufacturer should opt for a long channel of distribution if his financial position does not permit him to sell goods on credit and the buyers are in the habit of making credit purchases.

Or A channel of distribution usually consists of three types of flows, which are

(i) Downward flow of goods from producers to consumers.

(ii) Upward flow of cash payments for goods from consumers to producers.

(iii) Flow of marketing information in both downward and upward direction, i.e.

(a) information moves downward in the form of information on new products, new uses of existing products, etc., from producers to consumers.

(b) information moves upward in the form of feedback on wants of consumers, suggestions, complaints, etc., from consumers to producers.

29. C = ₹ 3; P = ₹ 18; D = 7,500

$$\text{EOQ} = \frac{\sqrt{2 \times P \times D}}{3} = \frac{\sqrt{2 \times 7{,}500 \times 18}}{3} = 300 \text{ units}$$

Benefit of Calculating EOQ It ensures that there is no stock-out situation and the cost of carrying and placing the order is minimised.

30. (i) The idea field used by Mr. Smith to launch the business is 'natural'.

(ii) Two other idea fields are as follows

(a) **Existing Products or Services** Another field to generate new ideas can be improving the existing products or services.

A great business idea combines skills with imagination and market demand. Entrepreneurs who look at ways to make an existing product or service better can be as successful as those who create and invent products.

(b) **Trading Related Ideas** Trading simply refers to buying goods and services and selling them to the consumers at a profit. Advantages of trading are that it is easier to launch and is less risky.

(iii) Socio-economic benefits are

(a) Better utilisation of local resources using locally grown bamboo which was underutilised.

(b) Supporting environment/sustainability provide a simple replacement for harmful plastic with bamboo based products.

31. Following are the advantages enjoyed by a franchisee

(i) **Product Acceptance** The franchisee usually enters into a business that has an accepted name, product or service. He does not have to spend resources to establish the credibility of the business and create a market for his product.

The credibility already exists based on the years the franchise has existed.

(ii) **Management Expertise** The franchisor provides managerial assistance related to all aspects of operating the franchise, to the franchisee.

For this purpose, training programmes are conducted which includes classes in accounting, personnel management, marketing and production.

(iii) **Capital Requirements** Franchise offers an opportunity to start a new venture with up-front support from franchisor, which saves considerable time and capital of the franchisee.

In some cases, the franchisor also finances the initial investment to start the franchise operation. Savings in start-ups are also reflected in the pooling of money by individual franchisees for advertising and sales promotion.

This allows advertising on both local as well as national level to enhance the image and credibility of the business, something that would be impossible for a single operation.

(iv) **Knowledge of the Market** Franchisors are well aware of the existing market conditions. With their experience and knowledge, they can provide advice and assistance to the franchisees for carving out a market for themselves.

This is particularly important because of regional and local differences in markets. Also, franchisors constantly evaluate the market conditions and determine the most effective strategies to communicate to the franchisees.

(v) **Operating and Structural Controls** Generally, a new venture is faced with the problems of quality control and managerial controls.

The franchisor helps the franchisee to combat both the problems.

Standardisation in supplies and products/services offered helps to ensure that the entrepreneur will maintain quality standards. It also supports a consistent image on which the franchise business depends for expansion.

Or (i) **Penetration Pricing** Under this pricing strategy, the price of the product is initially set at a price lower than the prevailing market price to attract new customers and increase its market share.

Creaming or Skimming In this type of pricing strategy, entrepreneurs set their prices higher, so that fewer sales are needed to break-even. Selling a product at a high price, sacrificing high sales to gain a high profit is therefore 'skimming' the market.

This strategy is usually employed to reimburse the cost of investment on the original research and is commonly used in the electronics market where a new range, such as smartphones are initially dispatched into the market at a high price.

(ii) **Advantages of Penetration Pricing**

(a) It can result in fast diffusion and adoption, resulting in an increased market share quickly. This strategy can take the competitors by surprise, not giving them time to react.

(b) It can create goodwill among the early users and create more trade by word of mouth.

Advantages of Skimming Pricing

(a) It helps the entrepreneur to recover the research and development costs associated with the new product quickly.

(b) This strategy best suits an entrepreneur who caters to consumers who are quality conscious rather than price conscious.

32. (i) The supplier can claim Mr. Prasad's assets as unlimited liability exists in a sole proprietorship.

The proprietor and the business are considered to be the same and in case the assets of the business are not sufficient to pay liabilities, his/her personal property can also be used to pay-off the business debts.

(ii) Environmental scanning is important for an entrepreneur because of the following reasons

(a) **Identification of Opportunities to Get First Mover Advantage** By keeping in touch with the changes in the external environment, an enterprise can identify opportunities and find strategies to capitalise on the opportunities at the earliest. e.g. LPG rationing led the manufacturers to come out with induction cooker.

(b) **Formulation of Strategies and Policies** It helps in identifying threats and opportunities in the market.

These can serve as the basis of formulation of strategies to counter threats and capitalise on opportunities in the market.

e.g. The depleting reserves of petrol is a threat for car manufacturers. E-cars or solar powered engines are the outcome of such threats, which forced them to look for alternate sources of energy.

(c) **Tapping Useful Resources** If a company has a thorough knowledge of environment, the enterprise can tap resources like financial resources, human resources, physical resources, etc., from the market at economical prices at the right time.

e.g. Pasco Ltd. should buy wheat for its wide variety of biscuits when the new crop comes in the market, as it is available at cheap prices.

33.

Variety	**Cushion Covers** (per pair)	**Curtains** (set of two pairs)	**Bed covers** (Standard king size)
Selling Price (in ₹)	555	1,150	1,550
Variable Cost (in ₹)	275	550	750
Contribution	280	600	750
Sales Mix	30%	40%	30%
Weighted Contribution	84	240	240

(i) Total Weighted Contribution Margin

$= 84 + 240 + 240 = ₹\ 564$

(ii) Break-even quantity for each variety

Break-even Point

$$= \frac{\text{Total Fixed Cost}}{\text{Weighted Contribution Margin}}$$

$$= \frac{22,56,000}{564}$$

$= 4,000$ units

Cushion Covers $= 4,000 \times 30\% = 1,200$ units

Curtains $= 4,000 \times 40\% = 1,600$ units

Bed Covers $= 4,000 \times 30\% = 1,200$ units

(iii) Break-even in Rupees for Cushion Covers

= Break-even Quantity × Selling Price per Unit

$= 1,200 \times 555 = ₹\ 6,66,000$

34. (i) LIC of India has approached the primary market.

(ii) Following are the differences between primary and secondary market

Basis	Primary Market	Secondary Market
Meaning	Primary market deals with the trading of newly issued securities.	Secondary market is that part of capital market which deals in already issued securities.
Role of the Issuing Company	Issuing company plays an active role as shares are sold directly to the investors.	The company has no role to play as securities are traded between investors only.

(iii) Capital markets are the most important source of raising finance for the entrepreneurs as this market can

(a) mobilise the financial resources on a nationwide scale.

(b) secure the required foreign capital and know-how to promote economic growth at a faster rate.

(c) ensure the most effective allocation of mobilised financial resources by investing in projects capable of generating highest returns or by investing in underdeveloped priority areas so as to promote balanced industrialisation.

Or

(i) Angel investors are informal investors in the start-up in its early stages.

They are ready to invest when even the venture capitalist are least interested to make investments. Most angels are expected to dilute after the first few rounds of investment, expected to dilute after the first few rounds of investment, whereas venture capitalists are professionally managed pool of equity capital who undertake long-term investment, usually occurring over five years and have continuous involvement in the management of business.

(ii) Angel investor plays an important role in an entrepreneurial venture in the following ways

(a) Apart from investing funds, they also provide proactive advice, guidance, industry connections and mentoring start-ups in its early stage.

(b) Their objective is to create great companies by providing value creation and simultaneously helping investors to earn a high return on their investments.

(c) They have a keen desire to keep themselves acquainted with current developments and mentoring another generation of entrepreneurs by making use of their vast experience.

Sample Papers (1-3)

Sample Paper 1

A Highly Simulated Sample Question Paper for CBSE Class XII Examination

Entrepreneurship

General Instructions

Read the following instructions carefully and follow them

1. This question paper contains 34 questions. All questions are compulsory.
2. This question paper is divided into four sections—Section A, B, C and D.
3. Section A : Questions number 1 to 18 are Multiple Choice Type Questions. Each question carries 1 mark.
4. Section B : Questions number 19 to 24 are Short Answer Type-I Questions. Each question carries 2 marks. Write answer to each question in 30 to 40 words.
5. Section C : Questions number 25 to 29 are Short Answer Type-II Questions. Each question carries 3 marks. Write answer to each question in 50 to 70 words.
6. Section D : Questions number 30 to 34 are Long Answer Type Questions. Each question carries 5 marks. Write answer to each question in 120 to 150 words.
7. There is no overall choice. However, an internal choice has been provided in Section B, C and D of question paper. A candidate has to attempt only one of the alternatives in such questions.

Time : 3 hours **Max. Marks : 70**

Section-A

1. Which of the following factors is/are involved in sensing opportunities? (1)

   I. Ability to perceive and preserve basic ideas.
   II. Ability to read the environment.
   III. Ability to access the environment.
   IV. Ability to harness different sources of information.

   Codes

   (a) I and II (b) Only I
   (c) I and IV (d) I, II and III

2. What is the first stage in the process of innovation? (1)

   (a) Idea germination (b) Creativity
   (c) Preparation (d) Incubation

3. Sam Murthy has a coffee bean processing unit in Karnataka. During the pandemic he has learnt different styles to make coffee. He started improvising his product and range to make different premixes in different varieties like Latte, Mocha and Dalgona which will eventually help him to establish a place for his brand in the beverage industry.
   Identify the field of idea generation used by him. (1)

   I. Market driven II. Trading relevant
   III. Service sector IV. Creative efforts

   Codes

   (a) Only IV (b) I and II
   (c) Only III (d) All of these

4. The law states that the business and owner are same in the case of sole proprietorship. Which of the following characteristics is highlighted in the above sentence? (1)

   (a) Separate entity (b) No separate entity
   (c) Limited liability (d) Unlimited liability

5. Which of the following is not a public sector enterprise? (1)

   (a) Departmental undertaking
   (b) Public corporations
   (c) Sole tradership
   (d) Government company

6. Nitin studies automation engineering from a reputed college and was always fond of automobiles. He, on returning back to his hometown, took a loan from a bank to start a spare parts manufacturing unit in the locality. The spare parts will be used to manufacture automobiles.

He took help from lawyers, marketing consultants, and accountants to prepare a fine business plan for his idea and a detailed and structured plan for the management was prepared. The initial plan was not for the external stakeholders. Which form of business plan was used by Nitin? (1)
(a) Elevator pitch
(b) Pitch deck
(c) Written presentation
(d) Internal operation plan

7. From the following given information, calculate the return on investment for the company (1)
Capital = ₹ 8,00,000
Sales = ₹ 3,00,000
Gross profit = ₹ 80,000
Expenses = ₹ 56,000
(a) 4% (b) 6%
(c) 5% (d) 3%

8. Cod Limited is a popular enterprise dealing in health related and organic products. The company grew at the time of the pandemic when everyone was very cautious of their health and now it has become to be a successful venture. The management of the company has achieved its sales target and now wants to expand in other areas. The senior marketing manager suggested that the company should issue its shares as it will be a good start for it to become public. The management agreed and decided to issue shares for getting funds.

In which market will the shares of Cod Limited be issued? (1)
I. Primary market
II. Secondary market
III. Money market IV. Securities market

Codes
(a) I and II (b) Only I
(c) Only III (d) III and IV

9. Sumit garments manufacture three types of fabric for garments A, B and C. The total fixed cost of the firm is ₹ 1,00,000 and the weighted average contribution per unit is ₹ 20. The break-even point of sales mix is (1)
(a) ₹ 5,000 (b) ₹ 6,000
(c) ₹ 4,000 (d) ₹ 8,000

10. From the given factors of the macro environment in Column I and their elements given in Column II, choose the correct pair (1)

Column I	Column II
A. Political	(i) Inflation, new discoveries
B. Social	(ii) Lifestyle changes, population dynamics
C. Economic	(iii) Taxation, cultural norms
D. Legal	(iv) Innovation, unemployment

Codes
(a) A-(i) (b) B-(ii)
(c) C-(iii) (d) D-(iv)

11. **Assertion** (A) Capital markets are the most important source of raising finance for the entrepreneurs.

Reason (R) The capital market can be classified as primary market (new issues market) and secondary market. (1)

Alternatives
(a) Both Assertion (A) and Reason (R) are true and Reason (R) is the correct explanation of Assertion (A)
(b) Both Assertion (A) and Reason (R) are true, but Reason (R) is not the correct explanation of Assertion (A)
(c) Assertion (A) is true, but Reason (R) is false
(d) Assertion (A) is false, but Reason (R) is true

12. Which of the following forms of business model is represented in the below image? (1)

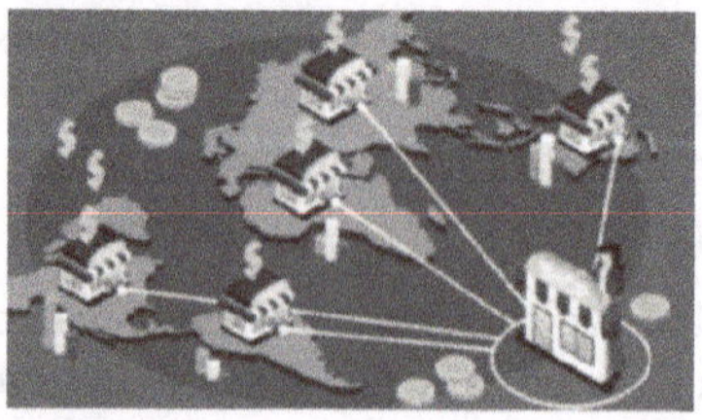

(a) Franchise
(b) Partnership
(c) Venture capital (d) Angel investor

13. This can be defined as the cost incurred by a company to produce, store and sell one unit of sale of a particular product or service. (1)
(a) Unit cost
(b) Margin cost
(c) Average cost
(d) None of the above

14. "Abhay, a new employee in the research and development department of Zylo Limited came up with an idea of manufacturing a security camera with a drone that will give a 360 degree view of the building or premises."
Which idea generation field is being utilised by Abhay? (1)
(a) Creative efforts
(b) Service related
(c) Market driven
(d) Natural resources

15. Neutron Corporations is involved in the manufacturing and selling of energy efficient electrical appliances. The general manager of the company, Ritu went on a trip to abroad and visited a similar factory that manufactured electrical appliances. She saw that their machinery was more advanced and easy to operate than Neutron's.
She sent an official mail to the board of directors and called a meeting in the next 2 days to discuss this. The board, after seeing the machinery of the foreign company, decided to purchase same machinery for their company. The new machinery was purchased and the production became more efficient and quick.
Which factor of macro-environment is being tapped by the company? (1)
(a) Social
(b) Technological
(c) Cultural
(d) Economic

16. Simon and Starlet are two foreigners wanting to start a business in India. They produce high quality; plant based organic cookies with a touch of Italian taste.
Simon and Starlet got an appointment with a group of venture capitalists in India and started developing a business plan to be represented. The business plan aimed at creating interest among the venture capitalists and contained the key graphics of the business in a written PowerPoint presentation.
Which business plan format is discussed above? (1)
(a) Internal operational plan
(b) Elevator pitch
(c) Written presentation for external stakeholders
(d) Pitch deck with oral narration

17. Sumit completed his masters in hotel management and was keen to open his own restaurant in Delhi. He has made a perfect business plan and has planned everything in advance.
He used his savings for starting the venture but was short on some money, so he decided to ask one of his faculties from his masters to provide finance for the venture.
The faculty is a .... (1)
(a) venture capitalist (b) stock fund
(c) creditor (d) angel investor

18. Which of the following is an example of the social environmental factor? (1)
(a) A popular news channel was sued by a viewer because of showing advertisements of a particular product that was banned by the government.
(b) The sale of flower jewellery increased in some specific months in India because of the marriage season. The sellers make special arrangements for meeting the demands in those months.
(c) The Covid-19 pandemic ended in a loss of economic strength of the country and increasing the unemployment rates.
(d) All of the above

Section-B

19. A comic book store has the following sales in a day.

Product	Unit Price	Quantity Sold
Batman Series	40	35
The Avengers	40	40
Action Figure	5	5
Superman Posters	15	10
Hulk Merchandise	10	5
Spiderman Comics	25	3

Total customers were 50 and cost of each item is 75% of the selling price.

If the customers are the unit of sale, determine the unit cost. (2)

Or Calculate the return on equity from the following information.

Capital = ₹ 10,00,000 Debt = ₹ 6,00,000
Sales = ₹ 5,00,000
Gross profit = ₹ 2,00,000
Expenses = ₹ 1,00,000

20. Anupriya wanted the youth to understand the importance and nutritional value of traditional food, therefore, she started a restaurant that only served traditional and healthy food and snacks to its customers. Anupriya went through a wholesome process to open the restaurant but at last the restaurant was a success and people enjoyed the traditional food.

Name the stages of entrepreneurial building process that may have helped in opening the restaurant. (2)

21. Nisha owns a small e-commerce business selling handmade skincare products. As her business expanded, she noticed discrepancies between stock records and actual inventory. To address this, Nisha decided to assign a unique code to each product based on its ingredients, weight and packaging. This helped her quickly identify and track items. Additionally, she categorised her inventory into raw materials (like essential oils and herbs), semi-finished goods (like soap bases) and finished products (like packaged soaps and lotions).

(i) Identify the two aspects that have been considered in the process of inventory control.

(ii) Explain the objective of an effective inventory control system. (2)

22. Explain the meaning of a business plan in regard to a business. (2)

Or

Organisational plan is very important for both, the entrepreneur as well as the investors. Justify this statement.

23. Identify and explain the growth strategy in which two companies combine for doing business. (2)

24. Refer to the images given below.

(a) (b)

(i) Identify the component of brand illustrated in the above images.

(ii) List any two other components of brand other then the one identified in (i). (2)

Or

What is a tagline in branding?

Section-C

25. Rash learned the art of Henna in college and was manufacturing natural Henna products and was always on the lookout to improve her products. She used social media and online surveys to understand the needs of customer.

Through the surveys, she found that the customers want natural Henna without any chemicals added for better colour. Responding to customers' needs, she developed a combination of Henna and tea leaves in an attractive package.

Her Henna pack was an instant success.

(i) Identify the way in which Rash spotted this trend.

(ii) Also, explain the method of trend spotting identified in (i). (3)

26. Explain any three factors affecting the working capital of a company. (3)

Or

Identify and explain the quantity of materials beyond which a firm should not exceed its stocks.

27. Akash belongs to a lower middle-class family with no business background. He, however, wants to venture into a business and has an innovative idea. He has approached various banks but due to his family background, he is unable to avail any finance.

(i) Identify the financial options that can be used by him.

(ii) Explain any two financial options identified in (i) in detail. (3)

28. "Pricing strategy refers to the method that the entrepreneur uses to price his/her products or services. There are various methods of pricing, such as cost-plus pricing, variable pricing, price penetration, etc."

In the light of given statement, distinguish between cost-plus pricing method and variable pricing method. (3)

29. "Partnership firms in India are governed by Indian Partnership Act, 1932. While it is not compulsory to register your partnership firm as there are no penalties for non-registration, it is advisable."

With regards to this, mention the drawbacks associated with non-registration of a partnership firm. (3)

Or Explain three characteristics of a company.

Section-D

30. What do you mean by place mix? Explain any two channels of distribution. (5)

Or Advertising is a paid form of non-personal communication designed to persuade potential customers to choose a product or a service over that of a competitor. Explain the rules of advertising.

31. "Start-up Boosters Pvt. Ltd." is a group of experienced entrepreneurs and business professionals who provide financial and strategic support to budding start-ups. The group consists of high net worth individuals and retired business executives who not only invest funds but also mentor early stage businesses. They believe in creating value by offering industry insights, strategic guidance and networking opportunities to help start-ups meet industry standards.

Understanding the risks involved, 'Start-up Boosters Pvt. Ltd.' expects a significant return on their investment, as their shareholding may be diluted in later funding rounds. The group is committed to fostering innovation and stays updated with the latest industry trends to help emerging entrepreneurs succeed. Their main objective is to build successful businesses while ensuring high returns on their investments.

Quoting lines from the above text, identify five features of angel investors. (5)

32. It is that part of the business which describes the proposed venture's form of ownership, i.e. whether it is sole proprietorship, partnership, joint hindu family, company or corporation. It plays an important role both for the entrepreneur as well as an investor.

(i) Identify the component of a business plan being discussed in the above statement.

(ii) Explain any three key elements included in this component of the business plan. (5)

Or A joint stock company is a voluntary association of individuals for profit, having a capital divided into transferable shares, the ownership of which is the condition of membership. A company is an artificial person and therefore cannot sign.

(i) Identify the legal document that helps a company overcome this disadvantage.

(ii) State any three other disadvantages of a company form of business.

33. Social media networks such as Facebook offer a promising way of fast, cost-effective and direct communication between enterprises and stakeholders.

Employing this technology in entrepreneurial Public Relations (PR) may increase the success of new ventures. Yet, the adoption of social media for PR by start-ups remains understudied. To fill this gap, we conceptualise entrepreneurial PR within the framework of communication management theory and entrepreneurial marketing.

We developed three success factors for PR communication out of the literature and tested them empirically using a sample of 453 German start-ups.

Results indicate the social media PR positively contributes to communication outcomes in terms of building up brand and reputation. Perceived relevance, long-term planning and understanding-oriented PR were all relevant for communication success. This means that entrepreneurs benefit from social media, when they initiate dialogues with stakeholders, conduct environmental scanning processes and build up PR planning skills.

Moreover, findings indicate that social media PR is practiced differently depending on the start-ups' age.

Hence, its crucial for future research to integrate a dynamic perspective on entrepreneurial PR studies.

Source *Christian Rudeloffb Media Management, 2020*

(i) Which concept is emphasised in the above paragraph?
(ii) Explain the concept.
(iii) Also, explain the tools of the concept. (5)

34. A factory is engaged in manufacturing washing machines. The following information is available to you

Sales = ₹ 4,00,000
Direct labour cost (2,000 units) = ₹ 40,000
Direct material cost (2,000 units) = ₹ 1,00,000
Direct expenses (2,000 units) = ₹ 20,000
Fixed cost = ₹ 1,20,000

Find out
(i) Variable cost per unit
(ii) Total cost
(iii) Quantity to be sold at break-even point (5)

Answers

1. (c) I and IV
2. (b) Creativity
3. (a) Only IV
4. (b) No separate entity
5. (c) Sole tradership
6. (d) Internal operation plan
7. (d) 3%
8. (b) Only I
9. (a) ₹ 5,000
10. (b) B-(ii)
11. (b) Both Assertion (A) and Reason (R) are true, but Reason (R) is not the correct explanation of Assertion (A)
12. (a) Franchise
13. (a) Unit cost
14. (a) Creative efforts
15. (b) Technological
16. (c) Written presentation for external stakeholders
17. (d) angel investor
18. (b) The sale of flower jewellery increased in some specific months in India because of the marriage season. The sellers make special arrangements for meeting the demands in those months.
19. Unit Cost = ₹ 49.5 *Or* RoE = 25%
34. (i) Variable cost per unit = ₹ 80
(ii) Total cost = ₹ 2,80,000
(iii) Quantity to be sold at break-even point = 1,000 units

Sample Paper 2

A Highly Simulated Sample Question Paper for CBSE Class XII Examination

Entrepreneurship

General Instructions

Read the following instructions carefully and follow them

1. This question paper contains 34 questions. All questions are compulsory.
2. This question paper is divided into four sections—Section A, B, C and D.
3. Section A : Questions number 1 to 18 are Multiple Choice Type Questions. Each question carries 1 mark.
4. Section B : Questions number 19 to 24 are Short Answer Type-I Questions. Each question carries 2 marks. Write answer to each question in 30 to 40 words.
5. Section C : Questions number 25 to 29 are Short Answer Type-II Questions. Each question carries 3 marks. Write answer to each question in 50 to 70 words.
6. Section D : Questions number 30 to 34 are Long Answer Type Questions. Each question carries 5 marks. Write answer to each question in 120 to 150 words.
7. There is no overall choice. However, an internal choice has been provided in Section B, C and D of question paper. A candidate has to attempt only one of the alternatives in such questions.

Time : 3 hours **Max. Marks : 70**

Section-A

1. Which of the following plan helps to plan the work in such a manner that one can clearly form an idea about plan layout? (1)

   I. Operational II. Production
   III. Marketing IV. Financial

   Codes

   (a) Only I (b) II and III
   (c) I and IV (d) Only IV

2. Under this model of franchising, the manufacturer grants a store owner the authority to distribute goods manufactured under their brand name. (1)

   (a) Product franchise business opportunity
   (b) Manufacturing franchise opportunity
   (c) Business franchise opportunity venture
   (d) Business format franchise opportunity

3. Sam studies in Quantum University and is a student of MBA. He was reading an example of a business that successfully grew in one year by following the principle which stated that 80% of their profits came from 20% of customers.

   This is why the management of the business focused mainly on those 20% of customers. Sam was confused and wanted to find out the roots of this principle.

   Help Sam by identifying the above mentioned principle. (1)

   I. Profit principle II. Pareto's principle
   III. Harley's principle IV. Smith's principle

   Codes

   (a) Only II (b) I and II
   (c) Only III (d) All of these

4. Routing is an element of which of the following components of business plan? (1)

   (a) Production plan (b) Operational plan
   (c) Organisational plan
   (d) Financial plan

5. Which of the following is not a component of financial plan? (1)
   (a) Economic and social variables
   (b) Follow-up
   (c) Break-even analysis
   (d) Proforma investment decisions

6. Alia had established a homemade papad business in Pune. Papads made by her were very popular in her locality but being the sole owner and manager of business, she is unable to introduce many flavours because of limited financial resources.
   Which of the following characteristics of her business, does this situation imply? (1)
   (a) Individual management and control
   (b) Easy formation and closure
   (c) Limited area of operation
   (d) Unlimited liability

7. From the following given information, calculate the economic order quantity for the company. (1)

   Cost of product = 12,000 units at 1,000/unit

   Cost of ordering = ₹ 500 per unit

   Holding cost = ₹ 300 per annum

   (a) 400 (b) 250
   (c) 210 (d) 200

8. Hargold company is constantly improving on its existing range of breads and bringing out variants like atta bread, multi grain bread, garlic bread, etc. Its source of idea field in the market is/are (1)

   I. market driven II. creative efforts
   III. service driven IV. natural resources

   Codes
   (a) I and II (b) Only II
   (c) Only III (d) III and IV

9. Harold Bakers produce 50 cakes daily on an average and received orders up to 45 on a daily basis. On monday, the bakery set record sales of 49 cakes and the management was very happy. The accountant extracted that the gross profit per unit of the bakery on that day was 1,200. What were the fixed expenses of the bakery? (1)
   (a) ₹ 57,000 (b) ₹ 24,480
   (c) ₹ 58,800 (d) ₹ 59,000

10. **Assertion** (A) Idea generation is a process of creating, developing and communicating ideas which are abstract, concrete or visual.

    Reason (R) It includes the process of developing the idea through creativity and innovation and bringing the concept to reality. (1)

    Alternatives
    (a) Both Assertion (A) and Reason (R) are true and Reason (R) is the correct explanation of Assertion (A)
    (b) Both Assertion (A) and Reason (R) are true, but Reason (R) is not the correct explanation of Assertion (A)
    (c) Assertion (A) is true, but Reason (R) is false
    (d) Assertion (A) is false, but Reason (R) is true

11. From the given factors of the types of mergers in Column I and their description given in Column II, choose the correct pair. (1)

Column I		Column II
A. Conglomerate merger	(i)	Purchase of most or all of competitors shares.
B. Horizontal merger	(ii)	Businesses involved in unrelated businesses come together.
C. Vertical merger	(iii)	Combination of businesses in same industry.
D. Product Extension merger	(iv)	Merger between companies dealing in similar types of products.

    Codes
    (a) A-(i) (b) B-(ii)
    (c) C-(iii) (d) D-(iv)

12. Refer to the given image.

    Which type of trend spotting is highlighted in the above image? (1)
    (a) Talk trend (b) Watch trend
    (c) Think trend (d) Idea trend

13. ...... indicate the percentage of return on total capital employed in the business. (1)
(a) Unit cost (b) Return on equity
(c) Average cost
(d) Return on investment

14. Firefun Limited is an electrical appliances manufacturer and has come up with a new type of induction cooker that uses the least electricity and can be run on saved battery power. The production department has started producing the new product and soon a sample will be given to chosen customers for identifying the reliability and quality of the product.

Which idea generation field is highlighted above? (1)
(a) Service related
(b) Market driven
(c) Natural resources (d) Creative efforts

15. Tina is a young entrepreneur who sells hand-made hair extensions through social media and online platforms. She started her venture in 2010 when she saw that many young girls faced the problem of hair fall either due to genetics or any other reason. So, she researched about the solution and found that the extension business is very vast and these types of products are very costly. Therefore, she started her own venture which made extensions from real hair and sells them at a reasonable price.

Which importance of environment scanning is utilised by Tina? (1)
(a) Better performance
(b) Grabbing opportunities from the markets
(c) Resource allocation
(d) All of the above

16. Marshal Company is planning on expanding internationally.

The company manufactures and sells beauty and skin care products in India. Now, the management has decided to enter the UK market.

For this, the company has raised a round of funding through a television show where famous entrepreneurs and business owners invest in new and innovative ideas.

Which of the following funding was utilised by Marshal? (1)
(a) Public issue (b) Venture capital
(c) Borrowing (d) Angel investors

17. Reema has started her boutique in Karol Baugh with two tailors and three staff members. She is very social in the neighbourhood due to which her boutique has many customers. Reema wanted to renovate her boutique into something modern and unique and for this she decided to prepare a 3 minutes summary of her business and awaken interest of some investors to invest money for the renovation.

Which type of plan is used by Reema? (1)
(a) Written presentation for investors
(b) Elevator pitch
(c) Pitch deck with oral narration
(d) Internal operational plan

18. Which of the following is an example of talk trends? (1)
(a) Suman came up with the idea of customised face masks after analysing the market and its opportunities.
(b) Quantum Limited is a known company and always engages with its customers through forums, online platforms, events, etc.
(c) Ram reads the business magazines weekly to grab some idea about business industry as he wants to start his own venture someday.
(d) Manas regularly go to trade shows to analyse the taste and preferences of customers.

Section-B

19. Determine the break-even quantity and sales at break-even level from the following information
Fixed expenses = ₹ 2,75,000
Selling price = ₹ 50
Variable cost per unit = ₹ 30 (2)

Or

Alpha Limited consumes 100-120 units of iron in a month.

The re-order period of the iron material is 4 to 6 days. What will be the re-order level?

20. Amazon is constantly on the lookout for new trends. Amazon GO stores, for example, allow customers to select what they want and leave, with technology tracking what they've taken and billing their Amazon account.

Finery's virtual closet manager can organise and create outfits as well as keep track of clothing purchases via e-mail receipts.

Explain any two types of trends that can be utilised by businesses to spot new trend in the markets. (2)

21. TechGear Pvt. Ltd., a start-up specialising in smart home devices, recently upgraded its product line to include AI-powered voice assistants. This decision was influenced by the rapid advancements in artificial intelligence and automation. The company also invested in cloud computing to enhance the functionality of its devices. As a result, its sales increased significantly and it gained a competitive edge in the market. Seeing the trend, competitors also started integrating AI into their products.

The CEO emphasised that staying updated with technological changes is crucial for business success.

(i) Identify the macro-environmental factor discussed in the case.

(ii) Explain any one point of importance of understanding the environment. (2)

22. The business assets of an organisation amounts to ₹ 2,50,000 and its liabilities are ₹ 3,00,000.

What are the alternatives available to the creditors if

(i) It is a sole proprietorship business. (2)

Or

(ii) The organisation is a partnership firm with Raghu and Raghav as partners.

23. Differentiate between product franchise and manufacturing franchise. (2)

24. Given below is the cash conversion cycle.

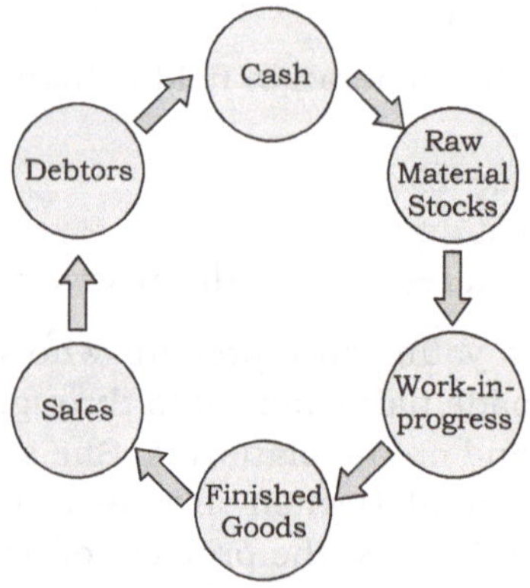

(i) Identify the type of business to which the above cash conversion cycle belongs.

(ii) Draw a 'cash conversion cycle' for another type of business other than that identified in (i) above. (2)

Or Explain the importance of unit of sales as a management tool.

Section-C

25. Raunak went on a trip with his friends to the forest of the Nilgiris hills. On his trip, he found that the forests were abound with various herbs that had medicinal qualities. Raunak decided to exploit this opportunity by developing medicines from these herbs.

(i) What is the source of Raunak's idea? Explain.

(ii) Give one more example of this source. (3)

26. Explain any three types of sales promotion techniques and give examples of each. (3)

Or Differentiate between packaging and labelling.

27. 'Fun Riders Automobile Company' is planning expansion after completing successful five years of operation.

For funding their expansion plans they plan to approach venture capital firms in India.

But they are also aware that venture capitalists invests in one in four hundred opportunities presented to them.

(i) Suggest them any two parameters on which they should impress venture capitalists.

(ii) State any feature of venture capital. (3)

28. "Finance is the life blood of any organisation and is the most important pre-requisite to establish any business. An entrepreneur makes use of several financial projection techniques and tools to draw up a financial plan."

Explain any three factors which affect the formulation of a financial plan. (3)

29. What are the drawbacks associated with skimming pricing method? (3)

Or "Promotion can be done for a mass or large audience, targeted customers and both by using different promotional approaches."

With reference to the given statement, explain the three promotional strategies or approaches.

Section-D

30. Anmol, a small entrepreneur is manufacturing portable fans with the brand name 'A-FAN'. These fans are in great demand. He finds that the cost of production of per unit of the fan is ₹ 800 and he can sell the same at ₹ 1,000 per fan. The competitors in the market are selling this type of fan at the rate of ₹ 1,200.

Anmol's objective is not to earn profit in the short-run but to capture the largest market share. His expectation is that the customers will be attracted towards the new brand because of lower price.

(i) Identify the method of pricing adopted by Anmol to capture the substantial portion of the market.

(ii) Also state any two advantages of this method of pricing. (5)

Or BrightVision Ltd., a newly established consumer electronics brand, is launching a marketing campaign for its latest product line.

The company ensures that its advertisements are engaging and persuasive while complying with industry standards.

To maintain credibility and consumer trust, BrightVision Ltd. follows specific guidelines while designing its advertisements.

(i) Identify the concept of promotion being discussed in the above case.

(ii) Briefly state the rules that must be followed while creating advertisements.

31. Number of people who took their meals and the total billing for each of the 5 weeks is in the following table.

Week	No. of People Taking Meals	Average Amount Billed (in ₹)
1	120	150
2	60	205
3	70	146
4	80	221
5	90	240

Based on the given information, answer the questions given below

(i) Calculate the unit price.

(ii) If the variable cost is 60% of the sale price, the gross margin per unit of sale.

(iii) State the meaning of unit of sale. (5)

32. State and explain the business plan that reflects the economic feasibility of an organisation. (5)

Or State and explain the formats available to design and develop a successful business plan.

33. 'Sauna Ltd' is a leading company for manufacturing of spa products for all genders. The company is in the process of developing a new organic mixture of various herbs that releases all types of body pain while getting a spa, 'All Gone', which would enable customers forget their stress and tensions and relax. All the ingredients are taken from famous herbal and ayurvedic practitioners.

Though it is an innovation for the company, imported versions of this product are already available in the market. The management wanted to devise a pricing strategy to target the 'switchers' present in the market.

(i) Identify and explain the pricing strategy that the management is thinking of using.

(ii) Keeping in mind the nature of the product, suggest the best distribution channel for the product.

(iii) Explain the benefits and liabilities of the channel suggested in (ii). (5)

34. Cool Breeze Pvt. Ltd. is a leading manufacturer of air conditioning units and cooling systems. The company planned to expand its operations in tropical regions where demand for air conditioners is high during summer. It ensured an adequate supply of raw materials before peak summer months to meet increased production needs.

To maintain smooth operations, the company streamlined its production process, reducing the time taken to convert raw materials into finished goods.

Additionally, Cool Breeze Pvt. Ltd. offered flexible credit terms to its wholesale buyers, allowing them to pay within 60 days instead of immediate payments.

The company also negotiated with its suppliers to extend payment terms, enabling it to purchase raw materials on credit for up to 90 days.

Furthermore, by adopting energy efficient production methods, Cool Breeze Pvt. Ltd. managed to reduce wastage and operational costs, improving overall efficiency.

Quoting lines from the above text, identify five factors affecting working capital that the company took into consideration while operating its business. (5)

Answers

1. (a) Only I
2. (a) Product franchise business opportunity
3. (a) Only II
4. (b) Operational plan
5. (b) Follow-up
6. (c) Limited area of operation
7. (d) 200
8. (b) Only II
9. (c) ₹ 58,800
10. (a) Both Assertion (A) and Reason (R) are true and Reason (R) is the correct explanation of Assertion (A)
11. (d) D-(iv)
12. (b) Watch trend
13. (d) Return on investment
14. (d) Creative efforts
15. (b) Grabbing opportunities from the markets
16. (d) Angel investors
17. (b) Elevator pitch
18. (b) Quantum Limited is a known company and always engages with its customers through forums, online platforms, events, etc.
19. Break-even quantity = 13,750 units

    Sales at break-even level = ₹ 6,87,500

    Or Re-order level = 720 units

31. (i) Unit price = ₹ 190

    (ii) Gross margin per unit of sale = ₹ 76

Sample Paper 3

A Highly Simulated Sample Question Paper for CBSE Class XII Examination

Entrepreneurship

General Instructions

Read the following instructions carefully and follow them

1. This question paper contains 34 questions. All questions are compulsory.
2. This question paper is divided into four sections—Section A, B, C and D.
3. Section A : Questions number 1 to 18 are Multiple Choice Type Questions. Each question carries 1 mark.
4. Section B : Questions number 19 to 24 are Short Answer Type-I Questions. Each question carries 2 marks. Write answer to each question in 30 to 40 words.
5. Section C : Questions number 25 to 29 are Short Answer Type-II Questions. Each question carries 3 marks. Write answer to each question in 50 to 70 words.
6. Section D : Questions number 30 to 34 are Long Answer Type Questions. Each question carries 5 marks. Write answer to each question in 120 to 150 words.
7. There is no overall choice. However, an internal choice has been provided in Section B, C and D of question paper. A candidate has to attempt only one of the alternatives in such questions.

Time : 3 hours **Max. Marks : 70**

Section-A

1. Contribution = (1)

   I. Cost Price + Variable Cost

   II. Selling Price − Variable Cost

   III. Fixed Cost + Profit IV. Fixed Cost − Profit

   Codes

   (a) Only I (b) II and III

   (c) I and IV (d) Only IV

2. A comprehensively written document prepared by the entrepreneur describing all the relevant internal and external elements in starting a new venture is called (1)

   (a) marketing plan (b) business plan

   (c) financial plan

   (d) operational plan

3. Ram and Ramesh are two partners owning a steel distribution business. The partnership deed of the company states that 'the business or operations of the company can be carried out by all partner or by one partner acting for both.'

   Ram and Ramesh represented which characteristic(s) of a partnership business? (1)

   I. Mutual agency II. Limited liability

   III. Ongoing nature IV. Utmost good faith

   Codes

   (a) Only I (b) I and II

   (c) Only III (d) All of these

4. A business needs capital for (1)

   (a) procuring fixed assets

   (b) meeting day-to-day expenses

   (c) growth and diversification

   (d) All of the above

5. Which of the following formats of business plan is not targeted towards the external stakeholder? (1)

   (a) Elevator pitch

   (b) A pitch deck with oral narrative

   (c) A written presentation for external stakeholders

   (d) An internal operational plan

6. Bishop Ltd., is in the fast moving consumer goods industry. They introduced a new variety of biscuits in the market. It has high fibre content with different new flavours incorporating various multigrains. State which promotion strategy should be used by Bishop Ltd.? (1)

(a) Below the line (b) Through the line
(c) Above the line (d) None of these

7. From the following given information of Larch textiles Limited, calculate the re-order quantity for the company.

Monthly consumption of wool = 200-310 units

Re-order period = 6 – 9 days (1)

(a) 2,790 (b) 7,200
(c) 3,120 (d) 3,000

8. Ankush was working with Vipul as a production manager. For smooth flow of work he has to pay attention to various elements and to ensure predetermined quality of products, he had to compare performance with established standards. The component(s) of business plan discussed above is/are (1)

I. operational plan
II. organisational plan
III. financial plan
IV. human resource plan

Codes

(a) I and II (b) Only I
(c) Only III (d) III and IV

9. Rita opened her beauty parlor a year ago with initial investment of ₹ 3,00,000 out of which ₹ 1,70,000 was her own savings. The parlor has been popular around the areas. The customers are happy with the services. Rita took a loan from XVB Bank for ₹ 50,000 with an interest of 6% per annum. The parlor earned a sales of revenue of ₹ 1, 00,000 per month with a cost of goods amounting to ₹ 60,000. Which of the following is the correct gross margin of the parlor? (1)

(a) ₹ 50,000
(b) ₹ 1,20,000
(c) ₹ 40,000
(d) ₹ 1,00,000

10. From the given factors of the elements of innovation process in Column I and components given in Column II, choose the correct pair. (1)

Column I		Column II
A. Analytical planning	(i)	Reward employee
B. Resource planning	(ii)	Human and material resources
C. Implementation	(iii)	Design and service features
D. Commercial application	(iv)	Delivering results

Codes

(a) A-(i) (b) B-(ii)
(c) C-(iii) (d) D-(iv)

11. Refer to the given image.

The given image represents which type of organisational plan? (1)

(a) Human resource plan
(b) Marketing plan
(c) Material plan (d) Financial plan

12. **Assertion** (A) Innovation is required to work out analytically the details of the enterprise, to develop marketing strategies, to organise, finance and strategies operations.

Reason (R) Innovation is the first step in entrepreneurial planning. (1)

Alternatives

(a) Both Assertion (A) and Reason (R) are true and Reason (R) is the correct explanation of Assertion (A)
(b) Both Assertion (A) and Reason (R) are true, but Reason (R) is not the correct explanation of Assertion (A)
(c) Assertion (A) is true, but Reason (R) is false
(d) Assertion (A) is false, but Reason (R) is true

13. .... is a process of creating, developing and communicating ideas which are concrete, abstract, or visual. (1)

(a) Creativity
(b) Environment analysis
(c) Innovation (d) Idea generation

14. Samuel is a post graduate in management and is fond of exploring different business ideas. Once, he came across a less known brand which produced and sold organic candles with aromas that relax mood and reduce stress. He appreciated the work of the owners and decided to help them.

Which was the source of perceiving the idea? (1)

(a) Problem (b) Innovation
(c) Change (d) Invention

15. Looks Limited is a beauty brand producing and selling various skin care products for both men and women. Lalit, the owner of Looks Limited is a good friend of famous and known entrepreneur who has lots of businesses around the world. Once, Lalit visited his friend and told him that he has come up with a new product idea and wants to go forward but he is in need of some funds. His friend immediately offered to help him in return of some equity in the company.

What is Lalit's friend for the company? (1)

(a) Venture capitalist (b) Creditor
(c) Angel investor (d) None of these

16. Farhan is the marketing manager of a company and is always indulged in making creative packaging for the products. The new senior manager wants to cut costs and decided to shorten the fund for packaging the products. Farhan did not like the decision and decided to meet the senior manager. He then, with his knowledge in business explained the manager the perks of marketing their idea and giving a smart package to the product. He also stressed upon representing the fact of eco-friendly product on the packets and assured that this will boost sales of the company.

The component of product mix highlighted in the above case is (1)

(a) labelling (b) packaging
(c) tagline (d) logo

17. Antler Limited started marketing their products on various platforms like social media, newspaper articles, etc. The new idea attracted many customers and the company also took a detailed online feedback from customers about their experience. All the analysis of the market and customer feedbacks indicated that the company is positively perceived in the market.

Which element of the marketing mix is highlighted in the above case? (1)

(a) Promotion (b) Product
(c) Place (d) Both (a) and (b)

18. Which of the following indicates that the idea is perceived through a problem source? (1)

(a) There is low power supply in small towns and villages; therefore, Beta Limited came up with heaters that can be operated on LPG.
(b) With the fear of Covid-19, many people turned to healthy lifestyles and many companies started making health conscious products to gain the opportunity.
(c) Samish got funding for his product from the Make in India scheme of the government.
(d) Both (a) and (b)

Section-B

19. Manish runs a grocery store in Nagpur. He started this store after his retirement and spent ₹ 5,00,000 to open the store.

The store generates a profit of ₹ 2,60,000 in a year. Determine the return on investment. (2)

Or Find the break-even point in units from the following

Average monthly output = 50,000 tons
Sales price per kg = ₹ 40
Variable cost per kg = ₹ 20
Fixed expenses = ₹ 50,000

20. The process of generation of idea can be streamlined by developing an awareness for different 'idea fields'.

This will help the entrepreneur in enlarging the scope of thinking. Thus, idea fields can be defined as convenient frames of reference for streamlining the process of generation of ideas.

(i) State the meaning of idea field.

(ii) Explain any one sources of idea field. (2)

21. Rama started her small-scale business of making pickles along with some of her neighbours using their free time at home.

They named the venture 'Home sweet Home' and were able to supply to the entire district. One of the members suggested that they should start expanding and sell to other states.

When she discussed it with her husband, he said that they will have to carefully analyse the environment of the target states.

State and explain any two sources from where they can collect information about the environment. (2)

22.

(i) Identify the form of business organisation highlighted in the above image.

(ii) State any one characteristic of the form identified in (i). (2)

Or Explain why private companies are more desirable in the present environment.

23. How meeting capital requirements is not difficult, when opting to start a business by buying a franchise? (2)

24. There is an adverse relationship between order size and ordering cost. Why? (2)

Or What is break-even quantity? How is it calculated?

Section-C

25. Ana Ltd. is a company that distributes gardening equipment. The company recently imported 5,000 testing machines to assess the rusting of iron. The company's chief executive officer convened a meeting of marketing heads from various zones to determine the marketing strategy. During the meeting, the local zone marketing head suggested that because the machines were sophisticated, they should personally visit the plants to explain how they worked, to the staff that would be using the machines. He also suggested that additional trained personnel be hired for the same purpose. Another zonal head stated that the company was short of funds to pay the additional staff because a large sum of money had been spent on the importation of the machines.

A newly appointed South zone zonal head suggested that because the order is not large, a detailed study of the factors determining the choice of distribution channels is required before making the right choice.

(i) State the meaning of channel of distribution.

(ii) Explain the factors influencing the choice of distribution channels. (3)

26. Explain the enterprise building process in detail. (3)

Or "If you don't adapt, you don't endure', is the core idea behind environment scanning." In the light of the given statement, explain the need for environment scanning? Explain.

27. Flipkart, an e-trading business giant, started operations with online selling of goods. People who wanted to buy at ease at anytime.

Through its quality service and timely delivery and return policy it has crafted a position for itself.

It has developed its logo very attractive. The brand value has increased a lot.

(i) What do you understand by 'brand'?

(ii) What is a logo? Give any two functions that logo serves. (3)

28. "Finance is a kind of solution that assists in the formation of new businesses and also allows businesses to take advantage of opportunities to grow and expand." In the light of the statement, explain some important sources of raising finance in business. (3)

29. What is meant by business plan? State any one advantage of writing a business plan for investors and entrepreneurs. (3)

Or

What is an operational plan? Explain its purpose.

Section-D

30. It relates to short-term incentives that encourage or promote the purchase or sale of a product or a service. These are often referred to as below the line activities and are designed to stimulate quicker or greater purchase of particular products by consumers.

(i) Identify the type of promotional tool discussed in the above lines.

(ii Explain the three types of activities involved in the promotional tool identified in (i). (5)

Or It involves oral presentation of message in the form of conversation with one or more prospective customers for the purpose of making sales. In this method, companies appoint salesperson who contact with prospective buyers to create product awareness.

(i) Identify the type of promotional tool discussed in the above lines.

(ii) Explain any three qualities of a good salesman.

31. Smart Stock Ltd.' is a company specialising in the distribution of electronic accessories such as mobile chargers, power banks and USB cables. To streamline its operations, the company implemented a robust inventory control system. It ensured that every product had a unique identification code that included specifications like voltage, capacity and compatibility, helping in efficient tracking.

Since the company dealt with a diverse range of products, including raw materials, spare parts and finished goods, it classified its inventory accordingly.

Recognising the space requirements for different items, the company allocated specific storage areas, ensuring that bulkier but low cost items did not take up unnecessary premium space.

To manage costs effectively, Smart Stock Ltd. carefully assessed the value of its inventory, prioritising high value items for secure storage and monitoring. The company also focused on lead time, ensuring timely procurement of products by analysing supplier schedules and production times to avoid stockouts.

Quoting lines from the above text, identify five aspects that were considered in the process of inventory control. (5)

32. What is a public company? Explain its features. (5)

Or Distinguish between private company and public company.

33. The fundamentals that guide e-commerce marketing, the four Ps of product, person, place and price are all essential in their own ways. The digital transformation that has guided the e-commerce boom in the last two years has helped brands and retailers hone optimising those core tenets, contributing to the drive towards expanded stores of first party consumer data.

With the eventual phase out of third-party cookies, there has been a divestment in those legacy identifiers, which has given smart brands and retailers more actionable, intelligent data. In short, better data has largely solved the first three of the four Ps; brands and retailers can now deliver the right product to the right person through the right channel with increased efficacy.

The only variable that is in desperate need of optimisation is pricing. As retailers begin mapping their holiday sales strategies, focusing on pricing can help on multiple fronts, including managing supply and demand as well as offering personalisation in an increasingly price sensitive consumer climate.

Source *Jonathan Treiber Contributo (Forbes–22nd October, 2011, 12:25 pm EDT)*

(i) 4Ps is related to which concept of entrepreneurship?

(ii) Explain the concept identified in (i).

(iii) Explain any one element/component of 4Ps. (5)

34. A factory is engaged in manufacturing coolers. The following information is available to you

Sales = ₹ 2,50,000

Direct labour cost (for 100 units) = ₹ 25,000

Direct material cost (for 100 units) = ₹ 62,500

Direct expenses (for 100 units) = ₹ 12,500

Fixed cost = ₹ 75,000

Calculate

(i) Variable cost per unit

(ii) Total cost

(iii) Break-even point

Are actual sales exceeding the sales required to break-even? (5)

Answers

1. (b) II and III

2. (b) business plan

3. (a) Only I

4. (d) All of the above

5. (d) An internal operational plan

6. (c) Above the line

7. (a) 2,790 **8.** (b) Only I

9. (c) ₹ 40,000

10. (b) B-(ii)

11. (d) Financial plan

12. (c) Assertion (A) is true, but Reason (R) is false

13. (d) Idea generation

14. (b) Innovation

15. (c) Angel investor

16. (b) packaging

17. (a) Promotion

18. (a) There is low power supply in small towns and villages; therefore, Beta Limited came up with heaters that can be operated on LPG.

19. RoI = 52%

Or Break-even point = ₹ 2,500 units

34. (i) Variable cost per unit = ₹ 1,000

(ii) Total cost = ₹ 1,75,000

(iii) Break-even point = ₹ 1,25,000

CBSE Examination Paper
2024 & 2025

CBSE Examination Paper 2024

Entrepreneurship

General Instructions

Read the following instructions carefully and follow them

1. This question paper contains 34 questions. All questions are compulsory.
2. This question paper is divided into four sections—Section A, B, C and D.
3. Section A : Questions number 1 to 18 are Multiple Choice Type Questions. Each question carries 1 mark.
4. Section B : Questions number 19 to 24 are Short Answer Type-I Questions. Each question carries 2 marks. Write answer to each question in 30 to 40 words.
5. Section C : Questions number 25 to 29 are Short Answer Type-II Questions. Each question carries 3 marks. Write answer to each question in 50 to 70 words.
6. Section D : Questions number 30 to 34 are Long Answer Type Questions. Each question carries 5 marks. Write answer to each question in 120 to 150 words.
7. There is no overall choice. However, an internal choice has been provided in Section B, C and D of question paper. A candidate has to attempt only one of the alternatives in such questions.

Time : 3 hours **Max. Marks : 70**

Section-A

1. During the rainy season, Subir observed that a large quantity of natural and free water was being wasted. Being a mechanical engineer, Subir started to work on a device that was to be installed in underground water tanks, for collecting the rain water, freezing it and creating a surplus water resource. He prepared a prototype and started the trials on this device. He was happy that he succeeded in converting his idea into reality.

   Identify the idea field that provided him an insight for developing the product. (1)

   (a) Market-driven idea
   (b) Natural resource
   (c) Service-related idea (d) Creative efforts

2. Which of the following is not a component of 'brand'? (1)

   (a) Brand name (b) Brand mark
   (c) Trademark (d) Tag line

3. 'Anarya Ltd.', a company manufacturing cars wants to enter into e-car business in the next few months. For this it needs additional funds. To speed up financing it decides to sell some of its shares to institutional investors. The company also does not wish to disclose this information in the open market.

   From the following, identify the method of floatation of new issues used by the company. (1)

   (a) Public issue (b) Rights issue
   (c) Private placement (d) Offer to employees

4. 'Nipro Electronics' was the leading player in the electronics industry for the last fifteen years. A few years back, 'Mobe Electronics', a smaller company as compared to 'Nipro Electronics' entered the market. 'Nipro Electronics' started losing its market share to 'Mobe Electronics' day-by-day due to its innovative products.

   To maintain or develop a competitive edge and to upgrade its technology, 'Nipro Electronics' decided to acquire 'Mobe Electronics' under friendly terms but that failed. Now it decided to buy majority shares of 'Mobe Electronics' and hence initiated the acquisition.

   From the following, identify the type of acquisition which 'Nipro Electronics' adopted after failing on friendly terms. (1)

(a) Friendly acquisition
(b) Hostile acquisition
(c) Reverse acquisition
(d) Back-flip acquisition

5. Selection of a product or service will depend upon many factors while assessing the market. The demand assessment is one of them. This assessment is based on (1)
(a) technological advancements in the field
(b) size of the market being targeted
(c) transportation delays, wastage, etc.
(d) level of operation

6. **Assertion** (A) Mergers and acquisitions is a potential strategy for ensuring the accelerated growth of business.

Reason (R) Growing through mergers and acquisitions usually turns out to be less expensive as compared with internal expansion, particularly when the replacement cost of asset is higher than the market value of the targeted assets.

Choose the correct option from the following (1)

(a) Both Assertion (A) and Reason (R) are correct and Reason (R) is the correct explanation of Assertion (A)
(b) Both Assertion (A) and Reason (R) are correct, but Reason (R) is not the correct explanation of Assertion (A)
(c) Assertion (A) is correct, but Reason (R) is incorrect
(d) Assertion (A) is incorrect, but Reason (R) is correct

7. Raghuram has been appointed as the stock incharge in a readymade shirt manufacturing company. The production manager asks Raghuram to ensure the availability of fabric without any interruption so that there is no stock-out situation. For this Raghuram wants to know the re-order point of fabric for the company, that is to determine when to place an order. For this he found out the procurement lead time, which is 2 months, and the demand during this period, which is expected to be 300 bales of cotton fabric per month. So the order should be placed when the stock reaches (1)
(a) 600 bales (b) 450 bales
(c) 300 bales (d) 150 bales

8. **Assertion** (A) Sales promotion relates to short-term incentives or activities that encourage the purchase or sale of products or services.

Reason (R) Sales promotion helps to create awareness about the companies' products.

Choose the correct option from the following (1)

(a) Both Assertion (A) and Reason (R) are correct and Reason (R) is the correct explanation of Assertion (A)
(b) Both Assertion (A) and Reason (R) are correct, but Reason (R) is not the correct explanation of Assertion (A)
(c) Assertion (A) is correct, but Reason (R) is incorrect
(d) Assertion (A) is incorrect, but Reason (R) is correct

9. Choose the correct formula from the following for calculating 'gross working capital'. (1)
(a) Gross Working Capital = Cash + Accounts Receivable + Fixed Assets + Other Current Assets
(b) Gross Working Capital = Cash + Accounts Payable + Inventory + Other Current Assets
(c) Gross Working Capital = Cash + Accounts Receivable + Inventory + Other Current Assets
(d) Gross Working Capital = Cash + Accounts Receivable + Inventory + Long-term Liabilities

10. Financial plan is a projection of key financial data about (1)
I. economic feasibility of the enterprise.
II. orderly movement of goods.
III. market opportunities and threats.
IV. the potential investment commitment needed for the new venture.

Choose the correct option from the following
(a) Only I
(b) I and IV
(c) I, II and IV (d) II, III and IV

11. **Assertion** (A) Public issue is the most popular method of raising capital these days by the entrepreneurs.

Reason (R) The capital does not have to be repaid and does not involve an interest charge.

Choose the correct option from the following (1)

(a) Assertion (A) is correct, but Reason (R) is incorrect

(b) Assertion (A) is incorrect, but Reason (R) is correct

(c) Both Assertion (A) and Reason (R) are correct and Reason (R) is the correct explanation of Assertion (A)

(d) Both Assertion (A) and Reason (R) are correct, but Reason (R) is not the correct explanation of Assertion (A)

12. Even after providing good food, excellent hospitality and other services, 'The Concept', a five star hotel, is facing problem of low demand for its rooms. To increase demand of the rooms in the hotel the chief executive officer of the hotel called the marketing manager for advice. The marketing manager suggested that with a booking for three days and two nights package the hotel should announce an offer to provide free dinner along with complimentary breakfast for one day, as well as a free stay for one day at a good resort for its clients within a month.

The promotion strategy or approach suggested by the marketing manager is (1)

(a) above the line (b) below the line

(c) through the line (d) None of these

13. 'Vision Ltd.' offers stock options to its employees. This enables employees to become shareholders of the company leading to higher efficiency and lower labour turnover.

The method of floatation of new issues being used by 'Vision Ltd.' is (1)

(a) public issue (b) rights issue

(c) private placement (d) offer to employees

14. Aditi successfully completed her studies at a famous institute of fashion designing. She is now eager to establish a manufacturing unit specialising in designer clothes for the youth in India. To achieve this, she started going to locations frequently visited by her target customers. Additionally, she has begun exploring local markets and actively participating in fashion shows. These efforts aimed at gaining a deeper understanding of the market and ensuring that the manufactured designer clothes are in sync with the prevailing fashion trends.

Identify the way in which Aditi is spotting trends. (1)

(a) Read trends (b) Talk trends

(c) Watch trends (d) Think trends

15. Samarya owned an airline business with a fleet of 20 aircraft operating between Nairo and Piere. She wanted to expand the business to other parts of the country. She was concerned about the rising oil prices which would impact the costs as well as the sensitivity of the airline revenues to fluctuations in business traffic.

Identify the factor affecting the macro environment under PESTEL model. (1)

(a) Political (b) Economic

(c) Social (d) Technological

16. Sarita got admission in Nadir Engineering College. After two to three months, she observed that the students of the college were facing problems in washing and ironing of clothes due to shortage of time. Sarita sensed the opportunity, analysed it and synthesised it to identify an opening. She suggested to her cousin, Hitesh to start a laundry service for hostel students. Soon, this service became popular, not only among the hostel students, but also among the nearby residents.

'Ability to perceive and preserve basic ideas which could be used commercially' was the factor involved in sensing this opportunity. The source which led to the emergence of this basic idea was (1)

(a) problem (b) invention

(c) innovation (d) competition

17. 'Air-Puro Ltd.' is engaged in manufacturing and distribution of air-purifiers. The company has four departments – production, marketing, finance and human resource. The quality of the air-purifiers is very good and these are handy also. Due to this the demand of air-purifiers started growing. To meet the growing demand, the production head informed the chief executive officer to recruit more employees.

The component of business plan which will help in deciding the number of people required is (1)

(a) marketing plan (b) production plan

(c) organisational plan (d) manpower plan

18. Manoj, Ankit and Nikhil are good friends and doing interior designing business at a small-scale. Their business is taking off in a big way. Now, there is a need to change their small-scale business into a large-scale business. The trio needs more capital to invest, to hire more employees and for other expenses. Due to the growing need they decided to re-organise their form of business. Now, they wanted to have an organisation in which members have a limited liability and minimum paid-up capital is rupees one lakh.

The type of organisation the trio wanted to form is (1)

(a) partnership (b) public company
(c) private company (d) sole proprietorship

Section-B

19. (a) State the elements in the innovation process. (2)

Or (b) Give the meaning of 'problem identification'. With the help of any two points, state how problem identification helps the entrepreneur.

20. Ariha loves eating good food and for that she generally visits famous restaurants. She is very fond of Kheer and after eating food she requests for Kheer as a dessert. Quite frequently she discovered that Kheer was not available in many restaurants. So, she decided to make instant Kheer-mix in various flavours like Mango, Kesar-Elaichi, Malai-Rabri, etc. and started selling these in the neighbourhood. The Kheer-mixes became popular in the neighbourhood, as they were easy to make and had a good taste. Now, one of her friends suggested that she should consider selling the Kheer-mixes to the retailers and also to the restaurants directly. To achieve this she had to keep a distinctive name to distinguish her Kheer-mixes from that of the competitors, if any.

(a) Identify and explain the component of product mix discussed in the above case.

(b) Also, identify and explain the term through which the name given by her to the product can get legal protection. (2)

21. Recognising the opportunity in the women's hair care, Prabhav conceived an idea to manufacture a multi-functional three-in-one machine for hair i.e., hair dryer cum curler cum hair iron. He felt that it would be comfortable to carry one machine instead of three. On the basis of this idea, interest and curiosity, the need was adjudged and he started looking for an answer to implement the idea. He then conducted a market research to foresee the future of this multi-functional three-in-one machine, hair dryer cum hair curler cum hair iron. The idea was considered very strong and he decided to go ahead.

Identify and state the steps in the creative process which were fulfilled by Prabhav. Also, state the two steps to be followed by Prabhav in the creative process. (2)

22. (a) Explain the advantages a franchisor gains through franchising which are related to 'expansion risk' and 'cost advantages' that result from extensive buying power. (2)

Or (b) Explain 'number of buyers' and 'types of buyers' as considerations related to market while selecting a channel of distribution.

23. (a) What is a 'business plan'? State any two points why 'business plans' are considered as decision-making tools. (2)

Or (b) Explain 'ability to harness different sources of information' and 'vision and creativity' factors involved in sensing opportunities.

24. A beauty parlour had varying number of customers during five weeks. From the given information, calculate 'unit price' per customer. (2)

Weeks	Number of Customers	Average Amount Billed per Customer (in ₹)
1	20	200
2	34	170
3	26	142
4	44	462
5	36	350

Section-C

25. 'Aircon Ltd.' manufactures and sells desert coolers with various unique features. There is no competitor of 'Aircon Ltd.' in the market. So, they decided to sell these at a high price. Inspite of having unique features its sale was not picking up. They tried to find out the reason for this. After market research they found that to raise their market share, they have to revise their pricing method. The company decides to adopt a pricing method based on manufacturing estimates which should cover the cost of producing the coolers plus a reasonable profit.

(a) Identify the pricing method 'Aircon Ltd.' decides to adopt.

(b) State one advantage and one disadvantage of this pricing method. (3)

26. (a) Explain the following elements of an operational plan.

(i) Scheduling

(ii) Follow-up

(iii) Inspection (3)

Or (b) One of the important methods for generating ideas is to carry out a 'market research'.

(i) What is meant by 'market research'?

(ii) Explain how market research helps an entrepreneur for generating 'market-driven or demand-driven ideas' as a source of idea field?

27. 'GRX Ltd.' has marked its presence for its 'Apple Cider Vinegar' on different social media platforms like Facebook, instagram, etc. by demonstrating features and benefits not available with the competitors' products without mentioning their names.

(a) Identify the type of sales strategy adopted by 'GRX Ltd.'

(b) Name and state the other type of sales strategy available with the businesses.

(c) List any two points of consideration required for creating an effective sales strategy. (3)

28. 'Mitsu Electronics Ltd.' was operating its business of electronic items in India. The Prime Minister announced relaxation in export duties on electronic items and the company started exporting its products to neighbouring countries. The company developed a better and cheaper video conferencing system to solve the problem, if any, and to replenish the stocks wherever and whenever needed. The demand for its electronic items started increasing day-by-day as there is an increase in the level of education and consumerism globally.

Quoting the lines from the above para, identify and explain any three dimensions of business environment. (3)

29. (a) Explain the following three stages in a company's development when an entrepreneur can seek venture capital.

(i) Seed capital finance

(ii) Start-up finance

(iii) Second round financing (3)

Or

(b) Who are called 'angel investors'? Explain any five features of angel investors.

Section-D

30. (a) What is meant by 'advertising'? State any four rules to be considered while planning any advertising activity and any four responses for developing effective advertising. (5)

Or (b) Give the meaning of 'franchise agreement'. Explain the four main ingredients of a 'franchise agreement'.

31. What is meant by 'primary market'? Explain the four methods used by an entrepreneur to raise the required capital in the primary market. (5)

32. (a) Give the meaning of 'company' form of business organisation. Explain the following features of a company.

(i) Separate legal entity

(ii) Limited liability
(iii) Transferability of shares
(iv) Diffusion of ownership and management (5)

Or

(b) 'Sensitivity to environmental factors is crucial for an entrepreneur.'
In the light of this statement, explain any five benefits of understanding the relevant environment of business.

33. Happy Hands Ltd.' manufactures liquid hand wash for children with minimal chemicals. They have three varieties of liquid soap. The fixed cost for the production process is ₹ 2,49,000.

Variety	Scrub Hand Wash	Gel Hand Wash	Foam Hand Wash
Selling Price per 100 ml in (₹)	155	175	195
Variable Cost per 100 ml in (₹)	75	95	105
Sales Mix	40%	30%	30%

From the above data, calculate the following
(a) Total weighted average contribution margin.
(b) Break-even quantity for each variety of liquid hand wash.
(c) Break-even point in rupees for scrub hand wash. (5)

34. Aneesh, a young entrepreneur, wishes to take his family business of designer fabrics to greater heights with the knowledge he has acquired at 'National Institute of Fabric Development'. His father gave him ₹ 25 lakh as a seed capital to start his own new product line under the family business.

Aneesh is venturing into leather and faux leather for which he needs to plan his business before he goes ahead with the execution. He knows that transformation of raw material into finished products takes place with the help of energy, capital, manpower and machinery. Further, he realised that manufacturing operations are highly complex and tedious, hence need to be well planned.

(a) Identify the component of business plan Aneesh is discussing about. Also, state its objective.
(b) Explain the three different options available before the venture. (5)

Answers

1. (b) Natural resource
2. (d) Tag line
3. (c) Private placement
4. (b) Hostile acquisition
5. (b) size of the market being targeted
6. (a) Both Assertion (A) and Reason (R) are correct and Reason (R) is the correct explanation of Assertion (A)
7. (a) Re-order Point = Demand per Month × Lead Time in Months
= 300 bales × 2 Months
= 600 bales
8. (a) Both Assertion (A) and Reason (R) are correct and Reason (R) is the correct explanation of Assertion (A)
9. (c) Gross Working Capital = Cash + Accounts Receivable + Inventory + Other Current Assets
10. (b) I and IV
11. (c) Both Assertion (A) and Reason (R) are correct and Reason (R) is the correct explanation of Assertion (A)
12. (b) below the line
13. (d) offer to employees
14. (c) Watch trends
15. (b) The rising oil prices and their impact on costs and revenue sensitivity are economic factors influencing the macro environment for Samarya's airline business.
16. (a) Sarita identified a problem "the shortage of time for students to wash and iron their clothes" and saw an opportunity to provide a solution through a laundry service.
17. (d) The manpower plan outlines the human resource requirements, including the number of employees needed, their roles and other relevant details to meet the business's operational needs.

18. (c) In a private company, the liability of the members is limited and there is usually a minimum paid-up capital requirement. Additionally, the shares of a private company are not freely traded on the stock exchange.

19. (a) The elements in the innovation process are

(i) **Analytical Planning** Carefully identifying the product or service, features, design and resources.

(ii) **Resource Organisation** Obtaining the required resources, materials, technology, human or capital resources.

(iii) **Implementation** Applying the resources in order to accomplish and deliver the results.

(iv) **Commercial Application** Provision of value to customers, reward employees and satisfy the stakeholders.

Or (b) When there is a road block in a situation which poses a conflict, then this road block is a problem and when this road block is identified, then it is called 'problem identification'.

Problem identification helps the entrepreneur in following ways

(i) It helps an entrepreneur to bring out new products in the market.

(ii) Understand the problems and needs of the market.

20. (a) **Branding** 'Branding' can be defined as a process, a tool, a strategy, an orientation whereby a name, a sign or a symbol, etc. is given to a product by the entrepreneur so as to differentiate its product from the rival products.

(b) **Trademark** A brand or a part of a brand that is given legal protection against its use by other firms is called a trademark. It is essentially a legal term. It confers upon its owner, the exclusive right to use the brand name and brand mark.

21. Steps in the creative process fulfilled by Prabhav are

(a) **Idea Germination** It is the seeding stage, where the new idea grows. The idea germinates from the interest and curiosity of the entrepreneur. He then explore and exploits it to its best potential. The ideas can also germinate from the need of a specific problem or area of study.

(b) **Preparation** Now, with the germination of idea, it needs to be implemented. For this, the entrepreneur takes up market research to see whether the product will have any future or not.

Two steps to be followed by Prabhav in the creative process are

(a) **Incubation** This is the subconscious assimilation of information. This is the transition period. The entrepreneur think about his idea, its pros and cons, process of its implementation in his mind. Here, the idea starts spreading its roots.

(b) **Illumination** The fourth stage or the illumination stage occurs when the idea re-surfaces in a realistic way. The entrepreneur comes with a viable plan to give practical shape to his idea by collecting raw materials, arranging for finance, etc.

22. (a) The advantages a franchisor gains through franchising are

(i) **Reduced Risk** One of the biggest benefits to the franchisor in a franchise agreement is the ability to expand without an increase in risk. Because the franchisee takes on the debt and the liability of opening a unit under the name of the franchise, the franchisor gets all the benefit of an additional location without taking on the risk themselves.

(ii) **Cost Advantages** The huge size of a franchised company offers many advantages to the franchisor. The franchisor can purchase supplies in large quantities, thus achieving economies of scale.

Or (b) (i) **Number of Buyers** If the number of buyers is large, then long chain of distribution should be opted, but if the number of buyers is small, then smaller channels should be considered.

(ii) **Types of Buyers** Buyers are commonly classified as general buyers and industrial buyers.

For general buyers, long chain of distribution should be used and short-chain for industrial buyers.

23. (a) A business plan is basically a written representation of an entrepreneur's vision for his business. It is a comprehensively written document prepared by an entrepreneur describing formally all the external and internal factors involved in starting a new venture.

Business plans are considered as decision-making tools due to the following (any two)

(i) Describe all necessary inputs for the enterprise.

(ii) Explain the mode of utilisation of the resources.

(iii) Detail the strategies for the execution of the project.

(iv) Outline the desired goals.

(v) Assess market sensitivity and the profitability of the venture.

Or (b) (i) **Ability to Harness Different Sources of Information** There are various sources from which information can be gathered like magazines, books, journals, seminars, friends, etc. Information from these sources should be analysed which helps in the identification of the right opportunity to start a new business.

(ii) **Vision and Creativity** The entrepreneurs should be able to creatively identify an idea to generate valuable solution to a problem. Creative vision helps the entrepreneurs to convert the solution into business opportunity. Through their vision and creativity, they constantly overcome adversity, exercise control over the business and make a significant difference.

24.

Weeks	Number of Customers	Average Amount Billed per Customer (in ₹)	Total Amount Billed (₹)
1	20	200	4,000
2	34	170	5,780
3	26	142	3,692
4	44	462	20,328
5	36	350	12,600
Total	160		46,400

Unit Price Per Customer

$$= \frac{\text{Total Amount Billed}}{\text{Number of Customers}}$$

$$= \frac{46,400}{160}$$

$= ₹\ 290$

25. (a) 'Aircon Ltd.' decides to adopt a cost-plus pricing method based on manufacturing estimates, which covers the cost of producing the coolers along with a reasonable profit.

(b) **Advantage of this Method**

The entrepreneur knows exactly the amount of expenditure that has been incurred in producing product and therefore, profit margin can be added accordingly, which helps in achieving the desired revenue for a firm.

Disadvantage of this Method

It can result in the company overestimating the price of a product because this method includes sunk cost and ignores opportunity cost of self-owned assets. Also, profit margin added to the cost can be biased.

26. (a) (i) **Scheduling** This means deciding the time frame within which each operation would be completed. It simply means fixation of time, day, date when each operation is to be commenced and when it is to be completed.

(ii) **Follow-up** This element relates to evaluation and appraisal of work performed. It is helpful in early detection of errors and helps all entrepreneur to

- Develop ways to review the present situation with regard to materials, work-in-progress and finished goods.
- Evolve ways to expedite the performance of those departments which lag behind.
- Remove obstacles in the way of production by suggesting remedial measures.

(iii) **Inspection** This means comparing materials, product or performance with established standards. Products can be tested in specified laboratories or new methods or strategies can be evolved to ensure pre-determined standard quality of the product.

Or (b) (i) Market research is a systematic process of collecting, analysing and interpreting information about a market, including details about potential customers, competitors and the overall industry. It involves gathering data and insights to understand market trends, consumer behaviour and preferences. The goal of market research is to make informed business decisions, identify opportunities, mitigate risks and develop effective strategies based on a comprehensive understanding of the market environment.

(ii) **Market or Demand-Driven Ideas** One of the important methods of generating an idea is market research. It is an organised effort to gather information about target markets or customers.

It includes social and opinion research and is the systematic gathering and interpretation of information about individuals or organisations using statistical and analytical methods and techniques of applied social sciences to gain insight or support decision-making.

Market research is a good source of generating ideas, as it gives information regarding

- Market needs
- Market size
- Level of competition
- General environment
- State of technology

Often, market research and marketing research are used synonymously. However, the distinction is that marketing research is concerned specifically about marketing processes, while market research is concerned with markets.

27. (a) 'GRX Ltd.' has adopted an **indirect sales strategy** by demonstrating the features and benefits of its Apple Cider Vinegar without explicitly mentioning names or features of competitor's products.

(b) **Direct Sales Strategy** Under this strategy, salesmen attack the competitors directly. While talking to the customers, they talk about each feature of the competitor's product and compare it to theirs. This strategy is also termed as negative selling approach.

(c) The following considerations should be carefully analysed and reviewed by a business before formulating a sales strategy (any two)

- Market knowledge.
- Awareness of competitor's activities.
- Awareness of current trends.
- Detailed business analysis.

28. The three dimensions of the business environment highlighted in the provided paragraph are

(a) **Economic Environment** "The Prime Minister announced relaxation in export duties on electronic items."

This policy decision influenced Mitsu Electronics Ltd. to explore new markets by exporting its products to neighbouring countries. The increasing demand for electronic items due to global education and consumerism trends further signifies the impact of economic factors on business operations.

(b) **Technological Environment** "The company developed a better and cheaper video conferencing system." Mitsu Electronics Ltd. adapted technological advancements to enhance its product offerings, addressing potential problems and ensuring efficient stock replenishment. Technological environment involves technological advancements and innovations that impact businessesses.

(c) **Socio-cultural Environment** "The demand for its electronic items started increasing day-by-day as there is an increase in the level of education and consumerism globally." This dimension includes social factors that effect businesses, like cultural norms, demographics, social values, etc.

29. (a) (i) **Seed Capital Finance** It refers to the capital required by an entrepreneur for conducting research at pre-commercia-lisation stage.

During this stage, the entrepreneur has to convince the venture capitalist, why his idea/product is worthwhile.

The venture capitalist will then investigate into the technical and economical feasibility of the idea.

Entrepreneur's ability, technological skills and competencies are closely scrutinised by the venture capitalist.

He may deny to assist if the findings and investigations are not upto his satisfaction.

(ii) **Start-up Finance** If the idea/product/process is qualified for further investigation and/or investment, the process will go to the second stage, i.e. the start-up stage. A business plan is presented by the entrepreneur to the venture capitalist firm.

A management team is then formed to run the venture. If the company has a board of directors, then a person or persons from the venture capitalist firm will take seats at the board.

The management team establishes a feasible production line to produce the product.

The venture capitalist firm monitors the feasibility of the product and the capability of the management team from the board of directors.

(iii) **Second Round Financing** At this stage, the idea has been transformed into a product and is being produced and sold. The entrepreneur at this stage, needs assistance from the venture capitalist for expansion, modernisation and diversification, so that economies of scale and stability could be attained.

Venture capitalist firm will be interested in financing this stage only if he is convinced about the capability of the management team to triumph against competition.

Or (b) An angel investor or angel, also known as a business angel or informal investor or angel funder, is an affluent individual who provides capital for a business start-up, usually in exchange for convertible debt or ownership equity. Angel investors, generally provide capital for a business start-up and early stage companies having a high-risk, high-return matrix.

The various features exhibited by angel investors are as follows

(i) Most angel investors are current or retired executives, business owners or high net worth individuals, who have the knowledge, expertise and funds that help start-ups match up to industry standards.

(ii) As angel investors bear extremely high risk and their share is subjected to dilution after second round of funding, therefore they expect a high return on their investment.

(iii) Apart from investing funds, they also provide proactive advice, guidance, industry connections and mentoring start-ups in its early stage.

(iv) Their objective is to create great companies by providing value creation, and simultaneously helping investors to earn a high return on their investments.

(v) They have a keen desire to keep themselves acquainted with current developments and mentoring another generation of entrepreneurs by making use of their vast experience.

30. (a) It is a paid form of non-personal communication designed to persuade potential customers to choose a product or a service over that of a competitor.

American Marketing Association defines advertising as, "Advertising is any paid form of non-personal presentation and promotion of ideas, goods or services by an identified sponsor."

Rules of Advertising Following four rules should be considered while planning any advertising

(i) **Aim** Before drafting out an advertisement, the primary or basic purpose of advertisement should be kept in mind.

(ii) **Target** Target should be considered, i.e. from which sector of the public are we trying to achieve a response? e.g. Male, female, adult, teenager, child, mother, father, etc.

(iii) **Media** Keeping in mind, the aim and the target, the next decision relates to which of the available media will be the most suitable? e.g. TV, radio, press or internet, etc.

(iv) **Competitors** The actions of the competitors should also be analysed. What are the competitors doing?, Which media channel do they use? Are they successful? Can you improve on their approach and beat them in competition?

Developing Effective Advertising (AIDA) Good advertising generally elicits the following four responses from its target audience, commonly denoted by the acronym AIDA

(i) **Attention** (A) An effective advertisement should catch the attention of the audience and stand out amidst the cluster of competing advertisements.

(ii) **Interest** (I) It arouses interest regarding the company's product or service and delivers a sufficient impact on its audience through its message or offering.

(iii) **Desire** (D) An effective advertisement should create a desire to gather more information on the offering or to crave for ownership.

(iv) **Action** (A) It spurs an action which prompts the potential customers to purchase the product or the service.

Or (b) **Franchise Agreement** It is a legal document defining the mutual terms and conditions between a franchisor and a franchisee. The agreement is designed to assure that all the franchisees within an organisation are treated equitably.

The **main ingredients** of a franchise agreement are as follows

(i) **Contract Explanation** It is the part of the agreement that defines the type of relationship, a franchisee is entering into with the franchisor.

(ii) **Operations Manual** This section of the agreement lays forward the guidelines that the franchisee must legally follow while operating the business, as specified by the franchisor.

From time-to-time, amendments may be made and the franchisee must be prepared to adjust operations accordingly. He should be aware that the contents of the document are confidential.

(iii) **Proprietary Statements** These statements outline, how the franchise name is to be used and also the marketing and advertising procedures required to be followed by the franchisee. It also states the proportionate share of franchisee towards national advertising campaigns.

(iv) **Ongoing Site Maintenance** This includes the types and time frames regarding various maintenance items and upgrades that must be made to the franchisee's location.

31. **Primary Market** It is also known as the new issues market, as this market deals with the new securities being issued for the first time.

By issue of new securities, primary market facilitate the transfer of investible funds from savers to entrepreneurs seeking funds for setting new enterprises, expanding or diversifying.

The 'new issues' may be issued by new companies, also called initial issues and old companies, also called further issues.

Methods to Raise Capital in Primary Market
An entrepreneur can raise the required capital in primary market by the following methods

(a) **Public Issue** It involves raising of funds directly from the public through the issue of prospectus. It is the most popular method of raising finance.

This method requires compliance to various statutory laws relating to prospectus drafting, listing agreements, etc.

(b) **Rights Issue** It is a method of raising additional finance from existing shareholders by offering securities to them on pro-rata basis, i.e. giving them a right to purchase certain number of shares in proportion to the shares they are holding.

In case the existing shareholders are not willing to purchase, then they can renounce their right in favour of another person.

This method is comparatively inexpensive as it does not require any brokers, agents, underwriters, prospectus or enlistment, etc.

(c) **Private Placement** It means the direct sale by a company of its securities to a limited number of institutional investors like Unit Trust of India, Life Insurance Corporation of India, General Insurance Corporation of India, Army Group Insurance, State Level Finance Corporations, etc.

This is an effective source of raising capital if the company do not wish to disclose information in the open market.

(d) **Offer to Employees** Stock options or offering shares to employees enables employees to become shareholders of the company and subsequently be able to share the profits of the company, leading to higher efficiency, low employee turnover, cordial relations, low flotation cost and wider/higher generation of funds.

32. (a) Company means a voluntary association of persons, formed for some common objectives, with capital divisible into units of equal value called shares and with limited liability. It is basically a creation of law, i.e. it is brought to life by law and can be put to death by law only.

In terms of **Companies Act, 2013**,
"A company means a company incorporated under the Companies Act, 2013 or under any of the previous company law, [Section 2 (20)]."
Features of a company are

(i) **Separate Legal Entity** A company has an entity or personality, which is absolutely independent and separate from the entity of its members.

This implies that a company cannot be held liable for the actions of its members and *vice-versa*.

(ii) **Limited Liability** It implies that the maximum liability of a member is limited to the unpaid value of shares held by a member or guarantee given by him.

e.g. If a member holds 20 shares of ₹ 100 each, on which he has paid ₹ 60 per share, then his maximum liability will be limited to only ₹ 800, i.e. @ ₹ 40 per share on 20 shares held by him.

(iii) **Transferability of Shares** Shares of a company are freely transferable, i.e. if a member no longer desires to hold shares of a company, he can transfer them to somebody else. In a private company, there are certain restrictions to transfer shares, but the right to transfer shares is not denied by the company.

(iv) **Diffusion of Ownership and Management** In this form of organisation, there exists separation of ownership from management. As the shareholders (i.e. the owners) are scattered across the country, they give the right to manage the affairs of the company to the board of directors. Hence, through the board of directors, the company is managed in a democratic manner.

Or (b) Sensitivity to environmental factors is crucial for an entrepreneur to succeed in the long-run. The following benefits arise by understanding the environment

(i) **Identification of Opportunities to Get First Mover Advantage** By keeping in touch with the changes in the external environment, an enterprise can identify opportunities and find strategies to capitalise on the opportunities at the earliest.

e.g. LPG rationing led the manufacturers to come out with induction cooker.

(ii) **Formulation of Strategies and Policies** It helps in identifying threats and opportunities in the market. These can serve as the basis of formulation of strategies to counter threats and capitalise on opportunities in the market.

e.g. The depleting reserves of petrol is a threat for car manufacturers. E-cars or solar powered engines are the outcome of such threats, which forced them to look for alternate sources of energy.

(iii) **Tapping Useful Resources** If a company has a thorough knowledge of environment, the enterprise can tap resources like financial resources, human resources, physical resources, etc. from the market at economical prices at the right time.

e.g. Pasco Ltd. should buy wheat for its wide variety of biscuits when the new crop comes in the market, as it is available at cheap prices.

(iv) **Better Performance** It can be increased with the timely action in dealing with threats and availing opportunities for the purpose of improvement in the performance of the firm.

e.g. The 'Make in India' scheme declared by the government (a part of political environment) opens new avenues for entrepreneurs to diversify.

(v) **Sensitisation of Entrepreneurs to Cope up with Rapid Changes** A keen watch on trends in the environment would help sensitise the entrepreneur to become proactive towards the needs of customers, changing trends, government policy, technology, etc.

e.g. Reliance Trends keep on changing its clothes with changes in fashion to gain an edge over its competitors.

33. (a) Weighted Average Unit Contribution Margin
= Scrub Hand Wash CM (Contribution Mix) Per Unit × Scrub Hand Wash Sales Mix Percentage + Gel Hand Wash CM Per Unit × Gel Hand Wash Sales Mix Percentage + Foam Hand Wash CM Per Unit × Foam Hand Wash Sales Mix Percentage

Product	Scrub Hand Wash	Gel Hand Wash	Foam Hand Wash
Sales Price Per Unit	₹ 155	₹ 175	₹ 195
(–) Variable Cost Per Unit	₹ (75)	₹ (95)	₹ (105)
Contribution Margin Per Unit	₹ 80	₹ 80	₹ 90
(×) Sales Mix Percentage	40%	30%	30%
	₹ 32	₹ 24	₹ 27

∴ Total Weighted Average CM

= 32 + 24 + 27 = ₹ 83

(b) Break-even Point

$$= \frac{\text{Fixed Cost}}{\text{Total Weighted Average Contribution}}$$

$$= \frac{2{,}49{,}000}{83} = 3{,}000 \text{ units}$$

- Scrub Hand Wash = 3,000 × 40% = 1,200 units
- Gel Hand Wash = 3,000 × 30% = 900 units
- Foam Hand Wash = 3,000 × 30% = 900 units

(c) Break-even point in rupees for Scrub Hand Wash = 1,200 × 155 = ₹ 1,86,000

34. (a) Aneesh is discussing about production plan.

The objective of a production plan in the words of **Alford** and **Beathy** is "Picturising ahead every step in a long series of separate operations, each step to be taken in the right place of the right degree and at the right time and each operation to be done at maximum efficiency."

(b) Being highly complex and tedious, the manufacturing operation needs to be well planned.

This venture mostly face the following situations

(i) **No Manufacturing Involved** If the new venture does not include any manufacturing function, i.e. it is a trading business, then this section is eliminated from the plan.

(ii) **Partial Manufacturing** If the entrepreneur plans to partially manufacture some of the parts and outsource or subcontract for other processes, then the production plan should describe

- name and location of subcontractors.
- reasons for their selection.
- cost and time involved.
- any contracts that have been completed by them.
- any other relevant information.
- a clear mention of what entrepreneur intends to do himself and what he plans to get done from outside.

(iii) **Complete Manufacturing** If the entrepreneur plans to carry out the whole manufacturing process by himself, then he/she needs to describe

- the physical plant layout.
- the machinery and equipment required to perform the manufacturing operations.
- raw materials and suppliers names, addresses, terms and conditions.
- cost of manufacturing.
- any future capital equipment required, etc.

CBSE Examination Paper 2025

Entrepreneurship

General Instructions

Read the following instructions carefully and follow them

1. This question paper contains 34 questions. All questions are compulsory.
2. This question paper is divided into four sections—Section A, B, C and D.
3. Section A : Questions number 1 to 18 are Multiple Choice Type Questions. Each question carries 1 mark.
4. Section B : Questions number 19 to 24 are Short Answer Type-I Questions. Each question carries 2 marks. Write answer to each question in 30 to 40 words.
5. Section C : Questions number 25 to 29 are Short Answer Type-II Questions. Each question carries 3 marks. Write answer to each question in 50 to 70 words.
6. Section D : Questions number 30 to 34 are Long Answer Type Questions. Each question carries 5 marks. Write answer to each question in 120 to 150 words.
7. There is no overall choice. However, an internal choice has been provided in Section B, C and D of question paper. A candidate has to attempt only one of the alternatives in such questions.

Time : 3 hours **Max. Marks : 70**

Section-A

1. "The business of partnership firm can be carried on by all the partners or any one of them acting for all." This statement indicates which of the following characteristic of partnership? (1)

(a) Agreement
(b) Implied authority
(c) Mutual agency
(d) Utmost good faith

2. Shivam is manufacturing hair straightening flat irons and supplying them to various beauty salons across the city. Over the last few months he observed that the sale of flat irons has decreased drastically. He tried to find out the reason. He found that the hair experts have started recommending ceramic irons which are now being sold by competitors in the market. So, he also started manufacturing ceramic irons based on new technology with added features like curling, crimping, etc.

Identify the source of idea field used by Shivam. (1)

(a) Trading related ideas
(b) Existing products or services based ideas
(c) Service sector ideas
(d) Market driven or demand driven ideas

3. In this method of pricing, goods are sold at higher prices so that fewer sales are needed to break-even. It also helps the company in recovering the research and development costs which are associated with development of a new product.

This method of pricing is (1)

(a) penetrating pricing
(b) cost-plus pricing
(c) variable pricing
(d) creaming pricing

4. Look at the given picture and state what it represents out of the following. (1)

State Bank of India

(a) Logo (b) Brand
(c) Brand name (d) Tagline

5. Sudershan has undergone skill development training for maintenance of electronic items, from an institute started under the 'skill development mission' by the Government of India.

He wants to start his own small business in his locality with ₹ 1,00,000 given by his father as capital. He himself wants to manage and control this business, employing some assistants, if required. Out of the following, suggest the form of business organisation he can adopt. (1)

(a) Public limited company
(b) Private limited company
(c) Partnership
(d) Sole proprietorship

6. A business opportunity can be described as an economic idea which can be implemented to create .... and earn profits. (1)

(a) customers
(b) competitors
(c) a business enterprise
(d) an economic environment

7. Match the given components of a business plan in Column I and their meaning in Column II. Choose the correct option from the options given below (1)

Column I (Business Plan)	Column II (Meaning)
A. Production plan	(i) That part of the business plan that describes the proposed venture's form of ownership.
B. Operational plan	(ii) That part of the business plan where transformation of raw material into finished product takes place with the help of energy, capital, manpower and machinery.
C. Organisa-tional plan	(iii) That part of the business plan which organises for the movement of material, performance of machines and operations of labour into a defined direction.
D. Marketing plan	(iv) That part of the business plan which provides guidelines regarding the marketing objectives, strategies and activities to be followed by the new enterprise.

Codes

	A	B	C	D		A	B	C	D
(a)	(iv)	(i)	(iii)	(ii)	(b)	(ii)	(iii)	(i)	(iv)
(c)	(i)	(iv)	(ii)	(iii)	(d)	(iii)	(ii)	(iv)	(i)

8. 'Payal Ltd.' is the manufacturer of high end costly water purifiers. Their water purifiers are unique and different from the purifiers available in the market.

For its marketing they appointed sales persons who will go door-to-door and explain the unique features of their product.

From the following, identify the channel of distribution adopted by 'Payal Ltd.' (1)

(a) Three-level channel
(b) Two-level channel
(c) One-level channel
(d) Zero-level channel

9. Patents .... (1)

(i) grant an inventor the right to exclude others from making, using, selling, offering to sell and importing an invention for a limited period of time, in exchange for the public disclosure of the invention
(ii) give the creator of the original work exclusive rights, usually for a limited period
(iii) are a recognisable sign, design or expression which distinguishes products or services of a particular trade from the similar products or services of other traders
(iv) protect the visual design of objects that are not purely utilitarian. It can be a two or three dimensional pattern used to produce a product

Codes

(a) Only (i)
(b) (i) and (ii)
(c) (iii) and (iv)
(d) (ii) and (iii)

10. A brand or a part of a brand that is given legal protection against its use by other firms is called .... (1)

(a) brand name (b) brand mark
(c) trademark (d) logo

11. 'Bharat Cars Ltd.' is the manufacturer of small cars in India and 'Swadeshi Ltd.' is the manufacturer and supplier of car parts. Both the companies decide to merge as such a merger would allow 'Bharat Cars Ltd.' to obtain better pricing on parts and have better control over the manufacturing process. 'Swadeshi Ltd.' would also be guaranteed a steady stream of business.

    The type of merger is (1)

    (a) market extension merger
    (b) vertical merger
    (c) horizontal merger
    (d) product extension merger

12. This is the title or cover page that provides a brief summary of a business plan's contents. (1)

    (a) Description of venture
    (b) General introduction
    (c) Production plan
    (d) Operational plan

13. **Assertion** (A) It is not compulsory to register a partnership firm as there are no penalties for non-registration.

    Reason (R) An unregistered partnership firm can file a suit in any court against the firm or other partners for enforcement of any right arising from a contract or right conferred by the Partnership Act. (1)

    Alternatives

    (a) Both Assertion (A) and Reason (R) are true and Reason (R) is the correct explanation of Assertion (A)
    (b) Both Assertion (A) and Reason (R) are true, but Reason (R) is not the correct explanation of Assertion (A)
    (c) Assertion (A) is true, but Reason (R) is false
    (d) Assertion (A) is false, but Reason (R) is true

14. 'Return on investment' is a critical profitability ratio. It is calculated as follows (1)

    $$\text{Return on Investment (RoI)} = \frac{\text{Net Profit}}{\ldots\ldots\ldots} \times 100$$

    (a) Equity
    (b) Debt
    (c) Total Capital Invested
    (d) Debt + Interest on Debt

15. Which of the following is not a current liability? (1)

    (a) Outstanding rent
    (b) Short-term investment
    (c) Trade creditors
    (d) Short-term loans

16. Which of the following methods of floatation of new issues is used by the company, when the company directly sells its securities to a limited number of sophisticated investors and at times does not want to disclose information to the open market? (1)

    (a) Public issue
    (b) Rights issue
    (c) Private placement
    (d) Offer to the employees

17. In .... acquisition, a public company is taken over by a private company. (1)

    (a) friendly
    (b) reverse
    (c) backflip
    (d) hostile

18. 'Techworks' is a company selling electronic products. To keep track of inventory and manage sales efficiency each and every item in the inventory is assigned a unique code which signifies certain aspects of the item. Its unique code is a combination of alpha and numeric and is used not only for data collection, but also for further manipulation for deriving meaningful statistics and decision-making.

    However, over time, due to advancement in technology, certain items may not be used and their demand drops-off. 'Techworks' faces a challenge of dealing with these products, particularly with technology evolving quickly.

    Some of the items that make up the inventory of 'Techworks' as discussed above are .... and .... (1)

    (a) Stock Keeping Unit (SKU) code, motley crowd
    (b) motley crowd, demand not uniform or not predictable
    (c) obsolescence, shelf life
    (d) Stock Keeping Unit (SKU) code, obsolescence

Section-B

19. What is a 'business opportunity'? List any two elements of business opportunity. (2)

Or Various factors are involved in sensing opportunities. 'Ability to perceive and preserve basic ideas' is one of them. Identify and state any four sources that lead to the emergence of basic ideas.

20. Manorama opened a retail outlet in Bengaluru selling readymade fashionable garments like t-shirts, skirts, kurtis, etc. for girls. Her decision was based on recent trends in clothing of young girls.
Since fashion changes very fast in the garments business, Manorama not only wanted to understand the business environment but also wanted to adapt it to succeed in the long-run.

So, she monitored fashion trends through social media and introduced sustainable clothing. A keen watch on the trends in the environment had sensitised Manorama to the changing needs of customers.

By doing this, Manorama is concentrating on one of the points of importance of environment.

(i) Identify the point of importance of environment discussed above.

(ii) Explain with the help of one more point how sensitivity to environmental factors is crucial for an entrepreneur. (2)

21. Deepa, Guddi and Vani are partners in a firm sharing profits and losses in the ratio of 3 : 2 : 1. Deepa wants to transfer half of her share in favour of her son Deepak without the consent of Guddi and Vani. Can Deepa transfer her share? Give reason in support of your answer. State the feature of partnership highlighted in the above case. (2)

Or Aruna, passionate about baking, opened a bakery shop. She borrowed ₹ 50,000 from her father and took a loan of ₹ 1,00,000 from a bank to start the business. To attract customers, she set the prices too low. Later on she noticed that the revenue earned by her was not enough to even cover the costs. When the loan amount became due, she was not in a position to pay.

The bank recovered the loan from Aruna's personal assets, including her savings and property.

Can Aruna's personal property be called upon to pay her business debts? Give reason in support of your answer. State the feature of sole proprietorship highlighted in the above case.

22. After completion of his training of cutting, tailoring and embroidery from a skill development institute, Sujit wanted to start his own business. He discussed this idea with his mother who advised him to identify the new trends in this area.

She also advised him to take the help of professional trend spotters for this. When Sujit contacted some of the best professional trend spotters, he found that their fee was too high.

So he decided to do this work himself, started reading the leading publications and visited websites related to the type of business he wanted to start. This way he was able to spot related trends.

Identify and explain the method used by Sujit to spot the trends. Also list two other ways in which trends can be spotted. (2)

23. Explain 'a pitch deck with oral narrative' as a format of a business plan. (2)

24. Given below is the 'cash conversion cycle'.

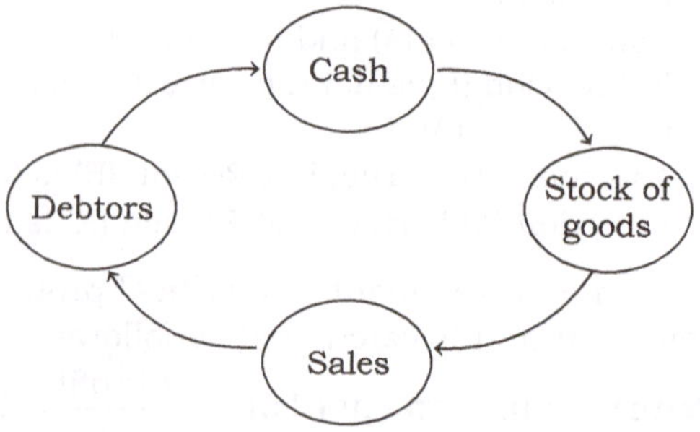

(i) Identify the type of business to which the above cash conversion cycle belongs.

(ii) Draw a 'cash conversion cycle' for another type of business other than that identified in (i) above. (2)

Or Give the meaning of ABC analysis technique of inventory control.

Section-C

25. 'Chai Cart', an Indian company, was set-up in 2021 near a prime office hub in Nurgaon. The company aimed to fulfil the high demand for tea among office goers. Within a few months, the demand picked up and the business started earning good profits. In response to the rising demand, the company decided to expand its operations. Expansion of its business could be based on activities or on acquisition of ownership and control of other business concerns.

'Chai Cart' expanded its present production capacity by adding more machines. Furthermore, it opened its branches in shopping malls, airports and suburban locations, allowing it to reach more customers and to increase brand visibility. They also introduced new products including a wider range of food items, coffee and other beverages to attract more customers. In this way, the company increased its business activities and broadened its present capital structure.

(i) Identify and explain the type of expansion discussed in the above paragraph.

(ii) Also explain one other type of expansion. (3)

26. 'Carefully identifying the product or service features, design, as well as the resources that will be needed' is an element in the innovation process. Explain its other three elements. (3)

Or The process of creativity involves various steps. One of the steps is related to transition period, 'where the entrepreneur starts thinking about the idea and implementation in his subconscious mind'. Explain the next three steps followed by this.

27. 'Golden Ice Cream Limited' is a manufacturer and supplier of ice creams.

They set the price of their various ice cream varieties based on manufacturing estimates. The company had been earning good profits over the last many years as there were no competitors in the market for their ice creams.

However, during the last year, the company incurred heavy losses. On investigation they noticed that while setting the prices, they did not take into account the actions of competitors, which may have led to these losses.

Additionally, the pricing method used by the company includes sunk cost and ignores opportunity costs.

(i) Identify the pricing method used by the company.

(ii) Explain any two advantages of the pricing method identified in (i) above. (3)

28. Explain any three product related considerations to be used by an entrepreneur while selecting the channel of distribution. (3)

Or

Explain 'above the line' promotion strategy used by a company to promote its products.

29. 'Kwality Book Store' sells 40,000 chart papers per year. The demand is constant throughout the year.

The purchase cost is ₹ 10 per chart paper. Holding cost per annum is 20% of purchase cost, ordering cost is ₹ 100 per order.

Calculate the economic order quantity. (3)

Section-D

30. 'Bharat Ltd.' is a manufacturer of electronic items. In 2022-23 the company decided to enter into manufacturing artificial intelligence based computers.

Being highly complex and tedious, the manufacturing process of these computers needed to be thoroughly planned.

(i) Identify the component of business plan discussed in the above paragraph.

(ii) State the objective of the component identified in (i) above.

(iii) List five points that are needed to be described in this component of business plan. If the manufacturing is to be carried out in whole by 'Bharat Ltd.'. (5)

31. What is meant by 'franchising'? Explain the main components of a franchise agreement. (5)

Or

Explain any five forms of 'synergy'.

32. 'Good Air Ltd.' is the manufacturer of different types of electric fans like ceiling fans, table fans, exhaust fans, etc. It wanted to start its operations in the recently electrified rural areas ahead of its competitors. It invested in research and development to adopt new technology so that it could produce energy efficient fans at lower cost.

The government was stable for the last many years and was focusing on electrification of rural areas. 'Good Air Ltd.' took advantage of this and started its operations.

The company complied with health and safety regulations, as well as environmental protection laws, to ensure customer safety. As its policy, the company also assures compensation to its customers in case of an injury or accident due to its fans.
Since the disposable income of the people in rural areas was low, the company offered an instalment scheme, making its products more accessible to them. Committed to sustainability, the company ensures that its production causes minimum environmental damage.
For this, it focuses on reducing waste by recycling production by-products and using biodegradable packaging materials whenever possible.
Quoting lines from the above text, identify five macro environmental factors that the company took into consideration while operating its business. (5)

33. 'Royal Fruit Juice Ltd.' are the manufacturers of different types of fruit juices. They do not use any artificial flavours in their products.

The fixed cost of the production process is ₹ 1,76,000. Given below is information about Mango, Orange and Guava fruit juices.

Type of Juice →	**Mango** (Per Litre)	**Orange** (Per Litre)	**Guava** (Per Litre)
Selling Price (₹)	150	135	100
Variable Cost (₹)	80	65	60
Sales Mix Percentage	20%	40%	40%

From the above data, calculate the following
(i) Total weighted average contribution margin per unit.
(ii) Break-even point in units of sales mix.
(iii) Break-even point (in ₹) for each type of juice. (5)

34. 'It is an equity based investment in a growth-oriented small to medium business to enable the investor to accomplish objectives in return for minority shareholding in the business.

This investment has to be carefully evaluated and analysed by an entrepreneur to find out the stage at which he/she requires this investment to assist in.
(i) Identify the type of capital discussed in the above lines.
(ii) Explain the three stages included in 'early stage financing' if the capital identified in (i) above is required at this stage. (5)

Or "An affluent individual who provides capital for a business start-up and early stage companies having a high risk, high return matrix usually in exchange for convertible debt or ownership equity."
(i) Identify the source to raise finance available to an entrepreneur discussed in the above lines.
(ii) State any four features of the source of raising finance discussed in (i) above.

Answers

1. (c) Mutual agency
2. (d) Market driven or demand driven ideas
3. (d) creaming pricing
4. (a) Logo
5. (d) Sole proprietorship
6. (c) a business enterprise
7. (b) (ii) (iii) (i) (iv)
8. (d) Zero-level channel
9. (a) Only (i)
10. (c) trademark

11. (b) vertical merger

12. (b) General introduction

13. (c) An unregistered partnership firm cannot file a suit in any court against the firm or other partners for enforcement of any right arising from a contract or right conferred by the Partnership Act.

14. (c) Total Capital Invested

15. (b) Short-term investment

16. (c) Private placement

17. (b) reverse

18. (d) Stock Keeping Unit (SKU) code, obsolescence

19. Business opportunity is an economic idea which can be implemented to create a business enterprise and earn profits.

Before setting-up a business, certain elements should be considered which are as follows

(i) Assured market scope.

(ii) An attractive and acceptable rate of return on investment.

Or

Four sources that lead to the emergence of basic ideas are as follows

(i) **Problem** Many times, a solution to a problem leads to idea generation.

(ii) **Change** Any change in social, legal or technological aspects, leads to a new business opportunity.

(iii) **Invention** New products or services lead to new business opportunities.

(iv) **Competition** It is often a source of new and better ideas that results in new business opportunities.

20. (i) The point of importance of environment discussed in the case is 'identification of opportunities to get first mover advantage'. Manorama monitored fashion trends through social media and introduced sustainable clothing.

(ii) **Formulation of Strategies and Policies** It helps in identifying threats and opportunities in the market.

These can serve as the basis of formulation of strategies to counter threats and capitalise on opportunities in the market.

21. No, Deepa cannot transfer her share to her son Deepak without the consent of Guddi and Vani as a partnership is based on mutual trust and agreement among partners.

The feature highlighted in the above case is 'restrication on transfer of shares'.

No partner can sell or transfer his shares to anybody else without the consent of the other partners.

If a partner wants to discontinue, he can do so with the consent of other partners.

Or

Yes, Aruna's personal property can be called upon to pay her business debts because she is operating as a sole proprietor. In a sole proprietorship, there is no legal distinction between the owner and the business, meaning the owner has unlimited liability.

The feature highlighted in the case is 'unlimited liability'.

The proprietor and the business are considered to be the same and in case the assets of the business are not sufficient to pay liabilities, his/her personal property can also be used to pay-off the business debts.

22. The method used by Sujit to spot the trends is 'read trends'.

The information available from the sources like reading the leading publications, industry publications, business magazines, etc. is vast and every piece of information may not be relevant for the entrepreneurs. They have to make an intelligent choice as to which source is valuable for them and which is not.

For this, they use tech-tools like RSS feeds, e-mails, newsletters or websites and forums to get the information that they want.

Two other ways in which trends can be spotted are

(i) Talk trends

(ii) Watch trends

23. **A Pitch Deck with Oral Narrative** This format presents the business plan in the form of an entertaining slide show complemented with an oral narrative.

It is meant to trigger discussion and awaken the interest of the potential investors and induce them to read the written presentation.

It includes executive summary, important graphs showing financial trends and key decision-making benchmarks.

24. (i) The type of business to which the given cash conversion cycle belongs is a trading concern.

(ii) Cash conversion cycle for a manufacturing company

It includes manufacturing, thus operating cycle will be longer, as follows

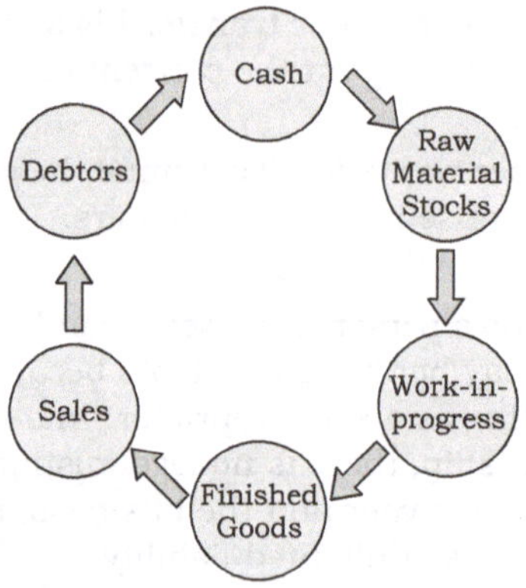

Operating Cycle or Cash Conversion Cycle for Manufacturing Business

Or

In ABC (Always Better Control) analysis, a company classifies all its inventory in three groups- 'A', 'B' and 'C'.

'A' group contains inventory which is 70-80% in terms of value, but only 10-20% in terms of quantity. 'B' group contains inventory which is 10-20% in terms of value and 15-25% in terms of quantity. 'C' group contains inventory which is 5-10% in terms of value and 65-75% in terms of quantity.

25. (i) The type of expansion discussed is 'internal expansion'.

It is a slow and time consuming process which is the result of a gradual increase in the activities of the enterprise.

A firm may expand internally by

(a) expanding its present production capacity by increasing the number of machines.

(b) replacing old machines with advanced technological machines.

(c) entering in new areas of production/ marketing or both.

(d) increasing the output of the enterprise.

Internal expansion is generally financed through long-term sources of finance and also through undistributed profits and reserves.

(ii) The other type of expansion is 'external expansion'. External expansion occurs when two or more business enterprises come together with a common objective of expanding their business.

A firm may expand externally by

(a) franchising

(b) mergers and acquisitions

26. The other three elements in the innovation process are as follows

(i) Resource organisation involves

(a) Human resources

(b) Material resources

(c) Technology

(d) Capital resources

(ii) Implementation involves

(a) Applying resources

(b) Delivering results

(iii) Commercial application involves

(a) Provision of value to customers

(b) Reward employees

(c) Satisfy stakeholders

Or The next three steps in the creativity process are as follows

(i) **Preparation** With the germination of idea, it needs to be implemented. For this, the entrepreneur takes up market research to see whether the product will have any future or not.

(ii) **Incubation** This is the subconscious assimilation of information. This is the transition period.

The entrepreneur think about his idea, its pros and cons, process of its implementation in his mind. Here, the idea starts spreading its roots.

(iii) **Illumination** This occurs when the idea re-surfaces in a realistic way.

The entrepreneur comes with a viable plan to give practical shape to his idea by collecting raw materials, arranging for finance, etc.

27. (i) The pricing method used by the company is 'cost-plus pricing'.

(ii) Two advantages of cost-plus pricing method are as follows

(a) The entrepreneur knows exactly the amount of expenditure that has been incurred in producing a product and therefore, profit margin can be added accordingly, which helps in achieving the desired revenue for a firm.

(b) It is the simplest method to decide the price of the product.

28. While selecting a channel of distribution, entrepreneurs should take care of following factors related to the quality and nature of product, which are as follows

(i) **Unit Value of the Product** If the product is very costly, like gold ornaments or industrial machinery, then it is best to use a small distribution channel. On the other hand, for less costly products, long channels can be used.

(ii) **Standardised Products** These are those products in which there is no scope of alteration and their cost is pre-determined, e.g. Thermos flask of Milton. For such products, long distribution channels can be used.

(iii) **Customised Products** These products are those which are made according to the discretion of the customers and there is scope for alteration, e.g. Furniture. For such products, direct channel should be used.

Or **Above The Line** (ATL) **Approach** This type of promotion focuses on advertising to a large audience. It uses mass media methods of promotion such as

(i) Advertisements in press.

(ii) Online banner advertisements.

(iii) Place advertisements on billboards.

(iv) Website development.

(v) Television and cinema advertising.

29. EOQ can be determined with the help of the following formula $EOQ = \sqrt{\frac{2PD}{C}}$, where

P = Cost of placing one order or ordering cost per order

D = Annual demand for the inventory

C = Inventory carrying cost per unit

Given, D = 40,000; P = ₹ 100

$C = \frac{20 \times 10}{100} = ₹\ 2$

$$\text{Now, EOQ} = \sqrt{\frac{2 \times 40,000 \times 100}{2}} = \sqrt{\frac{8,00,000}{2}}$$

$$= \sqrt{4,00,000}$$

$\therefore$ EOQ = 632.46 ≈ 632 units

30. (i) The component of business plan discussed in the given paragraph is 'production plan'.

(ii) The objective of a production plan in the words of Alford and Beathy is "Picturising ahead every step in a long series of separate operations, each step to be taken in the right place of the right degree and at the right time and each operation to be done at maximum efficiency".

So, a production plan helps to plan the work in such a manner that one can clearly form an idea about

(a) production schedule and/or budget.

(b) machinery, equipment required.

(c) manufacturing method and process involved.

(d) plant layout.

(e) time, motion and work study.

(f) manpower requirement.

(g) inventory requirement.

(iii) If the entrepreneur plans to carry out the whole manufacturing process by himself, then he/she needs to describe

(a) the physical plant layout.

(b) the machinery and equipment required to perform the manufacturing operations.

(c) raw materials and suppliers names, addresses, terms and conditions.

(d) cost of manufacturing.

(e) any future capital equipment required, etc.

31. Franchising can be defined as an arrangement whereby the manufacturer or sole distributor of a trademarked product or service gives exclusive rights of local distribution to independent retailers in return for their payment of royalties and conformance to standardised operating procedures.

Components of Franchise Agreement The main ingredients of a franchise agreement are as follows

(i) **Contract Explanation** It is the part of the agreement that defines the type of relationship, a franchisee is entering into with the franchisor.

(ii) **Operations Manual** This section of the agreement lays forward the guidelines that the franchisee must legally follow while operating the business, as specified by the franchisor. From time-to-time, amendments may be made and the franchisee must be prepared to adjust operations accordingly. He should be aware that the contents of the document are confidential.

(iii) **Proprietary Statements** These statements outline, how the franchise name is to be used and also the marketing and advertising procedures required to be followed by the franchisee.

It also states the proportionate share of franchisee towards national advertising campaigns.

(iv) **Ongoing Site Maintenance** This includes the types and time frames regarding various maintenance items and upgrades that must be made to the franchisee's location.

Or Synergy implies a condition wherein 2 + 2 = 5, i.e. the combined value of the merging firm exceeds the sum of the individual values of the merged firms. e.g. If firms X and Y merge, then the value of combined entity V(XY) is expected to be greater than (VX + VY). Synergy accrues in the form of revenue enhancement and cost savings.

It is the most common reason, why businesses opt for M&A. They aim to reap the benefits of synergy.

Synergy can take the following two forms

(i) **Operating Synergy** This refers to the cost savings that accrue through economies of scale or because of increased turnover leading to increased profits.

(ii) **Financial Synergy** This is the direct result of financial factors such as lower taxes, higher debt capacity or better use of idle resources.

Also, the new firm stands to gain in the form of 'tax shield', i.e. when a firm with accumulated losses merge with a profitable firm and the combined firm can sets-off such losses against its profit, a financial synergy occurs, known as 'tax shield'.

32. Five macroenvironmental factors considered by Good Air Ltd., along with the quoted lines from the case are as follows

(i) **Technological Environment** "It invested in research and development to adopt new technology so that it could produce energy efficient fans at lower cost."

The company focused on innovation to improve efficiency and reduce production costs.

(ii) **Political Environment** "The government was stable for the last many years and was focusing on electrification of rural areas." A stable government and rural electrification policies encouraged the company to expand its operations.

(iii) **Legal Environment** "The company complied with health and safety regulations, as well as environmental protection laws, to ensure customer safety."

The company followed legal requirements related to safety and environmental protection.

(iv) **Economic Environment** "Since the disposable income of the people in rural areas was low, the company offered an instalment scheme, making its products more accessible to them." The company recognised the low purchasing power of rural customers and introduced an installment scheme.

(v) **Ecological Environment** "Committed to sustainability, the company ensures that its production causes minimum environmental damage. For this, it focuses on reducing waste by recycling production by-products and using biodegradable packaging materials whenever possible." The company took steps to reduce its environmental impact by recycling and using eco-friendly packaging.

33.

Type of Juice	**Mango** (per litre)	**Orange** (per litre)	**Guava** (per litre)
Selling Price (₹)	150	135	100
Variable Cost (₹)	80	65	60
Contribution	70	70	40
Sales Mix	20 %	40 %	40 %
Weighted Contribution	14	28	16

(i) Total Weighted Contribution Margin

= 14 + 28 + 16 = ₹ 58

(ii) Break-even Point in Units of Sales Mix

= Total Fixed Cost/Weighted Average Contribution Margin per Unit

$= \frac{1,76,000}{58} = 3,034$ units

Number of Units of Mango Juice at Break-even Point = 3,034 × 20% = 607

Number of Units of Orange Juice at Break-even Point = 3,034 × 40% = 1,214

Number of Units of Guava Juice at Break-even Point = 3,034 × 40 % = 1,214

(iii) Break-even (₹) for Mango Juice = 607 × 150

= ₹ 91,050

Break-even (₹) for Orange Juice = 1,214 × 135

= ₹ 1,63,890

Break-even (₹) for Guava Juice = 1,214 × 100

= ₹ 1,21,400

34. (i) The type of capital discussed in the above lines is 'venture capital'.

(ii) Three stages included in early stage financing are as follows

(a) **Seed Capital Finance** It refers to the capital required by an entrepreneur for conducting research at pre-commercialisation stage. During this stage, the entrepreneur has to convince the venture capitalist, why his idea/product is worthwhile.

The venture capitalist will then investigate into the technical and economical feasibility of the idea. Entrepreneur's ability, technological skills and competencies are closely scrutinised by the venture capitalist.

He may deny to assist if the findings and investigations are not upto his satisfaction.

(b) **Start-up Finance** If the idea/product/process is qualified for further investigation and/or investment, the process will go to the second stage, i.e. the start-up stage. A business plan is presented by the entrepreneur to the venture capitalist firm.

A management team is then formed to run the venture. If the company has a board of directors, then a person or persons from the venture capitalist firm will take seats at the board.

The management team establishes a feasible production line to produce the product.

The venture capitalist firm monitors the feasibility of the product and the capability of the management team from the board of directors.

(c) **Second Round Financing** At this stage, the idea has been transformed into a product and is being produced and sold. The entrepreneur at this stage, needs assistance from the venture capitalist for expansion, modernisation and diversification, so that economies of scale and stability could be attained.

Venture capitalist firm will be interested in financing this stage only if he is convinced about the capability of the management team to triumph against competition.

Or

(i) The source to raise finance available to an entrepreneur discussed in the above lines is 'angel investors'.

(ii) The various features exhibited by angel investors are as follows

(a) Most angel investors are current or retired executives, business owners or high net worth individuals, who have the knowledge, expertise and funds that help start-ups match-up to industry standards.

(b) As angel investors bear extremely high risk and their share is subjected to dilution after second round of funding, therefore they expect a high return on their investment.

(c) Apart from investing funds, they also provide proactive advice, guidance, industry connections and mentoring start-ups in its early stage.

(d) Their objective is to create great companies by providing value creation and simultaneously helping investors to earn a high return on their investments.